THE SENSE OF THE *Song of Roland*

THE SENSE OF THE *Song of Roland*

Robert Francis Cook

Cornell University Press

ITHACA AND LONDON

Cornell University Press gratefully acknowledges
a grant from the Andrew W. Mellon Foundation
that aided in bringing this book to publication.

First published 1987 by Cornell University Press.

International Standard Book Number 0-8014-1930-1
Library of Congress Catalog Card Number 87-5407
Printed in the United States of America
Librarians: Library of Congress cataloging information appears on the last page of the book.

The paper in this book is acid-free and meets the guidelines for permanence and durability of the Committee on Production Guidelines for Book Longevity of the Council on Library Resources.

Peace is war's purpose.

—Augustine, *City of God*

Contents

PART TWO
The Sense of the *Song of Roland*

Preface

After a century and more of intense study, the reputation of the *Song of Roland* as a compelling epic poem scarcely needs to be established. But the student of epic literature may not be quite so sure *how* it compels. Why does this "great, shaggy, uneven masterpiece" (John Fox's words)[1] contain the material it contains? What story does it tell? How might it have impressed upon the early medieval hearer a sense of what it meant to be a knight and a defender of society in a young Europe? Most literary studies of the poem offer us a hero without a context, a Roland whose actions are obscure and whose words are irrelevant to the issues the poem raises, issues of which the hero himself is said to be largely unaware.

Interpreting the *Song of Roland* correctly is nonetheless crucial to our image of early medieval times. After all, the *Song* is not only the most famous of France's *chansons de geste,* but also one of the best-known titles in all epic literature. A book on medieval culture without a few lines about the meaning and contents of this poem would seem incomplete. The *Song* appears automatically in syllabi and studies on medieval history, comparative literature, and the history of French literature; it has often been the only epic *chanson de geste* used to illustrate the heroic spirit of its times. And the poem is also the object of something approaching veneration among literary medievalists, who add regularly to the dozens of books and articles dedicated to it. "The reason we are medievalists," Bernard Cerquiglini has even said, "is to study the *Song of Roland.*"[2]

[1]John Fox, *A Literary History of France: The Middle Ages* (New York, 1974), 70.

[2]Bernard Cerquiglini, "Roland à Roncevaux, ou la trahison des clercs," *Littérature,* 42 (May 1981), 40. The mass of studies thus generated, which Charles Knudson called

It is difficult to believe that a work on which so much is written can be a work incompletely explored. Yet though the *Song of Roland* is one of the medieval poems about which the largest numbers of scholars and readers know *something*, it is surprising how little critical attention has been paid to it as a story. Scholars have devoted much energy to studying such matters as its antecedents, the techniques by which it was composed, the ways it reflects specific historical events, and so on, but its subject, sequence, and significance have been much less thoroughly discussed. The venerable epic's considerable length, its antique style, its reputation (in some critical circles) for loose composition, and still other phenomena—even an entirely proper respect for its pioneer interpreters—have combined over the past century or so to limit inquiry into what it shows and why.

The result (as Cerquiglini also goes on to say) is that nearly all the books and most of the articles say much the same things about what happens in the *Song of Roland*. Nearly all of them also express reservations about its hero's conduct, if not outright disapproval. Pride and a fall; a rash Roland, blind to the consequences of his acts; his far-sighted and practical companion Oliver; a preventable disaster at Roncevaux—these motifs of criticism inevitably add up to an ironic or tragic view of the hero. The conviction that these motifs are central to the meaning of the work is reflected not only in older classics of medieval scholarship but also in valuable and important literary studies by W. T. H. Jackson, William Calin, Roger Pensom, Jules Horrent, and André Burger and in textbooks of undisputed excellence, such as those by C. W. Aspland, Alan Hindley and Brian J. Levy, and Daniel Poirion, despite calls elsewhere for its revision.[3] The traditional de-

"awe-inspiring" thirty-five years ago, has multiplied many times since ("The Problem of the *Chanson de Roland*," *Romance Philology*, 4 [1950–51], 2). The introduction and 615 notes to Gerard Brault's edition (*The Song of Roland: An Analytical Edition*, 2 vols. [University Park, Pa., 1978]; hereafter Brault, *Song*) constitute a remarkably thorough survey of problems in *Roland* scholarship and interpretation, one I have made no effort to duplicate. A full listing of the literature for the highly productive period between 1955 and 1976 (with major earlier works included) is in Joseph J. Duggan, *A Guide to Studies on the Chanson de Roland* (London, 1976). English translations of passages in other languages are my own except where noted.

[3] ". . . on y verrait à peine un problème, tant l'interprétation officielle est assurée," says Cerquiglini, 43. He is speaking of France; but see W. T. H. Jackson, *The Hero and the King* (New York, 1982), 63–67, 122; William C. Calin, *A Muse for Heroes* (Toronto, 1983), esp. 18–19, 21–24, 33, 44; Roger Pensom, *Literary Technique in the Chanson de Roland* (Geneva, 1982), e.g., in his discussion of Roland's psychological development, pp. 121–61; Jules Horrent, *Chanson de Roland et geste de Charlemagne*, in Hans Robert Jauss et al., eds., *Grundriss der Literaturen des romanischen Mittelalters*, 3:1, 2 (Heidelberg, 1981), 7–11; André Burger, *Turold poète de la fidélité* (Geneva, 1977), discussed in Chapter 5, below; C. W. Aspland, *Medieval French Reader* (Oxford, 1979), 38; Alan

scription of Roland's character and deeds has so permeated the literature on the *Song of Roland* that it is echoed to some extent even in the work of authors—Robert Guiette, Gerard Brault, Jean Misrahi and William Hendrickson, and William Kibler—who have tended to see Roland's fatal words and acts in a less traditional, more positive light.[4]

The elements of this interpretive description have been repeated, without fundamental change, for several generations, but that is no index of the interpretation's accuracy or value. What is more troubling is the long absence of hesitation or debate among its proponents. From Francisque Michel and Paulin Paris, through Gaston Paris, Léon Gautier, Joseph Bédier, T. A. Jenkins, and Edmond Faral, to Eugène Vinaver, Cesare Segre, and Pierre Le Gentil, there has been a confident uniformity of allusion and paraphrase that, far from inspiring confidence in the critic, might well give pause instead. This frame of reference is so pervasive that a strong disagreement, however carefully presented, may at first glance seem to border on sensationalism. Thus it is that Aspland, for example, describes Kibler's stance as an "extreme view."[5]

I am convinced that this situation stems in large part from a particular lacuna in studies on the *Song*. Though the poem has been summarized in print many times, and in part or by implication probably hundreds of times, there has never been any inclusive explication of its narrative content in the form I offer below. The work's standard

Hindley and Brian J. Levy, *The Old French Epic: An Introduction* (Louvain, 1983), 71–72, 113–14; Daniel Poirion et al., *Précis de littérature française du Moyen Age* (Paris, 1983), 68–69. Of the authors in this list, I think only Calin (p. 449, n. 15) and Aspland (p. 38) mention the positive interpretation, and none explains why he prefers the traditional reading.

[4]See Robert Guiette, "Les Deux Scènes du cor dans la *Chanson de Roland* et dans les *Conquestes de Charlemagne*," *Le Moyen Age,* 69 (1963), 845–55; Gerard Brault, "*Sapientia* dans la *Chanson de Roland*," *French Forum,* 1 (1976), 99–118; William Kibler, "Roland's Pride," *Symposium,* 26 (1972), 147–60; Jean Misrahi and William Hendrickson, "Roland and Oliver: Prowess and Wisdom, the Ideal of the Epic Hero," *Romance Philology,* 33 (1979–80), 357–72. There have been scattered but strong exceptions to this tendency; for more thoroughgoing justifications of Roland, see Alberto Del Monte, "Apologia di Orlando," *Filologia romanza,* 4 (1957), 225–34; Alfred Foulet, "Is Roland Guilty of *desmesure?*" *Romance Philology,* 10 (1956–57), 145–48; Norman Cartier, "La Sagesse de Roland," *Aquileia: Chestnut Hill Studies in Modern Languages and Literatures,* 1 (1969), 33–63; Emanuel Mickel, "Christian Duty and the Structure of the *Roland*," *Romance Notes,* 9 (1967), 126–33, and "Parallels in Prudentius' *Psychomachia* and *La Chanson de Roland*," *Studies in Philology,* 67 (1970), 439–52; Larry S. Crist, "A propos de la *desmesure* dans la *Chanson de Roland*," *Olifant,* 1 (1974), 10–20; Constance Hieatt, "Roland's Christian Heroism," *Traditio,* 24 (1968), 420–29. Positive statements in the same vein have also appeared sporadically in studies not directly concerned with Roland's character, many of which will be referred to in due course.

[5]Aspland, 38.

interpretation has been affirmed far more often than defended, and its occasional defense has generally been made on the grounds that the psychological and aesthetic assumptions *behind* the interpretation need no defense themselves. On the other hand, the standard interpretation has been challenged primarily on thematic or typological grounds rather than on the basis of extensive, sequential close reading. Thus many of the events in the story, though they have been used by numerous scholars for specialized arguments, have never been closely examined in the light of all that precedes or follows them. This observation is to some extent true even of the crucial episodes leading up to the battle of Roncevaux. The present analysis, and the quite positive interpretation of Roland's sacrifice that I have drawn from it, derive from uneasiness with both the original interpretation and with the situation of scholarship itself.

I will argue that Roland both knows and does his duty. His sacrifice is immediately understandable in the context of the poem's action. His responsibility to the emperor Charlemagne, to his comrades, and to his society precludes his sounding his horn at Roncevaux, for in effect he has given his sworn word to fight to the last when the expected attack comes, and the importance of that promise transcends the circumstances. Roland does not boast or belittle his fellows, nor does he express an unbounded sense of his own superiority. He does not even say he expects to win the battle of Roncevaux. The text supports those statements in a way it does not support the early interpretive hypothesis of pride and error.

I have had in mind, then, to account for features of the *Song of Roland* that are at least "known about," as I have put it above, but whose contributions to the work's narrative coherence are rarely discussed. The stakes (outside the circle of medievalists who assume the poem's artistic power as a given) are higher than is sometimes realized. If we continue to say, much as Gaston Paris did, that Roland brings on a tragedy through some error of his own, that "Roland's refusal to call Charlemagne to his rescue by sounding his horn is, in the poem, the true cause of the disaster of Roncevaux," then we may also agree with him (and with many other critics) in finding the poem ill composed and lacking in unity, since so much of it is superfluous to such a theme.[6] The work's references to the assassination of Basan and Basile, with the associated theme of vengeance; the pagan boasts before the ambush at Roncevaux; the lies Ganelon tells Marsile (and

[6]See Gaston Paris's *Extraits de la Chanson de Roland* (Paris, 1891), xix, 75.

Charlemagne); the heedless blow Oliver strikes Roland; the reappearance of Gautier del Hum on the battlefield—an analysis of the poem should make clear what roles these events and others play in what is in fact a deliberately and economically constructed story. Through an analysis of this kind, such widely cited elements as Roland's early refusal to sound the Olifant or his speeches of promise or Aude's sudden death take on new associations and thus new significance.

In the second part of this book, I situate the task of reading the *Song of Roland* in a practical, public, and humane—that is to say, historical—context. The supplementary chapters study, in broad terms, some of the ways a new interpretation affects our perception of the poem's themes and characters, of its place in history, and of its potential significance for today's reader.

Scholarship presents Roland's choices and actions as at best "splendid folly," inexplicable and unjustifiable by any human logic.[7] This failure to explain comes in part from our slowness to test the logic in the feudal ideal Roland espouses. In its turn, this reluctance stems largely from another scholarly reticence, a frequent unwillingness to allow that the feudalism we see in the *Song* was not only an abstract ideology but also an applied principle of social organization—a "method of government," as Joseph Strayer puts it. We have paraphrased correctly the question raised in the famous Roncevaux episode: Is Roland to call for aid or not? But in answering that question we have failed to make room for the antecedents of the scene and the practical implications of the horn-call, and have concentrated instead on the notion of a tragic error while neglecting the poem's construction as a whole.

Improving the reading is not, therefore, a simple matter of replacing a flawed hero with a good one. Our habitual ways of reading the *Song*—the plural pronoun, here and elsewhere, is a recognition that I have been struggling with it myself for more than twenty years—too often fail to recognize that its parts are related to one another through the ideas it illustrates. These ideas are not psychological but social: responsibility, including that of a king to his vassals; the impor-

[7]Scholars who have attributed some positive form of heroic folly or "folly of the Cross" to Roland include principally Guiette, 177; Crist, 18; Brault, *Song*, 1:245–46; Mickel, "Christian Duty," 133; Misrahi and Hendrickson, 370; Michael Wendt, *Der Oxforder Roland* (Munich, 1970), 279–80; and Pierre Le Gentil, "A propos de la démesure de Roland," *Cahiers de civilisation médiévale*, 11 (1968), 203–9. See also note 3 to Chapter 1 and note 11 to Chapter 2, below.

tance of principle; and the power of the given word to lend our deeds permanent effect in a mutable world. Thus the explanation of events in the *Song of Roland* begins here not with personal traits attributed to the characters—pride, stubbornness, vacillation, measure—but with the tasks and relationships that the bonds of homage and the demands of warfare assigned to important persons in the time of the audience. The fruits of steadfastness as the work shows and suggests them—an orderly society and protection for all its members against the arbitrary—are in no sense foreign to the ideals of feudalism. These are ideas that transcend the person, but they do so in ways we will not appreciate if we insist that the *Song* itself must above all else transcend its times.

Surprising though it may seem, there are only two full-length interpretive commentaries on the *Song of Roland,* by Edmond Faral and by Gerard Brault.[8] Faral's study (1934) is both out of date and out of print. Brault's 1978 study is neither; it is an invaluable work of scholarship, especially where iconography and typology are concerned, but its author has recourse to concepts and analogies drawn from Scripture and ecclesiastical writings to explain many passages where I think the text can be understood without appeal to analogy. My "Commentary on the Narrative," more compact than Brault's, makes more room for the relationship between the *Song* and the basic principles of feudalism in a period of consolidation, around the year 1100. On the other hand, it gives a fuller account of the text's contents, and a more sympathetic view of certain aspects of society in the poem's time, than do the studies by Pierre Le Gentil and Eugene Vance, which devote more space to aesthetic discussion and justification.[9]

This book is not, then, another general introduction to the *Song of*

[8]Edmond Faral, *La Chanson de Roland: Etude et analyse* (Paris, [1934]); Brault, *Song,* vol. 1. Joseph Bédier's well-known "Commentaires" (*La Chanson de Roland commentée* [Paris, 1927]) do not follow the full text line by line. They are concerned mainly with the clarification and defense of the Oxford text where earlier editors had rejected it. Bédier's famous interpretation in his *Légendes épiques,* 2d ed., vol. 3 (Paris, 1921), 410–45, breaks off, misleadingly, at Roland's death. T. A. Jenkins's rich stock of notes in *La Chanson de Roland: Oxford Version,* 2d ed. (Chicago, 1924), and Gérard Moignet's in his edition, *La Chanson de Roland: Texte original et traduction* (Paris, 1969), contain many interpretive statements and suggestions, but neither made a general interpretive argument. I cannot comment on all the many points of divergence and contact among the various interpretations cited here, in note 9, and elsewhere.

[9]Pierre Le Gentil, *La Chanson de Roland* (Paris, 1955 [2d ed. 1967], translated by Frances Beer under the title *The Song of Roland* [Cambridge, Mass., 1969]); Eugene Vance, *Reading the Song of Roland* (Englewood Cliffs, N.J., 1970). For examples of typological analogy applied to the interpretation of the *Song,* see Raimund Rütten, *Symbol und Mythus im altfranzösischen Rolandslied* (Braunschweig, 1970), and Wendt, *Oxforder Roland.*

Roland and does not replace the works just cited. It is an interpretation and a study in interpretation. The Commentary serves to furnish common points of reference and argument to all readers and to avoid gross errors of memory—this in preference to the "significant-scene" or "significant-line" methods often used in the interpretation of such a long poem. Both short articles and summaries of moderate length inevitably give a false impression of sequence and context by taking lines and speeches out of context and highlighting them as illustrations or proofs. The goal of many interpreters of the *Song* has been to make economically the kind of point that cannot be made without expense.[10]

To paraphrase a major work of literature, even one that counts great length and multiplicity of episodes among its outstanding features, may seem strange nevertheless. But to do so for the *Roland* is only to recognize that no complete canonical paraphrase exists and that much of the criticism of the *Song*, where both structure and ideas are concerned, is a response to traditional notions about the work as much as to what we may observe in it. In any case, nearly all interpretive work on narratives of great bulk is dependent on a periphrastic representation which, while perhaps not actually written, is in kind much like the restatements we find in Faral, Bédier, and Le Gentil.[11] There are, prima facie, clear advantages to making our paraphrase of reference as full and accurate as we can.

Thus, even if the *Song of Roland* were not what Cerquiglini says—one of those poems that most engage our attention as medievalists—it

[10]I realize I am repeating a caveat of Albert Pauphilet's: "When a work has been discussed, fragmented, pulled in every direction, to the degree the *Roland* has been, the most necessary thing, and the most difficult, is to learn once more to read it simply. . . . We have lent exaggerated importance to the most trivial details, when it was our pleasure to see them as evidence for our arguments; we have believed that a perfectly ordinary little passage could teach us more than an entire poem, on the grounds that the author had hidden a confession in it and thus given, to those who could grasp it, the key to his puzzle" (*Le Legs du Moyen Age* [Melun, France, 1950], 67). The approach Pauphilet describes is epitomized in Gustave Lanson's disdainful (and influential) dismissal of the poem's action: "'Roland is bold, but Oliver is wise.' That is all [our author] needs to define his characters" (*Histoire de la littérature française* [1894], rev. ed. by Paul Tuffrau [Paris, 1952], 30). It does not help, as Crist, 14, has noted, that the "significant line" is misquoted here.

[11]Lubbock has described the phenomenon well, though in another connection: "Nothing, no power, will keep a book steady and motionless before us. . . . As quickly as we read, it melts and shifts in the memory; even at the moment the last page is turned, a great part of the book, its finer detail, is already vague and doubtful. A little later, after a few days or months, how much is really left of it? A cluster of impressions, some clear points emerging from a mist of uncertainty, this is all we can hope to possess, generally speaking, in the name of a book" (Percy Lubbock, *The Craft of Fiction* [London, 1954], 1; I am indebted for this reference to Michael Issacharoff).

would still be an important case study in the reception of one culture's literary art by another culture. But such considerations must be grounded in a text—in this case, the Oxford *Song of Roland* with its references to early medieval society, that of its original audience. Thus I begin with an extensive re-presentation of what happens in the *Song of Roland,* including comments on how its content and action are related to certain feudal ideals of the late eleventh or early twelfth century.[12] It is not my purpose to apply new categories to the *Song,* either christological or Jungian (to take two recent examples). I hope only to make it sit more at ease with the social and military concepts that criticism has always associated with it, rather loosely at times. This can be done, perhaps, only at some cost to the claims of complexity, ambiguity, or mystery recently made for the work, but what the *Song of Roland* thereby loses in subtlety it may more than regain in heroic temper.

It is a pleasure to thank the University of Virginia Center for Advanced Studies for a semester's support, which allowed me to make considerable progress in the drafting of the Commentary. Particular thanks are due to Alice Colby-Hall and Gerard Brault for close reading and valuable suggestions for the organization of Part Two. Other debts to colleagues are detailed in the footnotes, but it would be wrong for me not to mention here the energetic and searching introduction to problems in reading Old French narrative that I received in the courses taught by Larry S. Crist at Vanderbilt University.

ROBERT FRANCIS COOK

Charlottesville, Virginia

[12]On the importance of acts, and their results, for interpretation, see Tony Hunt, "The Structure of Medieval Narrative," *Journal of European Studies,* 3 (1973), 295–328, esp. 315ff., despite Hunt's reservations about certain forms of causality (pp. 298, 304–6, 316); see also Hunt's "Character and Causality in the Oxford *Roland,*" *Medioevo romanzo,* 5 (1978), 3–33, esp. 3–4, 30–33. Cf. Bédier, *Légendes,* 3:409, with a different concept of "subjectivity" (Hunt, "Structure," 315), and also Eugene Vance, "Spatial Structure in the *Chanson de Roland,*" *Modern Language Notes,* 82 (1967), 612; Jacques Thomas, "La Traîtrise de Ganelon," *Romanica Gandensia,* 16 (1976), 97.

Preliminary Note

The text treated in the Commentary is the "Oxford version" of the *Song of Roland,* that found in manuscript Digby 23 of the Bodleian Library in Oxford. This is not the only version of the poem extant in the Middle Ages, and the other versions are themselves of literary and cultural interest. But the Oxford version, besides being the oldest (commonly dated around the year 1100) and the most concise of the complete texts, is also the common reference in matters of interpretation.

I have not been able to reproduce a full text of the *Song of Roland* here, nor is one necessary, given the existence of such complete and excellent editions as Gerard Brault's (now available in one-volume paperback, with revised introduction) and Gérard Moignet's.[1] The use of translations, as means of access to the *Song of Roland,* is a more delicate matter. Some of the most easily available translations contain modifications of considerable importance to the reading.[2] All of them are influenced to some extent by the traditions of interpretation that I intend to modify by reference to features of the original. Among the generally available English texts, the easiest to read, and in many ways the most accurate, are no doubt Gerard Brault's, W. S. Merwin's, and Frederick Goldin's. The excellent rendering by D. D. R. Owen is

[1]Brault's 1978 text and translation were reprinted under the title *La Chanson de Roland: Student Edition* (University Park, Pa., 1984); Moignet's 1969 text and translation have been reprinted several times, and the translation separately in the "Univers des lettres Bordas" collection (1970). Both scholars list other editions, of which Bédier's *La Chanson de Roland* (Paris, 1921; rev. ed. 1937, reprinted dozens of times) is the most often cited. See also Duggan, *Guide,* chap. 3.

[2]I have published a brief critique of several translations from this point of view: "Translators and Traducers," *Olifant,* 7 (1980), 327–42.

unfortunately more difficult to obtain. But the reader of a translation should bear in mind that any of the numerous English *Roland* texts is a work of interpretation, not the very words of the original.

This Commentary generally proceeds one stanza (or assonanced *laisse*) at a time. For purposes of analysis, I have treated the *Song* as a linear narration whose order as the audience would have heard it is an essential feature. Attentive members of this audience, I assume, would have had better memories than we sometimes attribute to them. Accustomed to the everyday need for reasonably accurate retention of oral bargains, oaths, and testimony, they also remembered the tenor of the vows and promises that occur in epic recitations.[3] The well-known "similar" and "parallel" laisses do not bring the narration to a halt, even when they appear to repeat themselves. These juxtaposed laisses almost always include some new information for the attentive listener (a name, a conditional adverb) even when they do not appear to advance the temporal sequence.[4] I have given examples at appropriate points in the Commentary.

The numbers of the laisses are given both in Roman (the traditional style, as in Moignet) and in Arabic (as in Brault). For strictly practical reasons, I follow the line numbering and laisse order given by Moignet, which is closest to that in the Oxford manuscript, the bulk of the Commentary having been done on the basis of Moignet's edition before the appearance of Brault's. Differences in arrangement be-

[3]The implications of an emphasis on the audience's knowledge and experience of the poem, rather than on how it was composed (orally or in writing?), cannot be pursued in the available space. In brief, neither oral poets nor their audiences should be refused credit for being able to remember significant events of a poem's beginning while approaching its end. They could thus consult their memories in order to recall, for example, that it was the group and not Roland that gave Ganelon his mission to Saragossa, despite the traitor's claims in line 3772 (cf. lines 321–22). On the importance of group memory in feudal affairs, see, e.g., Jean-François Lemarignier, *La France médiévale: Institutions et société* (Paris, 1970), 127; Marc Bloch, *Feudal Society* (1939–40; trans. L. A. Manyon, in two parts with continuous pagination [Chicago, 1964]), 360. Further discussion is now available in Brian Stock's *The Implications of Literacy* (Princeton, 1983), esp. chap. 1. On the informational potential of the formula, see Michael Nagler, "Toward a Generative View of the Oral Formula," *Transactions and Proceedings of the American Philological Society*, 98 (1967), 269–311. (I would not go so far as to insist that the hearers of an orally performed epic would retain details well enough to allow verbal patterning of the type Brault suggests [e.g., Brault, *Song*, 1:120–21].) Thus I do not intend to take sides in the current debate over whether the Oxford text was composed orally by means of improvisational techniques. To espouse unity in the work's general conception does not in my opinion require one to take a stance on formulaic composition. Whatever else that technique implies, it is increasingly clear that it does not imply a naive or shortsighted poet.

[4]Rychner admitted that these terms were inadequate to convey the subtlety with which the *Song of Roland* presents words and events (Jean Rychner, *La Chanson de geste* [Geneva, 1955], 93).

tween the two are not great, involving principally a disagreement about the position of Moignet's (and Oxford's) laisses 113 and 114 (CXIII–CXIV), which Brault places after Moignet's laisse 125 (CXXV), itself transposed with laisse 126 in the Brault text (cf. Brault, *Song*, 1:201–2). There is also an error in Moignet's line numbering, which omits the line number 1659. Parenthetical references in Arabic numerals are to specific lines under discussion.

As a translation would, a Modern English commentary on the text raises the question of how one is to refer to the characters. The relationship between medieval Islam and the enemies with whom the heroes do battle is tenuous at best. Charles, as he appears in the *Song*, is not the historical Charlemagne, and he is neither king nor emperor precisely, though the poem calls him both.[5] His men are certainly Christians by their lights, though not by everyone's, but they are neither eighth-century Franks nor Frenchmen. Neither are they knights in many modern-day senses of the word, and to call them soldiers is to introduce connotations more appropriate to the modern standing army. I have used the name Charles as I have used such terms as "emperor," "king," "Saracen," and "Christian," because they are cognate with the poem's own words and thus are less confusing than other terms when used to find one's place in the story, and also because it is difficult to find replacements for them that are not either cumbersome or jarring. The author's name poses similar problems. It may or may not have been Turold, but it does not much matter what we call him, since that name has no other associations whatever—there are no dates, places, or other writings attached to it, only the *Song of Roland* itself, for whatever that association is worth.

On the other hand, the *Song* is somewhat more specific (if not, perhaps, totally precise) in its use of terms that refer to institutions, social practices, and beliefs. I have discussed some of those terms briefly, with references to more detailed studies. Often the terms are false cognates, or partial cognates, and while I may not have used equivalents that will please all specialists, I hope at least to have provided sufficient warning against the sort of misinterpretations that distort our sense of how the narration is proceeding.

[5]Cf. Karl Uitti, *Story, Myth, and Celebration in Old French Narrative Poetry* (Princeton, 1973), 80–81. The image of Islam in the *chansons de geste* is given full and sympathetic treatment by Norman Daniel, *Heroes and Saracens* (Edinburgh, 1984).

PART ONE

Commentary on the Narrative

Before Roncevaux

Marsile's Council

1 (I)

The road to Roncevaux and beyond begins, for the reader or the medieval hearer, in an enemy camp in the midst of war. The war has been going on for a long time, we are told, but there is no preamble to speak of. As the tale unfolds, its characters will tell us most of what we need to know to understand what is happening. This is largely a self-contained or at least self-explanatory narrative, once we realize the situation in which it is set. The first scenes take place in what is called the Spanish city of Saragossa, but the geographic location is not crucial, and it does not matter who the Saracens are ethnically or culturally unless we are studying the origin of the poem and its own history, which is not my immediate purpose. The most important things about the people called Saracen or pagan are first that they are an alien enemy and second that they are beaten.[1] After a long war with an army under the emperor Charlemagne, or Charles (whose name, again, is not a reference to a historical person but the invocation of a positive, civilizing force in the world), the enemy are hemmed in and cannot escape. Nonetheless, they have no intention of surrendering.

2 (II)

After a single laisse of setting, the events come thick and fast.

The pagan Marsile is a feudal leader in this text, and (as does

[1]See Wolfgang Van Emdén, "Pro Karolo Magno," *Olifant,* 2 (1974–75), 176; Joan B. Williamson, "Trust and Kinship in the *Chanson de Roland,*" *VIII Congreso de la Société Rencesvals* (Pamplona, 1981), 553; Cartier, 37.

Charles) he calls upon the men who owe him allegiance for aid and advice. Without their willing support he cannot act. Neither man has any other instrument of war or justice besides this group. Here Marsile tells his lieutenants that he and they are defeated. He has no army capable of withstanding the Christians (19). Line 18, taken alone and literally, would mean that Marsile has no army capable of fighting at all, but line 19, which is much less restrictive, carries out the thought: Marsile's men are not good enough to break, with their charge, the front of the Christian army. (The "pagan" enemy is conceived as fighting the way medieval Europeans tended to do, depending heavily on cavalry charging as a unit.)

It is generally assumed that at this point Charles has been pursuing Marsile for some time, although these laisses do not say so. The two have met before as enemies (we will learn of one such occasion in laisse 14), and it seems that Marsile has gotten the worst of it all along. But he still has an army of considerable size. The figures in the *Song* express not precise counts but respectably large numbers. Later Marsile will appear at Roncevaux with four hundred thousand men (laisse 68), of whom one hundred thousand will attack the rear guard (laisse 78). The idea in laisse 2 is surely not that Marsile is helpless, but that he knows from experience that he cannot match the Christians on the battlefield, at least not in straightforward combat. "As in ancient tragedy," says Moignet, "everything is decided at the outset" (27). But the pagans, at least, do not think that way. Their chief does not consider surrender, but asks how he can avoid the fate of those who oppose Christendom. None of the members of his council has anything to offer, except Blancandrin.

3 (III)

It has been said over and over that the characters of the *Song of Roland* are all alike, whether pagan or Christian, Saracen or "Frank." It is true that both groups are equally dedicated to warfare and that they appear to belong to societies organized in the same way—the way familiar to the poet and his hearers. They dress alike, use the same equipment, and often talk alike, but they are *not fundamentally alike*, and the cliché of the handbooks can mislead us. The first event of the first episode of the poem—Blancandrin's speech at Marsile's council—proves that the pagans have attitudes that only infidels can have, attitudes that the Christians, to their misfortune, do not even understand. From the very first, the epic portrays the clash of two sets of ethical views.[2]

[2]The pagans are "felons," not only for the reasons Brault (*Song*, 1:208) gives, but also because they do not keep faith. This definition of *felonie* is M. Bloch's (*Feudal Society*,

Here is what Blancandrin proposes. If the Saracens cannot win fairly, then they must cheat: tell Charles they will submit, even though they do not intend to do so. The text is not verbally explicit here (it rarely is entirely so), but the development and sequence of Blancandrin's speech in laisses 3 and 4 clearly demonstrate that the promise suggested in lines 28–39 is a brazen, outright lie. Marsile should promise, but not make, feudal submission (29). *Fedeilz servises* and *amistez* can have no other implication in the political context of the late eleventh and early twelfth centuries, even if for some reason we were to say the poet is not using them as technical terms despite the context. They refer to the bonds of affection and steadfastness that are the fabric of feudalism.[3] Furthermore, the promise is to be sealed by a double appeal: to the Christians' cupidity (which the Saracens assume to exist as a matter of course) and to their credulity (which turns out to be limited, but sufficient for Blancandrin's scheme).

Lines 30–34 suggest a bribe: vast amounts of money and animals, perhaps more gold and silver than there was in the entire historical Carolingian kingdom. Of special interest is line 34, with its reference to the mercenaries whose presence in the Christian army Blancandrin seems to presume. The poet probably lived at a time when soldiers were already being paid in order to assure a ready fighting force not dependent on the various conditions placed on feudal duty.[4] Yet the mercenaries are never referred to in the *Song of Roland* except in Blancandrin's speeches, and we may think that his easy assumption—that the Charles of the epic is necessarily required to pay men to fight for Christendom—functions as a first example of the errors the Saracens, with their flawed view of the world, are destined to make.

In any case, lines 35–46 clearly are placed here both to show the profound iniquity of the foreigner and to suggest how that very iniq-

---

217, 228–29); cf. F. L. Ganshof, *Feudalism,* trans. Philip Grierson, 3d ed. (New York, 1964), 99–100.

[3]The meanings of these and other terms are studied in some detail in the various histories of medieval institutions (Ganshof's, Lemarignier's, M. Bloch's, David Herlihy's *History of Feudalism* [New York, 1970] and Robert Boutruche's *Seigneurie et féodalité,* 2 vols. 2d ed. [Paris, 1968–70]), and there seems to be sufficient agreement on their meanings to allow the general orientation for which I intend to use them. I have also relied on the standard dictionaries of Medieval French: Godefroy's, Tobler and Lommatzsch's, and Greimas's one-volume dictionary, which derives from them. More detailed work, highly suggestive for the *Roland* text, is found in G. S. Burgess, *Contribution à l'étude du vocabulaire pré-courtois* (Geneva, 1970) and in Burgess's specialized articles, cited below as appropriate. The notes to Brault's translation (*Song,* 2:253–82) are extremely helpful here as elsewhere. See also George Fenwick Jones, *The Ethos of the Song of Roland* (Baltimore, 1963), 9–95, and compare Chapter 6, below.

[4]See John Beeler, *Warfare in Feudal Europe* (Ithaca, N.Y., 1971), 42, and Philippe Contamine, *War in the Middle Ages* (1980; trans. Michael Jones [Oxford, 1984]), 32, for remarks on twelfth-century mercenaries.

uity might allow the pagans to preserve their independence and their religion. The first, small suggestion of fatigue among the Christians is here. Charles has been at war a long time and should go home. You will follow him in the autumn, at the date of Michaelmas, says Blancandrin to Marsile; you will be baptized—an essential promise—and you will swear fealty to him (this time, unambiguously, the feudal terms *hom* ["vassal"] and *honur* ["fief"] appear).[5] Blancandrin adds the key element at once. The proof of good intentions lies in the giving of hostages. And hostages Charles shall have. The fundamental evil of the enemy shows through his simple statement: he will send his own son, even if it means the son's death. The whole plan Blancandrin describes is a ruse. It is not the promised submission, but a lie, and a desperate one; but worst of all, it is an inhumane one, for Blancandrin is not planning to pay the price himself. He is ready to sacrifice the hostages' lives for the sake of his present status. He does not invoke beliefs, only his possessions. "It is better for the hostages to be killed than for us to lose our lands and fiefs, and be reduced to begging" (45–46; "lose fair Spain," 59).

4 (IV)

The fourth laisse is the logical extension of the third and serves to make explicit what the third only suggests. Blancandrin predicts—he swears—that the course of action he has described, bribes and the guarantee of hostages, will have specific results. The Franks, misled by a false promise, will disband. They are, of course, a host *banie,* called together for a specific campaign (cf. 211), and not a standing army; when they are not on campaign, they scatter to their fiefs and fortresses.[6] At Aachen, or Aix-la-Chapelle, his capital, Charlemagne will wait in vain for Marsile to carry out his promise. In his anger Charles will put the hostages to death. But in winter Marsile is beyond his reach. The host cannot be re-created, and the medieval Pyrenees, a nearly trackless waste in summer, are impassable for armies and baggage trains in winter. We may recall briefly that in the year 778 the historical Charlemagne lost his baggage and men precisely in the trek across the mountains. Even the highways of the twentieth century have been closed for days at a time by the snows that fall in the high Pyrenees. Desperate as it is, then, Blancandrin's plan is firmly rooted in the practicalities of medieval warfare. (The work does not record

[5]The *honur* was originally not the fief itself, but the associated functions; by the time of the poem the two had tended to fuse. See Boutruche, 1:186–213; M. Bloch, 176; cf. Burgess, *Contribution,* 78–79.

[6]On the temporary nature of military service, see M. Bloch, 220, 221; Beeler, 29–30, 41–42; Contamine, 133.

any discussion of what might happen the next summer or later; it may be that the Saracens are counting on the vagaries of organization and transport to protect them indefinitely.) Then Blancandrin repeats the most important element of his stratagem. The hostages are the key; they will make the plan politically practical, as it is militarily, and there is no doubt they will be sacrificed.

The laisse closes with a brief but indispensable expression of assent from the members of Marsile's council. This is the way the feudal gathering works, at least in principle. And though it is not surprising and need not be insisted upon, this acquiescence is not a filler or a simple stylistic device intended to round out a laisse. Marsile is presented as an evil and cowardly pagan, but he is not a tyrant; his court decides.

5 (v)

The council is over with that vote. The rapid and straightforward narrative continues. Blancandrin's proposal has been made in full and accepted by the group. Its execution alone remains. Marsile applies the group's will in detail, chooses ambassadors, and gives them their charges, which they accept in quasi-ritual fashion.

6 (vi)

This laisse overlaps with laisse 5; it is the first real "parallel laisse" we have seen. As is the practice with the parallel laisses, it also offers new material. The *Roland* narrative may contain repetitions of limited scope, but it never halts. Now Marsile's charge to his ambassadors is set out in specific detail. It corresponds to Blancandrin's plan. We should not, perhaps, make too much of the term of less than a month that Marsile mentions as the time until his submission, since we do not know exactly at what time of year the action of the poem takes place. The intention may be to suggest a reassuring desire for promptness on Marsile's part. In a very short time the conversion will take place, and Marsile will take his feudal vows. Again the terms are unmistakable: *amur* does not designate an emotional state, it is a term for a sociopolitical relationships, just as *feid,* "fidelity," is a social and not a religious term in this context. The hostages are mentioned again specifically; they are clearly part and parcel of the plan. Blancandrin approves the restatement of his stratagem.

7 (vii)

Another necessary narrative element, the equipping of the messengers and their departure, is given a twist at the end by the somber intervention of the narrator's voice (not frequent in this text). Charles, it is said, cannot possibly protect himself against the treachery of these men.

The first change of scene takes place at this point. We have learned that Marsile does not expect to resist Charles, and we have seen him arrange, at Blancandrin's instigation and upon the affirmative vote of his council, to stave off defeat by false promises. The falsehood will derive its effect specifically from the giving of hostages, whose lives are to be deliberately forfeited. The audience knows all of this, but it has also been obliquely reminded (95) that Charles and his men do not know it. All we have seen so far is the enemy's intentions. The next episode will show us what the Christians do when they are faced with Marsile's proposal.

Charles's Council

8 (VIII)

Now we are in the midst of Charles's army, where he is rejoicing at the taking of a city, the destruction of its fortifications, and the forced conversion of the inhabitants. The latter action. a distasteful one to the modern mind, is a theoretically requisite solution in more violent and less stable times, when the sworn word was a primary guarantee of behavior. A defeated enemy who made a public submission might in theory be spared; any who did not might logically be put to death at once rather than be left behind in a state of rebellion.[7] Charles, it will soon be seen, does not intend to occupy Spain.

The emperor is seen here surrounded by his men, some of whom are named. The names may have meant something to the *Song*'s hearers, who (it is generally thought) had some familiarity with epic legends beyond the text at hand. But we cannot identify them all with certainty, and the narrative does not require that we know precisely who they are as individuals. On the other hand, it is obvious who their leader is. The messengers go directly to him.

9 (IX)

Blancandrin speaks immediately, saluting Charles diplomatically in the terms of the latter's religion and not that of the Saracen (which was schematically presumed to involve worship of Muhammad, or

[7]This form of coercion was a traditional element in the ideology of kingship; see Paolo Cherchi, "Un Dovere della 'pietas' regia: L'Uccisione del nemico," *Modern Philology*, 73 (1976), 244–56.

"Mahum," as a rival of God). The message is transmitted almost word for word, a distillation of the (false) promise proposed in laisse 3 and agreed upon in laisse 4. Charles does not reply. Like Marsile, he cannot act alone in any case. But before submitting the offer to his barons, he insists on fuller information.

10–12 (x–xii)

After some reflection, Charles seems to accept the message Marsile and his council sent as being superficially logical. But (as Blancandrin has apparently foreseen) the Franco-Christian leader does not trust the pagan's bald assertions. He asks for guarantees beyond the simple statement, which is understandable enough in dealings with a bitter enemy (144) whose habit (we will soon learn) is to lie. Blancandrin's answer is ready. It is the reinforced falsehood, bolstered by conditions the French would apparently never violate themselves. We will give hostages, says the Saracen, as many as you wish, to hold as warrant that we will keep our word. Not now, but in the autumn, at Michaelmas, we will come to your capital and convert. Charles now knows what to tell his council. In laisse 11 he calls the barons together; we are told he will not proceed without the consent, and thus the guidance, of the men who are in fact his strength (167).[8] They are again summarily named in laisse 12, and the audience is told or reminded of Ganelon's treachery and warned that what follows is going to go wrong, indeed has already gone wrong as a matter of epic history. Thus the hearers are aware what reaction is proper during the next scene, that of the meeting in which the group surrounding Charlemagne decides what to do about Marsile's offer.

13 (xiii)

Charlemagne now restates the terms of Marsile's promise—money and presents, and eventual submission and conversion if the Christians will make the first move and go home (187). But he does not give any indication of his own opinion of this conditional surrender, saying only (perhaps with a nuance of suspicion), "I do not know what he really means to do." For reasons that are not immediately clear, he does not mention the hostages at first. Perhaps that is because his men have already heard Blancandrin (Naimon at least knows of the offer, to judge by his speech; 241), or perhaps it is because they do not really need that detail, but only a general knowledge of the situation, in order to make the right decision. The response given by the French

[8]Cf. M. Bloch, 410.

councilors shows that they share Charles's mistrust of the enemy: "We had better watch out" (192; cf. 143–46).

14 (XIV)

When the emperor has finished, Roland speaks first. The poet tells us he does not like Marsile's proposal (194), and Roland himself tells us why not. It is here, in the first speech Roland makes, that we must begin to look carefully at exactly what he says, and in what context. At first glance the poem seems to be implying that Roland is both aggressive and impolite. In line 195 he seems to be "contradicting" his leader. This is the obvious cognate of Old French *cuntredire* in both English and Modern French. But as is the case elsewhere, the reality of what the text conveys is not what our habits of language and our traditional approach to Roland's personality may lead us to believe.

First, the verb *cuntredire,* like *amur, feid,* and other words to be discussed as they appear, has changed in meaning and connotation more than in form over the centuries. *Cuntredire* did occasionally mean "contradict" in the Middle Ages, but it often meant one of several other things instead, notably "to express one's opposition to something."[9] And that is surely what it means here. Despite our likely first reaction, Roland cannot express any sharp disagreement with his leader's opinion, because his leader has not given any opinion. It is not possible to contradict him, despite the usually personal object *li* in 195, which Moignet was surely right to translate as *y,* "it" (cf. Brault: "to voice his opposition" [i.e., to the proposal]). Roland is the first to speak, and when he speaks against acceptance of Marsile's proposal, he is not "contradicting" anyone. He merely responds to Charles's implicit request for discussion, thus exercising his right, indeed carrying out his duty, to give his opinion for his leader's guidance and the group's.[10]

[9]See Greimas, 137; Tobler and Lommatzsch treat this example as intransitive under the gloss "widersprechen" ("contradict"), but cf. the examples given under "bestreiten," 'contest,' 'oppose' (2:791).

[10]On the duty of counsel, see Lemarignier, 135–36; M. Bloch, 92–93; on Roland's speaking first, see William Kibler, "Roland versus the Barons," in Raymond Cormier, ed., *Voices of Conscience* (Philadelphia, 1977), 53. Roland's motivation here has been said to be "an excess of heroic pride" (Vance, *Reading,* 5). "A whole lifetime for the taking of Saragossa is a bit much," says Italo Siciliano ironically in *Les Chansons de geste et l'épopée* (Turin and Paris, 1970), 351. But Hunt is surely right to say that this speech is "not provocative" ("Character and Causality," 5). Roland's simple syntax has been compared with Ganelon's deceptive use of language by Léopold Peeters, "Le 'Faire et le 'dire' dans la *Chanson de Roland,*" *Revue des langues romanes,* 81 (1975), 376–93. Frederick Goldin has studied both the language Ganelon uses and the language the text uses to present him and his acts, see his "Die Rolle Ganelons und das Motiv der Worte," in Kurt Baldinger, ed., *Beiträge zum romanischen Mittelalter* (Tübingen, 1977), 128–55. Cf. Pensom, 87–88; Vance, *Reading,* 32–34; J. Thomas, 96.

And second, this is a denser passage than it has sometimes been thought to be. We learn something vital both about the situation and about Roland from his argument. First, we are told the circumstances in which Marsile's offer is being made. It is not the first of its kind. He has been on the defensive for a long time, and he has already tried treachery—not just any treachery, but specifically a false offer of peace. His fifteen envoys said exactly the same things then (201–4), but it was a lie, and the council should have rejected the proposal. When Charles sent two of his officers, Basan and Basile, to the enemy, they were beheaded. The logic of that result is not immediately clear. What did Marsile have to gain by slaughtering the French ambassadors if he wanted a truce? But that uncertainty is less important than the function this reference has in the narrative. It is presented not as some chimerical imagining of Roland's, but as a true event with obvious relevance to the present situation. It is referred to as both true and important by Ganelon and the emperor later on (329–30, 488–92). The dead men's names are the symbol and guarantee of the enemy's evil nature. The hero represents the voice of experience here, reminding the council and the audience of something both already know in fact.[11] The barons know that Marsile's promises cannot be trusted (192), and the audience knows that the offer presently under consideration is simple treachery, a fact made clear from the outset. The point is not just that the Saracens are unchivalric in the accepted (and often trivial) sense of the word. They are people with whom one cannot deal normally because they do not follow the rules that allow such dealings.

Thus Roland, arguing from common experience, is right to say that trusting Marsile is a mistake.[12] That fact has not prevented readers from seeing laisse 14 as early proof of his nastiness. One possible reason is a misunderstanding of what vengeance means. It is not vendetta here, but a duty of leadership.[13] When Roland calls on Charles to avenge Basan and Basile, he is expressing a not-so-subtle

[11]Cf. Cartier, 38; Williamson, 555.

[12]Cf. Calin, 17; Le Gentil, "A propos de la *démesure*," 204; Williamson, 555; Cartier, 60; Crist, 17; Misrahi and Hendrickson, 361–62; Jean-Louis Picherit, "Le Silence de Ganelon," *Cahiers de civilisation médiévale*, 21 (1978), 265–66; J. Thomas, 96–97.

[13]"The primary duty of the kinsman was vengeance. *The same was true of the man who had done homage or received it*" (M. Bloch, 225; emphasis added). This duty of lord and vassal is distinct in concept from private feud; see M. Bloch, 125, 412. On the importance of vengeance, see Fern Farnham, "Romanesque Design in the *Chanson de Roland*," *Romance Philology*, 18 (1964), 147, 150; Del Monte, 227; Terence Scully, "The Ordeal at Roncesvalles," *Olifant*, 7 (1980), 228–29. For confusion with vendetta, see Jones, *Ethos*, 82–83, and John Halverson, "Ganelon's Trial," *Speculum*, 42 (1967), 661–62. The overlord's duty of "warranty" or protection is presented by M. Bloch, 225, and Ganshof, 94–95.

structural necessity. As the chief of a warrior group, who has accepted responsibility for his men in return for their homage, the king is moved to vengeance by political realism and not by spite. Roland is once again reminding his real and fictional hearers of something they probably already knew. Ideally, a feudal leader brings the weight of the group he commands to bear against anyone who attacks his subjects, and thus the machinery of which Roland, Charles, and the army are all part functions at its best to ward off harm before it occurs. But here one of the principal conditions controlling events in the *Song of Roland* appears in the text for the first time clearly.[14] A leader cannot, in all circumstances, protect the men who are his allies. Charles could not protect Basan and Basile (cf. 329–30), nor indeed will he be able to save Roland, though he knows the risk. Yet he will eventually make it clear that anyone who harms his men will not escape in the long run. Thus vengeance in 210–14 is a political act with abstract implications, and not an emotional response. Our knowledge of the risk that vengeance may degenerate into mere feud should not obscure the logic of the act, which is essentially defensive.

Roland's uncompromising call for consistency in policy—"fight the war in the spirit in which you began it!"—is thus, in the broad view, a call for commitment to the logic of a system. This does not mean that his speech here is given without energy and passion, as he recounts a sad event in the order of its occurrence and comes to a justifiably angry conclusion. The anger is directed toward Marsile. The only way to deal with him is by force. That is not an *a priori* assumption on Roland's part, but an empirical conclusion.

There remains an element in this laisse which might be taken as an expression of pride on Roland's part. Prefacing his mini-narrative, Roland uses the first-person pronoun and verbs to tell of the army's victories: "I won Nobles; I took Valterne, and the other cities" (199–200). It is too early for me to claim that the appearance of pride here should be discounted, but at least it is clear that the passage as a whole is concerned with something besides these victories, mentioned in passing. We should also note what Roland is not doing. His claim is not exaggerated. He is, demonstrably, Charles's chief lieutenant and apparently acts as his field commander (see, e.g., lines 662–63, where Roland alone is named by the narrator as having "taken" the city of Galne). It is not too much to suggest that he acted in the emperor's

[14]On the guarantor's role in the *Song,* see Wolfgang Van Emden, "E cil de France le cleiment a guarant: Roland, Vivien, et le thème du guarant," *Olifant,* 1 (1974), 21–47; also in *Société Rencesvals, VIe Congrès International: Actes* (Aix-en-Provence, 1974), 31–61.

stead on the occasions referred to, which could mean that the statements in lines 198–200 are as accurate as the rest of what he says. By synecdoche, as Charles's designated agent, he won those cities by leading the Franco-Christian army that attacked them.[15]

15 (XV)

For better or worse, no one agrees with Roland.[16] Charles is not a tyrant any more than Marsile is. It is not up to him to respond to any proposition until his council, the legislative body, has discussed the matter, and he says nothing in reply to his nephew. And the French, for whatever reason, do not vote. The easy way out, for the modern commentator, is simply to say that if they agreed with Roland without hearing Ganelon there would be no Roncevaux, indeed, no *Song of Roland* at all. This sort of narrative necessity sometimes requires characters to respond to the story line as a whole rather than to the immediate context, and it is an occasional temptation to invoke such an obvious necessity in the discussion of such a laconic text. But it has also been pointed out that the army, as characters, may not be in the same position that we are in as spectators to give immediate assent to Roland's counsel. First, they do not know for sure, as we do, that accepting Marsile's offer this time does not mean peace. Second, they have been at war for many years, as the text will soon remind us, and they are not all heroes of Roland's stripe. Although it is not said openly, they may be suffering from the inevitable fatigue of war, and their zeal may be just weak enough to allow them to consider what might be taken to be an honorable conclusion to the struggle.[17]

Ganelon, on the other hand, contradicts Roland sharply and insultingly. Without any attempt to counter his argument, and with no reference to past experience, he simply insists that Marsile's offer be taken at face value, adding that anyone who counsels its rejection "does not care how we will die" (227). That is a curious conclusion, and it may explain why Ganelon is so cutting in his reference to Roland's speech. First, of course, a soldier fighting for a supreme cause, social or religious, may not have much thought for how he will

[15]"When [Roland] uses the first person pronoun it denotes, not himself as an individual, but as a defender of public priorities, as an aspect of the whole" (Pensom, 113; the point will be further developed in connection with laisse 83). The entire army, presumably, attacked the cities mentioned in lines 199–200; these actions should be distinguished from the rear-guard action at Roncevaux.

[16]Although Jacques Thomas, 95, suggested that Roland is here expressing the feelings of the group.

[17]But for Van Emden the army is not tired ("Guarant," 27). Brault (*Song*, 1:106–8) argues that the council of Franks is unreliable.

die, and surely should not make survival a central element in an argument about policy. Second, if Ganelon is a Christian, then he should not give much weight to the prospect of physical death. Third, and perhaps most important, Ganelon has (to his own peril, as it turns out) failed to counter Roland's appeal to experience. Basan and Basile died, in degrading fashion, precisely because Marsile's earlier plea was accepted rashly (206), and if they could be slain with impunity, the precedent thus set will mean that all of Charles's men may risk further attack.

Does Ganelon's expressed concern with death then suffice to explain why he is moved to insult Roland so bitterly and suddenly when the hero calls for further sacrifices? He calls him *bricun* (220) and *fol* (229), at least by implication, by linking these pejorative terms to the counsel Roland has just given and by calling the hero's advice outrageous (*cunseill d'orguill,* 228). The text shows no overt motivation sufficient for the modern reader, but several have been posited. It may be a way of showing Ganelon's depravity that he should speak out, in haste and without reflection, against Roland's prudent suggestion and call the latter a fool in the same breath. On the other hand, it may be that he thinks he sees an immediate way out of the war in which he is risking his life and jumps at the chance eagerly, without realizing where the real danger lies, both for the French and (as it shortly turns out) for himself.

Early critics insisted that Ganelon must have hated Roland for some reason before the action of the poem began.[18] That is not necessary if we understand Ganelon to be a semi-hieratic figure, tending to error, rather than an attempt at reproducing in fiction the complexities that may be discerned in the motives of real persons. He may function usefully in a complex narrative without being multidimensional himself. By approaching him as functionally wrong, we may well run a lesser risk of anachronism, and for the nonce we will be freed from the obligation to decide what may have happened outside the text. It is true that at one point, much later, Ganelon says Roland once mistreated him, but that is when he is on trial for his life (3757–60), and

[18]See, e.g., Louis Petit de Julleville in his edition, *La Chanson de Roland* (Paris, 1878), 67; Bédier, *Légendes,* 3:413; Guy Mermier, "More about Unity in the *Song of Roland,*" *Olifant,* 2 (1974–75), 94; Auguste Demoulin, "Ganelon désigné pour l'ambassade," *Les Etudes classiques,* 45 (1977), 227–46, 377–89; and Moignet, 45. Siciliano, 353, claims for good measure that Roland also hates Ganelon. But the text gives adequate reasons for the conflict; see Hunt, "Character and Causality," 10–11, 16, and cf. Robert A. Hall, Jr., "Ganelon and Roland," *Modern Language Quarterly,* 6 (1945), 263–70; J. A. Stranges, "The Character and the Trial of Ganelon," *Romania,* 96 (1975), 333–67; Williamson, 556.

there is certainly no reason to think he has suddenly stopped lying at that point. His betrayal of Roland seems abrupt and unmotivated only if we think of Ganelon as a worthy man who requires great provocation to do and speak evil. The text gives no basis for such a concept, treating him, from his first appearance (178), as a traitor and an unpleasant comrade. There is no real need to look for his motivation in any circumstance outside his own shortsighted reactions.

One of the more misleading tics of *Roland* criticism is surely the habit of saying or implying that Ganelon, especially in the Council Scene, champions a course of action that will lead to peace and security.[19] Ganelon surely desires peace, but so, in his way, may Roland. That is not where their disagreement lies. They disagree about whether peace is within their grasp. To describe the traitor as representing a "peace faction" in the Franco-Christian army, and Roland as obsessed with warfare ("l'homme de la guerre à l'outrance," Le Gentil),[20] is to misunderstand not only the inevitability of war as the poem presents it, but also the facts of the matter to be decided upon in the council. The hero is not saying war is desirable; he is saying it is unavoidable. His first words are "Do not trust Marsile"; his last words are "Avenge your men, whom the evil foe killed" (196, 203).

It is therefore not accurate to describe Ganelon as an advocate of peace, if by that we mean that the course of action he recommends will bring an end to the war in which Charles is engaged. It will bring only a respite at best. Peace is what Marsile uses as bait: his promised submission and conversion to Christianity. Ganelon thus appears at first glance to be speaking in favor of peace—Naimon, bemused by the hostage offer, certainly thinks he is ("Since [Marsile] offers hostages as security, this great war should not go on," a significant hypotactic construction [241–42]).[21] But the issue before the council is not peace; it is the question Roland is right to raise, the question of

[19]For examples, see Le Gentil, *Song*, 87; Tony Hunt, "Roland's 'vermeille pume,'" *Olifant*, 7 (1980), 203–11; Jean-Charles Payen, "Une Poétique du génocide joyeux," *Olifant*, 6 (1979), 228; Jules Horrent, *La Chanson de Roland dans les littératures française et espagnole au Moyen Age* (Paris, 1951), 269–70; Calin, 16; Jacques Ribard, "Y a-t-il du 'pacifisme' dans la *Chanson de Roland?*" *Charlemagne et l'épopée romane: Actes du VIIe congrès de la Société Rencesvals* (Paris, 1978), 2:529–38.

[20]Le Gentil, *Chanson* (1st ed.), 122.

[21]This is true whether the link expressed by the relative adverb *U* is with the following line (242) or the preceding line (240): "It would be a sin to do him further harm, since he offers hostages." It is not clear how Naimon and the others know about the hostages, whom Charles does not mention; but the army's agreement in line 243 implies that the hostage offer is the key to the proposal's acceptability. If we decide Naimon is not yet aware of the entire offer, then *U* in line 241 may be translated 'If' or 'Once.'

whether the promise of submission is the truth. It is not, and the only way to attain the objectives for which the war has been fought is to refuse to be taken in. Ganelon's reply, to the effect that Roland is a fool to counsel refusal (see again lines 220–29) is not a substantive argument but an ad hominem outburst.

16 (XVI)

The laisse that concludes the discussion is given to Naimon. (I prefer the object form of his name, as for Ganelon's, while for both Charles's and Marsile's the subject form is much more widely used and hence less distracting than the object.) This warrior is traditionally said to be the king's wisest adviser, the Nestor every epic needs, and the text says clearly that he excels in the performance of his duties. "There was no better vassal in the court," states line 231, which implies he is both brave and wise, giving excellent aid as well as good counsel. *Vassal* means "courageous" first and foremost, but the feudal officer must be wise as well as brave, and so the word enfolds both aspects of duty at once.[22] As we shall see, *vassal* is only one of several words that can express this combination of early medieval virtues.

Naimon's role here is not that of simple arbitrator. First he does not adopt Ganelon's suggestion, although some readers think that he does.[23] What Naimon says is more subtle than a mere exhortation. "There is wisdom in what Ganelon says, but we must understand it properly" (234). In other words, there is indeed some truth in Ganelon's assertion (does this imply that it is strange?), but it cannot be accepted without certain conditions. What matters, Naimon says, is not that Marsile has been defeated, has lost his cities and armies. Rather, what counts is the hostages. It would be a sin to do further harm to a man who has asked for mercy *and who is willing to give a guarantee,* one that Naimon's feudal-Christian mind apparently perceives as iron-clad. To give up one's comrades or friends (the concept of friendship being closely related to that of alliance, in practice), and even one's heirs, the tokens of the future, as pledges, and with them

[22]See Burgess, *Contribution,* 20–23, 106–9, and cf. Jean Dufournet, *Cours sur la Chanson de Roland* (Paris, 1972), 142–51.

[23]E.g., Moignet, 41–42; Le Gentil, *Song,* 80; Siciliano, 354; Stranges, 337; cf. Pensom, 86, Bédier, *Légendes,* 3:413; but Picherit, 267, disagrees. It has also been claimed that Naimon does not understand the fate of Basan and Basile (Cartier, 40; cf. Van Emden, "Guarant," 27, n. 23, who omits the pair from consideration), but Williamson, 555, notes the importance of the hostages in his decision, and Hunt ("Character and Causality," 9) considers that Naimon's "strained" argument "completely begs the question at issue."

the right to take their lives if one proves false—all of this Naimon sees as a civilized man of his time naturally would. The promise thus secured must be valid, and if Marsile cannot be trusted under other circumstances, he can be here.

The French make and announce their decision at once: "He has spoken well." It may seem abrupt and summary, but their vote is the necessary conclusion to the debate and the only one required. Here the text shows clearly for the second time how the councils of its rulers work. Charles does not decide policy; his men do that. If we were to put things into approximate modern terms, we might say that legislative power lies with the assembly, which is only logical because their futures are all affected by their decisions. Charles, however, holds something like executive power and has some discretion in how the decisions of the group are to be carried out. Shortly he will use that discretion, and thus will reveal his trepidation at the course of action chosen, for line 243 means that Blancandrin's ruse has worked.[24] The French have taken the bait and in the process sorely underestimated the enemy's resolve. The offer of hostages is as false as the rest, although the French are unable or, in their fatigue, unwilling to imagine that. Their wisest sage has been tricked. Naimon agrees with neither Roland nor Ganelon, but he stresses what to him must seem the only safe (or moral) path. In classic fashion, the forces of evil have played on the very humanity and sense of decency of good men to put their enterprise in jeopardy. And in a moment's time the discussion is over. The council approves the speaker (Naimon, not Ganelon), and there is no more to be said on the question of policy. With that absolutely necessary but totally sufficient acclamation, the die is already cast—just beyond the poem's threshold—and it is time to carry out the decision, with its consequences.

The Nomination of Ganelon

17 (XVII)

Hence Charles's next question, which presumes that the matter is closed. An emissary will go to Marsile; who will it be? The next few laisses show the division of powers in the poem. On the one hand, Charles calls on the barons to speak up on matters of policy. On the other hand, custom or tradition apparently authorizes the king to name agents and control certain other circumstances. This is an ad

[24] Williamson, 553.

hoc, heuristic distinction only, but it does not lack empirical grounds. If we are willing to remain on this general level, then our sense of such constraints may be derived from what the chieftains actually do. The long-standing temptation to compare Charles, in his majesty, with the monarchs of different times must be resisted. On the other hand, though it is less immediately clear, we should not and need not base our critique and expectations of the text on any specific medieval system of distribution of political responsibility either. No matter how sophisticated the history behind them, no matter how prestigious in hindsight the court we take as a model, such *a priori* insistences on how well or how poorly the poem matches some documented practice of eleventh- or twelfth-century France or England are ultimately misleading. The *Song of Roland* is about ideals and attitudes rather than specific local practices.

And yet Charles's power is not an abstraction. It takes the form it does because it is incarnated in the people around him. The act of consultation makes that explicit. Charles does not merely *wish* to act in concert with the "men of France," as the text has it (167). He cannot, one realizes, act as king without them, for they are his army and his court of justice, and in theory also his administrators and his police.[25]

This arrangement explains much of what has been taken as weakness or vacillation in Charles's personality. It is a constraint of circumstance, and we will be able to grasp that constraint as part of a system as long as we are careful not to judge it merely as a historical prelude to the consolidation of kingly power in France. The centralization of the French state throughout the Middle Ages and beyond is certainly a phenomenon of paramount importance, but when we use phrases like "weak king" or "impaired royal authority" to describe Charles's situation in the *Song of Roland,* we may be falling victim to our own nostalgia for the future. Charles may not have the power to impose his conception of order on his comrades, and in fact the medieval author and audience may not even have thought such power desirable. But more to the point, within certain restraints, which he apparently accepts, Charles in the *Roland* acts decisively. He has the operative right to refuse permission to those individual soldiers who volunteer for the mission to Marsile, and he does so in the strongest of terms, repeatedly, without appeal or contradiction. Naimon volunteers immediately, as he no doubt should, having given his support to

[25]See Kibler, "Roland versus the Barons," 56–58; Pensom, 90. On military *auxilium* and the relationship of *consilium* and justice, see Lemarignier, 133–137; M. Bloch, 410. Thus it is actually the barons, not Charles himself, who have decided to "bargain with the forces of evil" (Mickel, "Christian Duty," 130).

the proposal of an embassy to the pagans. But Charles turns him down with an oath. "By my beard and mustache, you'll not go so far from where I am; sit down! No one has called your name" (250–51).

18 (XVIII)

Charles's question rings out again, repeated in its essence but with different wording to fit the new assonance. And now that Naimon has been eliminated from consideration, Roland volunteers. It is difficult to say whether there is some expected order of precedence, although there have been ingenious guesses.[26] In any case, Roland is Charles's lieutenant and apparently his field commander (197–200, 662–64), and there is at least nothing suprising about his coming second. More surprising, perhaps, is that the hero's second speech in the *Song of Roland* is only six words long and fills only one hemistich. *Jo i puis aler mult ben,* "I can go, of course" or "I might well be the one": Roland's volunteering for the mission shows he has accepted the group's decision, but the text's one clause and lone adverb reveal nothing of the spirit in which he volunteers.[27] Like the first, Roland's second speech provokes an immediate negative reaction from someone nearby. Oliver, about whom we know nothing, breaks in at once, before anyone else can respond, to nominate himself instead, claiming that Roland's character is not suitable for the job: he is cruel and fierce, and that could lead to strife. Charles's reply is made to both men equally, and to both on the same grounds, which have nothing to do with their characters. Like Naimon, they are valuable. They are peers, which means approximately that they are among the elite and perhaps belong to the king's household or his personal guard. There is no remark from anyone about Oliver's peremptory challenge to Roland's ability to perform. Charles swears again: none of the peers shall go.

19 (XIX)

Archbishop Turpin of Reims speaks next, stepping forward to propose himself in the warriors' stead, asking for the tokens of embassy. Charles is clearly angry by now, and it is time to ask why. The answer is obvious, though it is sometimes glossed over. We have been both shown and told that the decision the council has made is wrong (cf.

[26]For examples, see Anthony Beichman, "Ganelon and Duke Naimon," *Romance Notes,* 13 (1971–72), 358–62.

[27]Despite Vance, *Reading,* 14. The concept of honor Vance uses is one I will argue is inapplicable (see Chapter 2, below). Roland is going along with the majority here: Cartier, 40–41; Kibler, "Roland's Pride," 148; J. Thomas, 98.

179). Like Marsile's earlier offer, this one is dishonest. There is nothing to be gained by repeating what happened at Haltilie (cf. 201–9). And to be more specific, whoever goes on the embassy to the enemy is risking his life, and probably for nothing. Ganelon will escape, but only through treason and by changing the rules of embassy. Charles cannot override his soldiers' vote, but he has not forgotten Basan and Basile, as we shall see.

20 (xx)

There are no qualified volunteers. How is the impasse to be broken? By the selection of someone acceptable both to the assembly and to Charles. The king, once again, does not say who that might be, but he asks the group to choose him a messenger from among the border barons. He seems to be saying he will agree to that. Roland immediately responds (in five words this time) by suggesting Ganelon, and critics have marveled that Ganelon has not volunteered, after having argued so vehemently that the mission now offered him would lead to survival and peace. The council votes at once, as it did when Naimon made his suggestion, and as the pagans voted, briefly but decisively, on Blancandrin's plan (61, 243). Thus it is the group that gives Ganelon his mission, and not Roland.[28]

The motives of the two men in this laisse have been discussed intensively. This is unlike the way narrative proceeds in its more explicit modes, and several questions naturally come to us as readers. Why does Roland name Ganelon? And at least as important, why doesn't he give his reasons? Why did Ganelon not volunteer to carry out the policy he advocated? Why is Ganelon angry, and why at Roland specifically? Does he not think of himself as a logical choice even though his comrades all do (278–79)? Why is Roland *not* particularly angry, on the evidence of his minimal statements? And what are Roland and Ganelon arguing about in this laisse and the following one?

Scholarly uncertainty about these matters has led to considerable

[28]This was recognized early, in Paulin Paris's summary of the *Song*, in "Roncevaux," *Histoire littéraire de la France*, 22 (1852), 744; on the legal form of Ganelon's nomination, see Hunt, "Character and Causality," 23–24; Pietro Gibellini, "Droit et philologie: l'ordre des laisses dans l'épisode de la colère de Ganelon dans la *Chanson de Roland*," *Revue romane*, 7 (1972), 233–47. Neither Charles nor Roland makes the decision, despite many statements to the contrary: Moignet, 77; Horrent, *Chanson de Roland dans les littératures . . .*, 215–17; Demoulin, "Ganelon désigné pour l'ambassade"; Kibler, "Roland's Pride," 148; André Burger, "Le Rire de Roland," *Cahiers de civilisation médiévale*, 3 (1960), 8–9; cf. Hunt, "Character and Causality," 13–15. On Ganelon's failure to volunteer, see Faral, *Chanson*, 66–67; Picherit, 267–68.

hypothesizing.[29] The text has been said to be wrong, or incomplete, which leads us to study it backward, starting from our conclusions and working to set forth a poem that satisfies us instead of struggling to see why the one we have contains what it does. Commentators have felt the need to supply the motives and reasoning that Roland does not give in line 277. He wants to honor Ganelon as a man worthy of the task, or conversely, and more slyly, he wants to point out Ganelon's cowardice in failing to volunteer. And in turn there is a temptation to reach far beyond the text and to invoke some old quarrel, or the legendary relations between Charles and Ganelon's wife (who is also Roland's mother) to explain Ganelon's sudden flare of temper.

Despite all this, it may still be possible to see some logic, both situational and narrative, in the sequence itself. Charles has, of course, set conditions for the nomination of an ambassador, and those conditions exclude a certain number of people who would otherwise be qualified. As a matter of strict sequence, Roland is responding directly to the king's stricture, and not necessarily thinking of his own relationship with Ganelon at all. That is borne out, at least in part, by the fact that his opinion, far from depending on private considerations, is shared: the group backs him up at once. Ganelon, they say, is simply the best choice within the limits given. "If you skip him, you'll send a lesser (or less wise) man" (278–79). No one seems surprised except Ganelon and the critics. Ganelon, however, is definitely surprised and upset, perhaps even frightened, *anguisable,*[30] affected by the sort of emotion he accuses Roland of succumbing to; he has seen his peril.

Yet Ganelon's reaction, while uncalled-for, may explain a great deal. It implies that he has never associated himself with the actual carrying-out of the embassy. He knows the story of Basan and Basile

[29]Summarized, e.g., by Burger, "Rire," 2–9, and more recently by Hans-Helmut Christmann, "'Le Cunseill que mal prist': Zur ersten kaiserlichen Ratsszene des *Rolandslieds,*" in *Romanisches Mittelalter,* ed. Dieter Messner and Wolfgang Pöckl (Göppingen, 1981), 45–63; Zara P. Zaddy, "The Problem of the Two Ganelons," in *The Medieval Alexander Legend and Romance Epic: Essays in Honour of David J. A. Ross,* ed. Peter Noble et al. (Millwood, N.Y., 1982), 269–88; Jean-Charles Payen, "Encore le rire de Roland," *VIII Congreso de la Société Rencesvals* (Pamplona, 1981), 387–91; cf. notes 18 and 26 above.

[30]"Il est clair que dans cette querelle Roland est l'offenseur et que Ganelon, l'offensé, a droit à la vengeance" (Burger, "Rire," 11, with no mention of the barons' vote; even Ganelon's supporters do not condemn the decision itself [see line 355]). On the word *anguisables,* see Brault, *Song,* 2:257; Picherit, 266–67; cf. Burger, "Rire," 7. Ganelon is indeed the natural nominee at this point; see Faral, *Chanson,* 67; Leslie Brook, "Le Forfait de Roland dans le procès de Ganelon," *Société Rencesvals: IVe Congrès International* (Heidelberg, 1969), 122; Cartier, 41; Picherit, 269; Pensom, 90–91.

as well as everyone else (329–30), and when in essence he proposed sending someone else down the same path, he can hardly have been expecting to be the person to go.[31] And yet Charles has refused every volunteer under the circumstances of laisses 13–20. Ganelon is enraged now, judging by his rounding on Roland, who has not yet insulted him (*parastre,* in line 277, is the literal truth, whatever its overtones).[32] Calling the hero crazy (*tut fol*), Ganelon seeks justification outside the full and sufficient sequence of claims and refusals that has finally led to his nomination. He pays no attention to the procedure at all, but shifts his ground, saying that Roland hates him. But it is Ganelon's function to misunderstand. He is dangerous because he is unperceptive and not only because he is evil, and he has failed to admit the consequences of his earlier arguments just as he will refuse to admit that his treachery reaches far beyond Roland and that it cannot succeed.

The audience thus is given the chance to realize that Ganelon is caught in a revealing contradiction. Either Marsile intends to submit, in which case peace will be made and the ambassador Charles sends will face no danger, or else the mission is risky, and that implies it should not be undertaken. The only possible source of risk in an enemy who promises submission is the very treachery that Roland denounced, picking up the barons' note of distrust (*Il nus i cuvent guarde,* "We had better watch out," 192). It is difficult to say whether the future traitor is malicious from the outset, but there is no doubt he is mistaken,[33] insisting on a course of action without proper regard

[31]Cartier, 39: "Ganelon n'a pas oublié Basan et Basile." Lonigan states the opposite: "One may rest fairly certain that the same thing will not happen this time" (Paul Lonigan, "Ganelon before Marsile," *Studi Francesi,* 14 [1970], 277), but that is not what Ganelon says in lines 329–30. Ganelon's lack of logic is pointed out by Cartier, 41; Kibler, "Roland's Pride," 148; Pensom, 93 ("ontological contradiction"); J. Thomas, 100–101; Williamson, 556.

[32]*Parastre* is not necessarily pejorative; see Alice Planche, "Roland fils de personne," in *Charlemagne et l'épopée romane* (Paris, 1983), 2:598. Thomas, 99–100, claims that *parastre* is ambiguous and may mean Roland does not think Ganelon is the best choice, but cf. Hunt: "There is nothing in the text to suggest that Roland intends ill" ("Character and Causality," 18). Joseph Donohoe speaks of Roland's "spontaneous provocation of Ganelon" ("Ambivalence and Anger: The Human Center of the *Chanson de Roland,*" *Romanic Review,* 67 [1971], 258); Stranges claims that Ganelon is here "forced [by Roland's insults] to lose control of his emotions" (p. 341; cf. pp. 338–39); Burger ("Rire," 11) does not distinguish between vengeance and vendetta. Janet Boatner also says Roland causes Ganelon's treachery ("The Misunderstood Ordeal: A Re-Examination of the *Chanson de Roland,*" *Studies in Philology,* 66 [1969], 577; cf. Hall, "Ganelon and Roland," 266). But Picherit, 266, disagrees, as does J. Thomas, 96.

[33]Uitti, 79; Hunt, "Character and Causality," 26; J. Thomas, 96. Cf. the traditional statements that Ganelon is wise: Le Gentil, *Song,* 87, 114 (*Chanson,* 134: "lucide et réfléchi"); Van Emden, "Pro Karolo Magno," *Olifant,* 2 (1974–75), 179n. But the

for the possible consequences. But despite his expressed distaste for an embassy he himself recommended, Ganelon persists in his error and seals both his own doom and that of others with every step along a path whose logic is that of confusion between his own fears and the public interest. Ganelon makes no advance attempt to protect himself from the punishment he earns. The simple explanation is that he does not see where his contradictory attitudes—opposition to further combat (226–27), fear of the fate that befell Basan and his brother (329–30)—are leading him.

In sum, the story itself requires that Ganelon hate Roland (though not necessarily the converse) and that the traitor find himself in a position to harm the hero through treachery; and the Council Scene, as constructed, is sufficient in itself to explain both these things. Roland need have no ulterior motive at all in mentioning Ganelon's name, in response to the king's limited and specific request. The army. which actually makes the proximate choice, surely has no such motive. Ganelon is simply the logical nominee. On the other hand, there are good reasons to think that Ganelon never realized that would happen. If he had, the situation would never have arisen. The danger of the embassy is obvious even to its champion, and yet to his agonized embarrassment Ganelon must be the one to go. He does not admit that any of it is his own doing, but it is clear what he has let himself in for, now that the council has spoken, and he grasps at a straw. Roland is his stepson, as Roland himself has just mentioned; that is why Roland has selected him, he says.[34] And Ganelon, while admitting the risk, brings his own doom closer through this persistent failure of observation and logic. He threatens Roland with great and irreparable harm if ever he returns (289–91).

Roland has done his duty in advising the king, and Ganelon has impugned his motives. The slander and the threat arouse him to reply. Ganelon's outburst is foolish; Roland is not afraid of threats (292–93). But there is more. Ganelon is impetuous. He has lost his temper without cause. The embassy is a job for a levelheaded man. And for the only time in this exchange Roland here refers pejoratively to Ganelon by offering to take his place, which we may take as a renewed reminder that Roland has spoken reasonably all along, de-

inadequacy and the worldliness of his attitude are often stressed: Pauphilet, *Legs,* 81; Cartier, 39; Williamson, 555; Brault, letter to the editor, in *Olifant,* 3 (1975–76), 133; Le Gentil, *Song,* 81; June Hall Martin McCash, "*Scientia* and *Sapientia* in the *Chanson de Roland,*" *Medievalia et Humanistica,* n.s. 11 (1982), 134, 142; cf. Lonigan, 279–80, and Hunt, "Roland's 'vermeille pume,'" 203.

[34] I think this is a red herring, but cf. Williamson, 556–57.

spite what other characters may have said about him for reasons of their own. Is he withdrawing his nomination, recognizing that Ganelon is proving less wise and competent than the council said? In any case, it is too late. All questions of personality and personal honor aside, the vote has already been taken.

21 (XXI)

Ganelon admits that he must carry out the assignment, saying that Roland cannot act as his agent. The order will come from Charles—Ganelon will go—but now he makes another threat, an open promise of harm to come, and (if the adverb *i* "there," "in Saragossa" of line 300 is not an error)[35] he even refers to the treason he will soon commit. Roland shows no sign of fear, but laughs or smiles. (The verb *rire* can mean either.)[36]

22 (XXII)

Roland's reaction inflames Ganelon further, indeed, to the point of no return. The future traitor, we hear, has nearly taken leave of his senses (304–5). Again he drives a wedge between himself and the hero, this time using the verb *aimer:* "I have no love for you, none at all" (306). It is traditional to think of "love" here as some form of the modern concept, but the word remains a technical term used for the bonds (originally emotional) between men of the same group.[37] We have seen the Saracen leader use it to evoke a feudal relationship. (86). It recurs in the poem in its feudal sense in lines 494 and 635. Ganelon's threat is brief, but as much charged with significance as are the brief acquiescences of the two royal councils. He rejects, and will shortly reject again, the public, official relationship between himself and his comrades. It is not an exaggeration to say he is breaking an alliance. His pretext for the rejection is, again, false: "You, Roland, have brought an unjustified (or evil) decision upon me" (307). Once again, we must not allow any stirrings of sympathy we may feel for Ganelon to obscure the inconsistency in his reaction: this nomination is for an embassy he himself championed energetically. He does not use political terms to express his resentment; he does not take up the cudgels for some philosophy or minority view; he is simply mistaken, curt, and angry. Now Ganelon turns to Charles.

[35]Cf. Lucien Foulet in Bédier, *Chanson de Roland commentée,* 404.

[36]See Barbara N. Sargent, "Medieval *rire, ridere:* A Laughing Matter?" *Medium Aevum,* 43 (1974), 117; on the laugh (if it is one) as cause of Ganelon's anger, see Burger, "Rire," 11; Siciliano, 354.

[37]See Herlihy, 68–69; Lemarignier, 126–31; Jones, *Ethos,* 36–40.

23 (XXIII)

When Ganelon speaks to the king, he first admits that he must go to the enemy and allows that there is no way to survive the mission, then refers to his wife, Charles's sister, and to his own son, saying he will never see him again. Charles finds this unsatisfactory, a sign of weakness (*tendre coer*), and commands him to stand forward.

24 (XXIV)

The king insists on an important point, which Ganelon refuses to accept. "You heard the vote: it was the council that named you" (321). Perhaps to make it even more memorable, the poem emphasizes the reference to the group by placing the word at the assonance: *sur vos le jugent Franc.* But the traitor persists in his error, and claims: "Roland did it!" (322) He does not allow that his own hasty advice and his colleagues' will are causes of his predicament. He compounds his iniquity by what can only be conceived as a formal challenge to men who should be his comrades. The verb *aimer* is used again, and again negatively, applied now not only to Roland but to Oliver and the twelve peers as well. Ganelon is renouncing his place in his own social group, now using the even clearer verb *desfïer,* signifying his rejection of the feudal bond.

This term, like other sociopolitical terms in the *Song of Roland,* may slip past us if we do not look closely. It has implications and resonances that transcend the immediate situation. Ganelon is technically claiming to have been wronged, and thereby to have been released from his formal obligations to his fellows.[38] The word "defy" implies challenge to us, but in the eleventh century and for some time thereafter it was certainly closer to its roots. Etymologically, it meant to unpledge, to renounce one's fief and the associated promises. In context, it is a strong statement that Ganelon is contemplating a shift of allegiance or even betrayal. Its strength is not lost on Charles, who censures Ganelon's exaggerated resentment and for the third time orders him to get on with his mission. Ganelon's reply again contains a word whose significance we should not underestimate. "I will have no

[38]See Ganshof, 98–99, and M. Bloch, 228, for a discussion of the breaking of feudal ties. (Is Ganelon's throwing down of his cloak symbolic of the *desfi,* as Bloch indirectly suggests?) Cf. Lemarignier, 138: "[Sometimes] a man who considered himself wronged would act unilaterally by issuing . . . a form of *desfi.* Finally attempts were made to give some organization to these mechanisms of punishment which, if left to the whims [of individuals] . . . would have engendered anarchy." Ganelon's *desfi* may actually be "a breach of the pactum pacis or pax Dei extended to crusaders to encourage them to leave home . . . without domestic anxieties and fears for the safety of their property" (Hunt, "Character and Causality," 22).

guarantor," he says, "no more than Basan and Basile had" (cf. 329–30, and notes 13 and 14, above). This recognizes the correctness of Roland's initial call for vengeance, for the *guarant,* or protector, is ultimately the overlord, here Charles himself, who must respond when his men are threatened or harmed.

25 (XXV)

Finally Ganelon's appointment is to be consummated. Charles is to give him his own glove, an item associated with his person, to show the envoy is no imposter. The gesture goes explicitly wrong. In what is universally recognized as a presage of evil, Ganelon drops the glove, and it hits the ground, signifying the failure of his mission. What is less widely noticed is that even the French say as much, using the first person: "This embassy will cause us great loss" (335); and Ganelon's reply to them indicates, for the third time, that he has plans of his own: "You will hear more of this" (336). There can scarcely be any doubt in any hearer's mind, at this point, that these events are leading not to peace but to renewed danger.

26 (XXVI)

In the very brief twenty-sixth laisse, Ganelon asks Charles's permission to depart and (perhaps to our surprise) receives the king's blessing and absolution, along with a symbolic wand and a letter to Marsile. His mission is beginning under unpleasant auspices, but like other public functions the knights have in the text, it may not be suspended on grounds of suspicion or uneasiness. Charles is not ruled by auguries, even accurate ones. He will express his private fears about Ganelon's untrustworthiness later on. But acting on his capacity as chieftain, he proceeds as though his barons' choice was as correct as it was proper, and treats Ganelon as a trusted companion. Ganelon is apparently expected at least to deliver the letter and bring back a reply. Again, the expectation is structural in nature: that a knight must be counted on to do his duty as his king and his fellows describe it. The constraints deriving from that rational principle may not be set aside lightly or with any appearance of arbitrary intervention, even by an emperor—for the sake of the principle itself. This is an ethos of social necessity and not a manifestation of character.

27 (XXVII)

Ganelon retires to his tents or pavilions to prepare for his departure. This passage is sometimes treated as though it involved the whole army, but the attitudes of the speakers are biased by their close association with Ganelon. The men around him in this scene are a group apart: his uncle (348) and perhaps other relatives, and his knights, who call him "lord" and ask to accompany him. They weep and utter threats against Roland. Ganelon refuses any company, ostensibly to spare other men's lives, though he has promised harm to Roland and the peers, and the enemy with whom he will now treat is a natural instrument for that harm; hence, perhaps, he may prefer to have no witnesses. He commends his family to his men. These lines, with their specific reference to Pinabel (who will later be Ganelon's champion) foreshadow the later disruption in the court's deliberations over Ganelon's punishment, a disruption caused by the intervention of his powerful family and allies.

Ganelon's Treasons

28 (XXVIII)

The events leading to Roncevaux continue in rapid sequence. Here Ganelon is already en route toward Saragossa with the enemy envoys. At once, Blancandrin draws near him. They speak warily. The Saracen does not counsel treason now or later, and though his questions and remarks are pointed, it is difficult to argue that he plants the seed of treachery in Ganelon's mind. Ganelon has already promised harm to Roland; although it can be argued that Blancandrin is manipulating the Frank, it seems instead that in this and the following scenes Ganelon is using the enemy's desire to be rid of Charles as the lever of his promised vengeance.[39] It is he who controls the information the Saracens need, which is why Blancandrin is asking leading questions, and in reply Ganelon says about Charles and Roland only what he wants Blancandrin and Marsile to hear. The progression of questions and answers in this first conversation bears that out, for each of Blancandrin's questions after the first refers to what the traitor has just said. Blancandrin's first remarks are quite general and insinuate nothing. Charles is a remarkable conqueror; why is he making war on us? And Ganelon's first reply is equally general, without

[39]On the movement of Ganelon's scenes with Blancandrin and Marsile, see Hunt, "Character and Causality," 24–26; Lonigan, "Ganelon before Marsile"; Picherit, "Silence de Ganelon." Horrent's analysis (*Chanson de Roland dans les littératures . . .*, 234–40) brings out pertinent points concerning Blancandrin's function and the message Charles sends via Ganelon. Cf. Knudson, "Problem of the *Chanson*," 4ff. Siciliano, 334n., claimed Ganelon was Blancandrin's dupe; cf. Goldin, "Die Rolle Ganelons," 145–46. But Bédier described Ganelon as ready to betray at this point (*Légendes*, 3:415; cf. Pensom, 95).

any sign of his obsession: because it is the emperor's nature to make war.

29 (XXIX)

But Blancandrin makes a second and somewhat more pointed remark. No feudal leader, however belligerent, fights or decides alone. Someone among the king's counselors (Blancandrin may or may not already know who) is advising Charles to fight, and Blancandrin suggests that is not in Charles's best interests. There is no way of telling whether or not Blancandrin witnessed the council in Charles's camp—logically he should not have been admitted—or was somehow informed of the disagreement between Ganelon and Roland. His comment is in any case natural enough, since Charles cannot campaign without warlike companions. And yet the false offer of peace was accepted, and here is the man sent to negotiate. Blancandrin's ruse was designed to find such a weak point in the Frankish will. His allusion to Charles's best interest (and other men's) in line 380 leads indirectly to his discovering where Ganelon stands in the scheme implied by Blancandrin's own strategy.

The reply confirms that there is a division of opinion and commitment among the Christians. Blancandrin's thrust triggers a revealing response from Ganelon. The name that is uppermost in the traitor's mind comes out immediately. "No one is pushing Charles to fight on," says the latter, "except Roland," and he openly states that Roland is to suffer for it (382). The anecdote that follows has given rise to some commentary. In what is apparently intended as an illustration of his contention, Ganelon tells the story of the red apple Roland gave Charles—only the day before, he says—and of the nephew's proud claim that he is thereby giving his uncle the crowns of all the kings there are. The peculiar nature of this story, with its parallels to the motif of temptation and its interesting reference to what seems to be the symbolic Apple (or Mound or Orb) of Dominion, does not need full discussion here.[40] Like the offhand allusions to Charles's imaginary conquest of England and southern Italy in laisse 28, it is historically intriguing in ways that are not essential to our sense of how Ganelon's words fit into the narrative. We need not even grapple extensively with the question of whether Ganelon is uncharacteristically telling the truth here.

[40]See esp. Gerard Brault, "Ganelon et Roland: deux anecdotes du traître concernant le héros," *Romania,* 92 (1971), 392–405, and Brault, *Song,* 1:141–43; cf. Kathleen Capels, "The Apple Incident in Laisse XXIX of the *Song of Roland,*" *Romance Notes,* 14 (1972–73), 599–605, and Hunt, "Roland's 'vermeille pume,'" 203–11.

It is more important to grasp what Ganelon has done in his response taken as a whole. He injects Roland's name into the discussion for his own purposes (and not to the Saracen's advantage, since it will be ever more clearly seen that Roland is not the real cause of this war). He will do the same thing again shortly, in more subtle fashion, before Marsile. But beyond that, Ganelon immediately reveals, on purpose or because he cannot help himself, his immense hatred for a fellow knight (389–91), and he lies to the pagan emissary as he will later lie again and again to friend and foe alike. His first betrayal, in fact, is the virtual one in line 391, where he openly suggests killing Roland, one of his comrades (or former comrades) in the feudal system. And it is a futile and hopeless treachery, for his claim is false. Ganelon says that killing Roland would mean complete peace for everyone (391), but the text shows the contrary. The fatal ambush at Roncevaux seals both Ganelon's doom and that of the Saracens. That, at least, Blancandrin does not foresee. He will take up Ganelon's suggestions, and the Saracens will carry out the traitor's treason for him—to their misfortune. Thus the two men intrigue, each apparently seeking to use the other for his own ends. But Ganelon alone goes to the length of denying the rules of his society and risking great harm to Christendom, his own civilization, for the sake of a grudge. For that act, the text has given him no plausible justification.

30–31 (XXX–XXXI)

Blancandrin now seizes on the name Ganelon has furnished him and asks a second question. How does the infamous Roland (who, it is recognized, cannot make war alone either) expect to win his victories? The reply may or may not be a further treason. Ganelon names the *franceise gent,* the French or Frankish people, as Roland's allies and instruments. Later the men who die at Roland's side will be *Francs,* the victims of Ganelon's indiscriminate treason, and it may be that the third level of questioning in laisse 30 is meant to remind us that Ganelon's actions do not harm Roland alone.[41]

Now Ganelon and Blancandrin, riding together, solemnly agree to seek Roland's destruction. The wily Saracen has thus himself become

[41]Line 400, *l'emperere meïsmes ad tut a sun talent,* has been explained by Burgess in two articles, "La *Chanson de Roland,* Line 400." *Romance Notes,* 13 (1971–72), 165–67, and "*Talent* in Early Old French," *Romania,* 95 (1974), 433–66, esp. 447–48. It does not mean Roland has the emperor under his thumb, but rather that Roland "has the emperor constantly in his thoughts." Cf., however, William Kibler, "Again *La Chanson de Roland,* Verse 400," *Romance Notes,* 14 (1972–73), 621–23, who argues that *emperere* is the subject of the verb.

an agent of Ganelon's private resentment. Soon they stand before Marsile.

32 (XXXII)

Upon arriving in Marsile's presence, Blancandrin greets his king as he did Charles, invoking the gods of the ruler's own religion. He reports on his mission and introduces Ganelon as the bearer of Charles's message. We may marvel that, having agreed to arrange Roland's death, Blancandrin and Ganelon do not simply walk up to Marsile and announce the agreement, especially since Blancandrin will shortly say that he thinks Ganelon is committed to helping the Saracen cause. However (though speculation of this sort is always risky), it can at least be pointed out that the next scene reveals several things that Ganelon's simply going over to the enemy would not reveal. One is the precise nature of Charles's reply, which (unlike Marsile's offer) has not so far been spelled out for us; another is how Ganelon incites the enemy to kill a man of whom they have apparently never heard, thus continuing a war that is already lost, a war to which this embassy is supposed to put an end.

33 (XXXIII)

Ganelon's way of carrying out his embassy has not always been given close enough attention to allow us to understand what he does.[42] His is a complex and multilayered betrayal, and it develops slowly both here, in its virtual or potential form (i.e., in words of engagement), and later (laisses 54, 59), in fact. Ganelon is not a negotiator here, but a messenger. He has a letter, we recall, but he does not deliver it. Instead, he speaks, and the text presents his words as carefully chosen and deliberately offered (425–27). They are both a provocation and a lie.[43]

The first thing Ganelon does is insult Marsile by greeting him (as the Saracen diplomat did not) in the name of the Christian God whom Marsile abhors (cf. laisse 7). Ganelon's statement of Charles's intention (preliminary to the fuller one in laisse 36) makes it seem that Marsile's conditional offer has actually been rejected (which is not true). He may not keep Spain, not all of it, the traitor says, but only

[42]But see the very useful studies by Picherit and Lonigan referred to in notes 12 and 31, respectively.

[43]On Ganelon's lies to Marsile, see Brault, "*Sapientia,*" 101; Hunt, "Character and Causality," 26 and n. 40; J. Thomas, 105–7; Pensom, 102; Lonigan, 277–78; Horrent, *Chanson de Roland dans les littératures . . . ,* 28, 271–72. His "fermeté" (Le Gentil, *Chanson,* 135) is irrelevant; Jenkins, 45, did not grasp this.

half of his land, and only after first converting to Christianity; and in a second clause, Ganelon adds that if Marsile refuses these conditions he will be treated ignobly, taken and bound by force, to die a shameful death at Aachen, Charles's capital.

Predictably, Marsile is upset by this. He snatches up a weapon and starts to strike Ganelon. Why is Ganelon shown as taking such a risk? Two reasons come to mind. First, he has a plan, and this is part of it (425–27). The plan is, surely, to set up the ambush he will soon suggest to the Saracens. For that purpose he must turn their minds away from their offer (and the council's acceptance). He spurs them instead to further resistance, without giving them a chance to consider that they cannot, by their own admission (16–21), withstand Charles. Hence he stirs up their anger and resentment, at some apparent risk to himself.[44] He does not, it seems, know the contents of Charles's letter—it is sealed—and he seizes his best opportunity to precondition the enemy's reaction to it. On the other hand, he does know that Blancandrin is on his side, and in a moment the latter will intervene. Second, there may be a structural motivation for having Ganelon cause a quarrel, for the danger of a quarrel is exactly what Oliver invoked in order to block Roland's nomination to the embassy (255). The intratextual echo is too strong to be ignored completely. Though we cannot know what Roland would have done in Ganelon's place, at least Oliver was wrong to imply that if Roland was not sent there would be no quarrel.

34 (XXXIV)

Ganelon has apparently fallen short of carrying out his embassy, and he is now on the verge of drawing his sword to fight his insulted host. He apostrophizes his weapon and promises to make the pagans pay if they attack him. Instead, they pacify their king and put an end to the threat of combat.

35 (XXXV)

At his men's request Marsile again takes his seat. The *algalife* urges him to hear Ganelon out. The traitor insists on his mission. He throws

[44]For Bédier's influential claim that Ganelon seeks danger in order to justify putting Roland in danger later, see his *Légendes,* 3:418–19. Ganelon's motivation is more accurately grasped by Siciliano, 343n. ("If the Saracens make peace, there will be no way for him to destroy his hateful stepson"); Lonigan, 278; Pensom, 102; J. Thomas, 106; cf. Faral, *Chanson,* 210; Peeters, 391; Stranges, 350. Brault (*Song,* 1:147–48) states that Marsile's anger is feigned, as is Ganelon's haughty message, for they have already reached a (secret) agreement.

off his rich mantle, and Blancandrin takes it. The pagans see the gestures, or the cloak, and recognize that they are dealing with an important man.

36 (XXXVI)

Now Ganelon has the chance to make his statement clearer, and he does so in unmistakably traitorous fashion. First he repeats his arrogant first clause, but with an essential variant. Not only must Marsile give up half of Spain; he must also share his lands with none other than Roland—and a haughty partner he will be! Here the hero's name rings out again in a context guaranteed to provoke the Saracens' ill will toward him. The second clause follows, elaborated but unchanged. If Marsile refuses this humiliation, even worse will befall him. He will be thrown onto a packhorse and taken to Aachen to die.

But now the moment has come when Ganelon can control events no longer. He has said enough to stir the enemy up against the emperor, and specifically against Roland. Now he must hand over Charles's letter: if the pagans are going to act in such a way as to appease Charles temporarily and thus allow the treason to take place, then they must know what he is really asking of them.

37 (XXXVII)

Here suddenly the nature of Ganelon's words stands clearly revealed. The Saracen king breaks the seal that guarantees the letter's authenticity, and reads its astonishing contents. There is not a word in it about humiliation or punishment, no reference to a division of Spain. and above all nothing about Roland. Ganelon has betrayed both Roland and his king, for his provocative speech was a falsehood. Charles, surely uneasy, but bound to carry out his council's decision, has not rejected Marsile's offer or substituted a set of conditions of his own for those the enemy proposed and the council accepted. On the other hand, he has remembered the men he lost in the same circumstances before, when he could not protect them. He evokes the old crime that Roland brought forth as proof that Marsile could not be trusted. The emperor writes to tell his enemy that the deaths of Basan and Basile are not to be forgotten (this is the text's third reference to their embassy and execution). But he accepts Marsile's offer of peace, on one vital condition and one only. Following Naimon's advice—as sound as a Christian can give under the circumstances—Charles says he will not allow a bond between him and Marsile to be created (the term again is *amer,* Charles saying he will not "love" Marsile, as the pagan used the technical terms *amur* and *feid* in line 86) unless this time he receives a solid guarantee of his good intentions. And Charles insists on the best token available.

As Blancandrin had foreseen, the giving of hostages will set the Christians' mind at rest. But not just any hostage will do. The wary Charles insists on the one man closest to Marsile, his uncle (presumably matriarchal), the *algalife*. It is a smart move, but only his due. Charles has been tricked before, and if Marsile really intends to do as he says this time, then his uncle will be safe. Furthermore, Charles has in effect won the war, and Marsile is (or should be) in no position to pick and choose the hostages he will send. In fact, as we shall see shortly, even this wise and apparently effective precaution is useless because of Ganelon's treason. But for the moment Charles's proposal, when at last it is revealed, is reasonable and proper, and a long way from the insolent claim Ganelon makes in his name. The traitor is playing his own game.[45]

These facts are not lost on Marsile's son, who turns to his father in indignation, saying that the Frenchman has spoken words of folly and forfeited his life, that it is only just to slay him at once.[46] This is, curiously, a healthy reaction, for Ganelon is engaged in betraying the pagans themselves to their deaths. But the speaker knows only that Ganelon is unreliable despite the solemnity of the embassy. Such a man may indeed seem to have no right to live (497). Blancandrin, however, under the influence of his earlier talk with Ganelon, now intervenes, the treason continues to run its course, and Ganelon is given one more chance to harm his stepson.

Critics often assume that Ganelon delivers Charles's message accurately, or at least part of it.[47] But what he proposes in laisses 35 and 36 is not what Charles expects (laisse 54 will further make that clear).

[45]Le Gentil (*Song*, 85) seems to think Charles's letter is itself provocative. Moignet, 55, among others, seems not to have grasped that the oral message Ganelon gives is part of his treason. He confuses the traitor's statement, which is a virtual contradiction of the letter, with the letter itself, which is apparently intended to be authoritative. The reliance on a written document is the reverse of the "dichotomy of writing and act" mentioned by M. Bloch, 81, and is no doubt better explained by the movement toward reliance on the written described by Stock.

[46]It is for lying, not arrogance, that Jurfalet says Ganelon should die; see J. Thomas, 107; Lonigan, 278; Peeters, 391.

[47]The idea can be traced to Paulin Paris, 733: "Ganelon, when brought before King Marsile, presents his message faithfully." Bédier (*Légendes*, 3:416) also seems to have thought that Ganelon delivered the message correctly, that only his arrogance is wrong (p. 417); cf. Moignet, 56, 59; D. D. R. Owen, *The Song of Roland* (London, 1972), 20–21; Christian Gellinek, "A propos du système de pouvoir dans la *Chanson de Roland*," *Cahiers de civilisation médiévale*, 19 (1977), 40; Per Nykrog, "La Composition du *Roland* d'Oxford," *Romania*, 88 (1967), 512; Stranges, 349–50, 352; Siciliano, 334, thought his betrayal of Charles was at least not deliberate, but cf. the commentary to laisses 270–73, below.

The Franks in council do not speak of driving the Saracens out of Spain or of occupying their lands. They must be made to convert and submit, but this is no *Reconquista.* Charles's war is not a war of territorial aggrandizement, despite Blancandrin's assumptions (370–74, 392–94) and Ganelon's failure to correct him.[48]

We must also allow for the reaction of Jurfalet (Jurfaleu), Marsile's son, in line 496. He uses three abstract terms (the latter two at least are technical) with immediate and clear application. Ganelon has spoken *folie,* wild words (and not merely incomplete ones). By right (*dreit*) he should die, and to slay him would be *justise.* He has betrayed his own lord's trust with his falsehoods. Here, as before, the Saracens, whatever their ethics, think and act superficially as feudal officers with a sense of right and wrong procedure. Ganelon has perverted his embassy; he was, it seems, given no oral message to deliver, and moreover, what he has said was nearly a contradiction of the real message. The words in laisse 37 (and the events to come) cannot be reconciled with Ganelon's insistence that Marsile is to give Roland half of Spain. Charles makes no later attempt to seize any part of Spain or to leave Roland in charge there, even though Ganelon reports, in effect, that Marsile has accepted his terms (692–97). Had the emperor's counselors recommended such an occupation, it would again have been tantamount to refusing Marsile's offer. To set such extravagant conditions is not the clemency Naimon recommended and is not what the army approved. It is out of line with any desire to go home and to have peace. Hence, while Ganelon shows undeniable courage in baiting the Saracens, there is in it none of the righteousness sometimes claimed for him. He begins with an insult and finishes with a lie, and only his status as a sworn traitor (403–4) saves him.

38–39 (XXXVIII–XXXIX)

With the real offer at last in hand, Marsile withdraws to consult his council. Blancandrin speaks up at once. If it is not already clear from his own proximity to Ganelon as the knight spoke, or from the tenor of Ganelon's unauthorized message, Blancandrin now openly states that the Frank is disloyal and has agreed to help Charles's enemies. Now they can plot their lawless treason (*sanz dreit,* 511) together, the pagans against Charles, and Ganelon against both his fellow soldiers

[48]And despite such claims as Jean-Charles Payen's: "Une Poétique du génocide joyeux," 228–29 (cf. Uitti, 85). In particular, crusades were not considered offensive wars (Contamine, 278–80).

and the men he will soon swear to aid. Marsile, now fully informed, apologizes and offers Ganelon a gift. It is accepted, and they are ready to parley.

40 (XL)

As Blancandrin had done when first alone with Ganelon, Marsile begins with the question the pagans presumably consider vital. Although it is not said, he may even be aware that Blancandrin's ruse, though successful, can win him only temporary respite. Is there no way Marsile can rid himself of Charlemagne entirely? After promising Ganelon some further reward (*amer* is used again; the pecuniary aspect may be dominant here, as it was in 397–99), he asks for information on Charles. The man is old, he says, and has fought long and hard. When will he tire of war? Ganelon's first reply is quite general, as before (cf. 375–76): the pagan does not understand Charles; he is a valiant man indeed.

41 (XLI)

But that is not precisely the answer to the question. The text repeats Marsile's question almost verbatim, in a brilliant use of juxtaposed-laisse technique, suggesting rather than quoting the conversation, for Marsile will not be put off. But as they talk, Ganelon shifts his ground. When, he is asked again, will this aged man (who, whatever his real age may be, looks to Marsile as though he were two hundred years old or more) ever give up?[49] And this time the reply suggests a reason such that a pagan can grasp. The reason Charles is fighting, according to Ganelon here, is not that it is God's will that he defend his people and his religion. It is because someone is pushing him to make war. He will not stop as long as his nephew (at first unnamed) is alive. Ganelon may not even realize how wrong he is at this point, but the entire *Song of Roland* is designed to show that there is no chance that

[49]We do not know the characters' ages, and despite some assertions ("Roland est jeune": Le Gentil, "A propos de la démesure," 207) it may not matter. Though Marsile's "two hundred years" is often taken as accurate, it is only a statement about how Charles appears to the pagan. Cf. Julian Harris, "How Old Was Charlemagne in the *Chanson de Roland?*" *Romance Philology*, 25 (1971–72), 183–88. Roland is putatively younger than his uncle and probably (not necessarily) younger than Ganelon, his mother's second husband. But this does not get us anywhere as far as character or social age is concerned. Roland has been Charles's field commander on the whole long campaign—not a job for a stripling, though at the time one was no longer a youth at sixteen. He is unmarried, but, as Duby has shown, many bachelors were relatively old and experienced (Georges Duby, "Dans la France du Nord-ouest au XIIe siècle: Les 'jeunes' dans la sociéte aristocratique," *Annales*, 19 [1964], 835–46). Cf. Brault, *Song*, 1:401, n. 23.

Charles will falter, with or without Roland. For the moment, however, the insinuation is there, and it is clear. There is a way to end Charles's career. And for good measure Ganelon names in the same breath Oliver, and the twelve Peers, whom he has also promised to harm (323–26).

42 (XLII)

The answer is still not quite complete, and we hear the question for a third time. When will Charles tire of war and leave the field? At last Roland's name is pronounced openly. As long as Roland lives, Charles will fight, and with Oliver, the Peers, and the twenty thousand Franks the emperor cannot be beaten.

43 (XLIII)

Marsile now changes his tack slightly, asking a question to which he presumably knows the direct answer (see again 16–19). Perhaps he is seeking an alternative; in any case, Ganelon will offer him one. He has a huge army: four hundred thousand men. Can he meet Charles on the field of battle? Ganelon immediately answers that he cannot. Such a course is foolish; he knows a wiser one. And Ganelon describes the treason as he plans it.[50] Roland is the key, and Roland can be killed without engaging the Christian army in pitched battle. The Saracens must carry out their offer, giving Charles money and hostages. Charles will then withdraw. But he must have a rear guard; that goes almost without saying. That inevitable duty will isolate Roland, Oliver, and the others. They are as good as dead then, and without them Charles will lose his will to fight. He will never make war again. This, then, is the realization of the double betrayal Ganelon has been working for since his first meeting with Blancandrin. But once again, whether Ganelon is aware of it or not, his prediction is wrong. Roland's death actually arouses Charles to vengeance, and by serving Ganelon's ends the pagans ensure their own destruction.[51]

[50]This is not what Moignet, 55, calls a "skilful and thoughtful diplomatic game . . . played at the margin of service to the emperor," but rather a plan opposed to and potentially harmful to the interests of Charles, and indeed of all Christendom.

[51]Bédier (*Légendes,* 3:444) early noted that Ganelon's promise to the Saracens is wrong. Brault thinks he is deluding himself (Brault, *Song,* 1:154–55, and 306 with another emphasis). Roland's death leads to the capture of Saragossa and to victory for Christendom: Foulet, Crist, and Rütten; William Kibler, "Roland and Tierri," *Olifant,* 2 (1974–75), 32; Kibler, "Roland versus the Barons," 58.

44–45 (XLIV–XLV)

Marsile's question now takes the precise form that shows he has risen to Ganelon's bait. He uses Roland's name himself, and adopts Ganelon's goal as his own. How can I kill this man? Ganelon is ready to reply. Send one hundred thousand men against the rear guard at the pass of Cize. They may not prevail; then send as many men again. One or the other of the waves will be the death of Roland, and then you will have no more war. The statement goes on into another laisse. If Roland can be killed, Ganelon once more explains, Charles will lose his right arm, and his armies will melt away. Marsile accepts this claim, to his misfortune (he will lose his own right hand as a result of his decision, in laisse 142). He seals his assent with a kiss and calls for his treasure. Ganelon, often described as a lover of peace, has arranged to prolong the war.

It is worth noting Ganelon's reasoning in this attempt to convince the pagans to act as his surrogates. His argument is based not on Roland's character but on Charles's need for a rear guard, which is also one of the first things to come up in both laisses 43 and 44. Once he is satisfied and turns for home, Charles must cross the pass. He will need a rear guard. Roland will be there, and he will be vulnerable because of his position, not his turn of mind. Ganelon speaks of this as a matter of obvious necessity, not as something he will be at pains to arrange. There is no need to wonder at this point whether Ganelon foresees, for example, that Oliver will insist that Roland call for help when attacked or that Roland will refuse. It is enough for now to note that Ganelon presents the circumstances of Roland's last stand as self-evidently fatal and that the Saracens see it the same way. Attacking a rear guard is not the same as attacking the entire army.

Thus it is not difficult to know what the pagans expect to gain by ambushing Charles's rear guard. We read the *Song of Roland* with some foreknowledge of its end, but these Saracens do not share that sense of their own doom. They have, we may wish to recall, seen that they could slaughter Basan and Basile with impunity. They may expect the same with Roland. In any case, they have only Ganelon's lie to go on, and Ganelon says that to kill Roland is to win a final victory.

46 (XLVI)

The meaning of what Ganelon is doing is brought home by a typical device: a promise, symbolic as an early medieval man's oath must be, but nonetheless binding Ganelon solemnly to the ironic breaking of his prior oaths, the promises of fealty and service he unquestionably made when he became a knight and a baron of Charles's frontier. He swears here upon the holy relics that are part of his sword, and so his oath has all the seriousness of a quasi-religious gesture as well.[52]

47 (XLVII)

In turn, Marsile swears on his version of holy writ that if Roland is assigned to the rear guard he will fight him and try to kill him. The pagans have clearly accepted Ganelon's claim that Roland's death will be to their advantage; their remarks in the next two laisses reinforce that notion. These three speakers, Valdabrun, Climorin, and Bramimonde, do not promise, as their comrades will when the battle is imminent, to kill Roland. They merely insist that he must be in the rear and that he must be attacked.

48–49 (XLVIII–XLIX)

For the first time the narration spreads a little thinner. The rapid-fire density of the first laisses gives way to a brief series of parallel gifts and ritual promises. Yet though they may not contribute much to the advancement of the plot (not everything in the *Roland* does), these gifts and oaths have a strong and sure effect. They remind us that Ganelon is totally wrong and totally perverse. He imagines himself wronged, and he is not (cf. laisses 20–24). He plots vengeance, and his plot destroys him. And no affront, no slight, can make it conceivable that he would take money and gifts as a reward for the twisted pact he has made to ensure the death of comrades who are guided by the trust they put in him. If we had any lingering doubts about Ganelon's morality, this display of greed should dispel them.[53] There is no nobility in his treason. And it is clear also what he represents. This is not just money, but payment for service analogous to the rewards Charles, Roland, and Western feudal chiefs in general give to faithful vassals. But Ganelon is the opposite of faithful. He is a Frankish Christian knight, and yet in his blindness he can sin against his comrades and against the rules that shape his culture, even using the very forms of symbolic commitment that are part and parcel of that

[52]Uitti, 71, notes that "declaration of fealty is a kind of rite . . . that the narrative of the poem is designed to explain and explore." On the solemn, preexisting contract between Ganelon and Charles, see Judith Kellogg, "Ganelon: The Poetics of Guile and Greed," *Olifant,* 8 (1980), 162; D. D. R. Owen, "The Secular Inspiration of the *Chanson de Roland,*" *Speculum,* 37 (1962), 398.

[53]Brault (esp. *Song,* 1:100–103) has argued at length that avarice is Ganelon's motive; cf. Kellogg, 161, 166–67, 179.

culture. He is more dangerous than any sworn enemy. He is not merely different from Roland, he is Roland's opposite in most ways, the weak link that threatens the chain of vows and performance holding society together. And yet by an epic miracle the chain proves stronger than he.

Valdabrun, smiling, gives Ganelon his extremely valuable sword and offers him *amistiez,* a personal engagement, if Ganelon will arrange to put Roland in the enemy's power. Ganelon promises that he will, and they exchange the kiss that vassals and their lords exchange when the time comes to seal their promises of mutual dependency. Ganelon has thus formally linked his person to that of an enemy. Valdabrun is the enemy of his overlord, to whom he was originally linked in the same way, as a baron; he is also the enemy of the other barons, to whom Ganelon is indirectly committed via Charles. In laisse 49 (XLIX), Climorin (or Climborin) repeats the smile, the gift, the request, and the gesture.

50 (L)

Bramimonde (also Bramidoine), Marsile's queen, follows suit, saying that her lord's promise implies hers. She also uses the term of personal contract, *aimer;* her gift of two gold collars goes to Ganelon's wife. Ganelon squirrels them away.

51 (LI)

Marsile makes sure that the tribute is ready to be sent to Charles. His treasurer tells him that twenty hostages are ready also. They are part of Marsile's original offer, but they do not satisfy the terms of Charles's letter, which, we will recall, mentioned the *algalife* specifically.

52 (LII)

Marsile finally sums up his agreement with Ganelon one last time, promising him regular payments in the future if he will only put Roland within his grasp, so that they may fight to the death. Ganelon expresses impatience to be on his way.

53 (LIII)

The emperor has, it seems, turned for home, but he is still on campaign. He comes to the city of Galne, and Roland, acting again as his lieutenant, reduces it. (Or is this a reference to an earlier victory?) The Franks are anxious to hear from Ganelon. Now he is among them again.

54 (LIV)

Ganelon has come to carry out in practice the betrayal he committed in principle when he swore an oath to an enemy lord, and this laisse is where he does it. He salutes Charles correctly, of course, and shows him the keys of Saragossa, the tribute, and the twenty hostages. Then he lies to him, explicitly, at length, and to devastating effect.[54] Marsile cannot give you the hostage you asked for above all, says Ganelon, slyly (*par grant veisdie,* in the narrator's words, 675). The *algalife* is dead; he rebelled, with many others, and refused to convert. Having taken ship, he was drowned, with all his men, by a sudden storm. If he had still been alive, says Ganelon, I would have brought him (691). But Marsile is to come to France, convert, and do homage to you for his land of Spain. Again there is no reference to any expected division of that country (cf. laisses 33, 36).

This is a long and circumstantial lie, perhaps deliberately made so, to drive home the enormity of what Ganelon is so glibly doing. In the first instance, we know the *algalife* did not drown, because the story did not show it; it showed quick preparations and Ganelon's hasty departure. Unlike Roland's earlier, twice-corroborated story of Basan and Basile, the *algalife* episode (had it been real) would have had to take place immediately before its recounting, within the lapse of time covered by the narration, and not before it started. We could imagine that a narrator might include an episode of the *algalife*'s drowning in a *Song of Roland* and then have Ganelon summarize that episode in a typical reminder laisse (such as laisse 55 or 189). But it is not typical of the text to have a character report, in a summary laisse, events that are not otherwise reported and are not shown at all, even though they fall within the temporal boundaries of the action. Ganelon's tale of things unseen is a lie (one common sense of *veisdie,* line 675, is "trick" or "ruse") analogous to his earlier lie to Marsile about the destiny of Spain. The story of the drowning is no more honest than the claim that Marsile intends to submit (692–97); in fact, it is part of the evidence for the claim. Furthermore, an uncle of Marsile's (not called *algalife*) will appear later in person (1914ff.), though it does not do to put too much emphasis on such a detail.

Although this major lie of Ganelon's is usually recognized as a falsehood (see note 54), its consequences for the narration have rarely received any comment. It is in fact the operative treason against Charles. Ganelon's treachery succeeds, and it allows the pagan king to

[54]Moignet, 149; Brault, *Song,* 1:159–60, 320; Peeters, 391; Pensom, 105; Stranges, 363; J. Thomas, 109; and cf. the works cited in n. 43, above.

sacrifice his money and hostages as he planned to do from the first, in order to obtain Charles's withdrawal. Charles suspected the ruse (191) and demanded a hostage so close and so important to Marsile that he could hope the pagan would not dare play him false. His plan might have worked if it had not been undone by his own man. Yet in justice Charles must continue to trust one of his sworn barons in the absence of firm and public evidence sufficient to show that his trust has been betrayed. If he is to act as a true leader he cannot act arbitrarily.[55] Consequently, whatever his suspicions—he expresses none here—the king accepts the story, thanks God for Marsile's submission, promises to reward Ganelon, and orders the army into motion.

We never hear of the hostages again, nor Blancandrin, nor the *algalife* for that matter (at least not by that name). They have played their roles, triggered the mechanisms they are supposed to set off, and, like Lear's fool, they disdain to return once the maker is through with them. Their interest lies in the way they contribute to the construction of the story, not in the way we recognize them as personalities. Ramón Menéndez Pidal, reading the scholarly tradition and not the structure I am attempting to describe, thought they made no sense. Failing to allow for the status of these characters as narrative functionaries, Menéndez Pidal concluded that their presence in the poem was an accident. "This is a startling detail of historical reality, whose survival is due to chance and carelessness," he claimed, and he saw in this inconsistency evidence for his famous contention that the poem in effect had no individual author.[56] Thus the controversy over origins, with its important aesthetic overtones, was for a long time tangled up with the statements critics made about the content of the poem. It seems likely that Menéndez Pidal's desire to defend his thesis may have led him to seek such putative inconsistencies in the text with unusual eagerness.

The Nomination of Roland

55 (LV)

Charles has laid waste the land of Spain, taken its strongholds and cities, the narrator says; and, he adds, the king (not the narrator) now

[55]"Like God, Charles is not free to override the rules by which he works" (Van Emden, "Pro Karolo Magno," 181). See also John D. Niles's important study, "The Ideal Depiction of Charlemagne in *La Chanson de Roland*," *Viator*, 7 (1976), 129–39, esp. 131–36.

[56]Ramon Menéndez Pidal, *La Chanson de Roland et la tradition épique des Francs*, 2d ed. (Paris, 1960), 267. The scholarly tradition according to which the work is incoherent is considered in Chapter 4, below.

says the war is over. There is no attempt to occupy any part of Spain; Marsile's promised submission is enough. Charles heads for home, and Roland carries his banner. As the French make camp, the enemy—four hundred thousand strong—ride for the mountains. In another direct intervention the narrator's voice bemoans the Frenchmen's ignorance of precisely what is happening.

56 (LVI)
Until now the action has involved no extrahuman agency or power, if we except the accurate providence that caused Ganelon to drop Charles's glove in lines 334–35. Now Charles has two inspired dreams, metaphoric in nature, which refer paranormally to the future and convey a sense of danger. The first of the two dreams is the clearer warning. Charles dreams that he is at the pass he must cross the next day, lance in hand. Ganelon himself, named explicitly, seizes Charles's weapon and breaks it so that the splinters fly. Charles sleeps on.

57 (LVII)
The second dream is at first glance more obscure, so much so that even critics, who know how the story comes out, have disagreed on its meaning.[57] Charles dreams that he is at home, which seems to refer to the trial of Ganelon at Aachen. He is being bitten by an evil animal, a bear or a boar, and a leopard from the Ardennes region attacks him, but a dog races to his aid, wounds the bear, and fights ferociously against the leopard. The parallels with the later Trial Scene are strong but not perfect. In the dream, the French say they do not know who will win. Charles sleeps on; he has had two epic premonitions, informative but not evidential, like Hamlet's visions of his father. He has seen the culmination of Ganelon's treason, the destruction of the rear guard, in an image, and he will immediately recognize the real thing when it happens. But his dreams are his alone. His men do not share them, and he cannot impose his suspicions on the group. The operative betrayal of Roland happens at once, and Charles cannot stop it without taking improper action.[58]

[57]For the various studies on the dreams in the *Song*, see Duggan, *Guide*, nos. 254–62.

[58]Charles is not authorized to act on dream evidence; see Herman Braet, "Réflexions sur les rêves dans les chansons de geste," *Société Rencesvals: Proceedings of the Fifth International Conference* (Salford, Eng., 1977), 216–18; Pensom, 108. In any case, the dreams are imprecise and may have only a general significance; see Braet, 222; Mermier, 93; Hunt, "Character and Causality," 27 and n. 42; Frederick Whitehead, "Charles's Second Dream," *Olifant*, 3 (1975–76), 189–95; and cf. Brault, *Song*, 1:163–65.

58 (LVIII)

Laisses 58 and 59 are among the most important in the poem because they control most directly what is to happen at Roncevaux. The first is Ganelon's abrupt nomination of Roland to lead the rear guard; the second is Roland's promise, his commitment to his task. Both text and context require attention.

Laisse 58 reveals one of those contextual elements that the passage of centuries may too easily obscure or weaken. It is not a matter of ideas, social or political, this time, but of practical necessity. Charles and his host are on their way out of Spain and France, and of course they must cross the Pyrenees, the mountains that even today are to some extent taken for granted as a natural barrier between two countries. What we may forget, if we read too hastily (the text does not dwell on it) is how difficult the crossing really was for a medieval army on foot, with baggage. And yet that fact is both unquestionable and essential to an understanding of the scene.[59]

Charles puts the question with deceptive simplicity; it is not a matter for discussion: "Gentlemen, here are the mountains; choose me a rear guard" (740–42). Ganelon's moment has come; in the last effective step of his treachery, he names Roland at once. Unlike Roland in the earlier Council Scene (277–79), Ganelon acts alone. This one time there is no vote. What Ganelon falsely claims Roland did, he in fact does himself: he sends Roland on a risky, potentially fatal mission. The barons do not elect Roland; they are not in council, they are on campaign.

Charles understands. His dream would have been enough to warn him, but he, like everyone else present, knows of Ganelon's specific threats as well (lines 289–91, 300–301, 334–45). The characters are nearly as well informed as we—where Ganelon's intentions, if not his secret acts, are concerned.[60] The king cries out angrily to Ganelon, "You are a living devil, the devil incarnate. You are prey to a fatal

[59]On the necessity for a rear guard, see Cartier, 42–43; J. Thomas, 111.

[60]Despite claims that the characters here are unaware of what is going on (e.g., Le Gentil, "A propos de la démesure," 204; Moignet, 77), it is clear that they know something of Ganelon's dangerous intent. See Bédier, *Légendes,* 3:422; Joseph Duggan, *The Song of Roland: Formulaic Style and Poetic Craft* (Berkeley and Los Angeles, 1973), 176; Cartier, 42; Mermier, 94–95; Thomas, 111–12; Brault, *Song,* 1:165; Salvatore Battaglia, "La Glorificazione di Orlando," *Filologia e letteratura,* 17 (1971), 355–67, first published in *La Formazione della lingua francese* (Rome, 1945). Cf., however, J. Thomas, 102, and Brault's statement (*Song,* 1:398) that "the tragedy . . . stems in part from the failure of Roland, Oliver, and the Twelve Peers to take Ganelon at his word." Williamson insists on the importance of trust in this scene, but with an emphasis on kinship rather than social bonds.

madness!" It is true, of course; Ganelon's obsession has brought him well past the point of no return.

And yet the king still has no proof, only exceptional knowledge, and he accepts the nomination and closes the question in the same breath, asking immediately who is then to lead the vanguard. Ganelon nominates Ogier of Denmark. The decision is complete.

Despite a strong strain in the literature, we need not be too preoccupied with the question of why Charles refuses to risk the men who volunteer in the Council Scene (244–76) but accepts Ganelon's nomination of Roland at once in lines 746–48. The two nomination scenes are symmetrical, but they are not parallel. The conditions are different in the two cases. First, no council is assembled in the latter case. The rear guard is needed for practical reasons, and there is no question of policy to be decided. Moreover, the dangers of both Ganelon's and Roland's missions are obvious to at least some of the participants in each scene, but that does not mean these men are equally free to act on what they know. There is direct evidence of Marsile's earlier perfidy, but as far as the army can tell, Ganelon has only hinted at his intent. Officially, at least, at the time of the second nomination, Charles and Ganelon are still linked by the same bonds of trust that link any overlord with his vassals.

Thus, though Charles knows Ganelon is Roland's enemy and suspects this is his treason, as his bitter words show, he still does not refuse the nomination as he refused to accept volunteers for the embassy to Marsile. This time the job, dangerous as it is, really does need to be done, and done well. The embassy to Marsile was an unnecessary risk, but the rear guard is important. We must not forget, as Charles perhaps has not, that there is an armed and undefeated enemy in the rear. No one in the text has shown any sign of knowing exactly what form the danger thus implied might assume, but no one shows any signs of ignoring it. The characters in this scene are aware of potential danger, and if they are unable to avoid the danger through some radical action, it is because of the situation and not because of some limitation in their psyches. The retreat has been voted in council and must be carried out; Ganelon's embassy is suspect for many reasons. including his accident with the glove (333) and his overt statements. Yet Charles cannot act, not because he is a weak man but because his strength depends on his understanding and accepting the constraints of a common cause.

The principle is not made explicit in this poem; I derive it from the simple logic of feudal relations, and beyond that from a conviction that behavior in a feudal context may survive certain logical tests. In the absence of positive evidence of betrayal, the leader must maintain the structure of trust. The time will come when Charles has proof that no one can doubt, and then he will act at once.[61]

But for the time being it is not true that Charles does not try to protect Roland. In a moment he will offer him half the army. The circumstances prevent his doing more. His men are entering the mountains and will be vulnerable during the crossing, and Marsile has not surrendered, but only said he would eventually. The rear guard is as necessary and important in lines 745ff., after Roland has been named to lead it, as it was in lines 741–42. It is necessary because the barons chose to risk leaving without defeating their foes, and because Ganelon has threatened harm to his comrades (322–26, 336). Charles's trust in the man he leaves behind will not be betrayed this time. The assigning of the rear guard is not, then, a pretext for development and revelation of character; it is a necessity created by the circumstances in which it occurs, and it is a strong element of narration. These troops and their leaders have a key task, and as Naimon will say, they had better be equal to it.

59 (LIX)

We learn what the nature of that task is from Roland himself. Critics often describe Roland as though he had sought out combat with a larger force.[62] It is as though he had broken ranks, heedless of orders, like the knights of Mansourah or Bannockburn. What he actually does is quite different. He agrees to stay behind and promises to stand his ground. His discipline comes from his own promises and not from any orders. He is given no orders, and with the mountains before the army there is no need for any. It is his right—perhaps more precisely his function—to establish the expectations he will meet. Roland's responsibility is implicit in the lines Charles has already spoken. There must be a rear guard because the high passes and the enemy are there. This requires the Franks' attention but

[61]Charles's attitude in this scene, see Pensom, 109–13: "For Charlemagne to attempt to impose his will as a private person and uncle of Roland would have the effect of damaging the social order [that] it is his duty to uphold." Cf. Mermier, 94; Brault, "*Sapientia*," 113; see also note 55, above. Charles's anxiety is sometimes explained by the hypothesis that Roland is his own son; on this idea, see the works cited in Duggan, *Guide*, nos. 394–98; Demoulin, "Ganelon désigné pour l'ambassade."

[62]For example, Boatner, 578, says Roland chooses "fearful odds" for no reason; Hunt defines as a *hamartia* his "miscalculation of the military odds in the ambush" ("Character and Casuality," 31); Renoir says "he simply refuses to consider the odds" (Alain Renoir, "Roland's Lament," *Speculum*, 35 [1960], 572–83). These claims are based on the idea that Roland does not decide to fight until the First Horn Scene (see Commentary on laisses 65, 83).

needs little elucidation. Thus Roland does not need to be told his duty; he states it himself because it is self-evident (cf. laisses 43–45), and he insists in observing the necessary discipline even in the face of reproof. These facts do not make him "impetuous," but rather the contrary.

Roland and Charles both accept the nomination—in anger, because this matter, procedurally a routine one, is not what it appears to be—but with full respect for the procedure in the abstract. Charles curses shortly and goes on; Roland speaks *a lei de chevaler*, "as a knight should" (752). His first duty is to accept or reject the nomination. In words that guarantee his attitude from that moment until his death, he accepts. He first thanks Ganelon for choosing him. He does not repudiate Ganelon, as Ganelon earlier disavowed him, though Ganelon has acted alone. I ought indeed to cherish you, says Roland, and ironic (as they are generally thought to be) or not, his first words are quite different from Ganelon's. As Bédier put it, the traitor's reaction to his perilous state "oozed anger and fear." Roland's vow is simple, straightforward, and realistic, with no overtones of either fear or exaggeration. He says he will indeed do what is expected of the leader of a rear guard, and neither more nor less. "I say Charles will not lose a single horse, nor riding mule, nor even a pack animal that has not been fought for first" (755–59).

We should not assume that because it is Roland who offers his own interpretation of the matter the interpretation may not be trusted. Here as elsewhere, that begs the question at issue. One might more logically argue that because Roland is never contradicted, and receives no orders from any other source, there is every chance he is right to formulate his function as he does: to fight to protect the king's property. I have already stated my own conviction that this duty is evident from laisse 58 onward. Even more important, there is little to criticize in Roland's formulation, which promises neither victory nor even ultimate success in his task as he conceives it, but only resistance. It would not appear that there is any misunderstanding between him and Charles. The king gives him his blessing, with strong suggestions of uneasiness and no harsh words (cf. 317–21, 327–28).

The traditional interpretation of Roland's character would lead us to read something into these lines—some boast, some grandiose claim.[63] But there is a great deal to be gained by looking at both the

[63]"Roland . . . promised to triumph without any help" says Van Emden, "Guarant," 35; cf. (among others) Le Gentil, "A propos de la démesure," 205; Stranges, 357. Hunt

precise wording and the literal sense of everything Roland says from this scene until that of his death. First, his statement here is not absolute but qualified. He says only what the leader of a force detached to protect the rear of an army might well say: that whoever harms Charles will have fought a battle first. This is the promise, the commitment that makes Roncevaux inevitable, and it is nothing but a description of what a rear guard logically does. It fights if the army it is guarding is threatened. And here at least no one shows any sign of disagreeing. The rear guard's mission is not to carry out a scouting expedition. A few unarmed men would suffice for that. But the army will soon be fully occupied by the struggle to cross the Pyrenees on foot. It will be in no position to defend itself. Yet an attack is far from unlikely, as Roland, Charles, and Naimon know. They need not anticipate Ganelon's treachery in any detail. It is enough for them to know Marsile, and I must insist again that they do know from experience that he cannot be trusted; this is not some manifestation of bloodthirsty prejudice, but a fact established by events the audience has heard described. (See again 201–9, 329–30; is it worth repeating that Marsile has not surrendered?) Scouts can warn the army of a sudden attack, but only a determined fighting force can buy it time in an emergency. In sum, we should not take the rear guard's assignment for granted. There is a job to be done; its nature and importance do not derive from considerations of honor or personal vanity. This may be a convenient way for Ganelon (and the narrator) to separate Roland from his uncle, but it is not gratuitous in the medieval cultural context. Nor are things ever secure for those who must bring up the rear. What Roland has done in lines 755–59 is predict the future, not by some vain *litotes* but by literal statement. Ganelon knows it even better than anyone else here. He responds: "You are telling the truth. I know it well."

It is not difficult to understand that under certain circumstances the most important thing a medieval knight could do was stay put—to maintain his formation as ordered, whether in a charge or in a retreat. The military logic is that of any engagement: individuals and small groups are vulnerable where the mass is not; flanks must be protected; maneuvers may come to grief unless they can be carried

claims that Roland is not thinking of the future here ("Character and Causality," 30), but lines 755–59 refer to it explicitly. Renoir recognizes that Roland dies because of his oath, but he claims the oath is "far from unequivocal"; see Alain Renoir, "The Heroic Oath in *Beowulf*, the *Chanson de Roland*, and the *Nibelungenlied*," in Stanley B. Greenfield, ed., *Studies in Old English Literature in Honor of Arthur G. Brodeur* (Eugene, Ore., 1963; reprint, New York, 1973), 240–41, 251.

out without letting the maneuvering troops come under heavy attack. Historically, the logic applies particularly well to medieval cavalry, whose success in battle (and thus perhaps its ethos of combat) involved simultaneous participation in the charge. This implies a maturity of discipline (for example, on the Crusaders' march across Asia Minor in the years, 1147–48, Baldwin III's expedition to Bosra, or the Arsuf campaign in 1191)[64] that traditional military historians once failed to recognize in the feudal soldier. Yet it is such discipline, the stringent discipline of orderly withdrawal, that is at the heart of Roland's ordeal.

We must accept the fact that the trek through Roncevaux and beyond is a strategic withdrawal, not the triumphant progress of a victorious host through submissive lands. The reality is partly masked by Marsile's feigned surrender, but it is a fact nonetheless. Charles must move his army through difficult terrain with an armed and hostile force behind him. This recalls one aspect of the decision that went against Roland in council, with its attendant risks, which his advice would have avoided, and it also explains the need for a rear guard with a determined leader.

Roland's original commitment is the crux—often unrecognized—of the Roncevaux episode. If we are to describe Roland as blind, then we must understand what it is that he claims he is doing so that we may contrast that with lucid behavior. It is not in the "Horn Scenes," after his dark duty has been laid upon him and he has spoken his words of acceptance, that we will learn what he faces and how he makes up his mind. We have misled ourselves to a certain extent by failing to consider, first, that it is the accepting of the task itself that counts in the structural sequence, and second, that how the task is carried out is controlled by that choice. Yet the structure of assent to a task before the fact, and the explicit statement of such assent, are phenomena that match the concept of feudal duty remarkably well. We should allow ourselves to suspend the long tradition that says Roland is free to make up his mind in the First Horn Scene. If we instead consider how his own consent effectively seals his doom long before that scene, then we will have gone far toward understanding, without Roland's telling us, just why he is obliged, as a character and as the representative of a class, to fight when attacked rather than call for aid.[65]

[64]See R. C. Smail, *Crusading Warfare 1097–1193* (Cambridge, Eng., 1956), esp. "Fighting on the March," 156–65; J. F. Verbruggen, *The Art of Warfare in Western Europe during the Middle Ages* (Amsterdam, 1977), 81–82, 91–96.

[65]Le Gentil expresses the traditional link between the Horn Scene and *démesure:* "In

In fact, the Nomination Scene makes it clear (as has often been recognized; see note 60) that Ganelon's motives, and the very great danger of Roland's assignment, are known to the participants at this point. And yet the decision is made, and Roland accepts this duty as he earlier accepted the king's order to remain in camp. The choice, like the earlier acceptance, is made in a climate of apprehension. It appears that everyone considers the danger to be part of the assignment.

Thus it is important for what is to come that we note the rhetorical form Roland's first promise takes. It is, once again, typical of him in that it is neither personal nor absolute. Charles will not lose a single chattel *that has not first been defended.* Roland promises resistance, but does not claim that he himself will defeat or destroy the pagans, and he never will make that claim, although he will later refer broadly to their ultimate doom (laisses 83–85). Finally, the promise he makes in laisse 59 and the one he is to make in laisse 63 are both accurate—that is, as literal statements they come true within the text. Charles does not lose any of his train through any failure of Roland's to stand his ground.

On the other hand, the traditional notion of Roland's character as impetuous and haughty requires him to speak willfully and without regard for the consequences.[66] Yet his actual promises, while they are strong affirmations, contain no element of exaggeration unless we read them as reiterated and extensive understatements, as a strange sort of *litotes* whose irony ultimately turns against the hero, as if he were confidently claiming—but only by implication, between the lines, as it were—what he cannot deliver. We must assume that he has an intent conveyed by something besides his words, though how the text might otherwise convey it has never been explained. His minimal

---

fact, nothing has been decided when the enemy suddenly appears, and Roland and Oliver begin their moving debate. Roland is still free to change his destiny. He has only to sound the oliphant, and Roncevaux will not be Roncevaux" (Le Gentil, *Song,* 88). The same lack of attention to context recurs in Le Gentil, "A propos de la démesure," 203: the "perspective the poet himself adopts," which Le Gentil invokes here, must include the poem's earlier scenes. See, in contrast, P. Kirsch, "La Condition du héros dans la *Chanson de Roland," Mélanges de philologie romane offerts à Charles Camproux,* vol. 1 (Montpellier, France, 1978), esp. 391–93, 396. The same failure to recognize that the commitment to fight happens as early as it does has occasionally led to an inversion of the poem's structure; this is clearest in a statement by Vance, which refers only to the First and the Second Horn Scenes: "Oliver . . . is as devoted to heroic honor as Roland and believes that this code does not permit any second thoughts once a commitment has been made" (Vance, *Reading,* 51).

[66]As in Gérard's statement that "by seeking his own glory, Roland temporarily plays the Saracens' game" (Albert Gérard, "L'Axe Roland-Ganelon: Valeurs en conflit dans la *Chanson de Roland,*" *Le Moyen Age,* 75 [1969], 449; cf. Gérard's reference to Turold's "double-think," 464).

statement "Charles will not lose a horse" (755–56) has undoubtedly been taken to mean the grandiose promise "I will win a great victory"; and later, when he says "The pagans are doomed," he must mean "We will destroy the pagans ourselves." Indeed, these words have been translated into English in precisely that vein, and the important qualifier of line 759 (not a packhorse *that has not been fought for first*) has been left untranslated entirely.[67]

So strong is our adherence to the image of a prideful Roland that this interpretive manipulation, however risky, has always gone without saying. At the very least, the endowing of Roland's speeches with a rhetorical twist has never been fully recognized for what it is and has never been analyzed as a key part of what modern readers have brought to the text. Still I think it important to realize that Roland's words do not form a vain boast unless we apply the presuppositions that the deeply rooted *démesure* hypothesis of interpretation has always applied to them. They may be thought litotic (though not vain) only in the largest context, since everyone in the text knows that the fight Roland refers to as a possibility is likely and the audience knows it is inevitable (710–16). Nonetheless, Roland does not boast, here or later, in immediate context. What he says he will do is what he does and no more. The vainglory is supplied by the hypothesis. The text's statements may legitimately be examined and judged in their literal senses, if we agree to try another hypothesis. At the very least, given their careful qualification and given the contexts I shall now examine, Roland's promises are sound.

To begin with the present case, the *litotes* in laisse 59 is not Roland's but Ganelon's, for when Roland in literal essence promises to fight before any loss takes place, Ganelon replies with heavy irony, "You are telling the truth," which, as I have said, is a truthful statement in itself. He adds "I know it well," which is the truth in a sense that only Ganelon and the audience can completely fathom, since they alone know for sure that the ambush has been arranged.[68]

60 (LX)

Having spoken as a knight, Roland speaks again, as a man, in the mixed pain and anger the old language called *ire*. It is the same angry

[67]Of the authors I have consulted, I think only J. Thomas, "La Traîtrise de Ganelon," 112, notes clearly that Roland's first promise is a qualified one. See also Chapter 3, below.

[68]It would be possible in theory to construct the passage as a double *litotes*, which Roland's statement as *démesuré* and thus an incomplete expression of his intent, hence *not* as true in its implications as Ganelon says it is, but the attendant complexity, though implicit in various published analyses of the passage, does not seem warranted.

sorrow that overcame Charles when he thought of the assassination of his two counts, Basan and Basile (489); as it did then, it often occurs in combination with *dolur.*[69] It is important, if Roland's choices are to have their full heroic resonance, for us to follow the implications of the word *ireement* and realize that he, like Charles, is angry for a reason. He mistrusts or suspects Ganelon. Here, for the only time in the work, Roland uses directly insulting terms against a fellow Christian. (He described Ganelon's threatening words as foolhardy in line 292.) He calls Ganelon wretched and base, as the emperor just did; and in a master stroke the poet has him declare his own awareness of the situation by referring to the evil omen accompanying Ganelon's embassy, and thus obliquely to the evil nature of that mission itself. The hero draws at once a clear contrast (which the text will bear out) between Ganelon's investiture and his own. "Did you expect the token would fall from my hands, in public, as from yours?" (764–65).

The place and propriety of this laisse have been much discussed, though (as is the case for laisse 54 also) doubtless more in the context of arguments about the appearance of unity in the poem than with interpretation in mind. Of course its pasts and conditionals seem wrong, since Roland has not yet had a chance, as he will shortly, to receive the symbolic token, which is a bow not a glove, while what Ganelon dropped was a glove and not a staff. It has also seemed strange that Roland speaks in apparently contradictory fashion of his stepfather in two successive laisses. I do not think the two adverbial elements that introduce his speeches (*a lei de chevaler* [752] and *ireement* [762]) are necessarily opposites. Nevertheless, these lines may be those of a redactor anxious to emphasize the drift of the entire passage.

Let us recall that none of this passage (laisses 58–65) has any narrative, psychological, or ideological function at all unless the characters, including Roland, are aware something is wrong. If peace is thought to be assured, there is no need to insist at length on the formation of a rear guard. If the rear guard is not a dangerous or even potentially fatal mission in everyone's eyes, then there is no need for Charles's tears, Naimon's intervention, Gautier del Hum's assign-

[69]Though it is difficult to be precise about this semantic field (as Georges Kleiber clearly shows in his *Le Mot "ire" en ancien français* [Paris, 1978]), *dolur* and *ire* are closely associated, and either could express the combination of anger and sorrow. See George Fenwick Jones, "Roland's Lament: A Divergent Interpretation," *Romantic Review,* 53 (1962), 8; anger and sorrow are mixed, despite Jones's statements in *Ethos,* 45–46. Cf. the remarks on *doel, Ethos,* 178–79, and also Lucien Foulet's glossary to the *Song,* in Bédier, *Chanson de Roland Commentée,* 372, 407.

ment (discussed below), or Roland's promises. Yet all these elements are there, and Roland's anger is part of the sequence. It is a consequence and not a cause of the nomination. All this takes place without any reference to personalities (that is something we must choose to add if we dare), but with several references to the constraints of the situation. Someone has to guard the rear, and Roland is the obvious choice. Ganelon has not only nominated him, but also created a situation where Roland, Charles, and the others must acquiesce both for the army's safety and as a matter of principle. Roland accepts the danger on both these counts, and he accepts it willingly (hence laisses 59 and 61) yet not blindly, but rather in sorrow and irritation. In a famous remark, Bédier called this a drama of human will, not a tale of fate, but consideration of its setting shows that fate and will are intertwined in it, in high heroic style.

61 (LXI)

Repeating his reference to Ganelon's earlier failure, Roland now turns to the king and asks for the token of his mission, a hunting bow. In his first reference to the exemplary nature of his commitment, Roland says this time not just that he will not drop it, but that people will not be able to say he did. No one will be able to offer such a reproach, for he will not disgrace himself (768–70). But Charles does not yet accomplish the symbolic gesture. He weeps and casts down his eyes, twisting his mustache and pulling his beard. I think we are being led to recognize what Charles will say himself in lines 835–40: that the responsibility he will give his nephew may mean his death.

62 (LXII)

It requires the intervention of Naimon to make Charles act. That best of vassals (775) reminds the king that the decision is already made and cannot be changed. It is sometimes assumed that there is some reference here to Roland's character, but what Naimon is trying to do is persuade Charles to get on with a process that no one can reverse, in a situation that cannot be changed without arbitrary violation of a set of rules more important than the immediate circumstances. Thus he says nothing about Roland's impetuosity, but only states what the text has already said, that he is in a state of *ire* (see the discussion of laisse 60, above). But Roland did not volunteer for his task, Naimon adds: the rear guard has been assigned to him (*jugee sur lui*), which is another matter, and no baron can undo that now. It may have happened quickly, but it is done. Give Roland the token, says Naimon, and do the best you can do for him now: choose him good companions. Charles hands over the hunting bow without a word. Roland takes it, and of course the omen is good: the bow does not fall.

63 (LXIII)

Still, Charles does not quite accept Roland's assignment to what he appears to consider a highly risky mission. He calls him to his side and makes an offer whose strangeness is rarely recognized. I will leave half my army with you here, he says. Accept them, they will be your salvation. (The latter word, *salvement,* is further indication that Charles knows the risk and is trying to avert it.) This notion is, first, unusual tactics.[70] Half a host is not a rear guard; the men left behind will have to cross the mountains too, and who will then guard them? The poignancy here is not in Roland's refusal to allow such a thing to be considered, but in Charles's having been induced to forget a matter of ordinary military logic—of the type of logic so natural to commanders that it is not easy to think it would have been set aside even in the interests of timelessness in literature. Charles is trying to avoid the situation already established by his own announcement in lines 741–42.

But Roland properly refuses, cursing the man he would be if, having taken the assignment, he were now to cast it aside, in effect, by a transparent accommodation. He does not argue tactics, but rather invokes principle. God damn me if I fail the *geste,* he says. The latter abstract term (788) can have several meanings and has been translated in various ways. Roland is referring to something greater than himself, whether it be his family (and thus Charles's) or (as I think probable) the tradition of service, the meaning of a knight's commitments as shown in history or past deeds. If Roland can back down, though the danger be patent, then his word is worth no more than Ganelon's, and if a baron can go back on his word, then there is no other constraint strong enough to ensure that this society's needs will be met. As the battle approaches, Roland will say these things again, but the essence of the First Horn Scene is here. His reasons are the same later as now, and lines 1049–1109 will add no major element. A promise is a promise, we should recall, not only in matters of personal integrity but also in customary law. I will take twenty thousand good Franks, says Roland. This is something he has already said he would do. And he adds his second qualified and accurate promise (790–91).

[70]Cartier, 42–43, alludes to the meaninglessness of a rear guard that consists of half the army; he also suggests, following Bédier, that even that large a force might still be destroyed in an ambush.

Cross the passes without fear, he says, and we shall soon see that Charles and the army do so. You need not be afraid of any man as long as I am alive, the hero adds, with no reference to victory and no claim of superiority, but only the dogged insistence of a man who knows the implication of his commitment for those he is to protect. Roland does not even say he expects to live, but only that he will do the job while he can.

Why will the fight at Roncevaux take place? Why does Roland not recall Charles and thus change the balance of forces there? Because the pagan attack is not a surprise, and because as part of the preparations for it Roland has made promises of resistance in the presence of people who are aware that those promises may be tested. He promises aloud and by gesture, for the sake of witnesses who cannot necessarily read and do not keep written documentation, but who know the implications of what is said. That is what makes the promises binding beyond any immediate considerations of personal survival or safety.[71] The idea of pride, whether legitimate or criminal, has no explanatory value here. Any feudal warrior who knows his business might make such promises in the line of duty, whatever his character. The next laisse demonstrates exactly that point.

64 (LXIV)

Roland is not alone. As he mounts, Oliver and the twelve Peers, Charles's finest men, come to join him in what is shown as silent assent. Roland does not exhort them, and there is no discussion. They simply come, and the text lingers over their names. Archbishop Turpin also volunteers, with an oath. But it is given to Gautier del Hum to lend a shape and sense to their action, in one of the most moving and significant lines of the whole work. These men have been listening, or at least do not need to be told what is going on, what the mission before them is. They must separate from the army and remain in Spain under the conditions just discussed. None of the men so far named is ordered to take the risk by any other character. They go because (as Naimon said, line 781) it makes sense for good men to do this deed.

[71]Oral oaths or promises are treated in the textbooks primarily as they establish vassalic ties in general, not only specific duty, but to allow Roland to treat his promises as not binding here, the principle would actually have to be reversed; cf., e.g., Ganshof's discussion of vassalage and fealty, 69–81; Lemarignier, 127. "Within this interwoven system of word, symbol, and act, it is important that each of the participants fully understand the meaning of each pledge and that each verbal or symbolic exchange have a single meaning. . . . The face value and the true value of an exchange must be identical for the system to function" (Kellogg, 162).

It is Gautier who says openly that there is logic in their choice, stating the context that supports the entire scene. "I am Roland's man; I must not fail him" (801). This is not some gratuitous afterthought intended to enliven the obligatory presentation of the rear guard's departure, but a summary of the episode's portent. Whatever the nature of the mission, even if it means his death, Gautier will go with Roland now because, when he became his *man*, his vassal, he said he would be ready to serve when his leader needed him. Exactly like Roland, Gautier has a concept of his promises and a sense of responsibility that transcend circumstances. He responds to Roland's gesture as Roland responded to Charles's earlier decision, with a straightforward adherence and an invocation of a paramount ideal that makes it all seem simple. This goes a long way toward explaining one of the superficially curious things in the text: why Gautier is later brought into the battle of Roncevaux and is given the honor of sharing Roland's last stand.[72] Now the Peers and Roland select the twenty thousand men of the rear guard.

65 (LXV)

It is interesting that the legendary Roland does something that might have saved the historical Roland from the ambush the chronicler Einhard describes. He sends a detachment to protect the high ground (it is from above that the perfidious Wascones descended to attack Charles's rear guard in 778). This tactic may serve as another sign that Roland in the poem is a competent soldier and not the unthinking egotist of criticism.[73] Gautier is given the command of this new detachment, and he commits himself to the task, using the preposition *pur* to say "I will do it for your sake." Like Roland, he carries out his promise; he remains fighting on the heights without retreating or calling for help until it is too late and he has been overwhelmed.

It will be clear from this discussion that we can only deduce what a

[72]For discussion of Gautier's mission and the associated secondary literature, see Dufournet, *Cours*, 198–205; Wendt, 247–48; Horrent, *Chanson de Roland dans les littératures . . .*, 172–77.

[73]On the rear guard's rear guard, see D. J. A. Ross, "Before *Roland:* What Happened 1200 Years Ago Next August 15?" *Olifant*, 5 (1977–78), 171–90, and Ross, "Gautier del Hum: An Historical Element in the *Chanson de Roland?*" *Modern Language Review*, 61 (1966), 409–15. Ross rejected the idea that the Roland of the *Song* can have "ordinary military sense" ("Before *Roland*," 178) and thus was led to explain Gautier's mission as a reminiscence of a historical event. On the other hand, Paul Bancourt cites Roland as an example of the wise tactician in his "'Sen' et 'chevalerie': Réflexions sur la tactique des chevaliers dans plusieurs chansons de geste des XIIe–XIIIe siècles," *Société Rencesvals: VIe Congrès International* (Paris, 1974), 628. Einhard's description of the battle of Roncevaux is given in Moignet, 290–91.

rear guard was for or, to be more precise, what the audience would have thought a rear guard was for. The poem does not ever tell us explicitly, except in Roland's voice, and we cannot discover the rear guard's tactical functions by consulting Jean de Meun's Vegetius or John of Salisbury's *Policraticus.* It is possible that those functions were never codified, but rather decided on the spot—logically, not in the moments just before battle but at the time when plans are being made and assignments accepted. However, the deduction is incumbent upon us as readers: it would not be correct for us simply to assume that Roland is being asked to do something other than what he insists on doing.

Nevertheless, in spite of our loss of contact with some of the presuppositions that made the poem work in the hearers' consciences, it is still possible to state that the Nomination Scene, and not the later scenes of argument, is the crux of the Roncevaux episodes. We have generally considered the Horn Scenes as being those where the decisions about what will happen are made, and thus as being the linchpin of the poem's first part. But I have already argued, and I think the poem continues to show, that tactical decisions are not up to Charles's emissaries, whoever they may be, but up to Charles himself, as commander-in-chief. There is little to gain by considering Roland as anything but a lieutenant; he is not an autonomous commander.[74] Whatever the duties of the rear guard may be precisely, its leader's choice (when those duties are laid upon him) is made at the time he accepts them, and not in the field. Roland might conceivably refuse to undertake the rear guard's mission, although he does not, but he cannot refuse the actual accomplishment of the agreement he made with his commander and suzerain at the time he took on the assignment. There is enough logic in that to make the Nomination Scene the controlling one, and the logic is also clear enough to make surmises about hidden states of mind in the laconic characters unnecessary.

66 (LXVI)

The narrator does not fail to tell us how difficult the crossing of the bleak and rocky mountains is for the army. Again, while important, his description does not have to be lengthy. We may find his empha-

[74]The idea that he is some sort of general is clearly expressed by Bédier: "In what period of history, in what country, what leader, when taken by surprise and outnumbered by the enemy, has ever hesitated to ask for reinforcemens?" (Bédier, *Légendes,* 3:433; cf. Williamson, 558; Misrahi and Hendrickson, 367; Renoir's references to Roland's "army" in his "Roland's Lament," 572, 582). Van Emden offers important nuances, but still insists that Roland is a "chef" (Van Emden, "Guarant," 37ff., 43ff.).

ses inadequate, but we are foreigners wandering in the text without the knowledge that acclimated readers or hearers are likely to have had. The description omits little. It first evokes the lofty peaks and their shadows, and the awesome road to be trod, neither of which is ornamental here in a strict narrative sense. Then it tells us (816–17) that the French must struggle to cross, *a grant dulur.* The noise of their passing is clearly heard over some distance.

These lines (814–17) are indeed powerful in their suggestive sobriety, but they must also be understood as part of the setting for the action.[75] Many of us must make a certain effort of imagination if we are to see what lines 816–17 evoke, as clearly as the lines preceding them evoke a landscape. Others of us may have experienced the weary travail of campaigning and know precisely what the "pain" (*dulur*) and noise are like. "That day the French went through at great cost; for fifteen leagues around, the sound was heard." Put in context, the beginning of laisse 66 refers (as did lines 583–86 and 740–42) to something that has grown more and more obvious as the text unfolds. The army actually needs a rear guard. It is in disarray, occupied with its journey through inhospitable places, taking the risk of movement with an enemy at its back, working out the choice implied in the Council Scene. Close attention to these preliminaries—reading for situation rather than for character—shows Roland's real motivation in the scenes to come.

Now one of the hero's promises comes true. The main body of the army reaches friendly territory, Gascony, Charles's holding, in safety. The men think first of their homes and their women, but their leader has not forgotten that the story is not over. He fears for Roland—as well he might, given what everyone knows (cf. 843).

67 (LXVII)

Confirmation of Roland's peril and of the larger group's awareness of it comes quickly. First we are again reminded that, though the army is no longer in Spain, the twelve Peers and a large number of others still are.[76] Given their peril, it seems logical for line 828 to

[75]The mountains are more than "a physical manifestation of the atmosphere of tension and anxiety" (Fox, *Literary History,* 73; cf., e.g., Siciliano, 338–39). Cartier, 50, may have been the first to emphasize the fact they are a real physical obstacle; see also my "Roncevaux symbole de la nécessité," *Olifant,* 8 (1981), 352–66. Bédier shows a characteristic lack of consideration for the army's situation when he states: "At Roncevaux, it is not a matter of defending the homeland—no one is threatening it—but only of saving Charles's best men from a nasty ambush" (Bédier, *Légendes,* 3:433).

[76]Brault points out, following Smail, that it would be usual procedure for the rear guard to stay "close to the main body of the army" (Brault, *Song,* 1:407). It is the terrain

remind us that these men do not fear death. Charles is downcast; when Naimon asks why, the emperor reveals his true thoughts fully for the first time. I have argued that there was no point in his mentioning his dream before: its use in the nomination decision would not have been legitimate. But now the die is cast, and Charles reveals his private and privileged knowledge and the conclusions he has drawn. Summarizing his dream of Ganelon and the breaking of the lance, Charles proceeds as well to interpret it symbolically, in expected fashion, and with the expected result. Ganelon will destroy France, says Charles (835); he (and he alone) chose Roland for the rear guard (838); Roland may be lost.

68 (LXVIII)

The scene broadens to include the army, and we find that one hundred thousand men are moved by Charles's tears, now public. What is more, they are all deeply afraid for Roland's sake (843). They may or may not have heard Charles tell his dream, but they know the situation. The rear guard is a dangerous assignment in everyone's estimation. The scene changes again, quickly, reminding us exactly what the situation is. Ganelon has betrayed Roland for money (honor is not mentioned). Now Marsile is calling his armies together. In three days they outnumber Roland's detachment twenty to one. The pagans ride hard, until they have caught up with the departing Frenchmen and can see their pennants.

---

that precludes this, although in the compressed geography of the poet's imagination Charles's men can see Gascony while Roland is still at the pass of Cize. On Charles's attitude in this scene, see Burgess, "Old French *contenance* and *contenant*," in Raymond Cormier, ed., *Voices of Conscience* (Philadelphia, 1977), 21–41; *cuntenance* (830) has associations with grief.

The Battle of Roncevaux

The Pagan Boasts

69 (LXIX)

Now begins yet another scene of vital importance for our comprehension of how the work portrays Roland. Over against the twelve Peers, the pagans set twelve of their number. Before these twelve warriors begin their attack, each makes a traditional battle-boast, or *gab,* promising, all in similar terms, to defeat the Christians. Each uses a first-person formula of some kind (there are two possible exceptions to this uniformity) and promises to be the personal agent of the Franks' death, destruction, and disheartenment through some great and specified deed. Psychologically speaking, they might merely be pumping up their courage, but their boasts are rhetorically essential, not to be dismissed as extraneous ornament or as superfluous to the narrative, for they contrast with Roland's words in the scene immediately following. The pagans promise what Roland does not, and yet each and every one of them fails.[77]

[77]On the contrast between Roland's promises and those of the pagans, see my "Translators and Traducers." Stephen G. Nichols, *Romanesque Signs: Early Medieval Narrative and Iconography* (New Haven, 1983), 166–67, has come to similar conclusions about the pagans' promises and their ironic outcome (though he thinks Roland is also mistaken, for other reasons [p. 173]).

Given the vital importance of feudal ritual, it is surprising that criticism has neglected to distinguish between the stylized exaggerations of the *gab* and the binding solemnities of the true promise or vow (cf. Jones, *Ethos,* 63–65, 69–70). Promises are not exhortations, they are personal engagements. Unaware of the symmetry here, Moignet went as far as to exclude the pagan *gabs* from pp. 41–42 of the separate edition of his translation. Siciliano, 352, took the pagan boasts to be an attempt at humor by Turold. There is a tendency to minimize or excuse what are taken to be boasts on Roland's part; see

Marsile's nephew, the first to speak, is Roland's precise counterpart, at least for this episode (and he too points out that he has won battles for his uncle [863–65]). He parades before the king, asking as a boon (called a *fief*) permission to strike Roland, and he says, "*I* will kill him with my spear" (*Jo l'ocirai,* 867), adding that with Mahum as his *guarant* he will drive the Franks from Spain. Charles and his men will abandon their cause, he says, and Marsile will have peace. None of this shows any understanding of the situation, of Charles's motives or his determination, on the Saracen's part, and in fact what happens is something like the opposite of what he predicts. He makes no reference to Ganelon's false claim (laisses 43–45) as the source of his prediction that killing Roland will mean peace, but whether he got the idea from Ganelon (as seems likely) or thought of it himself, the pagan peer's boast is wrong in every particular.

70 (LXX)

Marsile's nephew brandishes the token of his mission and calls out fiercely for others to join him. Falsaron is first, and he too makes a statement: "It is fated that *we* shall kill Charles's rear guard" (*nus les ocirum,* 884).

71–78 (LXXI–LXXVIII)

Like the gifts and vows in laisses 47–52, the pagan peers' promises now come thick and fast. For unknown reasons, the wizard Corsalis is not quoted, but the speedy Malpramis cries out, "If I meet Roland, I will strike him down" (893). The bold *amurafle* goes him one better: "If I meet Roland, he will die, and Oliver too, and the twelve Peers" (901–3). He then repeats the prediction that such a feat will end the war and bring peace to Spain. The evil *almaçur* says, "If I meet Roland, I guarantee him death" (914). Turgis of Turteluse states, among other putative doctrinal errors, that Mahum is of greater worth than Saint Peter. He promises that he will fight Roland and that no man can save the hero from death. Showing his sword and promis-

Brault, *Song,* 1:92; Misrahi and Hendrickson, 367–68; Kibler, "Roland's Pride," 151 and n. 21. Horrent saw that the pagan *gabs* are meant to contrast with Roland's attitude (Horrent, *Chanson de Roland et geste de Charlemagne,* 5; and Horrent, *"Chanson de Roland" dans les littératures . . . ,* 226), but he compares them only with the scene in which Roland accepts the rear guard, not with the Horn Scenes that follow; cf. Ross, "Before *Roland,*" 177. The concept of the *gab* is discussed in general by Brault, *Song,* 1:171–76, 283 (with anthropological considerations); Van Emden, "Guarant," 44–45; Matthias Waltz, *Rolandslied, Wilhelmslied, Alexiuslied* (Heidelberg, 1965), 37–38; Pensom (pp. 116, 123, 128) points out that Roland's promises are impersonal while the pagans' are individual, and, like Brault (*Song*), he notes (p. 117) confusion and anarchy in this scene.

ing to cross it with Roland's Durendal, he says: "If the French fight us, they will die" (928).

In a variegated cascade of names and descriptions to which a prose summary cannot do justice, the narrator repeats this form of promise eleven times. For ten laisses, 124 lines, the litany does not slacken. Escremiz promises to cut off Roland's head if they meet (935) and adds yet another, more obscure falsehood. Charles will be short of good vassals then, claims the pagan, and yet the course of the war and the Trial Scene will eventually prove him wrong even in that claim. Esturganz, Estramarin, and Margarit all say they will kill the hero—the latter says that almost word for word (963), and for good measure also promises to capture all France and sleep within the walls of Saint Denis.

The last of the exaggerated promises is made in a laisse of unappreciated poetic merit by the most awful Saracen of all: Chernuble de Munigre. In his land the sun does not shine. Nothing grows, no rain falls, and no dew; the very stones there are black; some say it is a land of devils. This is the enemy that Roland, the mortal man, must face. "I'll dye my sword red at Roncevaux," says Chernuble, and he adds that he will win Roland's sword from him. This ends the string of vows, and the pagans (who like Occidental knights travel unencumbered by armor) go to equip themselves for battle.

We have heard Roland promise, and this is not his style. He says briefly that he will do his best, though loss may be inevitable (755–59). He could break that promise by doing less than his best, but as we shall see, he keeps it. The pagans are vain men who have no second thoughts. Their promises are unqualified, or wrongly qualified, and when the time comes to carry them out, they cannot do so. They promise victory, pure and simple, and they are mistaken. That is their nature as imaginary infidels, and it is not Roland's. Not one of the men just named survives the very first encounter at Roncevaux. Whatever their claims, they cannot kill Roland. He and his peers kill them. But only a few lines further on, Roland will swear his great triple oath, and the juxtaposition itself makes evident, as no critical argument can, how clear a vision the hero has of his duty.[78]

[78]The other preserved versions of the *Song of Roland* are not studied here. Sometimes their redactors seem to have had models similar in structure to the Oxford text, and sometimes they seem to have had something else in mind. Without a full picture of the work's textual history (frustratingly elusive so far), we cannot borrow from the other versions to explain or complete the Oxford text. They are autonomous, as criticism generally recognizes now, and that means Bédier was right in saying Oxford is independent also. A good example of the difficulties involved is furnished by the little

The First Horn Scene (or Scene of Argument)

79 (LXXIX)

The pagans arm and mount, the sun on their armor. They spur to the attack and sound their horns. The French hear clearly. Oliver proposes, perhaps ironically, that it might well be the Saracens. Roland's reply is his fullest speech so far, a ringing statement of principle. The "feudal credo" of lines 1008–16 has often been described as a legitimate statement of the vassal's duty; it is difficult to conceive of it as exaggerated or erroneous. What is less often recognized is its degree of generality: it is true in its essence, without respect to persons or to particular circumstances. Battle is coming, and that is only fitting, says Roland. Suffering (Roland uses heat, cold, and wounds as his examples) is the duty one owes to one's lord. (The subject of the major axiom is *hom* in line 1010, the impersonal pronoun but also the word for vassal.) Roland and his men are vassals and subordinates, and they are there at their overlord's behest (1009). Each one of them should strike hard—this is an exhortation, not an order—and ill fame will never come from such deeds. Victory is not mentioned. The pagans are in the wrong, the Christians in the right. And to summarize this, his one and only argument, Roland refers not to the glory of conquest but to the exemplary quality of what he means to do: *Malvaise essample n'en serat ja de mei,* "I will never be a bad example" (1016).

80 (LXXX)

But Oliver, though he does not contradict Roland immediately, is not listening. He rides or climbs to the top of a hill and sees the Saracens. He shows as yet no sign of surprise, but calls to Roland, confirming what he has guessed, that the pagans are coming to do them harm. Oliver also states what everyone suspects: that Ganelon has betrayed them. Roland's reply is sometimes misrepresented. He does not say that accusation is false, and very shortly he will reveal that he knows it to be true (1146–47). He says only that Ganelon has

conundrum of Corsalis, the only pagan peer who does not make a boasting promise. All the other medieval French versions but one furnish some sort of speech to go in the blank space that editors leave after Oxford's line 888. (They also add a lot of other things in places where editors of Oxford see no lacunae.) In the Châteauroux text, Corsalis is given no speech at all. Venice IV has him make a promise that fits stylistically into the scene of braggadocio, but it contains a suspicious verbatim anticipation of the following laisse. Like the others, Venice IV also makes him the only pagan to say anything as banal as "I am the third, now select the fourth." This cannot serve our interpretation of Oxford. See also Chapter 4, below.

married into his family and that he does not want Oliver to speak of the matter of treason.[79]

81 (LXXXI)

From the hilltop Oliver can now see the enemy plainly, their equipment and weapons gleaming, so many that he cannot count them, even by squadrons. And suddenly, explicitly, he is no longer himself. He is *esguaret,* says the text, "lost" in the literal sense, confused, beside himself, perhaps even frightened. The usual renderings are in any case not strong enough, to judge by the examples our dictionaries give us from other works. Oliver is not merely worried, he is upset. Even Modern French *égaré* (Moignet) might be better than Foulet's "*inquiet.*"[80] Line 1035 marks Oliver as an unsteady witness. He pounds down the hillside as hard as he can go, and comes to the French to warn them.

82 (LXXXII)

Oliver explains his haste by a reference to the large, very large, number of pagans, already an issue in lines 1021–22 and 1030–36. There are one hundred thousand of the enemy, an overwhelming force, more than ever seen before. One supposes that if numbers have ever mattered, they matter now. Oliver speaks to the rear guard as he first spoke to Roland, and calls for firm resistance (1045). But he and he alone also speaks as though he thought victory possible: "Stand your ground, lest we be defeated" (1046). The French, we already know, are not afraid to perish here (827–28); they reply as one: "A curse on him who flees! Not one of us shall fail you, though we die!" (1048).

83 (LXXXIII)

Oliver's attitude does not quite match that of the detachment, however. He speaks, probably in an aside, to Roland: the pagans are so

[79]See Brault, *Song,* 1:177–78. For examples of claims that Roland is unable or unwilling to admit Ganelon's treason at this point, see, e.g., Siciliano, 354; Cartier, 44; Pensom, 131. Williamson has described Roland's trust in his kinsman as the principal motive for his refusal to obey Oliver, but compare my commentary to laisse 60. The distinction between kinship ties and feudal ties is more or less artificial, depending on the period; see M. Bloch, 141–42, 233–34.

[80]For a similar interpretation of this word, see Brault, *Song,* 1:177, who imputes "bewilderment and consternation" to Oliver but adds that the gloss "grandement troublé" (Bédier, *Chanson*) "conveys more fear than the poet intended." Jessie Crosland draws a curious parallel between Oliver and Tedbald in the *Chanson de Guillaume:* the latter also climbs a hill, sees the enemy, and counsels flight (Jessie Crosland, *The Old French Epic* [Oxford, 1951], 82).

many, and we are so few! And in a proposal that the poem repeats twice afterward, rolling it over and over in the flow of its assonances, Oliver pleads with Roland to send a signal, to sound his horn: Charles and the army will return. This is a strange and contumacious reaction to Roland's feudal credo. A man must suffer on his lord's behalf (*pur sun seignur,* 1010), said the hero, and now he reacts sharply to Oliver's suggestion that suffering can be avoided. Roland avoids ad hominem invective, applying the strong adjective *fols* by a conditional clause to himself, as he would be, were he to agree. But his point is clear. To signal would be wrong, a foolish action. The French would never trust me again, or more precisely, I would lose the standing (*los*) I have earned. And then he promises again not imminent victory but a good fight and its inevitable results, outside the limits of temporal adverbs, verb tenses, or named agents.

What Roland says here is one of the most misunderstood predictions in all literature. His enemies all said, "I will kill, we will kill, at Roncevaux," and they were wrong. Roland names no time, no place, no agent, and thus he is telling the literal truth. "I will strike great blows, and the whole length of my sword will be bloody," he states. But his actual threat is in the most general of forms. The evil pagans were wrong to come here, he says, and his oath, when it comes, has all the sweep of the timeless, unconjugated adjectival participle. "I swear to you, *they are* all *doomed* to die" (1058).

Taken out of context, as they usually are, these lines can in fact be construed as expressing unwarranted confidence: Roland promising to do what he cannot and will not do.[81] That requires us to supply the verbal expressions of cause and effect that bring on some difficulty for us here by their absence. "The pagans will die *because* of my great blows," Roland might then be thought to say, and a localizing adverb or an agent is needed as well: "They are doomed to die *here,* by my hand." Translators have made those changes, but they are changes, alterations to the words of a text that is at the very least not explicitly consonant with the *démesure* hypothesis. The claims we might expect from the

[81]For the claim that Roland expects victory see, e.g., Bédier, *Légendes,* 3:434, 437, 442; Le Gentil, *Song,* 90, and "A propos de la démesure," 203, 205; Whitehead, "*La Chanson de Roland* et l'esprit héroïque," *Cahiers de civilisation médiévale,* 3 (1960), 115–17; Cartier, 47–48 (relies on chronicle figures to justify Roland's decision), 60–61; Waltz, 35; Van Emden, "Guarant," 29, 35; Burger, "Les Deux Scènes du cor dans la *Chanson de Roland,*" in the so-called "Liège colloquium," *La Technique littéraire des chansons de geste* (Paris, 1959), 113, 122 ("It is clear that Roland wants to triumph alone"); Hunt, "Character and Causality," 33: "[He seeks] to repair the damage by himself rescuing the rearguard"; cf. Hunt, "Structure," 306.

Roland of the handbooks are not here (any more than they are in lines 755–59 or 790–91). Another hypothesis may cleave better to the text by coming to terms with their absence.

There should be no mistake about what Roland is doing. He is not really arguing circumstances with Oliver at all; the circumstances are clear enough. He is referring back to a principle he has already stated, the only time he has spoken at length. He is at Roncevaux to represent Charles, and his first duty is not to save himself. His position needs no further explanation, and that is why he gives none. Still, it is essential to realize that this is not a moment of choice in any case. Roland has already committed himself to fight if attacked, and if he calls for help instead he will be breaking his word.

This is, rather, a moment of testing. It has been moderately clear all along that the decision to leave Marsile alone was a mistake, and close attention to the Nomination Scene has shown that the pagans' presence here at Roncevaux is at least half-expected. And yet the procedural rules of a great social system have committed Roland to this place, through the weaknesses of some of the men who must meet and apply those rules.[82] The army has faltered, and Ganelon has lied. Still, the rules are there: one suffers for one's lord; Charles cannot both move his army and defend himself. The rear guard is only too obviously needed. The question is whether the rules will finally work if they are followed despite such failures. What Roland is telling Oliver is that they will indeed work. That is the lesson of Charles's later vengeance, for every promise Roland has made will in the literal sense come true. The pagans are making a horrible mistake. They cannot win, and only too soon they will receive the wages of their sin.

Oliver does not understand, and neither, perhaps, do we, for the assurance that things will work out if only we act rightly may indeed often be scant comfort in the face of death. This is precisely why that notion requires a great poem and a great hero to affirm it. It is not enough to say it once; in three mighty parallel laisses, the epic, through Roland, says it again and then again. If we can admit that feudal duty, however crudely summarized, was once thought of as part of the structure of society; if we remind ourselves that the prayers and the alms of the church, the work of sowers and reapers, were once thought with some reason to be made possibly only by the valor of the knights who fought to protect them; if, finally, we simply

[82]Pensom (pp. 124, 128) makes a similar distinction between Oliver's attitude and Roland's. Nichols, 168–73, finds that both characters are mistaken.

recall that Roland has made a promise to fight if attacked—then all Roland's references to his people, his society, and even his honor are natural and correct, because all of those things really are involved.

And if we remind ourselves that Roland's credo comes first in the text; that Oliver is reacting to Roland's attitude, and not vice versa, when he suggests the signal; that Roland is not refusing an explanation, indeed has already expressed the only one that seems possible to him (one that perhaps should have occurred to Oliver too)—then we may even be moved to think that Roland's intensity has an understandable motive.

Of course the shadow of the old *démesure* hypothesis forms again in our minds when we hear Roland invoke his *los,* his standing, what people think of him.[83] By a well-known modern convention, reputation is mere frippery and no guide to what a person is: accident, not essence, in the terms of a philosophy alien to the times of the *Song of Roland.* And *los* is indeed reputation; honor is in certain senses always honor. But these are not the chivalric pretensions of Froissart's time or Tennyson's. The ideal knight of the early feudal age is trusted because he earns trust, the concomitant of reputation and honor, and where the feudal system is at home and functioning, then he earns it not by conforming to some detailed and arbitrary code but by acting as a knight. *Los* is then the opinion of those whose responsibility it is to judge trustworthiness on the basis of knowledge; it is close to its roots in the verb *loer,* which is to give counsel.

Roland actually does have something to lose here besides life. After having promised to defend Charles and the army, the king's favorite can call them back to defend him instead, but then the promise goes by the board, and what Roland is telling Oliver, what he has always been telling him, even as motley generations of readers rush past, is that the promise is more important than one might temporarily think. What we might like for Roland to do here—what Oliver asks him to do—is expedient: a response to immediate circumstances with no reference to what may be lost in the long run. And yet the entire structure of the given word now depends on Roland's constancy, and that structure is basic to the feudal bond. That is what *los* means here.

[83]"Reputation, good name, is all," says Halverson, 661, following Jones's thesis. *Los* is defined as "gloire personnelle" by Burger ("Deux Scènes," 113) and as "gloire cornélienne" by Gérard, 446. But if Roland speaks of his own role in the defense of society, it is not out of a desire for personal aggrandizement; he is already Charles's right-hand man, and that position actually does give him personal and public responsibility. *Los* should rather be seen in the semantic field of *loer,* which includes not only praise but also the vassalic duty of counsel, and hence involves public judgment and evaluation; see examples in Tobler and Lommatzsch, 5:546, 566, 668–72.

It means passing an especially rigorous conceptual test. All circumstances are irrelevant to the test except one: whether Roland's promise, as qualified, is fulfilled. Once it has been, then the future is as safe as one knight can make it. To act on that basis is Roland's greatness, and what sets him apart from Oliver.

84 (LXXXIV)

Oliver's entreaty is specific. Sound the horn: Charles will turn his army and rescue us (1060–61). Roland replies with full reference to the consequences of a change of heart: France itself would fall into a disreputable state (a wild claim indeed, if it were not that some of his society's underpinnings are at stake) and his family would be tainted. To avoid this unhappy result, Roland says he will fight instead and cover his sword with blood. But he still does not say, as our traditional hypothesis must assume, that he expects victory, in the short term, through his own deeds.

85 (LXXXV)

A third time the text presents Oliver's plea. We are not perhaps expected to think he actually repeats himself; there may well be only one discussion presented a little at a time. In any case, lines 1070–72 contain nothing really new. We may note that, although the audience has already heard that Charles is on his own lands, Oliver says (and Roland no doubt thinks) he is still in the Spanish passes. It may be on that basis that Roland replies, saying (like Oliver) the same thing he has already said, in a third way: "Please God, no man will ever claim that I blew my horn because of the enemy's presence." Once more we are faced with the need to reread a statement that may seem outlandish if we do not recall its context. The attack, which critics so often describe as a surprise, was expected, foreshadowed, and in a sense even promised. Roland accepted his task in sorrow and anger, but when he spoke, committing himself to attempt the defense of Charles's most worthless beast of burden, he said that he would do precisely what he is doing now. The fearsome proximity and vast numbers of the pagans have nothing to do with the matter, and it is their irrelevance to the larger issue of fidelity that makes it understandable for Roland to swear. To say he is free to change his mind, though it has generally gone without saying in *Roland* criticism, is to ignore the fact of his public and solemn commitment (confirmed by Naimon). Roland did not promise to send some signal that the pagans are there. The fighting force evoked in lines 780, 785, 802, 826–28, and so forth was constituted with such seriousness because there was good reason to expect the pagans would be there. Roland's own assumption, as the work presents it, was that Charles's goods and possessions, listed in lines 755–58, might well need defending and that it is his job to see to it that, if taken, they are taken only by the sword. I insist again, as I think the poem deliberately insists, that if Roland calls for help it will be in spite of his promise.

Again the hero promises to strike the necessary blows and to cover his sword with blood. The next two lines come as close as possible to promising some kind of success, if (and only if) we read them as linked, as cause and effect. "The French are good fighters and will attack bravely" (1080). And then: "The men from Spain will have no protector (*guarant*) against death" (1081). Once again the characteristic paratactic construction of these lines, a string of independent clauses, does not tell us what the logical relationship between lines 1080 and 1081 is. Editors working under the influence of the traditional reading nearly always furnish punctuation that makes line 1081 (another statement to the effect that the pagans cannot avoid death) into the result of line 1080 (another reference to fighting the good fight, this time on behalf of the entire rear guard). We should recall that the original is not punctuated (the commas and exclamation points in modern editions and translations are part of our interpretation), and we may ask ourselves whether the connection, obvious though the *démesure* theory made it seem, is in fact inevitable. I think these lines are like the conclusions to the two preceding laisses, just as the structures of the parallel laisses are alike in other ways. They are general statements like those in lines 1057–58 and 1068–69, and they are accurate because they are general. Roland is evoking the shape of the world, not his individual prowess.

86 (LXXXVI)

The argument, or discussion, is not over with laisse 85, and the First Horn Scene has several score lines yet to run before all its elements and their implications are put into place.

Oliver has no statement of principle to offer in reply to Roland's. He says *he* can see nothing wrong with calling for help (the use of a subject pronoun, naturally absent and easily omitted, may imply an emphasis on Oliver's expression of personal opinion). Then he states explicitly as his justification the fact that the Saracens are very numerous and the French are not. This is, once again, an argument based only on the immediate. It will appear valid or invalid as we choose or refuse to let our reactions be guided by the immediate situation rather than by what is beyond, including the rest of the poem. At first glance,

Roland may appear to reply directly, in reaction to Oliver's immediate terms, and it is impossible to show beyond question that he does not. But his reply is, as ever, couched in very general language. He does not speak of numbers; he refers to God, the angels, and France, whose honor (in the modern sense, this time) may be lost if he blows his horn. He again uses a term with feudal overtones, *aimer:* "Our bond with the emperor is the stronger for the blows we strike" (1092). And by negative implication he characterizes the proposed horn-call as shameful (1091) in a sense that requires some elucidation.

Huntage, "shame" in the abstract, is not just personal embarrassment here, any more than *los* is mere image. They both imply a network of relationships not necessarily implied by their cognates in Modern French and English or even in Middle High German and Late Latin. We have rarely tried to picture Roland's situation as one in which he *might* behave improperly, and we dissociate the loss of face to which he refers from any real professional responsibilities he has here. Yet every profession, every functioning caste, has standards of performance, and in the case of the soldier, feudal or not, they are often especially stringent. In short, I suggest that when Roland uses a word like "reputation" or "shame," he is referring to concepts that are already defined, things that the community has full knowledge of and a legitimate right to judge.[84] Oliver never counters his claims with any ethical argument. He does not say that proper knightly behavior is generally known to be something besides what Roland thinks. The hero's comrade is concerned with numbers and survival. That, of course, does not suffice to show that Roland has identified the proper action and that Oliver has not, but it certainly does not suggest that Oliver sees the ethical dimension of the matter clearly. If we are to decide, as latter-day readers, which of the two has a correct sense of propriety in this urgent business, we must continue to consult the poem as a whole.[85]

[84]Duby expresses this atmosphere in more positive terms than the debate has generally allowed for: "A knight who broke his sworn faith lost his right to hold his head high at assemblies of fellow warriors. At this level of the body social, the entire edifice of peace rested on a fabric of individual and collective oaths and the ties of solidarity that wove them tightly together. Boldness, vigor, generosity, fealty—these were the several aspects of honor, and honor in turn was the quintessential value, the most coveted stakes in that code of permanent emulation which was life at war and at court" (Georges Duby, *The Age of the Cathedrals* [1976; trans. Eleanor Levieux and Barbara Thompson, Chicago, 1981], 41).

[85]Statements implying that Roland's duty is to call for help may be found, e.g., in Bédier, *Légendes,* 3:433 (cf. 431); Pauphilet, *Legs,* 69; Jenkins, xxxiii; Faral, *Chanson,* 215, 230; Le Gentil, *Song,* 104–5; Burger, "Deux Scènes," 114.

87 (LXXXVII)

That Oliver is clearheaded and Roland wrongheaded is an idea sometimes said to derive from this very next laisse, in fact, from its famous first line (1093). *Proz* and *sage,* "that is all [our author] needs to define his characters," said Lanson.[86] But of course the *chanson de geste* does not proceed in that lapidary fashion. It depends too much on effects of scale and accumulation with which Lanson was not familiar, and the *Roland* in particular depends too greatly on showing rather than on telling, for a single aside, even in the narrator's voice, to have quite so much weight. The circumstances that form the context for action may be recalled in a few words (e.g., 740–41, 1134–35), but the meaning of the text itself unfolds only as the text proceeds.

Furthermore, recent lexical investigations have shown that the terms *proz* and *sage* do not express some sort of opposition in any case, but rather embody two aspects of the *vasselage* characterizing both Roland and Oliver (1094).[87] The narrator does not direct us to prefer one of these protagonists and his point of view to the other. We must derive, from their statements, a judgment about which of the two has a better grasp of the situation as a whole. Now, as the enemy approaches, Oliver says nothing new: if Charles were here, he claims, we would not be hurt (1102). One must ask, as reader or hearer, whether in the created context of the *Roland* or in practically any context, that can be the primary consideration in a rear-guard engagement. Oliver does add one element to his appeal. In line 1104 he makes the pathetic claim that the men Roland is leading are unhappy. "See for yourself," he says, but that is not what Roland sees, and he replies at some length this time.

Apparently Roland takes Oliver's reference to the detachment as an insult to his companions, just as his friend's earlier suggestions potentially raised the question of the hero's fitness for his task. His fairly sharp reply may be taken as referring to the subgroup as a whole, and it will be made more explicit in the next laisse. First Roland describes Oliver's statement (that the rear guard is in distress) as an impropriety, *ultrage.* (Moignet, curiously, translates that word by "paroles

[86]Lanson, *Histoire,* 30.

[87]See esp. Burgess, *Contribution,* 91–103; Brault, *Song,* 1:181–83; and note 10 to the Preface, above. To link *proz, sage, vassal,* and *curteis* all to the same semantic field of worthiness is not to deny the probable nuances among the terms, but only to recall that they do not have the divergent denotations of their modern cognates; cf. Brault, *Chanson,* xxiv–xxv. Thus the men of the detachment are not necessarily Roland's own vassals, despite Van Emden, "Guarant," 40; in line 1857 *vassal* means "fighters," though these men do serve Roland (1858). Cf. Dufournet, *Cours,* 142–60.

démesurées.")[88] Both Moignet and Brault, it is true, understand Oliver's *dolente* in 1104 as "pitiful," the passive present participle, rather than "unhappy" or "downcast." I prefer to stay, with Lucien Foulet,[89] closer to the secondary or modern meaning here, because Oliver invites Roland to use his eyes: *veeir poez,* he says, and his insistence on the evidence of things seen is consistent with his other arguments. The grief of the rear guard, if indeed it is grieving (but cf. 1047–48), is something that can be seen. But Roland, also in typical fashion, replies with an abstraction and a generality: "Cursed be the cowardly heart!" Then he affirms for the sixth time, in reply to Oliver, that the rear guard (now represented by an extended personal pronoun *nus*) will stand firm. Here he uses active verbs, not passive as he did in his initial promise to Charles. "We shall stand our ground, and when there is fighting, we shall be the ones to fight" (1108–9).

88 (LXXXVIII)

Roland summarizes and concludes the altercation with a final statement of his vassal's credo. He is growing fiercer now (that, and not "proud," is the sense of *fiers* in 1111),[90] as he cries out to his men and exhorts Oliver to remember that the rear guard is there at Charles's behest. All this is no mistake, he insists. (And how could the size of the pagan force make it one?) Charles acted deliberately in choosing these twenty thousand (1114–16). He thought none of them cowardly. And in a near replica of the opening lines in the debate (1008ff.), Roland again affirms that it is a vassal's duty to suffer discomfort and wounds on his lord's behalf. He asks only that Oliver use his weapon, and he will do the same. His sword was given to him for that purpose. I may die, says Roland—the *démesure* hypothesis scarcely gives him credit for envisaging this possibility—but it will be known that I was a noble vassal. Can we doubt that was the issue all along?

Se jo i moerc. . . "If I die, whoever has my sword may well say that it was a good vassal's" (1122–23). These words are no blind promise of victory, but an explicit reference to possible death. They are rarely if ever mentioned in commentaries, and having glossed them over for years myself I think I can say why.[91] It is because the interpretation

[88]Moignet, 99.

[89]Lucien Foulet's glossary to the *Song,* in Bédier, *Chanson de Roland commentée,* 370.

[90]Though *fierté* can be both pride and ferocity; see Burgess, "*Orgueil* and *fierté* in Twelfth-Century French," *Zeitschrift für romanische Philologie,* 89 (1972), 103–22.

[91]Van Emden ("Guarant," 38–39) seems to have been alone in pointing out that Roland, Turpin, and Oliver all mention their deaths at Roncevaux (cf. 1027–35, 1105).

comes to control the text, being set into place before we ever begin close study. Afterward, it does not matter how often or how deeply we read; as long as we fail to test the interpretive hypothesis extensively, we will fail to be struck by such lines as lines 1122–23. We scarcely even bother to explain them away as meaningless clichés, minor flaws in an otherwise great poem, to which they contribute nothing. It does not often occur to us to break this circle; to ask just how numerous such inconsistencies really are; to seek coherence in the work as if for the first time, and then to derive a meaning from that coherence. This reading habit is natural enough in the very first place, and it is also reinforced by its own product: the notion that the poem does not quite add up, as indeed in some details it does not. I have elsewhere described some of the effects of this "fallacy of hermeneutic necessity." By ignoring the slipping cogs in our interpretive machinery, it allows us to operate that machinery even when it is not well adjusted. Thus Moignet, though he had personally transcribed, edited, and translated these lines, still described Roland as "certain of victory"[92] and claimed that the hero becomes aware of impending doom (and of Ganelon's treason) only in lines 1455 and afterward.

89 (LXXXIX)

No other character besides Oliver shows any sign of doubt about what has to be done. (Again, Oliver's statement in line 1104, about the rear guard's pain or pitifulness is a revelation of his perception and must be seen in the light of his excited state of mind.) The fighting Archbishop Turpin does, however, speak of the impending battle emphatically.[93] He is the only one of the Christians to address the men of the rear guard at any length. Neither Roland nor Oliver offers them more than a brief exhortation, at least not in the form of direct address. But it is part of Turpin's priestly function to bless and absolve these men, who are fighting for their religion as well as for a social system, and as he gives his blessing he speaks clearly of both heaven and feudalism. The rear guard's duty is to earn the one and serve the other by dying.

The archbishop says precisely that, first echoing Roland's feudal credo, which of course is not "Roland's credo" but a broad statement of principles that every vassal in eleventh- or twelfth-century France putatively subscribed to. For that matter, every cleric presumably sub-

[92]Moignet, 123.

[93]Contamine, 269, notes that in Carolingian times, at least, it was normal for bishops to accompany armies. On the fighting-archbishop figure, see the studies cited in Brault, *Song*, 1:380, n. 568.

scribed to them too, though there is now some doubt about how they actually applied to clerics. Turpin's speech is in the first instance a recapitulation of Roland's. Charles, whose duty it was to decide, left the rear guard behind at Roncevaux, and it is the detachment's duty, "our duty," to die for the king's sake (1127–28). This is very nearly, if not exactly, what Roland has been saying, almost word for word but without the insistency lent Roland's words by the fact that the hero was replying to the hasty and perhaps repeated urgings of a worthy comrade temporarily not quite himself. Roland never specifically says "We must *die* for the king's sake," preferring to evoke the tortures of heat, cold, and wounds (1008–12, 1117–19), but he clearly refers to the risk of death in the context of those remarks (1122), immediately before the archbishop's summary. There can be little doubt that the two men, lieutenant and archbishop, are expressing fundamental agreement.[94]

What Turpin does say that Roland does not—most simply because it is his business as a member of the Second Estate—is that their battle is fought for Christianity's sake as well as for Charles's. Like the need for a rear guard, this basic element is no less obvious and no less weighty for being explicitly stated only once. The prelate reminds the soldiers that they are upholding their religion (1129). In the inevitable battle to come, they may die, but they will be holy martyrs and will sit in Paradise. He gives them absolution of all their sins and orders the work of the sword as the penance that will seal his blessing. The combination has been described as shocking, but this is just a bit hypocritical. Organized Christianity and warfare have always had, and continue to have, too many points of contact for us to express either bewilderment or condescension when faced with these men's bloodstained godliness. More important, the text offers them little choice: they are defending their comrades against a devilish foe.

90 (XC)

The archbishop has given the French soldiers absolution, and they rise. They are now in essence free of sin, and we may assume they die in a state of grace, or at least not the opposite. The rear guard, which was traveling light, now arms and mounts, ready for battle.

Roland calls to Oliver, telling him he agrees that Ganelon has be-

[94]Compare Le Gentil's claim that Roland shows no sign of realizing what he is fighting for (i.e., religion); Le Gentil opposes him to Turpin ("A propos de la démesure," 205), but cf. Brault, "*Sapientia,*" 112. For Turpin as a positive marker in the text, see also McCash, "*Scientia* and *Sapientia,*" 131–47; Faral, *Chanson,* 222; Siciliano, 344.

trayed them. This is not, of course, a contradiction of lines 1026–27, where Roland does not say he thinks Ganelon is innocent but only asks Oliver not to say such things about a man linked to his family. There is every reason to think Roland has known all along what the situation is. I have argued (as did Bédier) that his knowledge explains his reactions in the Nomination Scene. At the very least we can say that the text here does not show him receiving any new information or any impetus to change his mind. *Mult ben le saviiez,* he says to Oliver, "Your idea was quite correct" (or "correct, of course," 1145). Now Roland sums up the situation again, in terms less general and closer to the narrative this time, saying accurately what has happened and what will happen. "Ganelon has betrayed us, and has received payment for it." (He does not say that was his original motive.) "Marsile has brought our lives—but" (and the promise of resistance echoes the truth spoken in line 759) "he will yet have to pay by the sword." In passing, Roland also refers to the expected act of vengeance (1149).

91 (XCI)

Now Roland rides before his men in the narrow place where they must make their stand, in the doorway to Spain. His weapons are in his hand, his banner is whipped by the wind of his speed. The Franks are calling him their *guarant,* their leader and protector, but he does not claim he can save their lives. Still there is a promise he can make them, of equal or greater importance. This is not a vassalic engagement, but an incitement to combat. Roland uses one of the text's rare metaphors to express it. Looking angrily toward the pagans and tenderly toward the rear guard, he speaks *curteisement,* wisely, as a proper knight (1164).[95]

The pagans, Roland says, are seeking death ("martyrdom" may be too precise, or Roland's word *matirie* may have that connotation here, as Foulet suggests it has in line 1922).[96] The hero does not say whether they seek to suffer it or to inflict it. Our tradition naturally leads us to claim he means the former ("leur martyre," Moignet). If so, it is still not the same as a mistaken promise of victory (the pagans indeed lose many men before they triumph), but we may also miss thereby an important point about what he is saying. If Roland's vassalic promises are literal in a way that is generally unrecognized (and are therefore accurate), his promise to his comrades in the rear guard may be figurative. The

[95]The word *curteisement* shares, with *vassal* and other terms, the semantic field of worthiness (Burgess, *Contribution,* 21–22; cf. note 87, above).

[96]Lucien Foulet, in Bédier, *Chanson de Roland commentée,* 421.

context of this prebattle scene, with its several references to death (including Roland's own allusion [1122]), the close juxtaposition with Turpin's blessing, and with his promise of martyrdom's eternal reward, even the immediate juxtaposition with the word *matirie* itself in line 1166, all suggest that the *eschec*, literally "prize," "booty," that Roland mentions in line 1167, is a figurative reference to the martyr's privilege of heavenly acceptance. It is not some unprecedented vast treasure somehow to be won on this desert field, but a metaphoric treasure such as no king of France ever had, for it is not of this world.[97]

This runs, once more, hard against the grain of our reading habits, but it invites serious consideration. It is not as outlandish an interpretation of Roland's last prebattle speech as tradition might make it seem. All we really need to assume, in order to grasp it, is that Roland has heard and understood the explicit speech Turpin has just given and is echoing it as Turpin, in his own speech, echoed Roland's feudal credo. Whatever its intent, at least it cannot be denied that the statement has accurate connotations, for indeed no earthly king of France ever had a literal treasure equal to the seat in heaven mentioned in line 1135.

92 (XCII)

As the two armies draw together and argument is about to yield to action, Oliver speaks again, expressing his unshaken opposition to Roland's point of view. Once more, his remarks are limited to the specifics of the situation, and he takes no heed at all of the archbishop's intervention. Roland has not sounded his horn, Oliver says; Charles is not there. It is not the king's fault, for he knows nothing of what is happening—this statement is an error if it denies Charles's suspicions concerning the treason, correct if it means Charles does not yet know the battle has already begun. It is not the army's fault either. Oliver is still convinced a mistake is about to be made, and he will insist on that almost to the moment of his death.

But now he turns to the rear guard, exhorting the men to commit themselves firmly to battle and to fight hard. He never tells anyone except Roland of his misgivings, and never tries to call on the soldiers to support him in the dispute; he no longer refers to victory either. It is already too late, whatever Oliver might think. The rear guard is riding at the Saracens. They have no choice (1185), for a body of

[97]Brault also finds that the word requires elucidation (*Song*, 1:187–88). Bédier, *Légendes*, 3:435, took it literally. Cf. Ian Short's remarks in "Reinterpreting the *Roland*," *Romance Philology*, 34, Special Issue (February 1981), *55. The *matyrie* Roland mentions in line 1922 is clearly his own.

heavy cavalry has no effective means of defense, indeed, no battlefield function to speak of, except vigorous attack. Resistance here must be dynamic. Even at the very end of the battle, the last few Frenchmen charge into the press again and again. That is, of course, why knights have horses: to carry the shock of their charge to the enemy and "break" him (19). It is not until Roland and Turpin are alone, and Turpin has lost his horse, that their repeated charges come to an end.

The Battle Takes Place

93 (XCIII)

Thus the battle of Roncevaux is joined, and yet the time for affirmation of faith and principle is not past. Even in the thick of battle the men of the *Song of Roland* call out to each other and to their enemies. Furthermore, the promises of laisses 69–85 are about to be tested in detail. We see episodic breaks in the narration here (Moignet has subdivisions at laisses 79 and 88, as well as at 93), but it is really a seamless thematic fabric. The oaths of the Saracens, Roland's predictions, and the heroes' words and deeds in the field form a single resonant sequence. Now the first of the boasting pagan peers, Marsile's nephew Aelroth, rides forth to taunt the French with his claims. The Christians are betrayed, he claims, and by their own *guarant:* by Charles, not by Ganelon. But more than that, they are misled. Their king is a fool, and it was folly to leave them there (1193). As a result, what people know and think of France will be less good (lands as well as men can have their *los,* 1194). Charles will lose his right arm (as Ganelon promised [597] in almost the same words).

Roland's response to Aelroth is double. The Saracen swore only a short time before to kill him (867), yet in his anger the hero strikes the pagan's body to the ground, broken and lifeless, with a single blow. His cry is an exclamation of victory, for (in the hallowed manner of the medieval trial of strength)[98] his stroke has not only killed the Saracen but proven him wrong. Charles is neither fool nor traitor. His choice of a rear guard was a worthy deed (again *proz*) and will not cause France's decline. The first engagement is our victory, Roland shouts to his men, and he repeats his famous quasi-legal formula from line 1015: we are in the right, and these scoundrels are wrong!

[98]See Robert Delort, *La Vie au Moyen Age* (Paris, 1982), 116–17, and Scully, "Ordeal at Roncesvalles." The *gabs* after the Christians' victories are thus justified formally (Scully, 223; Del Monte, 232), despite Jones, *Ethos,* 19 (cf. 13–15).

94–104 (XCIV–CIV)

In a perfectly explicit and highly significant sequence, every one of the boasting pagans, in order man for man, engages a Christian knight in single combat, and not one Saracen is victorious. The symmetry between the two sides in the two scenes or subscenes is not absolute: one Saracen, Margarit, is not killed on the spot, but escapes Oliver's blow (1311–19); and the twelve pagans meet only eleven Frankish champions, since Roland strikes both the first and the last blow on his side.

The first of these differences is minor, but difficult to explain. Bédier studied it at some length, but inconclusively.[99] There may be something missing from the Oxford text, something that would explain where Margarit goes next. Other versions give him the role (not an absolutely necessary one) of messenger to the nearby Marsile, who has already been told that his first attack will fail (590–91). But, as ever, that may also be an ex post facto explanation that the Oxford redactor did not think necessary. The second asymmetrical element—eleven Christians against twelve Saracens—is easier to deal with from the point of view of its effect, whatever the maker's precise intent. It shows to the highest possible degree how foolish the pagans' promises were. The most fearsome of them all, the prodigious Chernuble, finds himself in Roland's path. The hero has smashed his lance in violent combat and has drawn his sword. He drives it with preternatural strength right through the Saracen and his horse, spine, armor, saddle and all, cleaving the man in two and killing his mount. Although the medieval sword was capable of inflicting horrible wounds, and similar marvels are attributed to other great fighters in epics and in chronicles as well, we need not pause to consider whether the poem's earlier hearers thought this a true description. What counts about Roland's terrific stroke is not its nature but its place and victim. Chernuble confidently said he would defeat Roland if they met (984–89); so said all his peers. And yet the opposite happens. The pagans' boasts are, in their error and blindness, signs of *démesure*, if I may borrow the term. Yet the text places Roland and the pagans in distinctly and deliberately contrasted positions. The enemy claimed immediate personal victory and were destroyed. Roland stops short of any such claim, yet he triumphs here, and his cause will triumph in the end.

The rest of this group of laisses presents that contrast in full detail.

[99]Bédier, *Chanson de Roland commentée*, 182–88; cf. Horrent, *Chanson de Roland dans les littératures . . .* , 220–22.

In a series of rapid single combats, Oliver, Turpin, and eight of the twelve Peers strike down the Saracens one by one, pausing on occasion to hurl the dead men's boasts back at them.[100] Oliver, true to form, claims victory, although only this first encounter may be meant (1233). Turpin, on the other hand, responds to Corsablix's slur against Charles (1240–41). When he sees his foe dead on the field, the archbishop insists that Charles is still (or is always) their *guarant,* thus echoing Roland's proud defense of the supreme commander in lines 1207–10. This claim is difficult to understand as a matter of immediate practicality, since the pagan is not wrong to say that Charles will not save the Christians from death. But if I am right to think that this passage, like others, is an illustration of principles and is not about the immediate at all, then Turpin is not saying he expects Charles to succor them then and there. His *tuz dis,* "as ever," is, like Roland's *il fist que proz* ("he was right to leave us behind," 1209), a reference to the fact that Charles has acted as a chief and protector rightly must, in choosing to protect his army even at the risk of losing the rear guard. When Turpin adds, again in words somewhat like Roland's, first, that this group of pagans (*voz cumpaignuns*) will be beaten (*restifs,* 1255) and, second, that the enemy must die, he is speaking the truth, though his reference to that death may foreshadow Charles's awesome double vengenace and not mean the battle of Roncevaux specifically. Thus Roland and Turpin, the warrior and the priest, echo each other, right up to the time when the dying archbishop, alone on the field with Roland after the fighting is over, claims victory for them both equally (2183).

The first part of the *Song of Roland* presents the causes of the battle of Roncevaux and the circumstances in which it takes place, but an epic is also a story of adventure and courage, and where it operates in that mode—as the several battles, Roncevaux and its consequences, unfold—the text requires less-intensive commentary. Henceforth (as has not been the case before) a large number of its lines are given over to matters of ornament: descriptions of the pagans' armor and horses, and lists of their horrible deeds. Thus, though the events continue to make sense and to signify what earlier laisses led us to expect, they are primarily the working out, in action, of what the exposition has prepared. The battle scenes, in grouping (for example) all the Christian successes together, then all the pagan victories, clearly fall under the

[100]The motif of the lance-attack is inevitable in the *chanson de geste* and has been given classic treatment by Rychner, 139–49, and Duggan, *Song,* 137–48.

sway of a coherent narrative impulse and are not mere scorekeeping. Still, they have a specifically epic function of displaying action at length and for present purposes require little detailed analysis.

There is not much new to be learned about Roncevaux at this point in the action anyway. We know that Roland and Turpin, as well as Oliver, anticipate death, and we have heard the archbishop promise the palms of martyrdom to the men of the rear guard. We know the importance of vengeance. All that remains is to confirm our knowledge in the event, and so the *Song of Roland* shows us the stout defense, the early French successes, and the slow turning of the tide as the rear guard tires. Then come the attack by Marsile's second wave, the many deaths among the Christians and the call to Charles for vengeance, when at last only sixty knights are left and none will be saved. In the end, Roland is master of the field, free to roam it at will while his strength lasts. The pagans have realized they cannot kill him. They have ceased to try, and have withdrawn, even before Charles quite arrives.

The themes remain the same throughout these scenes. One is duty to Charles, who was right to send the rear guard to its doom, despite what the pagans say, and who must be proved right by force of arms. Another is martyrdom, the prize to be won by men of courage and tenacity. Another is the necessity of vengeance, as appropriate a need now as it has been from the moment Roland first spoke. Numerous details in the illustration of these themes invite comment.

105–9 (CV–CIX)

We are shown first a new set of individual exploits. Roland and Oliver kill many, Oliver using the stub of his broken lance, which earns him Roland's grim, jesting approbation. Once his sword is out, he slices a man in two, as Roland did and will do again. Several Peers, and Turpin, each lay an enemy low. Then the focus shifts to the field as a whole, with an evocation of the pitched battle, and then to the Christian army beyond the passes, waiting in vain, and to Charles, whose tears (841) are recalled. But there can be no saving the rear guard, not because of Roland but because of Ganelon's treason, for which his punishment is forthcoming, as the narrator tells us in his own persona (1406–11).

110 (CX)

Again the text turns to the battle, and we glimpse the field as a whole. But next, as rapidly as before, it shifts its focus, this time to ancient Francia and to the first supernatural event we have seen outside Charles's troubled dreams. From one corner of the land to another, a tempest and earthquake strike, and the sky goes dark. It is, the narrator's voice tells us, a sign of Roland's death, and the first (but not the last) sign of God's involvement in Roland's final great deeds and his sacrifice. References to God, to the ultimate religious meaning of the battle, and to the supernatural will occur again, now that the men of the rear guard have done nearly all they can do as mortals and the time of their death draws close.

111 (CXI)

We are taken again to Roncevaux, where the fight goes on. Of one hundred thousand pagans, only two (or two thousand) survive. The Christians have held up under the attack of the first wave, as Ganelon predicted in what was perhaps his only true statement to the Saracens (588–91). Turpin reminds us once again that the rear guard is there to represent Charles: "No man has better soldiers." He affirms Charles's rectitude (or courage) in the same breath, though in curious terms. The reference Turpin makes here to a chronicle called *Gesta Francorum* (which the Oxford redactor cites elsewhere as his source, though it is probably imaginary) is less confusing than his use of the word *vassal* to describe the emperor (1444). Charles is no one's vassal in a literal sense, but as Foulet pointed out,[101] the word is not used in this poem in its literal sense. It is used as an adjective meaning "worthy" and is thus parallel with *proz,* applied to Charles in line 1209. Despite Bédier's objections,[102] the line only repeats and reaffirms what both Roland and Turpin have said before: that Charles is a fine lord and sovereign and that the French successes show he was right to put his trust in the men now fighting for his sake. The men of the rear guard will pass the test to which both sides have been referring (laisses 93–95, 104, 108). They will do everything expected of them, that is, what Roland promised in lines 789–91.

There is a brief lull, and then the second wave, under Marsile, reaches the Christians.

112 (CXII)

As Marsile's twenty battalions sweep down on Roland and Oliver, the hero introduces this new peripety with a summary of how things stand. It is not unlike the one the narrator gives in lines 1404–11. Although it is spoken by a character, its function is that of any such

[101]Lucien Foulet, in Bédier, *Chanson de Roland commentée,* 495.

[102]Bédier, *Chanson de Roland commentée,* 214–15; cf. Brault, *Song,* 1:200–201.

summary in the *Song* itself or other *chansons de geste,* to remind the hearers of the action's setting, and although it has been said to represent some sudden realization on Roland's part, it actually contains nothing he has not already said (e.g., in 1010–16, 1146–51). Ganelon has betrayed them, and that is obvious. Charles will mete out punishment (again, *venjance*). Roland and Oliver will continue to fight with their famous swords, which are worthy of good songs (assuming *en* has the same proximate antecedent, the swords, in line 1466 as in line 1465).

113–14 (CXIII–CXIV)

In Marsile's attacking company there is an exceptionally evil, atheistic, or heretical man called Abyss (Abisme). The better part of a laisse is given to a typical listing of his horrible characteristics. He must, of course, be killed. Turpin does it, in the name of religion. The archbishop opens the second combat by charging Abisme, smashing his shield (of diabolical origin) and piercing him through. The French acclaim the deed and state that Turpin's episcopal crozier is in good hands.

115 (CXV)

Then comes a moment of hesitation. The rear guard fails in its confidence for an instant, seeing the countless ranks of the enemy. The men call to Oliver, Roland, and the twelve Peers, their leaders, to protect them. But the archbishop, fresh from his clear-cut and symbolic victory over Abisme, in turn calls on them to remember what has been said before. "Let no unworthy thoughts tempt you to flight," he says (1515–16), insisting (as Roland has insisted) that it is imperative for them to stand their ground.

Turpin then recalls the importance of the example they are setting. By rights, a change of heart would be ill sung of (1517; cf. 1466, and note that the singer of the disparaging song is called *prozdom,* a good man). Then the archbishop repeats the firm promise he made in lines 1134–35: a seat in Paradise awaits the men of the rear guard after their deaths. This brief exhortation is all the Franks need to rekindle their spirits, and they send up their war cry again. They will fight to the death now without faltering.

116–17 (CXVI–CXVII)

From now on the detachment will need all its determination. The list of Christian exploits in the first combat yields to a growing number of losses. First Climorin—one of the Saracens who earlier gave and took treacherous vows and who is no *produme*—rides out to accomplish his promise (not reported in lines 629–31) to take away Charles's crown. He kills Engeler, one of the Peers; but Oliver soon avenges his comrade. Climorin's soul is carried off by devils (the equivalent, for pagan warriors, of the reward Turpin promises the Christians). In his sorrow and anger at Engeler's death (he is *irez,* says Roland [1558]), Oliver goes on to kill nine others. Roland sees that, whatever his earlier hesitations or weakness, Oliver has given his full effort to the fight, and the hero states that both men are equal on the field of battle. He adds another reference to the king's pleasure at such deeds and cries out to his men to attack.

118–25 (CXVIII–CXXV)

Once again a pagan, the sea captain Valdabrun, is described in some detail, and his evil deeds are recounted. He kills Samson, but Roland responds by killing the captain and his horse at one stroke. Again the hero shouts his defiance: the pagans are full of unjust pride. This two-part sequence is repeated twice. The archbishop (now clearly part of a warrior triad, with Oliver and Roland) avenges Anseis. Then, when Grandonie brings down five of Christendom's best, Roland kills the pagan with another prodigious blow. But he cannot even the score. Still, laisse 125 shows that the French are not dismayed. They fight with such intensity that the Saracens curse them and cry out to Marsile for speedy aid.

126–27 (CXXVI–CXXVII)

The great battle is still going against the enemy. The Franks are clearly superior fighters. Only the weight of numbers suffices to defeat them. They drive the Saracens back four times in a row, with great effort. Only then, as the fifth wave of the enemy breaks over them, do the men of the rear guard die. They are killed nearly to the last man. Only sixty are left, still standing fast. "Before they die, they will sell themselves dear" (1690). But that line implies the battle is over, and they cannot hold out long.

The Second Horn Scene

128 (CXXVIII)

It is in such circumstances that the "Second Horn Scene," the second debate between Oliver and Roland, takes place.

If we are to understand this scene, it is essential to recognize that while the characters' attitudes have not changed since their first argument, the situation is now different. We will recall that their first argument came before the battle was joined; the second comes not at some vague or undefined point within it, but at its end. Roland's initial promise to Charles has been carried out to the fullest extent possible.[103] The rear guard has been attacked, as was only too likely. Roland and his detachment have resisted, in effect, to the last man. In the context of the battle as a whole, the fighting is practically done and over. Roland sees that: he sees the "great loss," and though he does not say so, it must be clear that there is only a certain amount of time left. He calls to Oliver for advice. Many a good man has fallen and is forever lost to France. Charles is absent—a remark that takes the form of an apostrophe: "King, you are not here!" And Roland gives the obvious reason for mentioning his overlord: Charles should be informed and aware of his loss. That is the specific and literal sense of his direct question to Oliver: "Brother, how can we let him know?" *Cum faitement li manderum nuveles?* (1699).

This is not an admission of error or failure, for several reasons. First, Oliver's saying so does not make it so, and his saying so urgently does not make it compellingly so. It is now generally recognized that he is not the author's voice—that idea derives from the *démesure* hypothesis and not from what is said in these scenes—and the analysis of the work's earlier events has shown him to be fallible. Second, the powerful but neglected theme of vengeance (or perhaps better, retribution; see the commentary to laisse 14) is present, and its structural requirements must not be forgotten. Whatever the cause, Charles has again lost men to Marsile's perfidy. He must be notified at once, so he can carry out what has become his duty (to which Roland referred in line 1149): to show that he will punish though he did not defend. But, most important, the one governing condition has changed. Roland promised in lines 755–59 to resist if attacked, as befits the leader of a rear guard. His promise has doomed him, but it is fulfilled, and in a society where precedent counts it is important that the fact be known. The horn call proclaims success, not failure. It is good news for Western society. Charles's trust in Roland's promise has been upheld.

[103]See Owen, "Secular Inspiration," 393–94; Cartier, 45, 60; Bédier, *Légendes,* 3:441 (cf. 431). Roland must give battle before using the horn (Alfred Foulet, 147; Del Monte, 231). The rear guard's duty is to perish (Cartier, 49). Roland still does not grasp the situation (Renoir, "Roland's Lament," 578–79); he should have replied to Oliver's denunciation (Van Emden, "Guarant," 32). Cartier argues that for Roland to admit error would be bad taste (p. 56, n. 46).

It would be pointless to dwell on the fact that Roland makes no reference in laisse 128 to rescue or escape, but speaks only of informing Charles, were it not that our tradition of reading sometimes assumes those things and that Oliver just conceivably may read them into what Roland asks him.[104] The death of many good men does not imply rescue; it is forever too late for that, and there is no way, as the text shows (both through its sequels and by the narrator's intervention [1405, 1806, 1841]), for Charles to return in time to save a single man. Instead, a great loss implies vengeance, as it did in Roland's very first speech (Turpin will draw this conclusion in line 1744). The results of the battle are painful—"We may well grieve for sweet France"—but they are very much the results Roland always foresaw, the results he and the archbishop both had prepared the detachment for (see the commentary to laisses 89–91). It would be strange indeed if Roland found any of the things he then referred to surprising, now that they have happened. But for obvious reasons Charles should be told that his fears were well-founded. Turpin will shortly urge Roland to call the king back, not so that he can save anyone, which is no longer possible (and not even Oliver clearly seems to think it is), but to accomplish the all-important duty of avenging their loss (laisse 132).

Oliver's sharp reaction is quite different from anything these considerations warrant. He does not explain his reaction any more than Roland explains his questions and proposals. Oliver never says openly that he expects rescue or scorns vengeance. It is more difficult than before, not easier, to see why the two men are arguing here. But at least we may note that Oliver refuses, or fails to allow that the controlling circumstances have changed now that the battle has been going on for so long. As has often been pointed out, he uses now, at the battle's end, the terms Roland used when he argued against blowing the horn before it had begun. I don't know how to reach Charles, he says first, and adds (in what may be taken as a reference to possible rescue, but may be only a symmetrical echo of Roland's earlier words) that he would rather die than be shamed. He does not and will not say why a signal would be shameful at that point. Sometimes critics speak of this scene as though Oliver made an argument in response to

[104]For example, Pensom, 136, speaks of Roland's "childish desire to avoid the consequences of his acts"—a strong interpretation indeed of *mander nuveles*. For other examples, see Van Emden, "Guarant," 33; Horrent, *Chanson de Roland et geste de Charlemagne*, 179; Renoir, "Roland's Lament," 578; Crosland, 84; Boatner, 579, and citations in Chapter 2, below. Burger apparently thinks Roland expects both to survive and to be avenged: "Roland hoped . . . to see the traitor's punishment with his own eyes" (Burger, "Deux Scènes du cor," 122). But cf. Brault, *Song*, 1:210–11. It is not, then, surprising that Pensom, 137, should find the relationship of the First Horn Scene to the Second Horn Scene "inscrutably complex in its suggestions."

Roland here.[105] But all he says, with considerable embellishment, is that Roland refused to call before, when the battle could have been won, that calling now would be shameful, and that he cannot approve. He does not say why he thinks that, only that he does.

129 (CXXIX)

Here Roland's idea is given more precisely. I will sound my horn, he says. In the mountains, Charles will hear and the French will return—for what purpose is not stated. It is the same horn as in laisse 83, and Oliver claims at once that such a call would be cowardly: *n'ert mie hardement.* He still does not say why, only that it would shame Roland's family (1705–7, echoing 1063, 1076), that he had told Roland to call earlier and he did not (1709), and that Roland has already covered his two arms with blood (1710), a statement that may be an incitement to continue fighting, as Roland intends to do: *mander nuveles,* as the hero put it, does not mean ceasing to resist.

130 (CXXX)

Again we hear Roland refer to the horn, and to Charles's hearing, with no further comment. Oliver's reply adds the element of survival, if not precisely of rescue. *S'i fust li reis,* he says, in a hypothetical past subjunctive that contrasts with Roland's exclamatory present in the second argument's first lines. "If the king had been here all along, we would not have suffered," which is true enough, but without relevance for the rear guard's function. Neither is it the opposite of Roland's implied wish that the king were present now, to see the end. And Oliver hints that the suffering is no one's fault but Roland's (1718; *cil ki la sunt,* those he holds blameless, may be the main army, which in fact voted for a peace that has proven illusory). And Oliver further insults Roland by promising that if only he can see his sister Aude once more, he will arrange that Roland will never lie in her arms again. This may imply a renunciation of the bond between the two, since Aude is later portrayed as Roland's betrothed, a formal arrangement that her family must presumably support.

131 (CXXXI)

Now Roland asks—perhaps in surprise, especially since Oliver has made several heated affirmations but has made no argument—why Oliver is so angry (and possibly hurt; the term for his mood is *ire*

[105]Faral (*Chanson,* 110) for instance, has Oliver say "too late." Burger attributes to Oliver the notion that sounding the horn would cause panic among the Christians (Burger, "Deux Scènes," 120–21), but it is difficult to imagine that the few survivors are not aware of the situation.

again). Oliver gives a famous reply, whose relevance or irrelevance to the situation cannot be judged out of context. He has already said, and will reiterate now, that he is angry at Roland for not following the advice he himself gave the hero earlier.

But his explanation bears only on the first horn argument, and not on the present matter. He still does not say why it would be wrong to call now. Oliver insists, now explicitly, that the deaths of the men around them are Roland's fault entirely. His famous line 1724—*Kar vasselage par sens nen est folie,* "bravery that is sensible is not folly"—only begs the original question whether what Roland has done *does* make sense. Oliver thinks Roland is foolish. Yet that is only one character's resentful claim. The structure of the poem, I have argued, tends to dismiss Oliver's presumption that dying at Roncevaux is senseless. As for the equally famous line 1725, "Reasonableness is better than recklessness" (Brault), it is very much like line 1724: not so much a general appraisal of the situation, or an aphorism the author intends to apply to Roland, but the character Oliver's way of saying he still does not understand why his advice was not taken.

The only new element Oliver introduces to buttress his claim is often given some weight in studies espousing his point of view as identical to the sense of the poem. Yet when we look to later events, we find Oliver's reasoning is not borne out in the *Song of Roland.* His claim concerning the effect of Roland's firmness before the battle is put forth twice, in line 1727 and line 1732. Charles, he says, will never have our service again, nor our help, as he would have, had he been summoned earlier. It is no doubt the only practical objection that can be made to Roland's invocations of high principle, and that is perhaps why some readers have used it as an instrument to condemn the hero, rather than question the *démesure* hypothesis. Nevertheless, it is not quite accurate to claim, as Oliver seems to do, that it will make some difference whether Charles has Roland, Oliver, the twelve Peers, or the rear guard's twenty thousand men beside him at some future time. The rest of the *Song of Roland,* after all, shows precisely the future to which Oliver refers here, and it shows the inference sometimes drawn from Oliver's remark to be wrong.[106] When the supreme ruler of pagandom, Baligant, appears, Charles is more than a match for him without Roland. This may even be the primary purpose of the Baligant episode, in fact: to show that the Christian cause does not depend on any one knight or group of paladins, but on faith and on

[106]Jones (*Ethos,* 163) and Halverson, 665, both recognize that Charles does not need Roland but do not consider that Roland himself may be aware of that; cf. Cartier, 61.

God's willingness to intervene on behalf of those who keep the faith. Again the implication is bitter, almost totalitarian in modern terms, since it does not seem to matter whether any individual lives or dies as long as the right is upheld.

More germane for interpreting a late-eleventh-century text is a suggestion like the one Pierre Le Gentil makes: that Roland somehow may place "the greater interests of Christendom" in jeopardy by insisting that he and his men cannot go beyond Roncevaux (*Song,* 89). Things do not, however, work out that way in the text outside Oliver's accusation. First of all, peace on Marsile's terms can hardly be assumed to be in Christendom's interest. But above all, if we look to the latter part of the poem for a moment we will see that Roncevaux is in reality only a peripety, in a sense that Oliver's claims do not allow for. His death, Roland's, and those of the others, are much more important for their implications than for their results.[107]

Rabel and Guineman, who will be asked to take Roland's place and Oliver's in the battle against Baligant, lack their predecessor's indisputable superiority as warriors, but their cause and Charles's triumphs despite such details. Later, in analogous fashion, the right will triumph over Ganelon's champion and his kinsmen, who abuse civil procedure in an attempt to save Ganelon from the punishment he has (we know) deserved. If Roland had lived, the unfolding of the story might have been different, but its outcome would have been the same, a continuing affirmation of God's truth and of the superiority of Occidental Christian feudalism. Despite the apparent reasonableness of Oliver's reproof out of context, it is not true that Charles needs Roland, Oliver, or the Peers. Ganelon said that, in laisse 45, but he and Oliver are both wrong. The war Charles is fighting belongs to a whole culture and ultimately fulfills an eschatological vision. There is a hint of *démesure* in the notion that it depends on any one man or perhaps even one group. Roland makes no such suggestion, and Oliver in fact does barely more than imply it. Ganelon said something like it, but Ganelon is doomed because he does not speak the truth. Traditional readings of the *Song* are not quite to the point either. *A priori,* it would be difficult for any reader to say that a setback at

[107]It has been suggested that the poem is not so much a "Chanson de Roland" as a "Chanson de Charlemagne." See Pauphilet, "Sur la *Chanson de Roland,*" *Romania,* 59 (1933), 161–98; Williamson, 553; Uitti, 73ff.; Niles, "Ideal Depiction," 133–34, 137–38; cf. P. Aloysius Thomas, "The Structural and Aesthetic Heroes in the *Song of Roland,*" *Neuphilologische Mitteilungen,* 81 (1980), 1–6. Brault divides the poem into two parallel plots, a "Charles-plot" and a "Roland-plot" (*Song,* 1:47–51); Crosland, 70–91, tells the story twice in a row.

Roncevaux is a staggering blow to God's cause. We will learn that God can use such men as Thierry for his necessary ends, once Roland is gone.

That is, if we will accept it, the basic "message" of the *Song of Roland* in the form it takes in the Oxford manuscript. A sacrifice in the name of principle is its own justification. It does not matter that the sacrificed are mighty. To protect a divinely ordained social principle, God makes a victor even of the undistinguished Thierry (laisses 277–87). And Oliver is as much distracted as he ever was; indeed, he and his point of view have not changed significantly since line 1036. He is thinking of his own death and, for the moment at least, sees nothing beyond it clearly.

Thus, to sum up, Oliver's principal affirmations in the last argument remain *petitiones principii* or are of uncertain application to the situation. He affirms that blowing the horn would be cowardly or shameful, but he does not say why that is so, and he perhaps also implies that for him the situation toward the end of the battle is the same as it was toward the beginning (1701, 1705–7, 1710–11, 1715). He adds that Roland refused to listen to him earlier—an observation, not an element of proof (1709, 1716, 1728–31)—and he reinforces the whole with the obviously tendentious claim that their suffering is Roland's fault alone (1718, 1723–26, 1731–36). It may be, as a matter of speculation, that Oliver has always thought in terms of possible victory (cf. 1046, 1233) and believes that defeat is a shameful thing in itself, to be hidden if possible. But we will see at once that the news that reaches Charles and the army, borne on the horn's echoes, will bring the defeated rear guard not only swift vengeance but exceptional honors as well.

132 (CXXXII)

Hearing the pair's words, the archbishop rides to them and reproaches them, saying they should not argue. And he settles things by recommending the horn-call. It cannot save the rear guard, he points out, but it is much better to do it than not. If the king comes he can avenge us; the enemy should not leave here happy. And we can be buried in a churchyard, not eaten by scavenging beasts. Roland expresses his approval of the archbishop's reasons.

We are not in a position to speculate on what might be the effect on Roland of Oliver's last outburst, since the hero's reaction to it is not shown. If he is bewildered or hurt or somehow enlightened, we cannot guess. The archbishop intervenes and settles the argument in Roland's favor at once. The horn should be blown even though it cannot bring help (1742–43): what he says is emphatically not a compromise, nor is it the opposite of what Roland had in mind, nor even necessarily something different from what moved Roland to suggest using the horn.[108] Roland's motives are unknown and unstated, except for the desire to inform the king—to what end he does not say. He says only that many good men have died and that the battle is hard (1694–96, 1713). Thus he may well have been thinking of that same vengeance to which he referred in lines 213 and 1149. That at least is uppermost in Turpin's mind, along with the idea of proper burial. From the outside, we might speculate that it would not be to Charles's credit to abandon his dead to the animals any more than it would be to his political or military advantage to continue on his way without punishing Marsile. Whatever our reaction to those suggestions, we may at least consider that Turpin's words are both reasonable and farsighted. The rear guard has done its job; let Charles respond as he should. The pagans must not get away with this (1745). Only the horn-call can make it possible for the army to respond to what has happened. It is deferred no longer.

133 (CXXXIII)

Even as we pursue our incessant inquiries into sense and construction, the grandeur of the poem may still shine through. If it does, in the first instance, it will be in places like laisse 133, that pose no immediate problem of general interpretation. The power of the verse matches the power that is in Roland. Square and monolithic, the ten-syllable statements march past, one after another. Roland hefts his horn and blows it with great strength. The high mountains send back the echo over dozens of kilometers, over thirty leagues' distance. Charles hears it; the French all hear (1766–67). There is a fight, the king says at once. In this straightforward set of statements, only Ganelon's reaction is rhetorically complex, as his mind is twisted. Once again, a conditional clause helps reveal the quality of a character's thought. He does not state disagreement directly, but seeks to forestall the inevitable conclusion by a sinuous suggestion. "If someone else but you said that, it would seem a lie" (1760). We can only

[108]"It is the archbishop [i.e., neither Roland nor Oliver] . . . who clearly states the meaning of the Christians' deaths," says Brault ("*Sapientia,*" 102, 112), and thus Turpin (along with Charles) represents sapiential wisdom here (cf. Brault, *Song,* 1:12–14). Turpin sustains Roland (Misrahi and Hendrickson, 363; cf. Cartier, 61). Turpin's speech is a compromise (Crosland, 85; Pensom, 145, etc.). The vengeance to which Turpin refers is Charles's duty (Van Emden, "Guarant," 42; Cartier, 54). Williamson sees the importance of vengeance here, but does not think it goes beyond family; yet Charles mourns the loss of all his household knights (his *maisnee* [2397]).

guess whether Ganelon anticipated the marvelous horn-call, or planned for Roland and his men to be annihilated, many miles behind, in silence. If he expected the horn-call, then he must have been aware that Charles would learn of the pagan attack, which implies that he planned his own punishment. If, as seems more likely, he thought the rear guard would simply never be heard from again, then he was, as usual, grievously mistaken.

134 (CXXXIV)

Roland bends his efforts to the task. Though many of the preserved medieval horns are as large as they are because they are ceremonial instruments, we should perhaps think of the Olifant as being equally large, so that sounding it firmly was a feat of strength in itself. Suddenly fresh blood gushes from Roland's mouth. His temples, we are told, have burst. Thirty leagues is an epic exaggeration, more than one hundred miles by practically any of the various reckonings of the league. Charles, far off, hears the horn's voice and (as we have seen [1758]) understands at once what it means. Roland would never blow that horn if he were not in combat, says the emperor. Ganelon, his treachery nearly revealed now (for that is among the beneficial effects of the famous blasts),[109] responds rashly and without due respect this time. There is no battle, he says; you are an old, white-haired man and you speak as a child. And in the same breath, he refers to Roland's great and sinful pride with an obscure anecdote. But even as he speaks, the horn's voice is giving him the lie.

Charles is not senile, and even in the most extreme hypothesis Roland's horn is not being blown as a prideful gesture. The battle is real, and the audience is already informed of that. We may judge the story of the secret taking of the city of Noples as we will.[110] There is no other information on it in the poem. It may be a second or possibly third uncharasteristic truth of Ganelon's. But it is not relevant even if it is true. By a master stroke, the poet has found and exploited an impressively clear mechanism for breaking the impasse that held Charles back from intervention. Charles's suspicions, like his dreams,

[109]For the horn-call as proof, see Mermier, 94, and Pensom, 146. Burger says that for Roland to call Charles is to call Ganelon too, hence his earlier refusal (Burger, "Deux Scènes," 116), but when Charles hears the horn, what he does is put Ganelon in custody. McCash, 138–39, also notes that Ganelon panics (and thus insults Charles) when the horn sounds. I do not know why Siciliano, 353, and Calin, 22, take Ganelon's claim about chasing rabbits (1780) as valid. Brault (*Song,* 1:471) thinks it is meant to imply that Roland is a coward.

[110]Cf. Brault, "Ganelon et Roland: Deux anecdotes"; Brault, *Song,* 1:91, 471, n. 18.

were his alone, part of the burden of kingship and special knowledge. If he had mentioned them earlier, Ganelon might well have called him a dotard then also, and it might have been difficult indeed for Charles to respond to that allegation except by some form of coercion.

But every man can hear the horn. The sudden rattle of Ganelon's temporizing words cannot drown its compelling echoes. Roland has reached not just Charles but also all his anxious comrades (1757, 1766–67, 1788), and no one owes Ganelon a hearing anymore.

135 (CXXXV)

Here the reality of the situation, the secret Ganelon cannot forever hide, becomes public knowledge (as Roland has said it would [1458–59]), and the retribution Roland predicted (1149) will soon follow. Bleeding, Roland blows the horn again, and everyone hears: *Karles l'oït e ses Franceis l'entendent* (1788). Here is yet another line deserving of greater fame. It tells us that now, at last, Charles has evidence available to everyone equally and thus can act. Ganelon's final desperate attempts at manipulation are failing. Charles does not even have to interpret the horn-call himself, at the last. It is obvious to Naimon, and probably to everyone else as well, what the long blasts mean. There is fighting, says the wise duke, and the traitor is the one now telling you to ignore it. Rescue your man! There is no doubt what has happened. Roland is under attack, a thing that should never have been, but one that the army feared and at least half expected.

This, then, is what is meant in practice by Roland's *mander nuveles* in line 1699. The sounding of the horn is not a shameful act, and the army does not treat it as one, despite Oliver's insistence, but it is not just a call for vengeance either. It brings information and proof where before there were only doubt and suspicion. At long last, Charles is released from the prior constraints of systematic trust, and he goes to work at once; thanks to the horn, he does not need to make any arbitrary gesture. That may not be—and can never be shown to be—the idea that motivates Roland in the Second Horn Scene, but it is a direct result of what he meant to do. "Many good men are dead; and how is Charles to know?" he asked in lines 1693–99. Now Charles and all the Franks (cf. 1704) know there has been an attack, despite the agreement they had hoped to make with Marsile. The truth is out, and Ganelon cannot silence the Olifant. He has come to the end of the path he entered in the poem's second scene, when he called Roland a fool for mistrusting the same man the hero is fighting to hold at bay even now.

136 (CXXXVI)

The discussion once again comes to an abrupt end, and decisive action is taken. Naimon's statements have obviously been accepted as accurate. Charles signals his men to arm, and they are again transformed into a fighting force. They ride hard through the mountains, with words of sympathy for Roland (1803–4). The narrator, however, states that they have tarried too long—possibly meaning that Ganelon's delaying tactics have succeeded at least in holding the army back briefly, although in any case the hero is already bleeding from the wounds that will eventually kill him, the result of his own efforts and not of enemy action.

137–38 (CXXXVII–CXXXVIII)

Splendid in the late afternoon sun, the knights stream forth. Twice we are reminded of the majesty of the setting, we hear the horn-calls, we see the Christians' tears of frustration and anger. Charles is pained and angry, as Roland was when he vowed to defend his king, and so, as we are told through an explicit repetition of the elements of *ire, dolor,* and *curuç,* are his men. They fear for Roland, as ever (1815; cf. 843). There is certainly no sign of any resentment or dislike of the doomed chieftain among the comrades he is struggling to protect. They are too late, the narrator repeats, to reach Roland and fight by his side.

Meanwhile, Ganelon is handed over to the cooks as a prisoner and treated dishonorably. Charles uses the term *felun*—Ganelon has broken his vows (see note 2 above)—and explains that he has betrayed the very men closest to the king, his *maisnee* (roughly "household knights"). But Ganelon is to be tried, not executed summarily.

139 (CXXXIX)

In slightly different terms the opening of this laisse insists a third time on the angry state of mind of Charles and his men. The closing lines shift the scene again to the battlefield, where Roland and the sixty others, the finest of soldiers, will now make their last stand.

The Rear Guard's Last Stand

140 (CXL)

Roland voices a brief lament, mourning the dead as a proper (*gentill*) knight should. His words express the hierarchical nature of the feudal relationship, exactly as I believe his statements in laisses 14, 79, and 88 do. These men have served Roland for a long time (1858) and also won vast territories for Charles (1859), their keeper (1860). Here Roland is expressing the principle according to which a feudal warrior owes service to a suzerain ultimately, and simultaneously to an intermediary chieftain.[111] But the equilibrium of the relationship has been broken. That is the source of Roland's grief: in dying with Roland, in following him to Roncevaux (*pur mei* is variously translated but means roughly "because I am your leader"),[112] his men have gone where he cannot aid them. Roland and the men with him are in the same situation. He cannot protect them any more than he could save himself. He is not a supreme commander; this is not our impression, but literary history cannot be made of impressions. The commander-in-chief is Charlemagne; the rear guard's many invocations of the emperor are not meaningless; but now only God, not even Charles but the supreme Lord, can aid them. Roland calls out to Oliver, whom (he says) he must not fail. (Is it because Oliver has stood by him despite his doubts?) His grief is so great, says Roland, that it will suffice to kill him now. But he does not abandon the battle, hopeless though it clearly is.

141 (CXLI)

The issues of Roncevaux and of Ganelon's treason are effectively settled, and the forces that will avenge Roland and his men have been unleashed, but there is still fighting to be done. In his anger, the hero contributes to his own avenging (1875), driving the enemy like deer before him. The archbishop approves his fierceness. Still, the Christians' numbers continue to dwindle.

It is sometimes said, in the less-reliable descriptions of the *Song*, that Roland is killed at Roncevaux. Even well-informed critics sometimes

[111]On this passage, see Jones, *Ethos*, 175, though his conclusion avoids the implications of the hierarchy. It is regularly claimed that Roland fails in his duty as a *guarant* (e.g., Halverson, 663; Jones, *Ethos*, 186; Renoir, "Roland's Lament," 574–75; Peeters, "Le 'Faire' et le 'dire,'" 389), but Van Emden points out correctly that the *guarant* here is Charles and that "This protection cannot be absolute" (Van Emden, "Guarant," 39–40, 42). Van Emden does add that Roland is a "guarant ad hoc," but the term betrays the situation implied in lines 1863–64: Roland cannot both obey and protect. (Is line 1864, "Je ne vos pois tenser ne guarantir," addressed to the living or to the dead? Cf. Owen, "Secular Inspiration," 396.)

[112]Among others, Renoir ("Roland's Lament," 574) follows Jenkins in translating "through my fault," which derives from the hypothesis and supplies the substantive *fault*. Wendt, 279, notes that "the translation of *pur mei* depends primarily on the interpretation of the whole" and gives examples; he prefers "an meiner Stelle," "in my stead," because the troops precede Roland in martyrdom (p. 281). *Pur mei* is, logically enough, also used by Charles to describe the same deaths (2937); cf. Owen, "Secular Inspiration," 395, and note 111 above.

slip up in the matter, when they are talking of other scenes, perhaps with the image of the tragic blunder near the surface of their minds. But Roland dies because he begins to bleed as he blows the horn. To be precise, the text says that he suffers great pain, since he has burst his temple in using the horn (2101–2), and that his brain or something similar runs from his ears (2600). This is rather obscure in modern medical terms. However, the hero does not die from any wound inflicted by the enemy, but rather strikes down every pagan who approaches him, even when he is himself on the threshold of death. We should not overlook the fact that such ability is remarkable and such strength of will unusual.

142 (CXLII)

Marsile is still on the field. Now he has killed four French knights. But Roland counterattacks and strikes off Marsile's right hand. This is a traditional punishment for treason, and it effectively makes him powerless, since he cannot fight without it. Then Roland kills Marsile's son Jurfaleu (Jurfalet). Ganelon's suggestion of an ambush has led to the pagan king's destruction and that of his bloodline, though Charles and the army are not yet even near. The enemy recognize that the men Charles left behind are never going to retreat, even in the face of certain death. A full one hundred thousand of the Saracens take to their heels Marsile with them.

143 (CXLIII)

But the retreating band is only part of the vast enemy force. Now Marsile's uncle Marganice (is he meant to be identified with the uncle called *algalife,* whose death Ganelon falsely reported in lines 681–91?) attacks with fifty thousand men. Roland sees that there is little time left, yet he continues to call, as usual, for steadfastness, so that Charles will see that he and his men have done their duty, and France will not be shamed (1922–31).

144 (CXLIV)

Again Roland repeats his reference to approaching death (cf. 1456–59, 1867, 1923), and he and the remaining Franks charge once more. It might be noted that this description of fewer than sixty men resisting fifty thousand has (like Roland's destructive sword-strokes) at least some small basis in reality. In fact, not all of the enemy host could have engaged the small group of Christians simultaneously, as long as the latter stayed together and did not lose heart. The actual area of combat, given the style of hand-to-hand fighting described here, may have been no larger than the Franco-Christian front.[113] The battle may, at least temporarily, be reduced to the sort of single combat—between the few enemy men closest to Roland, and his remaining soldiers—that the poem continues to present. The Saracens must in the end resort to missile weapons thrown from a distance.

145–46 (CXLV–CXLVI)

Yet the pagans take heart on seeing how few Franks there are. Perhaps they are at last able to surround them. In any case, Marganice is in a position to strike Oliver a fatal blow from behind. Of course, that is both treachery (even, no doubt, in the context of a close encounter of this sort) and the only way a Saracen may be expected to triumph over an Oliver. It is the kind of stroke that does not prove Oliver wrong in his adherence to feudal Christian doctrine.[114] Nevertheless, the pagan adds a taunt. Like his men (1942) and like Corsablix (laisse 95), he refers to Charles, saying the emperor was wrong to leave the rear guard at Roncevaux.

The mortally wounded Oliver replies to Marganice in the expected fashion: with a blow that splits his helmet and skull, killing him, and also with words of defiance. Then he calls Roland to his side.

147–48 (CXLVII–CXLVIII)

Despite his wound, Oliver fights on, evening the score as Roland is doing, killing a number of Saracens. He calls to Roland, and the hero, realizing that his friend is dying, mourns his loss.

149 (CXLIX)

Now Oliver has lost so much blood that his sight is no longer clear. He can recognize no one, but he is aware of a shape near him. He strikes again with his sword, as he has been doing in his last moments, surrounded by nothing but enemies. This time, however, it is his companion who receives the blow. Oliver cleaves Roland's helmet, but does not injure him.

Roland recognizes his friend at once, and asks him softly for an explanation, as he did in line 1722. He says who he is, and adds, in something of an understated allusion to the situation as a whole, that

[113]Cf. Keegan's description of the French front at Agincourt, though the troops Keegan describes were fighting on foot (John Keegan, *The Face of Battle* [New York, 1976], 100–101).

[114]Cf. Scully, "Ordeal at Roncesvalles," 227–28, and the discussion of laisse 93, above.

Oliver has issued him no challenge, as we realize he had no reason to. There is, of course, no cause for the blow except Oliver's blindness.

When Oliver hears his comrade's voice, he immediately begs his forgiveness, explaining that he cannot see. Roland immediately replies that he is unharmed and gives his companion his pardon. They bow to each other, or bring their heads close together, and separate with *amur*.

This event, sometimes neglected,[115] is among the most significant moments in the entire text. It is a symbolic representation, on the physical plane, of the blind anger Oliver earlier showed in the scenes of argument. There, he wronged Roland with his mistaken claim and insulted him in unjustified *ire*. Here he actually strikes his comrade without knowing what he is doing. Roland questions him gently, without responding to his violence.[116] Oliver now admits his physical blindness and asks for pardon. Roland forgives him simply, "here and before God." His continued forbearance keeps the bond (*amur*) between them whole. And Oliver, his last strength spent, will die at once.[117]

150–51 (CL–CLI)

Now Oliver prays, asking God's blessing for his fellows, especially Roland, and dies. His companion is overcome with grief, and faints, but he cannot fall from the saddle.

Let us note that in line 2029 Roland states that Oliver never did him any harm (an echo of line 2006?) and that he never wronged his comrade either. The two terms Roland uses (*Nem fesis mal* and *jo nel te forsfis*) are probably equivalent formulas, as Moignet implies,[118] but there may also be a nuance between the two. What Oliver did has not harmed Roland physically (*fere mal*), but his anger may still represent the error implicit in *forsfere*.

[115]"A tragic mistake, but one with no dramatic consequences. . . . A poignant setting, costing little effort, for the discreet death of the modest Oliver," says Horrent, *Chanson de Roland et geste de Charlemagne*, 6.

[116]This is a matter of rhetoric, not of psychology or hidden intentions, despite Donohoe, 252–53.

[117]Wendt, 294–95, also sees Oliver as morally blind; Brault (*Song*, 1:212) suggests he may be near to succumbing to madness. Pensom, 155–57, thinks the two have exchanged roles. Attempts to reconcile Oliver's blow with the *démesure* hypothesis have led to several gratuitous claims: Donohoe's, 252–53, that Oliver's blind stroke is both deliberate and guided; Jones's, that Roland actually suspects Oliver struck him on purpose ("Lament," 14; *Ethos*, 186); Calin's, 24, that Oliver is "a sightless embodiment of Justice"; Boatner's, 581, that Oliver's blow "curiously re-enacts" Roland's "earlier faults."

[118]Moignet, 154.

152 (CLII)

Here again the poet picks up a thread from an earlier part of the narration, and thus reminds us of the important theme of fidelity at different levels of the feudal chain of command. Gautier del Hum, Roland's vassal, reappears. He has carried out the orders given him in laisse 65 and has held the high ground as long as he could. Now, like Roland himself, he is mortally wounded and cannot live long. But instead of simply disappearing from the story or being massacred along with his men, he returns to contribute to the last scenes of the battle. He insists on fighting as long as he can. Now that all his men are dead and there is nothing more to be done where he was, he rides into the very thick of the press, to die by Roland's side.

Critics have been nearly as unkind to Gautier as to Roland, whose sacrifice is mirrored in his vassal's. Bédier, Horrent, and others have described him as a coward and treated his last action as flight.[119] This surely misses the point both locally and thematically. Gautier has fought hard (*mult* [2041]), and he is forced out of his position despite hmself (*voeillet o non . . . s'en fuit* [2043]). But he does not leave in the midst of his fight or try to avoid further combat. Instead he comes to join his leader at the epicenter of Roncevaux, and he reports to him on an inevitable defeat, which he delayed through strenuous resistance. Though his armor and shield are battered and broken and his body is presumably wounded (part of line 2052 is, unfortunately, missing), he fights on, killing six more Saracens before he is struck down by a missile (2059, 2076). Though critics have hesitated, the narrator calls him a truly good knight, *bien bon chevaler* (2067), and so he is, in both an immediate and a broader sense, thanks to his skill and to his commitment to fight to the end. There is no need to think he requires any excuse.[120] On the contrary, he is part of the poem's network of positive examples.

153 (CLIII)

Roland has ridden to meet Gautier del Hum; now he attacks the Saracens again, pressing them hard, striking down pagan after pagan. Gautier and the archbishop join in the attack. The enemy pledge to kill them, and counterattack.

[119]The negative judgments applied to Gautier del Hum presumably derive from Bédier's remarks in his *Chanson de Roland commentée,* 190–91; cf. the works cited in note 72, above.

[120]Cf. Moignet, 157.

154–55 (CLIV–CLV)

Nonetheless, the pagan soldiers do not dare engage the three in close combat. Instead they throw spears and other missile weapons. Gautier is killed and Turpin is wounded. Unhorsed, the archbishop continues to fight, even though on foot, and it is said that he killed more than four hundred men that day. The "Geste" and the authority of Saint Giles are invoked as proof.

156 (CLVI)

Roland is bleeding to death even as he fights. He blows a last horn-call, weakly this time, but Charles hears and has his own horns blown in reply. The pagans realize he is coming: "We shall soon have Charles here!"

157 (CLVII)

Even at the end of the Roncevaux episode the Saracens remember Ganelon's lying claims (laisses 42–45). If Roland survives, the war will go on, they say to each other, not understanding that their ambush itself is what has brought Charles back and that they are doomed whether Roland lives or dies. In a last, desperate attempt to kill the hero, four hundred of the best Saracen warriors assail him. The fight is hard.

158–59 (CLVIII–CLIX)

Roland and Turpin, the last of the rear guard, now press their attack against the enemy. They too have heard Charles's horns, and they mean to stand together as long as they can. Roland is still mounted but the archbishop is not, and out of *amur* for Turpin the hero agrees to stay close by him, presumably to keep him from being overwhelmed by Saracens on horseback. As they choose a spot where they can defend themselves, the archbishop repeats that Charles is on his way. Again he says that they will be not saved but avenged (2145; cf. 1746).

160 (CLX)

The enemy at last realize that they cannot destroy Roland. Lamenting the misfortune that the "cruel day" of Roncevaux has brought them—the loss of their leaders and the approach of Charlemagne—they state that no mortal man can ever defeat Roland. Centuries later, Dante may have called the battle of Roncevaux a *dolorosa rotta* (*Inferno,* 31, 16–17), but in the *Song of Roland* the pagans call it a *pesme jurn* for themselves (2147). Ganelon was mistaken when he said Roland would not survive the crushing attacks of two waves of Saracen soldiers (cf. laisse 44). After a last shower of missiles (which smashes his shield and kills his horse, but does not harm Roland), the pagans give up trying to kill him and withdraw. We will never need to ask what might have been the consequences if Roland and his men had been overrun.[121]

161 (CLXI)

Not only is Roland still alive, he is still willing and able to fight and would pursue the fleeing pagans if he could. But his horse is dead. On foot, then, he goes to bind up the archbishop's wounds, then asks his permission to bring the Peers' bodies before him. The archbishop replies that he may come and go as he pleases, for the field is theirs.

162–64 (CLXII–CLXIV)

The archbishop gives the dead soldiers his blessing in terms that recall the promise of Paradise in his absolution before the battle (cf. 1133–35). A special laisse is dedicated to the blessing given Oliver and to Roland's lament for him. Then Roland faints again, from grief.

165–67 (CLXV–CLXVII)

In an attempt to bring water to Roland, Turpin collapses. The terrible thirst that overcame medieval men on the battlefield is well attested, and *mourir de la mort Roland* came to mean "die of thirst."[122] Roland comes to himself in time to witness the archbishop's last prayer. He praises the final survivor among his companions and commends him to God.

168 (CLXVIII)

Now it is Roland's turn to die, the last man of the rear guard. He prays for the others and for himself, and taking his sword with him he climbs a hill in the direction of Spain.

[121]It is difficult to say whether we are to think of Roland as having defeated the pagans (see Brault, *Song,* 1:236–37; Jones, *Ethos,* 50–52; Cartier, 55; Van Emden, "Guarant," 33). The pagans know Charles is on his way (2149–50; both Brault [*Song*] and Moignet think it is also they who say so in lines 2131–32, not Roland and Turpin, the protagonists of the laisse), but the pagans also state that they cannot kill Roland (at least under these circumstances) and should leave him alone (2152–54). It is easy to agree with Wendt (p. 336; cf. 352) that Roland's undefeated status is a sign of something beyond the worldly, for he can prove his earthly fidelity and still be defeated, but invincibility may well imply the supernatural.

[122]Discussion in Horrent, *Chanson de Roland dans les littératures . . . ,* 522–23.

169–70 (CLXIX–CLXX)

A Saracen has been hiding among the dead. Now, in his unthinking pride (the same *mortel rage* that afflicts Ganelon; see line 747), the pagan rushes to where Roland is lying and clutches at his sword. But Roland is aware of him, and with a last defiant cry he strikes the Saracen down with his horn, which is broken by the blow.

171–73 (CLXXI–CLXXIII)

These three laisses and the three following represent Roland's dying moments and serve to make his last thoughts clear. Le Gentil has pointed out the intensity that the parallel laisses give these supreme instants at the very end of the hero's career as servant of the emperor and of Christendom.[123] First, Roland strikes the great sword Durendal against a rock, hoping (in vain) to make it useless, because it should never fall into Saracen hands (laisse 171, lines 2300–303, 2309; laisse 172, lines 2312–15, 2335–37; laisse 173, lines 2338–42, 2349–52). The point is that Durendal is a special weapon: it bears precious relics (2345–49) and it was given by an angel to Charles, to serve as instrument of his conquests as Roland himself has served (2316–34). Roland never speaks of his victories without mentioning his king. In this enumeration (which has seemed prideful to some commentators), Charles is present constantly, either as a proper name or as an indirect object.[124]

174–76 (CLXXIV–CLXXVI)

In three famous laisses, Roland makes his final gesture and final prayer. He follows established ritual closely, even to the use of liturgical formulas in his ultimate prayer. Lying on the ground, his head toward the enemy as a sign of his steadfastness, he asks forgiveness for the sins he has committed in this life (2369–72). Then, in a symbolic gesture of contrition or submission, he holds out his right glove toward God.[125] Even as he is recalling the things for which he has lived—

[123]Le Gentil, *Song,* 147–48.

[124]Compare Le Gentil, *Song,* 104, with Farnham, 148. James Atkinson has claimed that Roland's victory over the rash Saracen symbolizes a repudiation of his own pride ("Laisse 169–70 of the *Chanson de Roland,*" *Modern Language Notes,* 82 [1967], 271–84).

[125]For a discussion of the possible meanings of such a gesture, see Brault, *Song,* 1:254–59; W. M. Hackett, "Le Gant de Roland," *Romania,* 89 (1968), 253–56; and Faith Lyons, "More about Roland's Glove," *Société Rencesvals: Proceedings of the Fifth International Conference* (Salford, Eng., 1977), 156–66, and cf. Jean-Charles Payen's treatment of these scenes in *Le motif du repentir dans la littérature française médiévale* (Geneva, 1968), 108–37. It is a difficult gesture to interpret, but apparently it is not primarily intended to show Roland as God's vassal so much as to show his humility. That humility may be

conquests, family, homeland, and lord—the archangels Gabriel, Michael, and Cherubin themselves come to take his soul to Paradise. We cannot and need not doubt that his exceptional reward has been fully earned. Faced with a challenge of great moral implications, Roland has succeeded in affirming a set of powerful principles, social as well as religious, that are here confirmed as being more important than life itself. Though Roland is gone, the poem's events continue to affirm these principles of commitment, solidarity, and trustworthiness up to the final laisse and even (by implication) beyond.

Charles's Vengeance on Marsile

177–79 (CLXXVII–CLXXIX)

Now Charles has come to the battlefield of Roncevaux, where the dead lie so thick. He and his men suffer great grief. But they cannot pause here. The time for exemplary vengeance, as the wise (*proz*) Naimon tells Charles, has surely come (2423–28). Without neglecting to leave guardians to protect his dead, Charles rides on after the fleeing enemy, following the cloud of dust they raise. The emperor stops only to pray for divine aid. His familiar angel promises him light by which to carry out his vengeance.

180 (CLXXX)

Miraculously the sun stands still. Using Roland's name now as a battle cry, the Christians ride against the ambushers. Their vengeance is total: the Saracens are killed or driven into the river Ebro, where they are drowned to the last man.[126] Marsile was right in the first place, and despite appearances Blancandrin was wrong. There is no way the pagans can defeat the host of God, even if they cheat.

181–84 (CLXXXI–CLXXIV)

Now there is a pause. The questions raised early in the Roncevaux episode—how the Saracens are to be dealt with, whether Charles will avenge his men—have at last been given forceful answers. The king

general in nature, and here, at least, it probably does not represent the acknowledgment of any sin. See Bédier, *Chanson de Roland commentée,* 311–12; Hieatt, 427; Owen, "Secular Inspiration," 397; Wendt, 256, 274, 334.

[126]It may be more accurate, though of no great importance for the general interpretation, to note that the pagans killed here are the men who remained on the field after Marsile's retreat (cf. laisses 142–43). The latter, at least, is still alive, though grievously wounded.

gives thanks for his victory, then returns to Roncevaux at nightfall. We see the horses rested and fed. The soldiers sleep on the ground; Charles lies down fully armed. His personal role as a warrior is just beginning.

Here we are given a description of the sacred sword Joyeuse, which Charles will shortly use to defend himself and his land against a deadlier foe than Marsile. But for now he and his men are safe. For the first time in the poem there is no undefeated enemy near. In a line that might serve as Roland's epitaph, the narrator states: "That night they posted no guard" (2495).

185–86 (CLXXXV–CLXXVI)

As before, at a turning point in the story, Charles dreams obscurely, metaphorically, of the future. God has sent Saint Gabriel to watch over him and transmit the dreams. The first of these announces the impending battle in which he will risk his life against Baligant to save his people. The second foreshadows the last event of the poem, the trial of Ganelon and the interventions of Pinabel and Thierry. The outcome is not shown to the dreamer (or to the audience) in either case.

187–88 (CLXXXVII–CLXXXVIII)

Now the scene shifts to Saragossa, where the pain-wracked Marsile and his distraught queen Bramimonde are lamenting their fate. An aside shows the pagans, conceived here as idol-worshipers, destroying and desecrating the statues of their various gods. Bramimonde speaks of the emir and her hope that he will come to fight the hated Charlemagne.

The Victory over Baligant

The next section of the poem is the "Baligant episode," in which the mighty emir, Marsile's overlord, leads his vast host against Charles, swearing to subjugate him. Empire meets empire, two religions clash on the battlefield, and again the Christian Franks are victorious, with God's aid, despite the absence of Roland and the Peers. Saragossa finally falls, and its surviving inhabitants submit and are converted.

There are various signs in the style, content, and conception of this section (roughly laisses 189–267, some 1,100 lines) that its origin is not identical with that of the beginning, and possibly the end, of the epic. On the other hand, whatever its age, and whether or not there were earlier versions of the *Song of Roland* without it, the authenticity of the Baligant episode is not precisely what is at issue.[127] The episode is simply part and parcel of the Oxford text, which I am studying here as a deliberate act of communication. Historically, it was an integral part of the Oxford text's effect on its hearers. It would indeed be difficult not to agree that its inclusion corresponded to an early-medieval conception of the poem, or to deny that it was meant to contribute to the work's meaning for some early "intended audience." Thus despite its anomalous features (some of which are patent, while others have been exaggerated) I have not hesitated to treat it as part of the

[127]"The vast bulk of the [*Song*'s] poetic material is a product of human imagination and must have been introduced at some point between the late eighth century and the late eleventh. . . . The Episode must be historically inauthentic, but like every other imaginative element in the work it is poetically authentic" (Duggan, "The Generation of the Episode of Baligant: Charlemagne's Dreams and the Normans at Manzikert," *Romance Philology*, 30 [1976–77], 59–82). A number of studies on the problem of the Baligant episode are listed in Duggan, *Guide*, nos. 279–84; see also Duggan, *Song*, 63–104, and Pensom, 163–77.

story. Most notably, it offers a context in which Roland's, Oliver's, and Ganelon's statements about the future of the Christian cause may be usefully judged.

But while the struggle with Baligant is an important and probably necessary element in the working out of the consequences of Roland's words and acts, it is not as complex or as dense as most of the Roncevaux section. Fitting it into the whole requires less commentary, and brief paraphrase often suffices for the purpose of global interpretation. I have not given it the same detailed treatment I think necessary for the first part, which is better known and more often alluded to and which sets the stage for this episode. On the other hand, the episode's relative clarity on the surface, and the resulting briefness of these remarks, should not detract from its significance as a confirmation of the rightness of Roland's moral and military stance.

189–93 (CLXXXIX–CXCIII)

Marsile long ago sent to his overlord Baligant, asking for aid against Charles. Now, after a long delay, the emir has assembled a vast army and fleet and has come to Spain. His intention, arrogantly spelled out in lines 2661–68 and 2681–84, is not merely to defend whatever rights he has there, but rather to invade France itself and force Charles to submit to him. The pagan overlord makes the same sort of promise that Marsile's peers made in laisses 69–78, and the events of the poem prove him wrong as they were wrong. Saying, "I shall not rest as long as I live, until Charles is dead or my prisoner," Baligant sends messengers to order Marsile to renew his feudal vows.

194–98 (CXCIV–CXCVIII)

The messengers find Saragossa in a turmoil. Bramimonde blurts out to them the story of her husband's misfortune and expresses her fear that Charles will come to rule all Spain. The envoys reply at once, in familiar terms that link this episode to what has gone before. Baligant is Marsile's *guarant,* his lord and protector, and now he is here with a great force, ready to invade France. Bramimonde replies that that is hardly necessary, since Charles is still in Spain.

But now Marsile speaks. He is helpless, his heir is dead. He no longer asks protection, but instead surrenders his fief: let Baligant defend Spain as his own. He explains that Charles is only a few leagues off, within striking distance. The messengers then depart.

One of the more widely accepted arguments for the appositeness of the Baligant episode, formulated by Bédier and compellingly summarized by Le Gentil, Aebischer, and others, states that the *Song* would lack completeness and symmetry without the climactic contest between emperor and emir. Each is at the summit of the feudal pyramid in his society, and each in his way embodies the cause for which the vassal armies are fighting.[128] What happens in laisses 194–98 tends strongly to bear out this view of the episode, for they refer explicitly to the theme of protection and the responsibilities of the overlord as *guarant,* which (I have argued) underlies much of the Roncevaux episode and its preliminaries. In laisse 198, Marsile explicitly hands over the future of the pagan cause in Spain to his suzerain; and since Roland's death, Charles has taken on personal responsibility for the leadership of the Christian host. The two supreme leaders are special in a way that their vassals are not. Each has no other *guarant* but the divinity he serves, and it is between those ultimate lords and their divinities that the greatest battle in the *Song* will be decided now.

199–200 (CXCIX–CC)

When the messengers return, Baligant asks for Marsile, only to be told that he is mortally wounded. The two men give a summary of the Roncevaux story as they heard it from Marsile and Bramimonde. It is continued in laisse 200: the Christians are still in Spain and can be attacked, says Clarien. Baligant's reaction is a joyous one. He calls to his men to be on their way and proffers a typical promise or vow, following the usual form. If Charles does not flee, then Marsile will be avenged. I will trade the emperor's head for Marsile's lost hand, Baligant says, linking (as Roland did at the beginning) the duty of vengeance with suzerainty.

201–2 (CCI–CCII)

Baligant arrives at Saragossa and enters the palace, where Bramimonde greets him. Marsile (whose men have had to help him sit up) gives up a glove to Baligant, symbolizing the relinquishing of his fief, and Baligant accepts it, along with the duty of vengeance. He will delay no longer, but rides after Charlemagne at once.

203–10 (CCIII–CCX)

Charles wakes up on the battlefield, where he has slept fully armed. Now he and his men disarm and ride toward the site of the rearguard action. Once there, the king goes forward alone to seek the body of Roland. He reminds his men of a promise Roland once made at a feast in Aix. The hero said that if he were ever to die in a foreign

[128] See Bédier, *Légendes,* 3:444–45; Le Gentil, *Song,* 94–97.

land he would be the foremost among his men and would be found with his head toward the enemy in the posture of a conqueror. Once more, the promise has been fulfilled. By the time Charles reaches the battlefield, in the Oxford version, there is not a single witness left alive, but Roland's attitude tells the story of the rear guard's trial of strength.[129] Charles finds Roland far beyond the others (laisses 204–5). His lament for his dead nephew is a classic of the literary complaint, or *planctus*. It continues for about ninety lines. Charles evokes their feudal relationship and his unhappiness at having been unable to protect Roland (or so I interpret the difficult line 2900: "How unworthy was the lord with whom you came to Spain").[130] The line occurs in the midst of a laisse heavy with technical terms that are by now familiar to the reader: *amur, feid, onur, ami, proz.* Charles continues with an evocation of the risks he will run in the future without Roland at his side. Finally (laisse 210) he speaks of his responsibility for the men who were killed in his service, "my household, killed for me." His grief is immense.

211–13 (CCXI–CCXIII)

Charles's standardbearer now calls on him to bury the dead, and it is done with great ceremony. The bodies of Roland, Oliver, and Turpin are given special preparations because they are not to be buried on the spot.

214–25 (CCXIV–CCXXV)

Suddenly the vanguard of Baligant's host is upon them, and two messengers have appeared, offering battle. Charles's only thought is for his recent loss (2983); he will consider this a new opportunity for vengeance. The emperor is now clearly leading his men in person, acting as his own field commander. He puts on his armor and takes up his sword, mounts his horse, and gallops vigorously across the

[129]The poem calls Roland's promise a *raisun* "speech," not a *gab* or boast. As Jonathan Beck says, Roland's dying attitude is an act of communication, though unlike Beck I find no falsehood in it; it is only the visual equivalent of Turpin's *cist camp est vostre* ("This field is yours" [2183]) and fulfills the promise of lines 1122–23. See Beck's expressions of disapproval for Roland's last acts in "Prist l'olifan, que reproce n'en ait," *Olifant,* 9 (1981), 49–52. The *planctus* motif, and Charles's lament in particular, have been studied with increasing interest lately; the pioneering study is that of Paul Zumthor, "Etude typologique des *planctus* contenus dans la *Chanson de Roland,*" in *La Technique littéraire des chansons de geste* (Paris, 1959), 219–35; cf. Duggan, *Song,* 160–83.

[130]For discussions of this line, see the studies cited in Duggan, *Guide,* nos. 277–78, and cf. Hans-Wilhelm Klein, "Was bedeutet 'Cum en Espaigne venis a mal seignur' . . . ?" in Manfred Hofer et al., eds., *Festschrift Karl Baldinger* . . . , 2 vols. (Tübingen, 1979), 258–65.

plain before his men (the *eslai* is a sort of practice run, and also a chance to show one's ability and the speed of one's horse). Before the battle of Roncevaux, his men invoked Charles himself; but he now calls on God and the pope in Rome, not on any worldly protector. The Frankish army is ready for combat.

Now Charles does something that may appear strange at first glance but is natural under the circumstances. He names two men, called Rabel and Guineman (not otherwise known as great warriors), to take the places of Roland and Oliver as leaders of his vanguard. He gives them a sword and the hero's horn. This is not some insult to the pair's memory, but a recognition of the fact that Charles must count on the best men he has. Both Rabel and Guineman are, if not fabulous paladins, at least willing and competent knights, and that is what the Christian cause needs.

Next Charles arranges his squadrons, one after another. The young Frenchmen or Franks form the first two, but there are others made up of men from throughout the empire, from both France and Germany, all led by Charles's sworn vassals and committed to his cause. Listing them and their leaders takes seven laisses; an eighth is given over to the seasoned Frankish soldiers led by Charles himself. They shout their battle cry.

226–27 (CCXXVI–CCXXVII)

Charles prays intensely, prostrating himself and repeating the evocations of great Old Testament events that are part of every epic hero's prayers. The thing for which he prays is specifically vengeance for Roland (3109). Then he mounts, and as he leads his men into battle they are weeping at the thought of Roland's death. He and his men ride forth from the hills even as the messengers reach Baligant again.

228–37 (CCXXVIII–CCXXXVII)

Now the pagans prepare in turn for the coming battle. The emir arms as Charles did, though he does not pray. His equipment, his past exploits, and his character are described at some length. He is a fine man and would be a great one if only he were Christian. Seeing his *eslai* (his horse leaps a fifty-foot ditch), his men boast that no Frenchman can meet him in combat without being destroyed: Charles is a fool not to flee.

Baligant's son Malpramis urges him to ride hard against the Franks and says he doubts they will find Charles on the field of battle. Baligant knows the emperor will be there, but at the same time he repeats

Marsile's fatal mistake, saying that without Roland the Christian lacks the means to withstand them (laisses 229–30). Then he puts his squadrons into order, in the same manner as Charles. All the peoples of his land are named; there are thirty battalions. Again and again he predicts disaster for Charles (3234–36, 3288–90). His vast army advances behind his banner and the idols that are their gods. There is a brief pagan invocation. The French are close enough to call to the enemy now. They dedicate their fight to God: "Let this battle be waged in His name!" Only a little open ground separates the two armies. The horns sound, and the pagans see they have a hard fight ahead.

238–39 (CCXXXVIII–CCXXXIX)

Each chief rides before his men, inciting them to combat. Baligant has recognized Charles at the head of his bearded barons; Charles has picked out the enemy's standard. Both pledge to fight in person.

240–51 (CCXL–CCLI)

The Franks attack first. Rabel strikes down Torleu, one of the enemy's leaders, and the men with him say that his victory is a sign that Charles is in the right. Next Guineman kills his man. Malpramis is trying to fight his way through to Charles; Baligant and his men follow. Never was such a battle seen; it will go on until nightfall, the narrator says. The leaders continue to urge their men on with words of inspiration. Baligant promises his men land and women. Charles recalls both the feudal bonds that link his men to him, and their victories in the past. Again he refers to the duty of vengeance for those who died at Roncevaux (3411–12).

Naimon now charges and kills Malpramis, but Canabeu attacks him; the first blow stuns him, and he would be killed but for Charles, who comes to his rescue and strikes the pagan down. Baligant himself attacks Guineman and kills him, then strikes down three other French knights. The pagans acclaim him as their *guarant.*

252–57 (CCLII–CCLVII)

The melee goes on, with great losses on both sides. Baligant now calls on his gods, promising to have golden statues made of them. He learns that his son and brother have been slain. At this news he calls on his adviser Jangleu and asks whether his army will indeed win the battle. Jangleu replies firmly that he is as good as dead: his gods are no *guarant.* But the fight must go on; Baligant rallies his men for another charge.

Now Ogier the Dane gathers his comrades and calls on Charles to counterattack: "Avenge the shame of this present loss!" Together they cut through the pagan ranks and bring down Baligant's standard. The emir realizes now that Charles has the right on his side.

258–62 (CCLVIII–CCLXII)

The day is over and the sun is setting, but the battle continues. It can be brought to an end only by the death of one of the chiefs. Shouting their war cries, they ride at each other in a climactic encounter. Both are unhorsed. Swords in hand, they face each other. Bereft of his lieutenant, Charles must defend his people and his faith in person. The emir calls on him, in the usual terms, to make his submission and become his vassal. Charles replies that he can have no such agreement with a pagan and in turn summons the pagan to serve not himself but the God he represents. Since neither will yield, the duel goes on.

They strike each other in turn, in the manner presumably dictated by the size and design of their swords. Baligant's blow nearly undoes the emperor: it smashes his helmet and cuts his head to the bone. Charles nearly falls, but in his distress he is visited again by Saint Gabriel. The divine emissary does not act directly, but only asks: "What (or how) are you doing?" His presence brings Charles's courage back. He strikes his blow in his turn, and splits Baligant's head in two. The battle is in effect won with this stroke. Naimon brings Charles his horse, even as the pagans flee, according to God's will.

263–65 (CCLXIII–CCLXV)

As he and his men pursue the enemy, striking with deadly effect, Charles calls one last time for vengeance and an end to his vassals' sorrow. In Saragossa, Bramimonde and her priests see them coming and call on Mahum for help, in vain. Hearing the news of this decisive defeat, Marsile turns his face to the wall and dies, overcome by his misfortune as he was at the beginning (line 3646 echoes line 15). The devils carry off his soul. The city is in Charles's hands by dark.

266–67 (CCLXVI–CCLXVII)

The emperor's second victory is even more complete than the first. His men destroy the remaining idols in Saragossa, and the surviving Saracens are given the usual choice between baptism and death (cf. laisse 8). Bramimonde is a temporary exception to this; Charles intends that she should be converted willingly (here *par amur* seems to mean "through love" in a religious sense). The events of the Roncevaux episode—the acceptance of Marsile's offer, Ganelon's treasonous plot and vows, Roland's sacrifice—have led to the result Roland called for so firmly at the outset. Charles has taken Saragossa, and his campaign is complete.

The emperor and his army return to Aix, leaving the Olifant in Bordeaux and the bodies of the three heroes in Blaye. Charles still has a duty before him, for Ganelon must be tried. He gathers judges together from all over the empire. The trial will begin after a brief interruption.

268–69 (CCLXVIII–CCLXIX)

The twenty-odd lines describing the death of Aude (Alda) have rarely been accepted for what they are. They have nearly always been taken as elliptical when in fact (like some of Roland's speeches; see above, laisses 59, 63) they may be understood as complete and specific once we understand what is being referred to. What they are not is sentimental, and the fact seems to have surprised and displeased even redactors (who were also readers) from the twelfth and thirteenth centuries, not to mention critics and philologists of the Romantic and post-Romantic periods.

In other versions of the *Song of Roland* (including the lost or ideal version sometimes postulated as a substitute for the Oxford text) we encounter the notion that Aude, presumably because she is a woman, brings feelings of tenderness into an otherwise hardy and masculine text. She dies for love, as modern literary criticism defines the term—an emotional, sentimental, and unreasoned attachment. If such a feeling be the thing Aude dies of in the *Roland,* then the Oxford *Song* is probably an inadequate evocation of it, and later *Roland* texts were perhaps right to expand this episode—up to 655 lines of circumstantial details about Aude, her feelings and her acts, in the version found in the manuscript called Venice IV. Still it is more than likely that what is involved in this version of the passage is not the "fleeting appearance" of an emotion or sentiment.[131] Aude is not skirting an inevitable reference to love, but is evoking a principle of the sort that an eleventh- or early-twelfth-century woman might publicly express, and she says all that is necessary for the other characters (and for us) to understand her.

The principle she mentions, clearly if indirectly, is that of fidelity,

[131]Martin de Riquer, *Les Chansons de geste françaises,* 2d rev. ed., trans. Irénée Cluzel (Paris, 1957), 192. Brault maintains the claim that Aude's tie to Roland is more than a formal one, which may be true, but it does not follow from *me jurat cume sa per a prendre* (see Brault, *Song,* 1:316; and cf. Brault, *Chanson,* xxii).

and far from being fleeting, it is (once recognized) identifiable as one of the themes of the poem as a whole. Before Roland's death, he and Aude had exchanged vows. When she refers to Roland, the vows are what she mentions, using the formal terms *jurer* and *per* (in the sense of "wife"). She does not speak of hers specifically, only of his, but it would be virtually impossible to maintain that their engagement was not mutual. About the vows themselves, we can know little except that they had every chance of being thought binding in principle. In laisse 268, Aude's vow is put to the test, as Roland's general and specific vows of vassalic service were earlier. Offered an alternative to what she promised, now that the circumstances have changed, she refuses as her betrothed did. That is natural enough if we accept the idea that an oral promise could sum up a binding commitment for the early medieval society in which the *Song of Roland* is set. Given the chance to live under conditions that do not correspond to her vow, Aude chooses instead to observe the vow strictly. She makes the sacrifice called for by the situation and dies rather than live without the man to whom she was promised. Like that of Gautier del Hum, her courage is an embedded echo of Roland's, and it ultimately mirrors the major theme of sacrifice for the sake of timeless principles.

Seen in that light, Aude's reaction to the news of Roland's death, and her brusque response to Charles's proposal of a substitute husband, need neither elaboration nor explanation. Each is predictable and correct behavior. Once again, the text stands alone, and the burden of expressing an overwhelming (but unmentioned) emotion is lifted from it. Aude's brief words (3709–10) bring Charles's sorrowful admission that Roland is dead. He offers his own son and the empire in exchange. Aude's reply is as simple as it is fitting. "God forbid I should remain alive after Roland is dead," she says (3717–19), and we may allow that by Roland she means a man to whom she is bound, and who bound himself to her, by a vow of betrothal.

There is no evocation of any emotional link between Aude and Roland (in this passage, at least; cf. line 1721) because none is required. Aude has accepted the immutable nature of the promises she has made and received, and she is ruled by them. At first glance her sudden death, from no explicitly stated cause, seems strange to us, but to her, as a character in the Roncevaux tale and as part of its sequence, it was Charles's proposed alternative that was *estranges,* foreign and alien (3717). In death, she is awarded great honors (3733). Perhaps it is the nature of her constancy that explains her being buried in a religious house by nuns, or it may be her unmarried state.

The Trial of Ganelon

The final episode of the *Song of Roland* is Ganelon's trial. Though it is brief—less than 300 lines—it reintroduces the question of feudal duty and procedure with enough subtlety to require detailed commentary. Indeed, the Trial Scene's various degrees of resemblance to documented forms of public justice in the early Middle Ages have been given several learned treatments, particularly Ruggieri's.[132] Occasionally these have tended to be apologies for Ganelon; that tendency may not be consonant with the narrative, but it does fit (in certain ways) the concept of Roland as an overbearing and heedless comrade.

The question of Ganelon's guilt has also been complicated by a failure to distinguish between the attitudes of characters and those of the narrator. Charlemagne the character intends to give Ganelon a fair trial, as custom and equity demand. He will not decide arbitrarily to put one of his barons to death here, any more than he could have acted unilaterally to save Roland before Roncevaux. Charles is not

[132]Ruggero M. Ruggieri, *Il Processo di Gano nella "Chanson de Roland"* (Florence, 1936). Following Ruggieri, the trial is often said (e.g., Vance, *Reading*, 83–86) to imply or embody a conflict between "prefeudal" or "Germanic" law and feudal law, or between individualism (Ganelon's) or clan loyalty and the nascent state. Marc Bloch, 123–25, implies that these two antinomies are not absolute; cf. note 138, below. The most recent summary of the legal aspects of the trial is Emanuel Mickel's highly detailed paper, "The Thirty *pleges* for Ganelon," *Olifant*, 6 (1979), 293–304. Mickel reminds us that our knowledge of "Germanic" codes is uncertain and promises a fuller study (p. 302, n. 20; p. 310, n. 10). Jenkins gives a lengthy note to line 3741, with anachronistic references to Beaumanoir and Philip of Novara. See also Duggan, *Guide*, nos. 285–90; R. Howard Bloch, *Medieval French Literature and Law* (Berkeley and Los Angeles, 1977), 37–40. Pensom, 179, unlike other commentators, finds that the trial lacks complexity, a view with which I concur for the reasons given here.

just the representative of central authority in the *Song of Roland.* He is also the guardian and symbolic guarantor of justice—a point not always fully dealt with by those who hope to link the work too closely to the consolidation of royal power by hook or by crook in the twelfth century.[133] Charles has a certain margin of initiative—he can have Ganelon bound and tortured—but he is ultimately required to heed the principles of order that I have argued are one of the central thematic concerns of the poem.

The narrator, however, does not hesitate to proclaim Ganelon guilty. He calls him an oathbreaker (*fels,* 3735), says he is not *leial,* not loyal or law-abiding (3765), and states that he is a traitor who deserves punishment (3740, 3748), thus recalling earlier explicit narratorial remarks (cf. 178–79, 1405–11). The complications of the Trial stem not from any ambiguity in what Ganelon has done or uncertainty about the guilt he bears, but from a renewed emphasis on the threat to feudal principles that human weakness and perversity can pose. The fair trial Charles intends to give Ganelon comes perilously close to being a miscarriage of justice, thanks to the threatening intervention of Pinabel in favor of the guilty man, undertaken on grounds that have nothing to do with the issues at hand.

270–71 (CCLXX–CCLXXI)

Ganelon has been tied to a stake before the palace at Aix. Servants beat him. He has deserved no better, we are told (3740). Now Charles has solemnly convoked his court. The men of the empire, having fought a war, are now to serve him by doing justice. The traitor is brought before the emperor.

272 (CCLXXII)

Just as we lack early-medieval manuals of tactics to inform us of the rear guard's function and explain the duty laid upon its commander, so also do we lack legal manuals contemporary with the *Song of Roland* and detailed enough to tell us whether Ganelon's trial is carried out according to the rules of procedure obtaining in the various places where the epic is most likely to have been composed and sung. This absence of precise legal documentation is at first glance every bit as bothersome as the lack of military handbooks. Medieval systems of public justice do not treat such concepts as truth and wrongdoing

133Wendt, 153, notes that vengeance is synonymous with *justise* in this passage, though the latter word is polysemous and may mean "punishment" or even "decision." Cf. Jones, *Ethos,* 13.

exactly as we do, and the ways of establishing technical guilt could be as far removed from ours as were the techniques of warfare.[134] It would be risky indeed to say that we can be sure the trial of Ganelon either does or does not satisfy the local rules of procedure that its maker was most familiar with.

Still, technical guilt and innocence are not the issues in the episode considered as part of the *Roland* narrative. It is not a self-sufficient courtroom drama, but a moral tale within another tale, with a well-marked traitor in it. The Trial is, in that respect, no different from the scenes preceding the battle of Roncevaux: through the device of the judicial duel, with its finality, the last episode clearly shows Ganelon's guilt in a broad sense. Charles accuses Ganelon, in solemn assembly, of having betrayed not just Roland and the Peers, but also himself. Ganelon's response may play on the meanings of the word *traïsun* (to judge by the later examples cited by R. H. Bloch).[135] He says that he had a right to bring about Roland's death, since he observed proper form in challenging him—this without reference to the agent he used, to the circumstances, or to the consequences. If this is legally correct (it is difficult to say), it openly begs the moral question.

Ganelon first defied without proper cause a man who did him no wrong; Roland did not send him to Saragossa, whatever he says. He then lied, destructively, to Blancandrin, Marsile, and his own sovereign; he arranged an ambush under the cover of concluding a peace. These acts were all deliberate and not inadvertent. Ganelon offers no explanation for any but the first. Even if it were possible to find a law whose letter permitted such manipulation of persons under patently false pretenses, there would still remain a consideration that makes Ganelon guilty beyond redemption. He has broken trust and betrayed comrades who counted on him explicitly.[136] That was the

[134]See Robert Delort's rapid but suggestive summary, *La Vie au Moyen Age* (Paris, 1982), 114–19.

[135]R. H. Bloch, *Medieval French Literature*, 34–37.

[136]Ganelon specifically breaks the "negative rules of fidelity" that forbid a vassal from harming his lord; they are given in Fulbert of Chartres's famous letter (Lemarignier, 128–29; Ganshof, 83–86). Cf. Hans Erich Keller, "The *Song of Roland* and Its Audience," *Olifant*, 6 (1979), 263; Mickel's résumé in "Thirty *pleges*," 294; J. Thomas, 108 (though we cannot know or guess what Ganelon's intention was). It is not clear that there was an early distinction between betraying one's comrades and betraying the king, despite Brault, *Song*, 1:319; cf. R. H. Bloch, 40. Gérard, 454, reads Beaumanoir backward: it *is* treason to take "vengeance" on anyone *de cex qui ne furent pas au fet* ("among those who were not involved"). Even if we were to grant that Roland has insulted Ganelon in the Council of Charlemagne, we should not be too hasty to attribute to twelfth-century men the idea that any slight or insult was the equivalent of an act causing harm and requiring vengeance, despite the connotations of our word

act that furnished the context for Roland's last fight, which is the heart of the story. It is also the act of which Charles in fact accuses Ganelon (*Les .xii. pers ad traït,* "He betrayed the twelve Peers" [3756]), as did the narratorial voice in anticipating this episode (1405–11).

Furthermore, Thierry points out that to harm Roland was to harm Charles, and in a judicial combat he proves the point by defeating Ganelon's champion, with God's help. This outcome leaves little room for any lingering suspicion that Ganelon may have been justified in what he did, even though we are told that the identification of treason with *lèse-majesté* is a later development.

Though he is the supreme ruler and a divinely inspired man, Charles must still go to court and state his case. His accusation is brief. On the campaign in Spain, Ganelon deprived him of twenty thousand men, including Roland, Oliver, and the twelve Peers: he betrayed them (strictly, perhaps, the Peers [3755–56]) for money. There is no doubt about any of this. It was indeed Ganelon's collusion with the enemy (an act of treason by any general standard) that caused the loss of the rear guard. The poem long ago announced this act as *traïsun* (178) and it was also treason according to certain ancient definitions. To cite R. H. Bloch's summary: "Treason, under Germanic law, meant either aiding the enemies of the warrior group, the *comitatus,* or flight from battle. Both required successful completion of an act of military betrayal or cowardice, breach of troth or *Treubruch.*"[137] Among other things, Ganelon aided the enemy against his comrades when he announced to Charles that Marsile had submitted and when he described the death of the *algalife,* both of which were lies (laisse 54). And if my analysis of laisses 53–63 is at all correct, then it was Ganelon alone who made the rear guard's mission both inevitable and fatal (cf. laisses 43–46). Furthermore, he received gifts and money from the pagans. The multivalent preposition *pur* in line 3756 makes it difficult to judge the portent and thus the accuracy of this last claim of Charles's. *Ad traït pur aveir* seems to mean "betrayed for payment," but *pur* could also express a condition or manner and may mean that Ganelon both betrayed his comrades and took money in return, with no implication that money was his motive. The money was not his sole or original motive—that was probably his embarrassed resentment at having to carry out the embassy he had suggested without adequate

"feudal" and some hints of Jones's (*Ethos,* 11). In any case, the twenty thousand men of the rear guard did not insult Ganelon at all. Finally, Ganelon is not just "any medieval knight"; he is Roland's comrade in a war against the infidel (despite Stranges, 338).

[137] R. H. Bloch, *Medieval French Literature,* 40.

reflection (cf. laisses 15–16, 20–24)—but Charles does not necessarily say it was, only that he profited by his act.[138]

Ganelon at first replies to the emperor's charge with what is almost certainly another lie.[139] He admits readily enough that he caused Roland's death: "I arranged Roland's death because he had done me material harm" (*en or e en aveir;* does Ganelon mean to claim Roland had taken money from him or defrauded him? Why does he not say when or where?)—"but I do not consider that treason" (3759–60). This counteraccusation is, first of all, extremely implausible. It is not easy even for Roland's most consistent critics to maintain that he might have needed or desired to cheat Ganelon in a matter involving money—a matter, one might add, to which no one in the poem ever refers except the traitor, and then only when he is on trial for his life.[140] I have argued above that nothing in the Council Scene requires us to posit any feud between the two beyond what the poem itself shows us. Beyond that (since the courtiers in the poem do not necessarily know anything about the relationship between Roland and Ganelon), it is even more difficult to argue seriously that the society here shown rendering a rather elaborate verdict would accept the notion that the valid settlement for a property dispute was for one of the parties to arrange, in secret, to have the other party ambushed and killed by a third under cover of a false treaty.

But in any event, such questions have no bearing on the situation, and even to consider them is to fail to recognize what Ganelon is trying to do. In fact, he refuses almost entirely to answer Charles's

[138]Let us recall the notion, treated by Jones, Gérard, Halverson, Gellinek, Pensom, and others, that Ganelon represents "family and clan" in tension with "state and church" (Pensom, 89). This opposition is made problematic by, among other things, the strong possibility that the kin-group includes kin by marriage, which would make Charles himself (Ganelon's brother-in-law) part of Ganelon's kin-group and not just the symbol of the state; see M. Bloch, 123–25; Wendt, 269; Williamson, 556. In any case, the age of the *Roland* is in principle posterior to the age of rampant clanism, as Williamson, 557, implies; cf. M. Bloch, 233–34, on the primacy of vassalic over kinship ties. On the alternate motivation of avarice, see Cartier, 40; Brault, *Song,* 1:100–103; Mickel, "Parallels," 449. In betraying, Ganelon does not act in the name of any subgroup—familial or political.

[139]Ganelon's defense is sometimes said to be sincere (e.g., Calin, 71; Gérard, 452–53; Horrent, *Chanson de Roland et geste de Charlemagne,* 9; Goldin, "Die Rolle Ganelons," 129, 149–54), but cf. J. Thomas, 115. Once in a while his claim that he has a right to vengeance is taken at face value (Stranges, 341, 344, 358, 360; Gérard, 455; cf. Payen, "Génocide," 228, and note 30 above).

[140]See, however, an interesting suggestion by Donald Maddox: Ganelon is afraid for his son Baldewin and his succession and suspects Roland had designs on the latter, which *is* a material matter (see Donald Maddox, "*E Baldewin mun filz:* la parenté dans la *Chanson de Roland,*" *VIII Congreso de la Société Rencesvals* [Pamplona, 1981], 299–302, esp. 302).

accusation.[141] Charles speaks of harm done to himself (and perhaps, by implication, to the peoples he rules; the link is logical if not necessarily part of customary law for the specific period). The emperor enumerates the twenty thousand men of the rear guard, and he names Oliver and the twelve Peers, these last, at least, betrayed for gain. Ganelon does not respond to any of this. He does not attempt to establish that he had some legitimate claim against the others or that settling things with Roland was a proper excuse for depriving Charles of the twenty thousand men.

273 (CCLXXIII)

Ganelon elaborates on his defense and modifies it in lines 3769–78. The narrator describes him as he stands before Charles. Like Baligant (3164), if Ganelon were of different stuff he would be (or seem) a worthy baron. Thirty of his relatives stand beside him, their presence recalling the importance of the kinship group and its loyalties in early medieval law.[142] The accused man cries out loudly to the assembled court. He may be describing the events at Saragossa to a group of men who were not there, or (as seems more likely) giving a slanted account to a group containing at least some eyewitnesses.

First Ganelon says that on the Spanish campaign he served Charles loyally and honored his feudal bond. This is a statement we cannot judge, if by it he means to describe the long period of warfare before the council at Saragossa; it is a transparent lie if it is meant to describe his actions in toto, for in fact he solemnly swore to aid Marsile instead (see laisses 45–46).[143] Next Ganelon claims that Roland came to hate him and hence singled him out (*si me jugat* [3772]) for death and suffering. This statement is clearly false, both in the circumstances it presents and in the cause-and-effect sequence it implies.

On the one hand, there is no sign that Roland hated Ganelon. He nominated him in five words that merely served to identify him (277). There is no expression of hatred, although it is marginally possible that the term *parastre,* "stepfather," could conceal some feelings of resentment.[144] But even if we posit some hatred between the two

[141]Cf. R. H. Bloch, *Medieval French Literature,* 39.

[142]Cf. Mickel, "Thirty *pleges,*" 297–300, and note 138 above.

[143]Marsile said at one point, "Swear to me that you will betray Roland," but that treason is only the means to the end described in laisse 45: "Charles will lose his right arm [597] . . . and never have such an army again [599]."

[144]It has been suggested both that Roland meant to honor Ganelon by proposing him and that he meant to shame him. Both ideas depend on multiple assumptions. I have preferred to think that Ganelon is simply the logical nominee at that point, as the Franks all say (lines 278–79); cf. notes 30 and 32, above.

men, some long-standing quarrel that the text does not show and to which no one ever refers except Ganelon, it is not that hatred that sent Ganelon to Marsile's camp. The embassy, with its risk of *mort et dulur,* was Ganelon's own idea—Roland opposed the idea—and it was a miscalculation, or an oversight due to haste on his part, that led him to propose it, apparently without thinking that he might himself be sent to carry it out. The text of the Council Scene shows, first, that Charles refused a series of volunteers before Ganelon was named and, second, that while Roland may finally have nominated Ganelon, it was the acclamation of the assembly, and Charles's acceptance, that actually laid the mission upon him.

By contrast with the preceding, line 3773 is a true statement. Ganelon was ambassador to Marsile, but his next claim (3774) is that he survived the mission thanks to his skill. Though ambiguous out of context, that is another outright lie in view of the events. He actually survived by pledging, with the most powerful oaths he could muster, to help the pagans rid themselves of Charles and Roland. He had already come to terms with Blancandrin before he ever saw Marsile (402–4). His testimony here is both self-serving and selective. (Perhaps we are meant to remember that no one in the court can possibly have witnessed Ganelon's bargain with the enemy.)

Ganelon now continues in the same vein. I challenged Roland, Oliver, and the others in public, he says. Charles heard it. (Ganelon does not add that Charles rejected his claim that Roland was responsible.) What I did was vengeance—a positive term—not treason, the traitor concludes.

This part of Ganelon's defense, considered only in itself, exhibits enough surface plausibility to have been given considerable weight in one or two scholarly studies on the *Song*. Leaving aside for the moment the important question of agent—the Saracen host that actually killed the rear guard (nobody killed Roland)—it is just barely possible that the public nature of Ganelon's *desfi,* however unwarranted the latter was, could under some procedural rules have served to show that his intent was not technically criminal.[145] Nevertheless, arranging the deaths of thousands at Roncevaux cannot be construed as an act of

[145]Mostly from later legal texts, R. H. Bloch derives the definition of murder as "equivalent to deception, either because of an attempt to hide wrongdoing after the fact" (as Ganelon does in lines 1770–84) "or because of an inferred malice in its enactment. It necessarily implies treachery, a killing in which the guilty party, through ruse or surprise, knowingly takes unfair advantage of his victim" (R. H. Bloch, *Medieval French Literature and Law,* 35). The ambush at Roncevaux may not be much of a surprise after the Nomination Scene, but it certainly qualifies as a ruse and as unfair.

personal vengeance. Nor is it correct to insist that Ganelon sees some distinction between betraying the twelve Peers and betraying Charles, or that he sincerely believes his act was lawful. His defense is either incomplete or simply specious. It is not some affirmation of an ancient and respectable legal code, one that Ganelon honestly thought he could follow. Such a code could in no way imply the skein of falsehoods and the unhallowed alliances that are the primary features of Ganelon's plot. No quarrel with Roland, no right Ganelon possesses, can justify his perversion of his mission to Marsile, his abuse of trust, or the destruction of the Franco-Christian rear guard. What the traitor is doing is seeking what we might today call a loophole, attempting to exploit the code, or his judges' expectations, in order to escape punishment for an act that was traitorous in intent, an act for which Ganelon possibly never expected to come to trial (cf. the commentary to laisse 134). There is no need to assume the portrayal of competing legal systems here.

The traitor's reply to Charles is, then, a mixture of verifiable lies, ambiguous statements, and claims whose relevance is at best dubious. Despite the surface detail of his recital, and his broadening of his targets to include Oliver and the "companions," Ganelon does not establish the legitimacy of his *desfi* or the validity of his having arranged a large-scale ambush by means of solemn vows exchanged with the enemies of Christendom. Nor (as Thierry will soon point out) does any of what he says explain why he might have thought himself justified in secretly providing for Charles's men, performing a necessary service during a campaign in wartime, to be attacked by an overwhelming pagan force.[146]

Ganelon may be either telling the truth as his bias suggests it to him, or (as appears more likely) trying to save his skin by misleading the court. Whichever it may be, and whatever our expectations, it is not on the basis of his arguments that the barons make their decision, but on other grounds entirely. As it turns out, Ganelon has a powerful friend or ally whose presence will have a decisive effect on the court's verdict. When it comes, the recommendation of clemency (not, strictly speaking, of acquittal) is based neither on consideration of whether Ganelon is telling the truth nor on a technical determination that his action was legitimate or warranted. It does not matter whether he acted rightly or not, as long as Pinabel is able to cow the assembly. The

[146]The ambush at Roncevaux could hardly qualify as legitimate under any of the rules discussed by R. H. Bloch. Strictly speaking, Ganelon does not even try to claim that his *deed* was overt (and thus he may be obscuring an important point of law; cf. ibid., 39), only that his *challenge* was.

Franks say, "We will take counsel among ourselves," but in fact there is no debate. The claims Ganelon has made in his defense are never discussed.

274 (CCLXXIV)

Trial by combat is not an arbitrary procedure for those who believe in a justice, divine in origin, that transcends our ability to perceive. The judicial duel, like the symbolic battles in Spain, is a way of making God's will visible.[147] The duel in the final episode of the *Song of Roland* is made necessary by the court's failure to give proper consideration to the matter at hand. It represents a risk, but it does serve justice in the long run. For a trial by combat to succeed as proof, however, there must obviously be at least one champion willing to commit himself to the defense of justice. If one comes forward, then according to the logic of the proceeding justice will inevitably triumph. By the devices of these final laisses, the maker of the *Song* both manages to show the possibility of abuse, with which we are all familiar, and also contrives to express confidence in God's ultimate intervention on the side of the right.

Seeing that the deliberation has begun, Ganelon turns to a member of his family, Pinabel, a leader among the thirty who support him, both a fine talker and an excellent fighter. Ganelon calls on Pinabel to save him from death, and Pinabel responds without any reference to public justice. "You will be saved," he says. "Any Frenchman who condemns you to death will have to face me, and I will give him the lie with my good sword" (3788–91). Pinabel's promise to Ganelon, like Marsile's involvement with the traitor, will mean his death.

275–76 (CCLXXV–CCLXXVI)

Now the courtiers are in council, but there is no determination of right and wrong, no weighing of arguments, and no attempt to discover whether Ganelon deserves exoneration: in a word, there is no judgment. "Because of Pinabel, they hardly speak" (3797).[148] In a faint echo of the first Christian council, Charles's men temporize,

[147]The presence of champions is apparently considered normal in this text, as it the prior submission of the case to the assembly, though Ruggieri described both as archaic features.

[148]I think this translation is consistent with the evidence thoroughly marshaled by Burgess, who translates "Because of Pinabel's intervention, the judges prove more favorable to a peaceful conclusion" (Glyn S. Burgess, "Remarques sur deux vers de la *Chanson de Roland*," *Société Rencesvals: Actes du VIe Congrès* [Aix-en-Provence, 1974], 63–78). It is difficult to think Pinabel's intervention could be anything but a threat; cf. lines 3788–91, 3804.

shunning the duty incumbent upon them.[149] Let us leave the matter as it stands, they say; we'll ask the king to let Ganelon off, this once, in return for faithful service in the future. After all, Roland is dead and cannot be brought back. Only a fool would fight Pinabel over this. And so they agree, and return to where Charles is waiting, without having decided whether Ganelon's arguments have any legal standing, whether his acts deserve censure, or what is implied if Ganelon is set free under these circumstances.

The barons now repeat to Charles what they have said among themselves. They recommend neither acquittal nor punishment, but clemency. Let Ganelon go, they say, for he is a noble man. Putting him to death, or even requiring a money payment of him, will not bring Roland back. The king's reaction is swift and sharp. "You are *felun,* oathbreakers." The barons are themselves betraying Charles. They have not rendered proper service; by implication, they have failed to keep their word. They do not constitute a sworn jury, but an ad hoc swearing-in is not what makes an early feudal court. As Charles's vassals. they owe him aid and counsel, and that includes deliberation in matters of justice.[150]

277 (CCLXXVII)

Charles is bitterly disappointed. His men have failed him (*faillir* [3815] may also mean breach of duty).[151] But his discomfiture is brief. A knight steps forward, Thierry, the only councilor who did not vote for clemency (3806). He is not a remarkable man physically; he is small, slender, and dark, and at first glance he may not seem much of a match for Pinabel.[152] Morally, however, and no doubt legally, his stance is clearly valid. He speaks correctly (*curteisement*), evoking his family's long service to Charles, and his own. His statement is both a formal challenge to Pinabel and an affirmation of principle that con-

[149]See Kibler, "Roland and Tierri."

[150]See Lemarignier, 136–40; Ganshof, 92–93. It is sometimes said that Ganelon is acquitted (e.g., Burger, "Rire," 9; Stranges, 361; Gellinek, 41; Gérard, 455; Karl-Heinz Bender, *König und Vassal* [Heidelberg, 1967]), 34 (though "the triumph of the extra-feudal law of reparations and of the . . . power of the family is . . . not final"); Mickel, "Thirty *pleges,*" 299 (cf. his n. 33, p. 304). On the failure to judge, see Brault, *Song,* 1:324 (who adds that the judges put their society at risk); Horrent, *Chanson de Roland dans les littératures . . . ,* 281–82; Waltz, 49; Halverson, 667; cf. J. Thomas, 115–16.

[151]Tobler and Lommatzsch (3:1607) treat *sunt failliz* as a past indefinite and enter this line under the gloss "jemanden im Stiche lassen" ("to leave someone in the lurch"), but cf. the (later) examples of the adjective *failli,* given under the gloss "treulos," "ehrlos," "feige" (3:1615).

[152]Uitti, 105, describes Thierry as "a kind of everyman, a typical Frenchman with whom a member of the audience might physically identify himself."

trasts with the court's prevarication. Thierry puts the ambush back into its proper context (3827–30). Roland may or may not have done Ganelon some personal harm, he says, but that is neither here nor there.[153] Roland was Charles's man and was actively serving him when he stayed behind at Roncevaux. Ganelon's act constituted treason and felony because it meant harm to his own overlord.

That is an issue neither Ganelon nor the court addressed. Any vendetta that might have lain behind the traitor's dealings with Marsile would be no excuse. Ganelon's act was criminal with respect to the collective interest represented by Charles, and hence with respect to the traitor's own status as a Christian knight.[154] It was contrary to the principle of feudal allegiance: *Vers vos s'en est parjurez e malmis* (cf. note 136, above). The duel is superfluous; that is one reason why the court's failure to judge the case on its merits qualifies as *felunie.* I judge that Ganelon should die as a traitor, Thierry concludes, and I am ready to face his champion in combat. The group belatedly approves this speech.

278–80 (CCLXXVIII–CCLXXX)

The preparations for the duel go forward briskly. Pinabel accepts Charles's jurisdiction, or his right to make a claim against Ganelon; then he responds to Thierry's challenge. The requirements of ritual are satisfied. The two men place their gloves in Charles's hand as tokens of the commitment they have made to fight each other. Each is pledged by a number of relatives (3848–49 [these are Pinabel's pledges, not Ganelon's, yet if he loses, as it turns out, their lives are all forfeit] and 3852). The two men perform an exchange of challenges, and Ogier the Dane lays out (I presume) the rules under which the duel is to be conducted. Both champions are shriven, take Communion, make offerings. They arm and mount. One hundred thousand knights weep as they look on, out of sympathy (*pitiet*)[155] for Thierry and respect for Roland's memory. The narrator reminds us that God already knows what the outcome will be.

[153]Thierry is not necessarily conceding that Roland harmed Ganelon (despite Brook, 124); *que que* is the indefinite "whatever" (with the subjunctive) and serves primarily to put the question aside.

[154]"No legal proof is needed to establish the criminal character of that vengeance" (Menéndez Pidal, 138).

[155]*Pitiet* can mean "worry," "solicitude," "sympathy" as well as modern "pity" (*pitié*) (Tobler and Lommatzsch, 7:982–86). The onlookers might have pity on the apparently overmatched Thierry for Thierry's own sake, but it is for Roland's sake that they are concerned about him in the text's lines 3870–71.

281–84 (CCLXXXI–CCLXXXIV)

Now the two champions are charging at each other. They meet, their lances smash each other's shields, and both are unhorsed. They continue the fight, predictably, on foot. Charles cries out to God to show where justice (*dreit*) lies. Pinabel calls on Thierry to change his mind, and Thierry in turn emphasizes his refusal to do so with his own appeal to God to show which of the two has justice on his side. He praises Pinabel and asks for his surrender in turn, but Pinabel refuses, invoking family loyalty. As has often been pointed out, this single combat presents obvious analogies with the duel between Charles and Baligant. Like the former, this one must end with the death of one combatant or the other (3914; cf. 3578).

285–86 (CCLXXXV–CCLXXXVI)

The combat reaches its climax with two mighty blows. Pinabel strikes such sparks from Thierry's helmet that the grass catches fire. His blade cuts into Thierry's cheek and rips into his hauberk. God protects Thierry from death (3823), as he did Charles (cf. 3602–11). Now Thierry returns the blow, slicing through Pinabel's helmet and into his head. Pinabel is killed instantly, and with that the duel and the trial are over. The onlookers recognize that God has manifested his will, and call for the traitor and the pledges to be put to death.[156] Thierry is not a paladin, apparently, but he does have the one quality that is indispensable if justice is to be done. Like Gautier del Hum and Aude, he exhibits a stubborn attachment to the principles he states (3824–29). His steadfastness, like theirs, is an echo of Roland's, and so is his victory. The ideal of justice is as harsh as the warrior's ethic or the binding promise, but constant adherence to these ideals means success in the poem's terms. The fears that seem to lie behind Oliver's last reproach (lines 1726–34), if they were real, were groundless. Charles and the things he serves will always find a defender, and God will help.[157]

[156]Marc Bloch, 125, includes this episode as an example of trial by combat; on the deliberate effect of contrast between the two sides, see Scully, "Ordeal at Roncesvalles," and cf. Paul Aebischer, "Pour la défense et l'illustration de l'épisode de Baligant" (1940, reprinted in *Rolandiana et Oliveriana* [Geneva, 1967]), esp. 218–20. This duel reproduces Charles's combat against Baligant (Brault, *Song*, 1:309, 328–29). It repeats, instead, Roland's disagreement with Ganelon (Pensom, 182, 185).

[157]Cf. Kibler, "Roland and Tierri," 32. Thierry is Roland's spiritual heir; a later poem in the same cycle, *Gaydon*, goes as far as to show him taking Roland's place. I think this is more important than the fact Roland has no children (cf. R. H. Bloch, *Etymologies and Genealogies* [Chicago, 1983], 105). He sacrifices his own chance at establishing a

287–89 (CCLXXXVII–CCLXXXIX)

To honor the victor, the king and four (or forty) barons come forward to cleanse his wound—Charles does this with his own fur cloak—and remove his armor. They return to the palace. Once there, Charles asks his supporters how the hostages, Pinabel's guarantors, are to be treated. The response is, as elsewhere, unanimous. They are to be hanged, all thirty. The sentence is carried out at once. Its message is clear. Pinabel and the thirty, themselves originally blameless, are caught up in the ambit of Ganelon's evildoing. Earlier the Saracens of Saragossa and their leader sealed their own doom by making themselves Ganelon's instruments. The narrator sums up that theme in a single line: "Whoever betrays a man destroys himself and others too" (3959). Marsile and Pinabel are the counterexamples, their deaths the mirror-images of the triumphant deaths at Roncevaux.

At last Ganelon, his guilt made strikingly clear despite the court's hesitation and Pinabel's intervention, is punished. Specifically, in an execution notable for its violence, he is torn apart by four warhorses, "as a proven oathbreaker" (*fel recreant* [3973]). Again the narrator's voice breaks in to remind us that a man who betrays another has no right ever to boast of it.

290–91 (CCXC–CCXCI)

Charles's vengeance is complete. The baptism of the converted Bramimonde underscores the triumph of Christendom.[158] The story of Roncevaux is over, but the epic goes on. That very night, as he sleeps, Charles is visited once more by God's emissary, Saint Gabriel. The archangel orders him to gather his armies again and to go forth to defend a Christian city under pagan attack. The people of Bire and Imphe—it still does not matter precisely who or where they are—are calling for his help. Roland's sacrifice and Charles's suffering are only local events in an even greater story. The subjunctive used as past conditional in line 3999 tells us what we expect: that Charles will indeed respond. "The emperor would have wished not to go," but even as he weeps and proclaims his life a burden, we see that with or without Roland, Oliver, the peers, and the twenty thousand he will go out and fight the invaders once again.

---

lineage, just as he sacrifices his own life, because larger issues are involved. Kibler says "it would certainly be excessive to pretend that Tierri is a 'second Roland,'" but goes on to establish parallels similar in function to those I present ("Roland and Tierri," 30–32); Mermier, 97, and McCash, 143, call Thierry a "new" or "neo-Roland."

[158]On Bramimonde's conversion and the name Juliana, see Brault, *Song,* 1:333–35, and the studies cited in Duggan, *Guide,* nos. 291–91A.

PART TWO

The Sense of the *Song of Roland*

[1]

Rereading the *Song of Roland*

As I suggested in the Preface, it can be a difficult task to discover what sort of hero Roland is in the Oxford *Song of Roland,* or how his story embodies (as it is said to do) the spirit of its age. He is surely an energetic man and a paladin, a great fighter. The reader scarcely needs a literary critic's help to notice that. But when one does read what critics have had to say about him, far more often than one reads of some perversity—a tragedy, a failure, built into his very character, making all his prowess hollow. Pierre Le Gentil, the most influential recent interpreter of the *Song,* implies that he puts his own civilization in jeopardy: "At the last moment, abandoning all caution, surer than ever of his prowess—perhaps unmindful of the fate of his men and of the greater interests of Christianity [*la Chrétienté,* Christendom]—he blindly rushes into a battle that from the start is doomed by his own fault. . . . Roland, in his eagerness to answer his stepfather's challenge, exposes Christendom to a catastrophe."[1] He does these things, we are told, because of a pathological concern for his reputation, a pathetic sense of his own superiority, a *démesure* that leads him to boast when he cannot perform, to scorn obviously reasonable advice, and to bring on a disaster that he could have prevented by the proper exercise of his leadership.[2]

[1]Le Gentil, *Song,* 89, 94.

[2]"Roland's braggadocio is the epitome of his haughtiness (2316–34)," says Jones (*Ethos,* 67; as Brault points out, the example is ill-chosen [Brault, *Song,* 1:97]). For the claim that Roland boasts, see, among many others, Cartier, 62 (who justifies it); Kibler, "Roland's Pride," 152–54; Siciliano, 348, 351; Boatner, 577; Jones, "Lament," 13–14; Owen, "Secular Inspiration," 391; Donohoe, 255; Renoir, "Roland's Lament," 576. For the claim that Roncevaux is a disaster, and the rear guard is wasted, see Van Emden, "Guarant," 31; Owen, "Secular Inspiration," 390.

Any reader curious about medieval life and thought may very well ask how such a tale of narrow, selfish pride fits the framework of a time like the late eleventh and early twelfth centuries—a time of endemic local struggles, of uncertain central government, of baronial privilege, all of which temporarily threatened Europe with political instability, economic stagnation, and a patchy cultural future. What sort of response is the self-centered heedlessness we find in Roland supposed to have awakened in the hearers for whom he was created? He is said to look upon man's deadliest occupation as a sport or game. What does this have to do with the ethos of the elite around the year 1100? A story of o'erweening pride may have held the interest of its hearers then, but did it do more than entertain them? Can "a tale of personal grudge and feud leading to treachery and national disaster" (Owen) have spoken to the age of Europe's emergence with any moral force?

The usual answer to such questions is to posit the poem of culpable rashness and then read it as an example of behavior to avoid. As Le Gentil puts it, "The Oxford poem criticizes Roland, or causes him to be criticized, in unequivocal fashion."[3] There have been apologists for Roland the character, including Le Gentil, who have argued that, though unthinking and prideful, the hero is not beyond redemption (eschatologically or aesthetically). But it is still traditional to claim that the text teaches us that the disaster of Roncevaux is the wages of Roland's pride: "It cannot be too often stressed that the drama of Roncevaux is at heart [*par ses origines*] a human drama, initiated by Roland's pride [*C'est la démesure de Roland qui l'explique*]."[4]

When we, at least, contemplate the announcement of Roland's failure and the statement that his humanity lies in his flaw, we are satisfied. It seems proper to us to express an ideal such as that of "measure" by showing the sad effect of its opposite; and, though

[3]Le Gentil, "A propos de la démesure," 204. Cf. Boatner, 575, 576: "In the name of feudal loyalty [Roland] betrays every aspect of the feudal code . . . his total misunderstanding of his feudal obligations is due to the blindness of pride." Roland "fails to live up to his contract; indeed, he perverts it." Scattered affirmations of the contrary have appeared in the works of critics not immediately concerned with refuting the *démesure* hypothesis in any detail. See Guiette, "Deux Scènes," 96; Battaglia, 126–40; Yves Bonnefoy, "Sur la *Chanson de Roland*," *L'Ephémère*, 4 (1967), 62–65; Farnham, 164 ("a great warrior whose martyrdom is a supreme act of feudal loyalty"); Williamson, 557; Picherit, 265; Owen, "Secular Inspiration," 398; Payen, *Le Motif du repentir*, 127 ("in an epic perspective, [Roland's] conduct appears nearly beyond reproach"). Mickel points out parallels between Roland's role and those of the Virtues in Prudentius (Mickel, "Parallels in Prudentius's *Psychomachia*," 440–42). See also the works cited in note 4 to the Preface, above.

[4]Le Gentil, *Song*, 87.

earlier medieval literature, and epic in particular, tend to a straightforward portrayal of heroism (or saintliness), that is indeed no reason to insist that a Turold could not have essayed, instead, a more familiar, apparently more sophisticated, negative form of exemplum.

Still, important questions remain, for some readers at least—questions that the tradition of scholarly interpretation of the *Song of Roland* has never answered and in some measure has failed to address. Are Roland's preternatural soldierly skills, his sublime prowess, his firm statements of feudal principle, his translation to heaven, really caveats? Is that how they link functionally with the other elements in the *Song of Roland* to lend weight and closure to the narrative? And more immediately important: is Roland really such a fool? Does he talk and act like one within the text and within what we know of the duties of his caste? If these and other questions of the sort no longer inspire perfect consensus among *Roland* scholars, it is not just because Roland's fate is what Le Gentil calls an "apparent paradox"; it is in large degree because so much of what happens in the *Song of Roland* seems to have little relevance to the theme of overbearing pride and its consequences, or no congruity with it at all. The disparity is quite large, as I have tried to suggest in the Commentary. Among its effects in criticism has been an exaggerated disdain for the way the work is constructed. Even so great a partisan of its unity as Joseph Bédier did not hesitate to call the Oxford *Roland* "enigmatic," to declare parts of the poem "obscure, nearly unintelligible," to claim that the poet, "too human to choose," never makes clear his own attitudes toward the "*preux*" Roland and the "*sage*" Oliver.[5] In the *Song of Roland,* then, the hero's misguided bravura is thought to be evident, but once that is posited, the narrative means used to express *démesure* are often described as vague.

The purpose of the foregoing Commentary and these supplemental essays is to explore how the *Song of Roland* makes sense as a different story. The intensity of scholarly commentary on this most famous of French epics has not always been matched by any great breadth of curiosity about why its contents and sequence are precisely what they are. The traditional reading of the poem was established and elaborated under the strong influence of late nineteenth- and early twentieth-century concepts of realistic narrative. Methodological innovations have since proceeded apace, both in criticism and in the writing of narrative itself. Yet the entrenched conception of the *Song* as a psychological drama, and the insistence on psychology—Roland's

[5]See Bédier, *Légendes,* 3:388–90, 439, 444, and below, Chapter 4.

character and his interaction with the others—as the main validating feature for interpretation, have survived even in the work of those who mistrust the philological methods of our predecessors.

Not that I mean to apply any innovative calculus to the narrative values of the *Song of Roland.* There are two reasons to stick to a more prosaic algebra instead. First, if a new reading is to gain acceptance, it must be put into terms accessible to the broadest possible interested audience. Second, my analysis is meant to form a contrast with the reading generally given from Léon Gautier's time (if not Fauriel's or Grimm's) to Le Gentil's, and to permit comparison with that reading it should be cast in a form compatible with it. For those reasons I chose to begin with an old exercise whose advantages should not be underestimated: that of the explanatory paraphrase. The foregoing Commentary is similar in form (though not in scope) to the summaries every reader learns when first encountering a lengthy and ancient work of narrative art. It resembles, as well, the sort of mental paraphrase on which readers tend to rely, for some purposes, as much as they do on the whole text. This is not, then, a "new reading" in the sense become traditional in some critical circles—applying some category of modern thought (Marxism, Freudianism, deconstructionism) to a poem created without overt attention to such things.[6] Behind the paraphrase lies instead a deep curiosity about the author's and the audience's habits of literary thought, and their attitudes toward heroic subjects.

If the *Song of Roland* is not primarily a study in pyschology, then what should we take it to be, and how should we take on the task of interpreting it, which (for an epic narrative at least) is the preliminary to other forms of understanding? My answer—temporary as all such answers are—is that it should be read as certain other works of art of its time are "read," as an ethical statement, embodying values in a framework that is no less aesthetically satisfying for all that it conveys ideas. Recognizing its power means admitting that our ancestors may have been moved, even excited, by ideals whose aesthetic status is greatly diminished today. Coming to grips with such historical particulars is a prerequisite for any reading that aims to discern where the poem's universal appeal may actually lie.

The appeal to history as a guide to interpretation is an important feature of philological method, and as such it has often been de-

[6]See Martin Steinmann, Jr., "What's the Point of Professional Interpretation of Literature?" *Philosophy and Literature,* 8 (1984), 267–68.

cried by proponents of various forms of New Criticism and by some structuralists. Some "Poststructural" theorists, on the other hand, have been less inclined to insist that something intrinsic to literary texts allows us to interpret them without ever referring to how their makers and audience thought and lived. The available space does not allow me to discuss at any length the ways concepts associated with reader-response criticism and reception theory echo the historical philologist's concern with the text's effects in the past. I can only note briefly that in the case of a work like the *Roland,* the practical, mediating interpretations medievalists give may be strengthened by considering such notions as the variability of communities or the implied audience.

Thus, for example, Stanley Fish has invoked the authority of "interpretive communities" to help explain how conflicting readings arise and come to supplant each other (an implicitly historical notion). In Fish's strategy, the concept of interpretive community permits us to avoid the impasse created by the insistence that meaning is specified either by isolated readers or by the text itself taken in isolation.

The solution will not seem particularly strange to literary historians who know, say, Gaston Paris's work on the relationships between Arthurian literature and the court of Champagne, Curtius's on vernacular literature and the medieval intellectual community, Robertson's on the milieu for which Chaucer wrote, or Stock's on textual communities.[7] Decisions about what counts in a text are made according to prevailing assumptions that stem not from individuals but from the "interpretive communities" to which they belong. As Fish puts it:

> What was normative for the members of one community would be seen as strange (if it could be seen at all) by the members of another. In other words, there is no single way of reading that is correct or natural, only "ways of reading" that are extensions of community perspectives. . . . This meant that the business of criticism was not (as I had previously thought) to determine a correct way of reading but to determine from which of a number of possible perspectives reading will proceed. . . . The business of criticism, in other words, was not to decide between interpretations by subjecting them to the test of disinterested evidence but to establish by political and persuasive means (they are the same thing) the set of interpretive assumptions from the vantage of which the

[7]See Stock, 88–240, esp. 88–92, and D. W. Robertson, *A Preface to Chaucer* (Princeton, 1962), e.g., vii–ix, 3–6; and cf. Daniel Poirion's measured remarks on literary communication in the Middle Ages in his introduction to *Précis de littérature française,* esp. 13–15.

evidence (and the facts and the intentions and everything else) will hereafter be specifiable.[8]

For the purposes espoused by the present community of readers of the *Song of Roland*—primarily a community of persons curious about other, medieval persons—the preferable reading is the one probably attributable to another community, a medieval one. The "perspective" or point of view from which the hermeneutical ball is set rolling is a perspective created by our knowledge of the past. It is often claimed that we cannot know the attitudes of the past, but such claims apparently stem from overarching philosophical assumptions about knowledge itself, rather than from any actual demonstration that history is a total failure. A different assumption unites such divergent theorists as Hans-Georg Gadamer and E. D. Hirsch, who allow us the capacity to recognize and grasp meanings that are not the meanings we originally had in mind—even if they come from the past.[9]

Fish, like most of his colleagues in reader-response criticism, does not put the question historically, but it is more important to note that, in his formulation, two communities' criteria for right reading differ and can be identified:

> Given the notion of interpretive communities, agreement more or less explained itself: members of the same community will necessarily agree because they will see (and by seeing, make) everything in relation to that community's assumed purposes and goals; and conversely, members of different communities will disagree because from each of their respective positions the other "simply" cannot see what is obviously and inescapably there. This, then, is the explanation for the stability of interpretation among different readers (they belong to the same community). It also explains why there are disagreements and why they can be debated in a principled way: not because of a stability in texts, but because of a stability in the makeup of interpretive communities and therefore in the opposing positions they make possible.[10]

[8]Stanley Fish, *Is There a Text in This Class?* (Cambridge, Mass., 1980), 15–16. It is not my present business to delineate the complex and interesting relationships between this statement of Fish's, the "literary anthropology," associated with Roland Barthes, the "traditions" associated with Hans-Georg Gadamer, or Jauss's various applications of the idea of "horizons of expectation."

[9]H.-G. Gadamer speaks of "mediation between past and present" and of the possibility of avoiding historical error (in connection with legal history), in *Truth and Method* (New York, 1984), xxi; E. D. Hirsch discusses "bracketing" of "alien meaning" in *The Aims of Interpretation* (Chicago, 1976), 3–6.

[10]Fish, 15.

Fish, therefore, does not merely postulate the interpretive community. He explicitly gives it a form of authority for textual meaning, and this decision has clear application in medieval studies. Indeed, it is easier to understand historically why two communities differ in their assumptions than it is to understand why contemporaries constitute more than one community (Fish seems to define communities pragmatically, more by the interpretations they give than by any other features they may have).

A formulation such as Fish's allows us to pursue our curiosity about authors and early audiences, not as ultimate arbiters of meaning, but as the putative authorities on what the text meant to them. Deciding how they would have exercised their authority, without confusing our own with theirs, remains a difficult task, but the difficulty itself is historical and subject to historical rules. Where there is little or no evidence of how medievals actually first reacted to a work—as is the case for the *Roland* among many others—there is at least evidence for the preoccupations and attitudes of a medieval community, and that evidence can be applied according to the usual canons of probability.[11] (In the Commentary, I have followed the rough working consensus according to which the overt content of the *Roland* implies a knightly, or soldierly audience, an idea to which I will return.) Error is possible in the exercise, and anachronism is specifically an error, since it means assuming an authority over medieval readings as historical events that belongs properly to medieval people. Before attributing a reading of the *Song of Roland* to Turold or Henry Plantagenet, the medievalist must do whatever can be done to specify anachronism—study language as the interpretive community under consideration used it; discern the place of the text's elements of reference in the community's mentality; and even judge the implicit claims of critics that the text corresponds to essentially postmedieval frames of reference.

A historical reading of the *Song of Roland*, then, seeks to reconcile the text with a time and place, with people not ourselves, as we know them. It is a type of reconstruction, not an immanent reading; what it tries to reconstruct is one or more versions of the text's meaning that have already existed—especially those likely to have been natural to the intended audience and the author, whose reactions and achieve-

[11]The crucial role of probability in historical reasoning is described by, among others, G. R. Elton, *The Practice of History* (New York, 1967), 83–87. For the equally vital distinction between the probable and the plausible, see Jacques Barzun and Henry Graff, *The Modern Researcher*, 3d ed. (New York, 1977), 125–46, esp. 133.

ments interest us profoundly. Intuition does not offer any form of guarantee that we are sharing anything; analogical criticism asks us above all to acquiesce in the analogy; but a historical reading can draw on what has become a considerable mass of studies on medieval habits and society. I have only scratched the surface of that mass, and yet in the preceding pages the constraints of terrain, time, and physical strength, the practicality of vows and hardihood have easily taken the place of assumptions and intuitions about personality and honor in the *Song of Roland*. The substitution allows parts of the work to be analyzed as functional where traditionally they were hardly analyzed at all. On the other hand, to posit a historical context and characterize a likely medieval audience does not solve all our problems.

It is essential for us to use the medieval predicate of meaning—to speak of "What the *Song* meant to a medieval audience"—but that is not entirely adequate. There is every reason to think that there were multiple meanings for real medieval people just as for us. One thinks of the heresies described by Stock, of the fourteenth-century disagreements about the *Roman de la Rose*, of clerical condemnations of apparently rather orthodox romances, or, more immediately, of the medieval remakers of the Roland legend, who gave parts of it length and complexity of a sort it does not have in the Oxford version and probably did not have in the *remanieurs'* models. One may even imagine, and not idly, that there were medieval hearers who sympathized with Ganelon and felt he was entitled to wipe the rear guard out.

In this sense we may still teach and describe more than one *Song of Roland*, within certain limits: a monastic one condemning the sin of pride in one or more characters; an individualistic one defending Ganelon's right to put personal interest above the group's; a monarchical one wherein Charlemagne's court in the *Song* is identified with the kingship of Louis VI or Louis VII of France. All we need to do, it would seem, is posit an audience that would most likely have heard the work as we wish to describe it, and then speak from that audience's vantage point.

The risk is that the interpreter will attempt (in Robert Crosman's words) "to impose on modern readers responses [the critic] is not certain of being able to persuade them to adopt on the evidence of their own reading of the text."[12] It is not enough to posit a likely past

[12]Robert Crosman, "Some Doubts about 'the Reader of *Paradise Lost*,'" cited by W. Daniel Wilson, "Readers in Texts," *PMLA*, 96 (1981), 857. The "fallacy of the homogeneous past" is discussed by Hirsch, 40–41. It is perhaps the error of which Joseph Duggan would accuse Brault; see Duggan's review of Brault's *Song* in *Speculum*, 56 (1981), 355–58.

community or "homogeneous past" and then derive statements about the text's meaning from the characteristics of that community rather than from the text's content and procedures directly. Here another theoretical concept comes to our aid: that of the "implied reader" (here, "implied audience"), which allows us to pay close attention to the text's allusions and to how the narration unfolds, without requiring us to abandon our curiosity about how the work was perceived in the Middle Ages.

The implied reader or audience is neither a hypothetical extratextual construct nor a real audience, but a feature of the text. In W. Daniel Wilson's handy definition, it is "the behavior, attitudes and background—presupposed or defined, usually indirectly, in the text itself—necessary for a proper understanding of the text."[13] A literary work will not always exhibit an imaginary reader (Wilson's "characterized fictive reader") to whom the narrator actually speaks. It is well known that narratorial asides are rare in the *Song of Roland,* although they do occur. But a text will always have an audience whose anticipated reaction guides the author.[14] That implied audience's characteristics will be discernible from the way the text goes about informing it—or not informing it—of things it needs to know in order to understand: in the Oxford text, the pagans' intentions at the outset, the dangers of the Pass of Cize, or the wording and results of Roland's promises, of Turpin's, or of Chernuble's.

The concept of implied audience is rooted in the study of literature as communication, not just in literary phenomenology. By definition, the implied audience of the *Song of Roland* is that with which it communicates fully and effectively; by inference, it is those hearers for whom it was designed. In my example above, a real reader sympathetic to Ganelon must consider what the text asks of the implied audience when it shows an angel guiding his accuser's hand. The angel's presence implies a religion, and his act implies a judgment. "An interpretation of the implied or intended reader's role in a work must aim at what the author intended (in a wider sense) to communicate, and historical circumstances will condition this intention," says Wilson.[15] On the other hand, the implied audience is, again, a formal

[13]Wilson, 848; I will follow here Wilson's useful summary and definitions. Reference to the medieval audience (a collectivity, not an individual) is inevitably clumsy in this context, but I have retained the term where it seems appropriate, even though "member of the audience" or "hearer" might be more accurate at times. One way of framing the question of interpretation, then, is to ask which points a medieval audience would have recognized and recalled as salient as the Oxford story unfolded.

[14]Ibid., 851–52.

[15]Ibid., 851.

feature of the text in that its state of knowledge about events is what the narrative communicates. (This is one of the ways in which it may differ from any real audiences that had heard a *Song of Roland* more than once.) To concentrate on it is to give ourselves the advantage of not having to postulate, as sole guides to a historical reading, either an author about whom we know nothing specific or an audience about whose actual composition we are ill-informed. We may rely instead, as we would in any reading, on observations and inductions.

A glance at my Commentary will show that what I have referred to as "the hearers" or even as "we" is often the implied audience, not a hypothetical one reading the *Song of Roland* through Freudian, structuralist, or even Augustinian categories. I consider the limitation an important one in the first stages of choosing a reading. It would be possible, though burdensome, to show that *Roland* criticism has at times shifted from the implied or intended audiences to hypothetical real ones and back for reasons of convenience. But when we have deliberately described what we think was the implied audience of the *Song,* it has not always been incongruous with the probable real one. The implied audience of which the text informs us is only a clue, "no more authoritative and restrictive on our own right to establish a new interpretation than other aspects of a work are."[16] But it is an important, even irreplaceable, clue to the existence of a definable group with which the author worked to communicate—a "most likely medieval audience," or a historical interpretive community, as we might put it with Stanley Fish's terms in mind.

Observation of the Oxford text then leads us to a picture of the audience, implied and probably real, that is not unfamiliar, since we have at least partly been guided by the text's implications all along. To judge by what the *Song* talks about overtly, its audience was knowledgeable about feudal practices; anyone who can follow the text's feudal allusions will also have certain historically real knowledge of the system that is its setting. I will also reason, in Chapter 5, from the presupposition that the audience was not only conversant with the rules of society but also interested in them, that is, that the poem did not bore its intended audience. (This assumption, a safe one in the case of the *Roland,* is coming to be acceptable for a growing number of other medieval texts, as indeed it should be.) Furthermore, on similar grounds, the implied audience grasps Christian eschatology, is comfortable with formulaic style, and is familiar with campaigning and fighting on horseback and on foot. Its interests do not seem, on the

[16]Ibid., 858.

face of things, to be primarily ecclesiological—another old observation—but it is neither pagan nor German nor even Carolingian. In short, the implied audience has interests a great deal like those that many of the Oxford redactor's contemporaries had: the needs of feudal society suffice to explain them. And—if we accept the account of its knowledge and likely reactions that I have given in the Commentary—the implied audience is not hostile to didactic concerns, any more than many real contemporaries of the Digby redactor were.

Gerard Brault has already argued at length that the numerous restatements of the traditional interpretation "fail to do justice to the poem's religious dimension or misconstrue its techniques of character portrayal,"[17] and I do not intend to attempt gleaning after him in the fields of iconographical or exegetical analysis. But I believe that one need not acquiesce entirely in Brault's postulate of a conflict between "Christian" and "feudal" values in this masterwork from an age notorious for its disinclination to separate religion from daily life. Thus, without any desire to minimize the importance of the religious atmosphere that is so clearly a major aspect of the poem, I have preferred to apply my curiosity principally to the nominally secular questions of responsibility, to the matters of government and social principle that furnish the immediate setting of the action. For convenience, I have called the set of relationships involved "feudal," though there is no great uniformity among scholars—especially literary scholars—in the use of that term. I understand by it the system of vassal and lord, of homage and mutual service, discussed more fully in Chapters 5 and 6.

The structural key to the Roncevaux episode is the relationship, through time, between promises and their accomplishment. (This is the general burden of Chapters 2 and 3 in this part.) Roland's promises are qualified ones, and their context is broader than the battle of Roncevaux. These facts, though not always appreciated, are essential. Roland carries out his promises as qualified, while his enemies neither limit theirs nor succeed in fulfilling them. There is little to be gained by contorting these elements of the text, or ignoring them, for the sake of a scholarly doctrine of heroic pride. Personal pride—even if Roland did exhibit such pride—would be irrelevant to the theme of responsibility and sacrifice in a context of promises and ensuing, related acts.

"The problem of vassaldom is at the very heart of the *Chanson de Roland*."[18] The construction of the work—Roland's context as a char-

[17]Brault, *Song of Roland*, 1:xiii.
[18]Dufournet, 142.

acter—has the highest possible likelihood of resonance with a larger context, that of a relatively early medieval society in which the oral vow, homage and its analogues, represented the knight's primary way of shaping the future. This resonance (treated primarily in Chapters 4 and 5) requires even more thorough consideration than *Roland* criticism has already given it. This is not to say that Roland, Oliver, and Aude "do not have" a psychology. Any human action can probably be described in the terms psychologists use. But the *Song*'s structure cannot be deduced from psychological categories, for the *Song of Roland* is not a drama of personalities. It is a drama of the sworn word. It exalts neither a nation nor a religion so much as the power and efficaciousness of faith: faith in the bonds of promises kept, between persons and God, of course, but also among persons.

Feudal ideas have been associated with the *Song of Roland* for a long time,[19] but to apply them in a systematic inquiry into its meaning is another matter. Breadth of definition is a strength rather than a weakness here, as I will argue in Chapter 5, since we cannot discern precisely when or where the *Song of Roland* took shape. Various forces coexisted uneasily within feudal society, throughout the period of the *Roland* and far beyond it, and we tend to emphasize the tension where we might with equal accuracy emphasize the coexistence.

Feudalism, as it pertains to literary interpretation, is a strong tendency for people who lived together under a common general arrangement to take the argument as natural. It is very much like what most historians now recognize as a "mentality" (or set of shared attitudes)[20] Any such set of attitudes will probably contain some profound contradictions, but experience, and numerous studies, show that the contradictions do not prevent the mentality from functioning—it, rather than some radically different system, will most likely occur even to highly intelligent and thoughtful people as a point of reference. Such a tendency of thought may manifest itself in literature in quite general terms.

That a mentality of reference, despite the great strength of its original appeal, may have lost the favor it once enjoyed is axiomatic in

[19]The most cogent discussion of this is by John Benton, "Nostre franceis n'unt talent de fuïr: The *Song of Roland* and the Enculturation of a Warrior Class," *Olifant,* 6 (1979), 237–58.

[20]For discussion and summary definitions, see Georges Duby, "L'Histoire des mentalités," in Charles Samaran, ed., *L'Histoire et ses méthodes* (Paris, 1961), esp. "L'Outillage mental," 952–57; Philippe Ariès, "L'Histoire des mentalités," in Jacques Le Goff, ed., *La Nouvelle Histoire* (Paris, 1978), 402–3; Jacques Le Goff, "Les Mentalités: Une Histoire ambigüe," in J. Le Goff and Pierre Nora, eds., *Faire de l'Histoire* (Paris, 1974), 3:76–94.

the history of ideas, but we have been slow in applying that insight to the study of *belles lettres.* Medieval ways of conceiving and idealizing a set of relations among people are surely as vital an element of "alterity" as are medieval genres or styles of composition. And (to borrow R. S. Crane's terms) they affect the "pre-constructional" and "constructional" phases of poetics as well as the "post-constructional" ones.[21]

At this point, the problem of reading for meaning overlaps with questions of history. The fact that the *Song of Roland* does not say explicitly how its parts are related to its themes does not mean that its construction is loose or confused. Many of the questions that arise as we read it can be answered by information about its historical setting. That is an obvious alternative to the postulate that the *Song* is an unclear or ambiguous work. Yet numerous critics have chosen to follow another tradition of explanation, that exemplified by Erich Auerbach's well-known claim that the paratactic line or sentence structure of the *Song* is mirrored in a mystifying absence of logic in the story itself. Paul Zumthor offers a convenient summary:

> Opposition between the stripped-down precision of the utterance, and what appears to be a lack of clarity on the plane of narrative causality, an ambiguity deriving from the uncertainty into which the hearer is plunged: which of the previous propositions gives rise to the one now being heard? Perhaps the order of causality and implication is reversed: because Roland must be avenged, he dies; because he is to die, he must be betrayed. The text can be understood only imperfectly, or not at all.[22]

This expresses both a hermeneutic stance and an aesthetic position. In the atmosphere created by such presuppositions, the characters' hidden motives and unspoken thoughts may come to seem as important as anything they actually say or do. The protagonists are seen as

[21]See R. S. Crane, *Critical and Historical Principles of Literary History* (Chicago, 1971), 11, and W. D. Wilson's remarks on the relationship between author and "implied audience" (p. 851).

[22]Paul Zumthor, *Essai de poétique médiévale* (Paris, 1972), 337. "*La Chanson de Roland* . . . is, on the political and psychological levels, a far more sophisticated, ambiguous work than, say, Auerbach would want us to believe," says Calin, 437. For further statements on the text's ambiguity, see, e.g., Frederick Whitehead, "L'Ambiguïté de Roland," *Studi in onore di Italo Siciliano* (Florence, 1966), 1203–12; R. A. Hall, Jr., "The Individual in Relation to His Society: *The Chanson de Roland*," in *Cultural Symbolism in Literature* (Ithaca, N.Y., 1963), 17–32. For Evelyn Birge Vitz, however, the poem is coherent on the level of narrative syntax or "plot in comprehensible human terms," despite features that undermine the "ontological solidity" of causality; see her "Desire and Causality in Medieval Narrative," *Romanic Review*, 71 (1980), esp. 222–23.

vehicles of a kind of complexity, even ambiguity, whose evocation lends the work a misleading air of aesthetic familiarity. Guesses about what Roland, Charlemagne, or Ganelon is thinking (when the *Song* does not say) may then replace scrutiny of sequence and juxtaposition, cause and effect as instruments for understanding it.[23] To analyze the *Song of Roland* has long meant assuming (as Auerbach in fact did; see Chapter 4) that uncertainty about circumstances is a real feature of the narrative, and one that any implied audience may presumably be expected to accept. On the other hand, arguments against incoherence and for the work's unity of structure have been made primarily in terms of psychological categories—Roland the proud (or, in Roger Pensom's terms, the neurotic), Oliver the wise, Charles the weak—rather than by reference to the situations the characters are in and to the potential for constraint those situations involve.

Furthermore, the reluctance to explore allusions to the situation, and the appeal to assumptions about the psychology of the characters, are intertwined with each other and with the *démesure* theory in the history of *Roland* interpretations, since any of the three can serve as a postulate apparently authorizing the other two. Whatever in the text does not match the requirements of the received interpretation can be laid to the incoherence of the narration. Concern for cause and effect can be transferred to the realm of character study. The three ideas of incoherence, psychological deduction, and foolish pride work together to make empirical, inductive, close reading seem either unnecessary, or unlikely to give significant results. For these and other

[23]Paulin Paris insisted early that the characters were consistent, and he stated their importance for interpretation ("Roncevaux," *Histoire littéraire de la France,* 22 [1852], 740). Cf. Le Gentil, *Song,* 82; "[the] lives of the principal characters . . . are psychologically intense lives" (Horrent, *Chanson de Roland et geste de Charlemagne,* 7); "emotions hidden beneath the [political] surface . . . never come directly into view" (Calin, 20). For surmises about the hidden thoughts or intentions of the characters, see, among many others, Bédier, *Légendes,* 3:418ff.; Siciliano, 334, 347, 352; Boatner, 577, 579; Crosland, 75–76, 78–79, 81, and passim; Faral, *Chanson,* 94–95; Burger, "Deux Scènes," 114–15, 122; Donohoe, 252–53; Foulet, in Bédier, *Chanson de Roland commentée,* 148; Pensom, 78, 80, 85, 98 (but cf. 99), 104, 131, and esp. 132ff.; Stranges, 338–39, 344, 365; Brault, *Song,* 1:110, 129, 133, 322 (the Franks), 141 (Blancandrin), 152 (Marsile), 160 (Roland), 168 (Charles). D. W. Robertson protested energetically against the assignment of psychological motivations to the characters (*Preface to Chaucer,* 162–71). Cf. Battaglia, 356; Goldin, "Die Rolle Ganelons," 134–35; Crist, 17, "[Roland] has no autonomous mental processes." Hunt also states the position I prefer: "The 'exposition' of the *Roland* consists of a chain of reactions to what is openly *said:* it is not a revelation of character" ("Character and Causality," 32). Hunt does not eschew surmise entirely (cf. pp. 8, 14, 19, and 22 of the same article), but his remarks on pp. 11–12 are questions rather than guesses.

reasons, there has never been a full-dress exposition of the *Song* from the vantage point of its likely historical setting—even in the simplified form I have adopted here. On the contrary, its place in history has usually been assigned on the basis of the often-repeated *démesure* hypothesis.

In other words, the interpretations found in the secondary literature of medieval studies are borrowed for use in other contexts *as though* their referents were historical. The use of imaginative literature as a tool for exploration of the past is a well-known tenet of the "*Annales* school," as Calin has recently recalled;[24] thus it is no surprise that, let us say, Philippe Ariès gives a particular interpretation of the *Song of Roland* status as an element of medieval culture. "The death of Roland," he says, "became the death of the saint" and was so regarded "by the clergy as well as the laity."[25] Neither is it especially surprising that Philippe Contamine can state that "the notions of sacrifice, and absolute devotion, seem alien to medieval mentality,"[26] although when he does so he is taking an implicit stance (perhaps unintentionally) against sacrifice as the rear guard's reason for dying at Roncevaux.

In an older but equally famous study, J. H. Randall adopted the *démesure* convention as an important element in his summary of premodern civilization. At the same time, he repeated the incompatible but equally traditional description of Roland as *bon vassal:*

> The knight was first and last a warrior. Hence valor, personal and physical, was his prime quality. The reckless courage of Roland, who from pride and confidence refused to blow his mighty war-horn for Charlemagne when the Moors ambushed the rear guard of the Frankish army, and thus doomed his fellows to destruction, had its counterpart in many of the great fighters, like Godfrey of Bouillon and Richard the Lion-Hearted; it was forever making impossible anything like sound military tactics. . . . Of equal importance was loyalty; for the performance of the numerous vows of medieval society, the very structure of feudal obligations, depended upon it. . . . Roland expresses this feudal loyalty admirably as he goes into battle.[27]

[24]Calin, 13.

[25]Ariès adds various statements on the meaning of details: "[Roland] does not have a single thought for Aude, his betrothed, who falls dead when she learns of his cruel end, nor for his fleshly parents" (*The Hour of Our Death,* trans. Helen Weaver [New York, 1981], 5, 14; cf. 143–46, 213).

[26]Contamine, 255.

[27]J. R. Randall, *The Making of the Modern Mind,* 2d ed. (1940; reprint ed., New York, 1976), 85–86.

Here Randall has in effect attributed literary *démesure* to a pair of Crusaders (one of whom may have shown it, one of whom, Godfrey, almost certainly did not). And so it is that the early Romanists' descriptions of literary texts find strong echoes in such diverse publications as the *Annales,* the *Dictionnaire de théologie catholique,* and Ezra Pound's *Spirit of Romance.*[28] In similar fashion but in a more literary context, Georges Duby and Erich Köhler have integrated accepted notions of courtly love into their discussions of twelfth-century French society.[29] "All critical schools adopt in practice, without question, the findings of literary history," says Goulemot.[30] He does not explicitly include interpretation in his definition of literary history (borrowed from Raymond Picard), but observation shows that literary historians rarely eschew interpretation, indeed probably cannot. In the context of their statements about authors' ideas, biographies, and achievements, their interpretations tend strongly to be passed on, as part and parcel of the history.

To reread the *Song of Roland* means to apply systematically the hypothesis that Roland may be strikingly right in what he does and says, even where that is not immediately clear. This heroic hypothesis of interpretation assumes the text is largely coherent and that it presents information about events that orients our reading, though inconsistencies may seem to occur or have habitually been posited in it. In other words, like its predecessor, the reading of the *Song* as exemplary is a tendentious reading. We may thank hermeneutic criticism for reminding us that tendentiousness is not some avoidable defect, but a feature common to all readings, at least all those that seek coherence in sequential narratives.[31] The question is which tendency of reading is most consistent with the contents of the text. In the case of a tale devised for an audience from a lost culture, we must ask

[28]For the *Annales,* see the following note; for the *Dictionnaire,* see L. Salembier's bitter denunciation of the *Roman de la Rose* in his article "Jean Gerson" (6:1324). Like Randall, Pound repeats the *démesure* hypothesis: the "bombastic" Roland, "splendid and absurd," is "Galliffet at Strasbourg," and he falls victim "not to the treachery of Ganelon, but to that pride which forbade him to sound the horn for aid" (Ezra Pound, *The Spirit of Romance* [New York, 1910], 74–75, 77).

[29]See Duby, "Dans la France du Nord-ouest au XIIe siècle"; Erich Köhler, "Observations historiques et sociologiques sur la poésie des troubadours," *Cahiers de civilisation médiévale,* 7 (1962), 27–51; and cf. Evelyne Patlagean on Köhler in Jacques Le Goff, ed., *La Nouvelle Histoire,* 257.

[30]Jean-Marie Goulemot, "Histoire littéraire," in Le Goff, *La Nouvelle Histoire,* 309.

[31]See the discussion of historical interpretation and criticism in Gadamer, *Truth and Method,* 258–74; David Linge's introduction to Gadamer *Philosophical Hermeneutics* (Berkeley and Los Angeles, 1976), xvi; and David C. Hoy, *The Critical Circle* (Berkeley and Los Angeles, 1978), esp. 141–46.

which tendency matches what can be known of the context in which the tale was designed to be heard. The answers to those questions are supplied by public testing of coherent readings that can claim a basis in the text and also in what we know of its times.[32]

My analysis does not, I have said, seek to apply any special method, but it does make some claims about the poem's content and its implications that have not been made frequently. A few words about the assumptions behind them are in order. I began with the suspicion, aroused by the work of Alberto Del Monte, Alfred Foulet, Gerard Brault, L. S. Crist, Norman Cartier, Emanuel Mickel, and William Kibler, that what is at stake in the *Song of Roland* is not persons and their short-term survival but a social system or set of ideas about society, thought to transcend immediate personal concerns. Rather than seek to explain *why* Roland would boast, or would pursue a course leading to an incomprehensible death, I have tried to show the important senses in which those things do not occur at all in the text. Arguments to that effect may seem forced or conjectural unless we distance ourselves from the secondary literature and take the measure of *démesure* in the poem.

That, in turn, requires us to remember that the *démesure* interpretation is itself a hypothesis, not an argument, and has a traceable history. It was affirmed very early without extensive confrontation with the text. Early specialist reports—those of Paulin Paris, Léon Gautier, Gaston Paris, and Louis Petit de Julleville—make roughly identical claims about the work's import and Roland's place in it, but they cite only isolated lines and psychological surmises as evidence. The ubiquity of the interpretive hypothesis of Roland's pride hides the fact that throughout the better part of the nineteenth century it was purveyed by authors who never thought to test it against any alternatives. By the twentieth century, the hypothesis seems to have been considered as having been established at some earlier time. It is assumed, as a basis for deductions and arguments, in the fuller analytical work of Bédier and Menéndez Pidal. Both the hypothesis and the confidence with which it is repeated lead us to expect elements in the poem—exaggerated claims, missed opportunities—whose presence is not revealed by close reading.

Upon examination, the poem appears neither to exalt heedlessness nor to express a grudging acceptance of it. The heroes often criticized

[32]I like to think that a reading capable of passing such tests could also be a "valid" reading according to the tests recently proposed by Armstrong (inclusiveness, "intersubjectivity," and efficacy or fruitfulness); see Paul Armstrong, "The Conflict of Interpretations and the Limits of Pluralism," *PMLA*, 98 (1983), 341–52.

for presumed errors are in fact, and in context, aware and foresighted, as leadership in any age requires. Neither Roland nor Charles is marked by any fatal flaw. But they are marked by their places in the story and in a fairly well known, historically localized structure of leadership. If Roland and Charles do not act to prevent Roncevaux, it is because their freedom to act is limited by military and political reality. There cannot be an immediate, iron-clad demonstration of this, less because society in a large sense has nothing to do with narrative literature than because there is no eleventh-century handbook of procedure—civil or military—with which the *Song of Roland* might be compared in detail. What I can do is examine the text for congruency with the feudal system as I understand it as a nonspecialist—through the general works of Frédéric Ganshof, Marc Bloch, Georges Duby, Jean-François Lemarignier, David Herlihy, Joseph Strayer, and others. In so doing, I use such terms as *rules* or *principles* in the looser senses applicable to historical feudalism as those authors describe it. These tendencies of thought stand as points of reference for reading the poem. They occupy the place usually occupied by broad claims about human psychology as a universe, or about the protagonists' own characters, which in my view are not givens but points at issue. I have tried to limit my assumptions to the nearly obvious, and my deductions to those that allow for a consensus of informed readers. Though I cannot speak with the authority of an institutional historian, I am convinced that a reading more closely related to feudal ideals is one that offers better textual and historical credentials than the *démesure* hypothesis can show. That is, in sum, a recognition that the latter reading had its own assumptions (Roland's autonomy in the field, the mutability of his promises, and the finality of his death, for example) and that these may be found anachronistic not merely in the abstract but in comparison with the text we know, the situations it contains, and the ideas it names.

The many forms and manifestations of the *démesure* hypothesis make testing it a particularly complex task. The idea that Roland causes a disaster at Roncevaux through self-destructive error is one of the oldest ideas in medieval literary studies. The tragic error is implicit in the summary Francisque Michel gave of the poem when he first published it in 1837: "The most prominent hero is Roland, who, through the advice he gives Charlemagne, brings about Ganelon's betrayal, his own death, and that of the twelve peers at Roncevaux."[33]

[33]Francisque Michel, *La Chanson de Roland ou de Roncevaux* (Paris, 1837), xi. On Roland's presumed responsibility (or guilt) for his own death and that of others, see,

The idea is made explicit at least as early as Gaston Paris's *Histoire poétique de Charlemagne* (1865): "[Oliver] asks Roland to sound his ivory horn.... Roland refuses out of an exaggerated sense of honor."[34] In Louis Petit de Julleville's edition (1878), it has taken on something like its modern form: "Roland destroys the entire rear guard, and himself, at Roncevaux, through his foolish obstinacy.... [Such flaws] lend his character [the effect of] life and truth."[35] Having attained the status of a given in *Roland* scholarship early on, the tragic principle of interpretation has served for generations as an element of argumentation or proof in studies on the poem's origins, poetics, politics, and genre. Now that *démesure* itself has come under occasional attack, it is not surprising that the aesthetic and historical arguments that *démesure* helped establish long ago are sometimes invoked themselves as givens that make it inevitable. This network of interdependent arguments in various areas makes the *Song of Roland* both a strikingly illustrative work to interpret correctly and a burdensome work to treat with anything approaching thoroughness.

Under most circumstances a summary or paraphrase of the *Song of Roland* would stand or fall virtually alone, depending on whether it is accurate, complete, and respectful of historical context. But to establish a reading where another, very different one has long been accepted and is so thoroughly enmeshed in a vast secondary literature is a more problematic business. To say practically anything about the *Song of Roland* is to repeat someone and to contradict someone else. To say anything about its content, organization, and meaning, in the context of such a complex set of critical reactions, is to imply some stance on its origins, its intended audience, their literary and social mores and outs, and so on. Heroism, obviously, and the feudal system, less obviously, have aesthetic standing, and their very importance in the *Song* can thus be denied on grounds that appear to override history. Merely to consider them is to raise the general question of how reactions are related to the text. It is incumbent upon the reinterpreter not only to state what lies behind the new reading but to explore the implications of his conclusions. Hence some closing arguments (Chapters 7

---

e.g., Vance, *Reading,* 3 ("his decision causes the destruction of all Charles's most beloved vassals"); Donohoe, 259 ("[Roland's] insufferable pride is the real underlying cause of the tragic occurrence"); Le Gentil, "A propos de la *démesure,*" 203; Van Emden, "Guarant," 31; Scully, 229; Siciliano, 348 ("the single responsible party"); Brault, "*Sapientia,*" 108; Hall, "Ganelon and Roland," 266n.; Stranges, 333; Kirsch, 390; Whitehead, 1206–11. But cf. Uitti, 112 ("Ganelon, not Roland, is guilty of the massacre").

[34] 2d ed., Paris, 1905; Reprinted ed. 1974. Quotation from p. 273.

[35] Petit de Julleville, *Chanson de Roland,* 59.

and 8) to the effect that the *Song of Roland,* as it is described here, deserves all our efforts of understanding and explanation.

I cannot pursue all the threads of this tangled skein to final conclusions, but it will be clear to anyone interested in any of the broader questions I have referred to that I would be remiss in my duty as an interpreter if I gave them short shrift. The reading is its own best argument, even if it cannot quite stand alone. Nonetheless, in the vast body of criticism specifically devoted to the *Roland,* there are elements that clearly must be treated in greater detail. Two aspects of the text need particular attention, following these general remarks on how the poem's structure, hero, and themes have usually been presented. One aspect is the structure itself, the other is the characters as they manifest themselves within it. I will discuss them in that order (though the separation of the two is artificial) before going on to the work's themes, to the question of its coherence, to its historical and social setting, and to some of the problems of reading and response that the discussion will raise.

[2]

Démesure and Choice

One purpose of the foregoing Commentary on the *Song of Roland* is to establish the importance of several neglected elements in the *Song;* another is to state the functions of several better-known features. I have had in mind to account for the very presence of these textual events, to explain why they occur where they do, and to suggest how they are related to a central theme of duty and sacrifice. Let me cite the following elements in particular:

The references to the murder of Basan and Basile (see the commentary on laisses 14–15, 24, and 37)
Charles's insistence on a specific hostage (laisse 37)
The discrepancy between Ganelon's oral version of Charles's message to Marsile and the version in Charles's letter (laisses 33–37)
Ganelon's lies to Marsile about the import of his mission, and to Charles about the drowning of the *algalife* (laisses 33, 36, 54)
The call for a rear guard (laisses 58–66)
Charles's condemnation of Ganelon (laisse 58)
Roland's first promises and his insistence on a fairly small force (laisses 59, 60, 63)
Gautier del Hum's assignment (laisse 65)
The pagan boasts (laisses 69–78)
Oliver's trip to the top of a hill (laisses 80–81)
The deaths of the pagan peers in the first encounter at Roncevaux (laisses 93–104)
The suddenness with which Charles acts upon hearing the horn (laisses 133–38)

The blow Oliver strikes Roland (laisse 149)
Gautir del Hum's abrupt appearance at Roncevaux (laisse 152)
The nomination and deeds of Rabel and Guineman (laisses 217, 241–42)
The stark manner of Aude's death (laisses 268–69)
Thierry's and Charles's speeches at Ganelon's trial, and Thierry's unlikely victory (laisses 270–86)

These elements of overt content have never been combined as I have combined them, even in recent defenses of Roland's character. Several of them have gone nearly unmentioned in studies on the *Song* and its interpretation. Nevertheless, their unfamiliarity as guides to reading the poem may result from scholarly habit and does not necessarily indicate that they are inherently negligible. It is difficult to reconcile their presence with, for example, Bédier's description of the poem as dominated by "the character of Roland alone," or with the idea that the *Song* is unified by (let us say) the *fortitudo-sapientia* topos.[1] But in the poem as I have paraphrased it in my Commentary, these events have a clear function. They serve to illustrate or to support the idea that the consequences of a feudal leader's choices are more significant than individual survival in the short term. Charles and Roland are both aware of what is happening around them, but when offered the opportunity to counter the arbitrary onslaught of fate and treachery with an equally arbitrary suspension of feudal principle, both refuse. Aude, Thierry, and Gautier, each in an appropriate way, echo this attachment to something beyond the immediate; even Rabel and Guineman do their best to support it. Oliver, Ganelon, and the barons in council are temporary obstacles to such commitment. The pagans show no signs of knowing about it at all. Applying these principles of reading (structural only in a very simple sense) means replacing the *démesure* hypothesis as a whole. To make clear why that is so, it will be necessary to sum up some of the features and assumptions of the latter.

The *démesure* theory has taken on various nuances over the course of time, but its essence remains a condemnation of Roland.[2] I do not

[1]Much perceptive work on the interpretation of the *Song* is vitiated by the failure to examine such presuppositions. The *fortitudo-sapientia* topos was first put forward as an explanation by Ernst Robert Curtius ("Zur Literarästhetik des Mittelalters, II," *Zeitschrift für romanische Philologie*, 58 [1938], 199–206, 225–28) and recurs in his famous *European Literature and the Latin Middle Ages* (1948; Eng. ed., New York, 1953; reprint ed., New York, 1963), 173–79.

[2]One may begin with the following selection of examples from various periods and types of studies. Paulin Paris, 741, spoke of "the blind contempt for danger that stands

need to go into any great detail about its various forms here, for statements of it are very widely available.[3] It is still the only explanation of the *Roland* to be found in textbooks, general introductions to the *Song* (except Brault's), translators' prefaces (except Goldin's and Harrison's), and general histories of medieval culture, and it is virtually the only interpretation known to nonspecialists. Elements of it appear in isolation in many works not concerned with the problem of interpretation in itself—in far too many for systematic discussion or even listing here.

The hypothesis runs like this. Roland dies and the men entrusted to his leadership are lost, because his pride leads him to make an error. His prowess is, then, fatally tainted either by *hamartia* or by *hubris,* sometimes equated with *superbia,* the medieval sin of pride. He is (still according to the hypothesis) the source of discord in the army and an obstacle to peace. *Démesure,* it has been pointed out, is a concept not named in the *Roland* text. (The adverb *desmesureement* in line 1425 describes the falling of heavy rain and hail.) As applied to Roland in critical usage, it is the Modern French word, with implications of deliberate and characteristic exaggeration.[4] Owen's definition of the

---

revealed in every word and every act of Charles's nephew," and Gaston Paris spoke of "heroic folly, of the sort one often encounters in France's military history" (*Extraits,* 75); Curtius spoke of "the foolhardy hero" and of "hubris" ("Uber die altfranzösische Epik," *Zeitschrift für romanische Philologie,* 64 [1944], 283); Gustav Gröber spoke of Roland's "youthful impetuousity, certain of victory" (*Grundriss der romanischen Philologie,* vol. 2, part 1 [Strasbourg, 1893], 464); Cesare Segre spoke of his "total confidence in his own strength" (*La Tradizione della Chanson de Roland* [Milan and Naples, 1974], 10). See also Del Monte's summary, 225; Bédier, *Légendes,* 3:431, 440–42; Faral, *Chanson,* 230; Calin, 23; Owen, "Secular Inspiration," 390, 394; Le Gentil, *Song,* 87, 106, 108; Jones, *Ethos,* 173–88, and "Lament," 14; Pauphilet, *Legs,* 73; Donohoe, 255–56.

[3]*Démesure* is given perhaps its most moving presentation in Le Gentil, *Song,* 82–89, 103–10. Payen implied that the old theory could not stand, but he did not argue the point systematically (see Payen, *Le Motif du repentir,* 108–37).

[4]See Le Gentil, "A propos de la *démesure,*" 203, 208 ("the word is too strong"; yet "there is something pernicious in the way his good qualities are pushed to extremes" [*dans l'excès même de ses qualités*]). It is difficult to know whether an eleventh-century person would have found *desmesure* a strong word, but *démesure* has been given the strongest possible pejorative value by nineteenth- and twentieth-century critics. Hence, surely, the attempts to distinguish "good" and "bad" pride, *fierté* and *orgueil,* in the text; see Kibler, "Roland's Pride," 147, 149, 150 (the word *orgueil* is frequent but is not applied to Roland by reliable characters); Jones, *Ethos,* 65–69, 175–77 (compares him, significantly, to Shakespeare's young Henry V; Gérard, 448, makes the comparison with Hotspur). As Foulet points out, Bédier did not use the word *démesure* (Alfred Foulet, "Is Roland Guilty?" 146n.). Gaston Paris did, however: "the hero's error . . . his *desmesure,* in Old French . . . a word which translates perfectly the Homeric idea of *hubris*" (G. Paris, *Extraits,* 75).

The notion takes on extreme forms in later criticism: Roland is "the prideful man punished by his own excess" (Siciliano, 351); he is "obviously wrong-headed in his

hero's fault is a relatively sympathetic formulation: "Roland was guilty of the sin of *démesure,* which is the pursuance of proper ends in an outrageously exaggerated way. . . . Perhaps it is a virtue exercised in so extreme a fashion as to become a sin."[5] Renoir's definition is less so: "The hero in the power of *desmesure* thinks his most outrageous acts perfectly normal and justified."[6] Le Gentil's original definition (later modified) even had eschatological overtones: "this failing is the one that our early authors condemn under the name of *démesure*: it is, first, opposition to reason, then a rejection of the human condition, or even a revolt of the created being against God."[7] Nevertheless, the word *desmesure* has not been found in those few French texts surviving from around the year 1100. Oliver's word *mesure* (1725) is compared with "foolishness" or "recklessness," *estultie,* which is neither revolt nor sin. But criticism has clearly gone well beyond Oliver. Roland (we are sometimes told) cannot understand the situation. He does not know his own limits; he expects, against all logic, to defeat his enemies then and there; he has an unrealistic concept of honor. His thirst for battle makes him not only morally blind but also technically incompetent. The men for whom he is responsible are utterly destroyed because his pride will not let him make the simple gesture of leadership, the horn-call, that would have saved them. The tragedy is avoidable; Roland causes it both proximately (he is too proud to admit help is needed and immediately available) and originally (by insulting Ganelon and turning him against his own comrades). He puts his own army and its mission at risk.[8] It is, further, in precisely such ways that he represents an entire nationality or historical period.[9]

---

attitude to the clear facts" (Van Emden, "Pro Karolo Magno," 177, n. 5); his pride prevents God's intervention on his behalf (Burger, "Deux Scènes," 124); his pride is "a spiritual distortion that makes black appear white" (Boatner, 575); "the world exists to be subjugated by his sword" (Donohoe, 259); lucidity "is totally foreign to Roland's nature" (Calin, 23); Owen, "Secular Inspiration," 394; Van Emden, "Guarant," n. 66. Some of these statements stem from a natural tendency to enliven one's prose; other motives are suggested in Chapter 7, below. Renoir too hastily identifies Oliver's presumed *mesure* with the later German courtly concept (Renoir, "Roland's Lament," 577 and n. 10).

[5]Owen, *Song,* 20.

[6]Renoir, "Roland's Lament," 577.

[7]Le Gentil, *Chanson* (1955), 124.

[8]"Roland . . . scorns all forms of prudence. It would be one thing if he were risking only himself, but he endangers the Frankish elite and the holy cause that the entire army is in Spain to defend" (Le Gentil, "A propos de la *démesure,*" 204; cf. note 2 to Chapter 1, above); Roland "pays excessive heed to feudal and family honor . . . endangers the sacred mission" (Calin, 19). See also Gérard, 451; Vance, *Reading,* 3.

[9]Le Gentil, *Song,* 106–7; Kibler, "Roland's Pride," 152, 156–57; Petit de Julleville, 58, 67; Jones, *Ethos,* passim. Gaston Paris, *Extraits,* 75, compares Roncevaux to the

But while the *démesure* hypothesis has often been presented, the numerous corollaries it requires have rarely been discussed. They appear to include these ideas: that honor is a strictly personal matter and an irrational force in society;[10] that the precise form taken by the vassal's promise is unimportant, whereas a generalized tendency of his character controls his acts; that the leader of a rear guard is an autonomous commander; that one function of a rear guard is to signal impending attack; that death is both final and tragic; and that Roncevaux is an unredeemed disaster. Sometimes these assumptions are stated per se, and sometimes they are the unstated postulates that form the logical basis for what is stated. Patent historical and textual difficulties attend their application, and yet they are difficult to separate from the *démesure* theory. I will argue that they may be abandoned, and replaced by other second-order statements about the poem that not only seem less startling upon reflection but are also simpler in some cases.

But first I would like to insist that recent attempts to soften the traditional condemnations of Roland as a character, without fundamentally revising them, have not seemed to me convincing. Despite the claims that Roland's vainglorious foolhardiness has a dimension of greatness,[11] or that it can be a path to self-awareness and redemp-

---

"national" disasters of Courtrai and Mansourah. Fox, 69, speaks of an "uncompromising spirit so characteristic of the French nation."

[10]Cf. Jones's definition of honor (*Ethos*, 46–55), which fails to give adequate attention to pragmatic questions (Is it proper or improper to associate honor with public opinion, as medieval people clearly often did? Is honor ever fairly earned, or is it merely a matter of appearances?).

[11]To take this stance usually means to argue that Roland's words and deeds make no sense—that they are excessive or paradoxical in everyday terms—but that they nonetheless have some extraordinary justification, to be sought outside the circumstances of the narrative. Thus he may be said to respond to a heroic code that ordinary mortals such as Oliver cannot grasp. Hence Faral: "The poet's intention was to show Roland as right, even in his exaggerated bravura" (Faral, *Chanson*, 234; cf. 231); Uitti (111–12), "Olivier's *sagesse* is certainly not 'wrong' . . . it is simply that Roland's *prouesse* is 'more right.'" Misrahi and Hendrickson, 371, speak of "Celtic, Germanic, Deuteronomic, Pauline views of heroic excess." See also Payen, *Le Motif du repentir*, 109, 128–29; Cartier, 51; Owen, "Secular Inspiration," 394, 398; Alfred Foulet, "Is Roland Guilty?" 148; Gérard, 445–46; Peeters, 387; McCash, 138; Le Gentil, *Song*, 92–93, 107; Mickel, "Parallels," 440; Battaglia, 365. Or else Roland's sacrifice is described as an imitation of Christ or as "folly of the Cross." The fullest statement is Wendt's (274–76, 284–85; cf. 316–17, 348–49); see also Del Monte, 231–32, following Battaglia; Crist, 18; Brault, *Song*, 1:40–44, 103–4, 211; Roland "personifies *humilitas*," Brault, *Song*, 1:97; Crosland, 70; Rütten, *Symbol und Mythus*. Roland was in fact treated as a saint; see Maria Chiara Celletti, "Santi Rolando, Olivero e compagni," *Bibliotheca sanctorum*, vol. 11 (Rome, 1968), 303–6, and cf. Wendt, 337–42. Burger posited a "passio Rotholandi" anterior to the *Song;* see André Burger, "La Légende de Roncevaux avant la *Chanson de Roland*," *Romania*, 70 (1948–49), 453–73.

tion,[12] the *démesure* theory leaves scant room for any defense of his actions as it conceives them. There are sublime failures; there are understandable errors; there are reasons why men feel they must attempt things beyond their strength. But the prideful Roland of criticism makes promises he should know he cannot keep. He willfully leads men who are needed, who are his charges and his alone, men who trust him, to their destruction. He speaks of what is not. His motivation is a groundless sense of his own invincibility. He means to cover himself with glory whatever the cost to his friends and his cause. All told, one is tempted to adopt Erich Auerbach's judgmental stance and say that his rising to Heaven is some sort of mistake. Roland's death might indeed redeem his character if he died alone, but what explanation would the laconic author give, if pressed, for the apotheosis offered a man who leads others to their deaths for perverse pride's sake alone?[13] It is difficult to imagine an excuse for Roland, if we accept the account of cause and effect we so often find in what has been written about the *Song*.

Hence the impulse to argue that the construction of the work is more straightforward than the scholarly tradition indicates. It presents an unambiguous tactical and moral situation, though one prepared with great economy. Beginning *in medias res,* with earlier events barely mentioned, the poem establishes the issues of Roncevaux in the first few hundred lines. This economy is not surprising in itself. What is perhaps more surprising is the realization that what follows—including the battle proper—falls within the dénouement and not within the crisis. What follows Roland's nomination is not problematic peripety but expository development, an extended demonstration of how issues already defined are to be faced and resolved. The Horn (or Argument) Scenes in particular, while of course crucial, present only the consequences of decisions that have already been made. We have introduced a certain amount of confusion into the description of the text by failing to see and state clearly that the Horn Scenes have antecedents. The work's narrative line is fixed in the earliest scenes. In particular, it is the form of Roland's response to his nomination as leader of the rear guard that controls his reactions later, and in my Commentary I have sought to bring out the parts of the text that make it clear that both Roland and Charles (at least) know the implica-

[12]The best-known advocates of this position since Bédier (*Légendes,* 3:434, 437, 442) are Le Gentil and Renoir. See also Ronald Walpole, "Le Sens moral de la *Chanson de Roland,*" in *Travaux de linguistique et de littérature* (Strasbourg), 4, 2 (1966), 7–21.

[13]See Erich Auerbach, *Mimesis* (1946; 1st Eng. ed. 1953; reprint ed., New York, 1957), 88.

tions of what Roland agrees to do. The battle scenes and the highly charged debate of the Horn Scenes expound the meaning of that choice.

It is important to recall that Roland and his men are not precisely ambushed. The literature varies, but Bédier gives in passing a summary of the Nomination Scene that scarcely differs from my own: "The instant Ganelon designated him, Roland realized what was going on. If he had not understood (as Jenkins argues) he would have been quite naive. If he accepted the order to stay at Roncevaux as a normal assignment, his sacrifice would be a sacrifice no longer; it would lose its noble quality entirely, and the *Chanson de Roland* would lose its *raison d'être*."[14] Like many other interpretive statements about the poem, however, this one was governed by its role in another argument entirely, one concerning the literary superiority of the Oxford text. Its implications for Roland's attitudes remained unexplored in Bédier's work, and Bédier is remembered instead as the sponsor of the *démesure* theory in the highly influential version to be found in his *Légendes épiques*. In that version, Roland's foreknowledge of the ambush does not mean he is sacrificing himself. He knows he will be attacked, but he expects to triumph.[15] I have stated that on the evidence of his own words the hero harbors no such expectation, but for the understanding of the work's structure it is enough to allow that Bédier is right in his judgment of the Nomination Scene itself and that Roland, aware of Ganelon's intentions, is taking a deliberate risk.

This leads to a new emphasis in the First Horn Scene or scene of argument: not on some presumptive spur-of-the-moment rejection, by Roland, of Oliver's suggestion that he call for help, but on the problematic sequence of choices in the preceding scenes. The decisions the Franco-Christian army and its leaders are forced to make at the outset, and the results of those decisions, need to be given greater weight in our descriptions of how the *Song of Roland* unfolds. Roland's acceptance of the rear guard is only one of several decisions (though it is the central one), each of which controls other decisions and later events to some degree.[16]

Thus the fight at Roncevaux does not result from a single decision about the use of the horn. It is the consequence of a series of choices, yet they are not to be taken as equally reasonable. The characters do not all have the same points of view, nor do they share the audience's

[14]Bédier, *La Chanson de Roland commentée,* 151.

[15]Bédier, *Légendes,* 3:433.

[16]Choices made at the outset fix the sequence of the rest (Horrent, *Chanson de Roland et geste de Charlemagne,* 10; Brault, *Song,* 1:40–44).

knowledge, and so they disagree, and choose both for good and for ill. For the army, to accept or refuse Marsile's offer is apparently to choose between going home or fighting on; for Charles, to accept or refuse Ganelon's nomination of Roland for the rear guard seems to mean choosing between exposing his nephew to evident danger or protecting him; for Oliver, to blow or not to blow the horn is to choose between rescue and senseless risk. Or so the characters seem to be saying at the time. But I have pointed out in the Commentary that accepting Marsile's offer does not mean putting an end to his enmity, as the audience already knows. Substituting half the army for the rear guard does not solve the very real problem of how the Pyrenees are to be crossed. Elsewhere, once the horn has been blown, Charles has no choice between responding and going his way, despite Ganelon's specious arguments. In the Trial Scene, finally, the traitor's claims deserve no better treatment than those he made when the horn sounded (lines 1770–84; Roland was not chasing rabbits then), and the only possible response to Ganelon is the one Thierry makes, at his personal risk in the short term.

Once choices are made, therefore, they create situations in which no similar choice is available any longer. The decision to treat with Marsile makes the crossing of the Pyrenees with the enemy in the rear unavoidable and therefore makes the rear guard's mission necessary. And in the same vein, once Roland has chosen to accept the rear-guard assignment it is too late to choose again, though his advice, had it been followed at the outset, would have made the detachment's task superfluous. Once his promise of resistance has been given, he must resist with the resources that the logic of the situation allows him. His opportunity for refusal comes when he hears the traitor's brusque words at the foot of the pass, and then he commits himself to the risky mission. Bédier recognized the import of the scene without realizing how pivotal it is. In the First Horn Scene, Oliver can only ask Roland to reconsider a decision that had been made with some degree of knowledge and deliberation and had been publicly and solemnly affirmed.[17]

Uneasy, perhaps, with the stark suddenness with which the decisive

[17]Cf. Le Gentil, *Song*, 88: "In fact, nothing has been decided when the enemy suddenly appears, and Roland and Oliver begin their moving debate. Roland is still free to change his destiny." Many statements about Roncevaux imply that Roland has a choice; for explicit claims that he makes a wrong decision there, see, e.g., Tony Hunt, "The Tragedy of Roland: An Aristotelian View," *Modern Language Review*, 74 (1979), 800–803; Misrahi and Hendrickson, 364; Williamson, 557; Renoir, "Roland's Lament," 578 ("[he] simply refuses to consider the odds"); Renoir, "Heroic Oath," 251–52.

episode of Roland's nomination is presented, critics have found various ways of making all choices ambiguous, of making Roland both wrong and right, or Charles partly wrong and Ganelon partly right—often on the basis of single lines or short passages. But these are compromises of hindsight; critical conscience allows for them by extending or reshaping the context of choice. Within the work, disagreements about future actions, even the famous one between Oliver and Roland, have two distinct sides, and only one right for the time and place. The promise made before the battle of Roncevaux is part of the battle's context.

Nonetheless, we must avoid confusing clear choices with simplistic conception and presentation. Through Roland and Charles, the poet drives his point home in a manner more direct than is sometimes admitted. Neither man can be said to make a mistake. Charles is bound by the limits of his power, and Roland by his vows, and for both heroes the path to glory is perfectly straight. But that does not mean that the poem shows it as an easy path. Straight though it may be, it is arduous in the extreme, and not every man can follow it. Roland offers the supreme example by rejecting the temptation to ease his own burden, and he dies in a fight he might indeed have avoided if he could only consent to cloud the simple issue and thus live a little longer, as Oliver advises.

Charles, however, has potentially an even more important moral challenge to face. His temporal powers are not absolute, but they are considerable, and so, no doubt, is the temptation to use them arbitrarily. The question is openly raised only once, and then by Charles himself. No Oliver ever argues that the emperor should refuse credence to his vassal Ganelon simply on grounds of strong suspicion, when he has no evidence of the sort he can share.[18] That is the burden of suzerainty, after all. Charles has no companion like Oliver, and he cannot have one. Succumbing to obvious fears, he offers Roland half his army without any prompting from anyone, and thus nearly breaks the rules of leadership unilaterally. Then it is Roland himself who reminds him that a principle is involved, with implications beyond one man's immediate security: "May God curse me if I behave wrongly in this matter!"[19]

[18]Cf. Bédier, *Légendes,* 3:422–23, and note 55 to my Commentary.

[19]*Deus me cunfunde, se la geste en desment!* If this analysis is correct, then *geste* here is not "family"—even including Charles—but "tradition" (that of service) or "noble behavior"; compare Moignet, 76. *En* is more difficult: "by acting as you suggest"? As might be expected, assessments of Charles's character have varied. He is called weak or guilty by Le Gentil, *Song,* 116–18; Crosland, 71 ("yields to temptation"); Gérard, 463; Mermier,

To say that Roland dies for principle is to banish from the study of the poem both the idea of a tragic flaw and the persistent metaphor of Roncevaux as a tragedy.[20] I say "metaphor" whatever the intention of critics who use the term tragedy, since Roland goes to heaven straight from the battlefield, and only some figurative use of the term (or refusal of Christian eschatology) can make that a tragic end. "A martyr is not a tragic figure; he is not marked by a tragic flaw."[21] But the metaphor is flawed even as an image. The Roland of traditional criticism does not have the lucidity that characterizes a powerful tragic hero. When, before the battle, he claims victory and exhales pride, he is simply unaware of the situation. That is pathetic enough, but catharsis, that is, pity and terror, do not arise from the contemplation of incompetence. Foolhardiness does not teach us anything, except that we must not overestimate our strength, or that tragedy is avoidable through attentiveness to one's surroundings.

But even if we allow that destructive *outrecuidance* can qualify as a tragic flaw despite Aristotle's insistence that "first and foremost, [tragic] characters should be good,"[22] even if we insist that *hamartia* is one of those universals to be found in early medieval literature, it must still be admitted that the Roncevaux episode does not measure

93–95 ("used bad judgement"); Siciliano, 341, n. 3, 342; Horrent, *Chanson de Roland et geste de Charlemagne*, 8 ("incertain"); Duggan, *Song*, 179; Owen, *Song of Roland*, 21–22; McCash, 137 ("has disobeyed his mission to rid Spain of the Saracens"). But Uitti (103; cf. 70ff.), Van Emden ("Pro Karolo Magno," 178–81), and Niles ("Ideal Depiction," 135) agree that he cannot act otherwise; cf. J. Thomas, 97, Mermier, 101 ("enlightened ruler"), and Brault's equation of Charles with Abraham (Brault, *Song*, 1:165, 245; cf. 35, 51–52, 82) or purely and simply with God (1:178; see also 184, 252).

[20]This is another idea that goes back at least to Gaston Paris: "In the poem, Roland's refusal to call Charles to his rescue, by blowing his horn, is the true cause of the disaster of Roncevaux: it is an act of heroic folly. . . . Through that act, the disaster assumes a truly tragic nature, since it is caused in large part by the hero's mistake" (G. Paris, *Extraits*, 75, cf. xx; and G. Paris, *La Littérature française au Moyen age*, 4th ed. [Paris, 1909], 58 [p. 55 of 3d ed., 1890]). The earliest expression of the idea I can find was Duval's, but he did not know the Oxford text (see Amaury Duval, *Histoire littéraire de la France*, 18 [1835], 718); see also Ernst Robert Curtius, "Zur Literarästhetik des Mittelalters, II," *Zeitschrift für romanische Philologie*, 58 (1938), 227 ("tragic guilt"); Siciliano, 356; Gérard, 445. Hunt ("Tragedy of Roland") has recently argued that *hubris* is the wrong term but that Roland commits a tragic error, or *hamartia*. On the latter, historically slippery term, see O. B. Hardison, "Tragic Flaw," in *Princeton Encyclopedia of Poetry and Poetics*, 2d ed. (Princeton, 1974), 864. Among others, Auerbach, *Mimesis*, 96, Vance, *Reading*, 64, C. M. Bowra (*Heroic Poetry* [1952; London, 1966], 75–77), and Farnham, 163, state that Roncevaux is *not* tragic. This is also Hunt's final conclusion ("Tragedy," 803–5), at least where the Oxford text itself is concerned.

[21]Farnham, 163.

[22]Aristotle, *On the Art of Poetry*, trans. T. S. Dorsch, in *Classical Literary Criticism* (Harmondsworth, Eng., 1965), 51. In large part this anomaly is what leads Hunt to replace the idea of tragic flaw with that of tragic error (see Hunt, "Tragedy," 797–800).

up to the requirements for tragic catastrophe. The men of the rear guard bear witness, through martyrdom, to their faith, which is an affirmation and not a disaster at all. They are volunteers, and they fight as willingly and joyfully as Roland does, without being given the chance to speak as often. (For what they say when they do speak, see laisse 82, lines 1047–48.) There is a strong tendency in recent studies to recognize the accuracy, for this text, of what Turpin says about the situation. "*Se vos murez, esterez seinz martirs*" ("If you die, you will be holy martyrs," 1134): the rear guard dies absolved of all sin. (Technically, if necessary, this would include Roland, since the First Horn Scene is over and he has already exhibited whatever pride, or tenacity, he has to show.) There is no reason to doubt that, instead of endless nothingness, they have seats in Paradise. The latter phrase is, of course, not "outside the text" (*Sieges avrez el greignor pareïs,* 1135). Roland himself is elevated directly to heaven by God's emissary angels. This is so clearly not a punishment that even before Payen's study on repentance, scholarship was tending to hedge its bets and say that God could somehow accept Roland's pride despite its consequences, or that Roland had suddenly become aware of reality in the course of the battle.[23]

But does the text require interpretation as a "complex" plot in that sense? Are the tragic consequences of pride, and thus the flaw and Roland's realization of it, real phenomena in the text we have? What kind of catastrophe is there in the unlocking of the gates of heaven for 20,014 men whom Charles, victor over Baligant, does not need for the defense of the right in any case? The catastrophe is, presumably, mass death. Yet Roncevaux, the death of mature warriors in the voluntary exercise of their profession and in the successful defense of their comrades, bears little relationship to the sinking of the *Titanic,* the earthquake of Lisbon, or even the battle of the Somme. In a concluding chapter, I will discuss the appropriateness of the battle of Roncevaux as presenting the apparent paradox of survival beyond transitory sufferings. For now, it is enough to consider that our second thoughts about death in the field are not part of the context Turpin and Saint Gabriel give the battle in the poem.

In the Oxford poem's sequence, then, as in Turpin's formulation,

[23]Hence the "Christian" argument that "only by supposing that the hero has now completely purified himself can we explain what might otherwise seem sheer theological audacity" (i.e., given the traditional view of Roland's acts; Renoir, "Roland's Lament," 582–83). Accepting the traditional idea that Roland does not at first comprehend the events in which he is involved, Hunt prefers to call his presumed realization *anagnorisis* ("Tragedy," 799–802).

Roncevaux is an incident and not an end. That is another thing that has surprised or irritated critical readers at times: that the story can continue without Roland, Oliver, and the peers, even at great length.[24] But that was what Roland was talking about all along. The Oxford text sets his sacrifice in a larger and positive narrative context, right down to the last laisse. Among the reactions that might have to be faced here is this one: that to envisage Roncevaux as a peripety, its causes as unproblematic, and its outcome as positive, is to diminish the work as literature. Most obvious, the pathetic grandeur of the horn's dying echoes, forever too late, may be thought lost, if we do not insist that Roland's last stand is indeed final. Still, it is difficult to maintain that either history or aesthetics requires such pathos as a sine qua non of literary success. In arguing for it, we may be arguing only for an atmosphere and a set of associations. This is a form of the fallacy of affect, saying that the greatness of the poem is in pathos because we habitually associate pathos with it, even if upon second examination that flies in the face of emphases found in the text. Pathos is (I will continue to argue) like *hubris,* part of an early hypothesis in *Roland* criticism, whose long-standing prestige is an inadequate argument for its presence in the work.

There is a less obvious but more positive reply to those who fear the work's reputation may be inseparably bound up with the battle's reputation as a *dolorosa rotta.* It is evident from my Commentary that in the poem whose themes are sacrifice and duty the Roncevaux episode is just as crucial for meaning as it is in the poem of blind pride. We cannot let pathos become our guiding light without the risk of thwarting our attempt to grasp the work as a whole. But the first battle remains essential to the expression of the theme, because it is the exemplary one. It is the event that sets before us the actions of the hero at the supreme test, and it binds up the largely open, contrasting arrangement of the earlier scenes of choice. It replies to Ganelon's implicit challenge to Roland, even without reference to victory, and it furnishes the answer to Roland's symbolic question: "Did you think the glove would fall from my hand?" (764–65).

The scenes of choice and commitment are continued and made complete by the Baligant episode and the justice done to Ganelon, and I do not think Roncevaux would be as clear a statement without Charles's final victory and Thierry's staunch insistence on the right. We would not otherwise know whether Oliver's doubt might not have a grain of justification. But the great rite of passage, where the mettle

[24]See the discussions of the Baligant episode cited in note 127 to the Commentary.

of the heroic man is tested and he does the simple, unthinkable thing he has to do, is found in the scenes of valor that we have always admired as their maker probably meant. Roncevaux is simultaneously the dénouement of Roland's agon proper and a peripety of eschatology. The combination is a replica of the paradoxes of service and of Christianity, and the dénouement is paradoxical itself precisely because its present, tangible importance is not comparable with the values of order and eternity. It is essential for Roland to realize how unessential he is; if he does not, he will succumb to Oliver's arguments, and an overriding question of principle will go unanswered.

[3]

The Characters: Words and Deeds

The narrator's voice in the *Song of Roland* is every bit as laconic about characters as it is about events and their causes or effects. With rare exceptions ("Ganelon . . . who committed the treason" [178]), we must derive our notions of them from a narrative that prefers showing to telling. But the characters are not mute themselves. "The knights are valourous, their words are noble" (1097): promises, boasts, battlefield taunts and scornful replies are part of the technique of representation in the work, and not a matter of ornament.

This brings me back at once to a point that any revisionist reader of the *Song* must face over and over. Just as we associate the structure of the work with pathos and tragedy, all experienced readers also recall the impression Roland's speeches made on first reading. That impression—as the secondary literature abundantly confirms—is negative. The hero's words seem brash, impetuous, and offensive. They appear to express a limitless self-confidence and an arrogant sense of superiority that refers every event and every character to itself.[1]

It has then been natural to assume that Roland makes rash promises and fails disastrously to carry them out. This aspect of the stan-

[1]Cf. Pensom, 126; Kibler, "Roland's Pride," 148, 152; Hunt, "Roland's 'vermeille pume,'" 207; Horrent, *Chanson de Roland dans les littératures* . . . ; Brook, "Le Forfait de Roland," 123. Renoir calls his "uncouth" speeches "embarrassing" ("Roland's Lament," 576). For Siciliano (p. 354; cf. p. 351), he is "trenchant, quarrelsome . . . rancorous . . . even . . . perfidious." Calin, 21–22, finds him impulsive and simple as well as tactless. Mermier, 101, speaks of his "rude impatience." For further expressions of irritation, see Burger, "Rire," 8–9; Boatner, passim; Donohoe, passim; Halverson, 662. Does this irritation explain the energy with which numerous commentators have defended Ganelon? ("It is not difficult for us to be in sympathy with Ganelon": Owen, "Secular Inspiration," 391).

dard interpretation requires a presupposition that has almost never been discussed explicitly before. Roland must be the victim of a well-known form of narrative irony. His martyrdom is at best the unintended consequence of an attempt at earthly conquest. The glorious victory of which he boasts is impossible, and the finality of death awaits him instead. If he is accepted into the company of the angels, it is because he has stumbled into sublimity by mistake. D. C. Muecke has called this "self-betraying irony," "where the false image a character has formed of himself clashes with the image that the work enables the reader to form."[2] I have suggested in the Commentary that this irony, like the pathos just discussed, has been supplied not by the work's events but by a prior hypothesis of reading, and that when Roland's speeches appear to reinforce the notion of an irony working against his expectations, our impression needs to be corrected.

It is true, once again, that sophisticated commentators, sensitive to the tension between the foolish Roland and the heroic legend, have combined the character and the legend in complex ways, a reaction that flows more or less naturally from our first impressions of Roland. We may then read that Roland is prideful or foolish, but not culpably so; or that he is guilty, but partly lucid; or that he is initially foolish but later humble and clearsighted.[3] As I have said, the presumption of complexity is then reflected in considerations of structure, and we are obliged to posit anagnorisis or ambiguity where they are not otherwise necessary. In fact, as I hope to show, we need not assume either structural ambiguity or confusion in the heroic protagonist in order to recognize the text's inclusion of human diversity. But the diversity is in the characters that surround Roland, not in him. The speeches of Oliver, Ganelon, and Naimon express precisely that diversity, not authorial disapproval of Roland's vision.

[2]D. C. Muecke, *Irony and the Ironic,* 2d ed. (New York, 1982), 87. Hunt recognizes that the traditional Roland must be a victim of irony ("Tragedy," 798; cf. Nichols, 166–68, 172).

[3]Roland changes his mind, or atones: Le Gentil, "A propos de la *démesure,*" 206; Le Gentil, *Song,* 90–93; Van Emden, "Guarant," 35; Burger, "Deux Scènes"; Renoir, "Roland's Lament," 579; Boatner, 580; Atkinson, 271–84; Calin, 19, 24; Mermier, 99; Jenkins, xlii; Nichols, 172–73, 177; Renoir, "Heroic Oath," 254, 258; Bernard Huppé, "The Concept of the Hero in the Early Middle Ages," in Norman T. Burns and Christopher J. Reagan, eds., *Concepts of the Hero in the Middle Ages and the Renaissance* (Albany, 1975), 1–26. Roland and Oliver exchange characters during the battle: Vance, *Reading,* 51 ("Roland is at last wise and Oliver is at last bold"); cf. Boatner, 581, and Donohoe, 261. For Pensom, 137, Roland is changed (but Oliver is not), but not transformed into a saint (pp. 154–59). Roland does *not* change: Owen, "Secular Inspiration," 393, 396; Alfred Foulet, "Is Roland Guilty?" 146–48. For Vance, Roland is "right for the wrong reasons" (*Reading,* 11–12). See also the works cited in notes 11 and 12 to Chapter 2, above.

It is axiomatic that, in the absence of explicit comments, the text will convey Roland's character to us by his words and deeds.[4] That makes it all the more imperative to examine these in detail without trusting to general impressions. I have said that some consequences of Roland's actions are comprehensible only with respect to certain ideas. The eschatological framework into which we are to fit the many deaths, though stated, is never systematically expounded. But the promises Roland makes are set in a complete narration, and, once we have examined their style closely enough to have gained a clear idea of their import, we may compare them with the textual events they refer to, and to other characters' claims about those events.[5] The results may well make us uneasy with the assumption that the hero's statements are designed to reveal an inadequate understanding of his fate.

In particular, if we do not take up Roland's speeches in the First Horn Scene with the presupposition that they will lead him into unexpected catastrophe, then we will realize that what he says contains no exaggeration. Roland is in fact more nearly given to understatement, even in the most flamboyant of his remarks: "I will strike great blows; my sword will be bloody along the whole length of its blade" (1055–56, 1065–67, 1077–79), when in the event he does not merely strike, but slays, and cripples even Marsile without having boasted of it as the pagan peers had done just before. The *gabs,* then, are on the enemy side.[6] Roland's promises are characterized rhetorically by a consistent meiosis, a reverse Delphism in which he raises minimal expectations and then exceeds them. *Démesure* characterizes the claims of his foes, and not his, as the comparison of laisses 69–78 with laisses 83–88 has shown. Here I would like to explore one of two ramifications of this presentation of the First Horn Argument.

Roland's replies to Oliver's suggestions are sometimes said to show not only his overconfidence, but also his overbearing nature. It is true

[4]Faral, *Chanson,* 229–30, clearly states the opinion I will refute: "Roland knows, and is not afraid to say, what he is worth. . . . He does not doubt the worth of his sword for an instant, and in the death threats he makes to the enemy, we find almost the same boastful mockery with which the insane challenges of the twelve pagan peers were filled." Again, Léopold Peeters argues that words and deeds cannot be separated for purposes of interpretation ("Le 'Faire' et le 'dire,'" 383–92; see also Pensom, 83; Hunt, "Character and Causality").

[5]On the audience's power of recall, see the Preliminary Note. Cf. Paul Zumthor's useful remarks (based, however, on a broader concept of public memory or commemoration) in *La Poésie et la voix dans la civilisation médiévale* (Paris, 1984), esp. 105–12. Peeters, 391–92, has also argued that the text shows Roland to have told the truth and that Ganelon has lied.

[6]For discussions of the concept of the *gab,* see the works referred to in note 77 to the Commentary.

that this is not the way we would like our neighbors to talk to us. Furthermore, our humanist sentiment is that it is not a good thing to be impatient with what we take for weakness in others. But the primary observation we must make on the text, one that goes far toward answering the claims of Roland's detractors, is that even in this emergency Roland speaks not to Oliver's character but to his suggestions: *Ne dites tel ultrage* ("Don't say such a dishonorable thing"; 1106; cf. 1113). His sharpest line, *Mal seit del cuer ki el piz se cuardet* ("Cursed be the cowardly heart"; 1107), is a generalization, though it may be read as a reference to a suspicion on Roland's part (in fact an accurate one) that Oliver may not be quite himself at the moment (cf. 1036 and the commentary to laisse 81). But Roland never indulges in the accusations that Oliver will employ against him in the Second Horn Scene. Roland's first-person pronouns, his references to his own honor and his own family (which appear only here), may be the better part of discretion in this sense, and not signs of egotism. After all, he has the choice between tempering his remarks by putting the problem in terms of himself ("If I were to do what you suggest, I would be wrong") or replying directly to his temporarily shaken friend ("*You* are wrong; you are making a shameful suggestion").

As for humanism and tolerance, if Roland is right in any degree, then there is every reason for us to accept his sense of urgency. The poem up to this point has led to this: when the expected attack has actually come to pass, will Roland carry out his promises? Will he, unlike Ganelon, meet the challenge of exemplary behavior? Oliver has just seen how very many pagans there are. We are not told what his reaction was to the nomination of Roland and the choosing of the rear guard, whether he understood the danger as Charles, Roland, probably Turpin and perhaps Gautier del Hum did, or whether he is only just now grasping it. But to judge by his way of describing what he has seen from the hilltop, Oliver is unsettled specifically by the large number of Saracens (1035–36, 1049–52). The issue in the First Horn Scene, as Oliver puts it (and as Bédier's interpretation, for instance, puts it by implication) is this: is Roland to carry out his promise to defend Charles and his goods even though the pagans are more numerous than Oliver expected? And the answer must be: yes, of course. Oliver is himself an important character, but his opinion on the number of pagans involved is an irritating side issue. Nothing else has changed. The statement of the meaning of Roncevaux was made when Roland accepted his task, with no qualifying reference to numbers. If he meant what he said when he made that statement, then it is no wonder Roland is adamant about holding to it now.

Let us recall the words of Roland's original, controlling promise, as they appear in lines 755–59. "Charles the king will, in my view of things, lose not a palfrey nor charger in the rear, not a mule, not a packhorse, without a decision of arms—unless things have been decided by the sword." These future tenses constitute an authentic prediction. Roland has not said that Charles will not lose a single warhorse or beast of burden at Roncevaux or in the mountains—though this prediction, had he made it, would have come true as the others do. He says, instead, that Charles will suffer no loss without a fight, without resistance. That is not a boast, but rather a minimal statement of assent, a definition of the rear guard's duty to which Roland will hold consistently. Given our knowledge of feudal proceedings and of the importance of form in fixing a vassal's responsibility, we may not assume such precision to be insignificant; indeed, we must give serious consideration to it, as we always have to the precisely worded oaths of Guenevere or Iseut.[7]

Only afterward, as if to suggest his awareness that he has been betrayed, does the hero speak three angry lines to Ganelon, echoing Charles's. "Evil man (renegade?), did you think the glove would fall from my hand in public, as the wand did from yours?" (763–65). The comparison with the earlier scene underscores what the text is about to show; that Roland's mission will begin with a good augury, not with an ill omen. He does not drop the token he receives (a bow, in fact, not a glove—hardly a telling inconsistency). Showing how strongly he suspects a risk whose existence he cannot prove, Charles offers his nephew half the army instead of a detachment. Roland refuses this expedient as unworthy and makes a final, precisely qualified promise: "Cross the passes in total safety. You need fear no man while I am alive" (790–91). Again, he has bound himself by a promise he can keep, if his will is strong enough, though he may not live, a possibility to which his last words allude. Roland is angry, perhaps deeply saddened (again *irascut,* Naimon's word, can mean both),[8] but there is no sign of heedlessness. To produce any such signs, we would have to modify what he says.

The issue is vitally important, for if Charles or Roland were to try to change the course of events (implicit from the Council Scene on), it

[7]Most recently in Barbara Nelson Sargent-Baur, "Truth, Half-Truth, Untruth: Béroul's Telling of the Tristan Story," in Leigh Arrathoon, ed., *The Craft of Fiction: Essays in Medieval Poetics* (Rochester, Mich., 1984), 393–421. On the importance of form in medieval law, see M. Bloch, 360.

[8]See Kleiber, *Le Mot "ire,"* 145–54, 329–31.

would mean in effect accusing Ganelon of the highest of crimes without proof. Circumstantial evidence indicates, early on, that any promise Roland makes here will be tested to the extreme limits he evokes, even to death. But that is the logic of a situation and not the dictate of personalities. Roland's character is no different from the ideal character of his whole class. He must, in the end, do as he says, with no regard for the immediate circumstances—betrayal, the overwhelming size of the army sent against him—or bend his vows to his own point of view, as Ganelon does.[9] Roland chooses the ideal, and when he might have modified his choice, in the Horn Scene, he reaffirms it explicitly again and again.

It is helpful to recall briefly what sort of limitations his commitment places on Roland. It is not, perhaps, until we review the histories of the art of warfare (at least the more recent histories, which allow the feudal age some tactical sense) that we realize how the limits on maneuverability and the difficulties of communication—the mountains and the breath that blows the horn—affected the medieval soldier's task. As noted in the Commentary, it could be of the utmost importance that one stick firmly to one's plan or assigned place. Chaos threatened the feudal army's line of march and its plan of battle as inevitably as fire threatened wooden cities. In the Commentary, I have taken the Crusades not as a direct explanation of the Saragossa campaign but as a well-documented, nearly contemporary example of the need for and the respect given to strict discipline among both footsoldiers and knights. The movements of the latter could, at need, be firmly subordinated to the needs of the army as a whole, as R. C. Smail makes clear in his discussion of what he calls "fighting on the march."[10] We may understand the habitual Turkish tactics of harassment as attempts to destroy a necessary order in the Western armies, and we may admire the discipline that allowed the retreat from Bosra in 1147 or the march from Acre to Jaffa in 1191, through hostile territory and under intermittent attack. Apparently (though it will not do to insist too strongly on the coincidence) the Muslims considered the rear of the moving army to be its weak point and directed their attacks especially against the rear guard.[11] Individual initiative could save the day, but to an extent that the *chanson de geste* rarely shows, it

[9]In another narrative sequence, Oliver might well be thought right, but his recommendation to Roland is wrong in this context. That is why it is not really a question of a hierarchy of values.

[10]Smail, *Crusading Warfare,* 156–65.

[11]Ibid., 164.

could lose it as well. Hence the period's slow movement away from autarchy in social organization may be thought to have parallels in warfare.

Therefore, once we remember that Roland is not a general but a lieutenant, and commands not an army but a detachment with its own function, we see that the question before him is eminently understandable in tactical terms. Is he to carry out his promise to stand fast, or is he to modify his position in difficult (but not entirely unforeseen) circumstances? The poem shows the former choice and its consequences, but it cannot simultaneously show what the consequences of the latter decision would have been. Criticism has often assumed that the consequence of the horn-call would have been a victory, and survival for the rear guard.[12] I have suggested that if we think of how the army as a whole (not the mounted force that accompanies Charles on his mission of vengeance) travels in the Pyrenees, we may find that conclusion overly hasty. But even if it is correct, it leads us back to a platitude that the *démesure* theory could never entirely hide: when attacked by a superior force, one should call for help, and live to fight another day. We must consider that the feudal system, as a set of social and political ideas, may have generated more sophisticated arguments than that.[13]

This raises an essential point for our understanding of what is expected of Roland at Roncevaux and of what he is referring to in his speech of acceptance. What is the function of a rear guard in general, and how does it govern this rear guard in particular? It is a question to which the poem gives only very limited space. That is not in itself proof that the question is negligible. There is an excellent chance that the brevity of Charles's allusion to the crossing of the Pyrenees is, rather, an indication of the intended audience's familiarity with the nature of Roland's task. Unfortunately for the application of that well-known principle of historical criticism, any such familiarity is long lost, along with a number of other things that our forebears neglected to write down. The personal and oral nature of the knightly apprenticeship may have made its codification in written form superfluous. But is is not quite true to say that the poem itself gives no indication of what the rear guard is needed for. If we are to understand the text's brief invocation of this crucial matter, however, we

[12]Exceptions are Cartier and Del Monte.

[13]I see I am approaching from its negative side a point made by Benton: "Even though disciplined retreat can sometimes be the best strategy, every commander wants troops who will risk, indeed sacrifice, their lives if necessary" (John Benton, "Nostre franceis n'unt talent de fuïr," 245–46).

will have to rely to a certain extent on historically conditioned common sense.

The mountains, the Pyrenees, may be in the work for any of a number of reasons, all well chronicled elsewhere, but it may also be that the poem makes a particular use of the Pyrenees as a locus of action, a use that we have not yet considered thoroughly. Edging toward the pathetic fallacy, we speak of the high peaks and the dark vales of Roncevaux as a poetically evocative setting for great and hopeless deeds. But the mountains may also have suggested something else to the minds of hearers with more immediate knowledge of campaigning in the age of muscle power.

The Pyrenees are rough mountains indeed, in many places bare and unforgiving. The medieval track that crossed such terrain was uncertain, steep, and narrow. Einhard's famous passage reminds us precisely of the dangers such a crossing may involve. It must have been a struggle to bring an army across a mountain pass in the eleventh and twelfth centuries, what with laden pack animals, problems of supply and organization, and no doubt dust, thirst, and heat in the best of seasons. Like many other tasks we no longer appreciate, that of moving an army efficiently or safely at the time the poem was written must have required skill and energy even when the terrain and weather were favorable. Any difficulty may have called forth in concentrated fashion the initiative and stamina which, in theory, had created personal leadership in the distant past.

But none of those considerations, now beyond absolute proof, is necessary for the understanding of what is involved in the return from Spain in the *Song of Roland.* We need only consider two obvious points. First, an army did not travel in armor ready to fight—even the pagans must arm and equip themselves before attacking Roland—and, second, it did not and could not travel through mountains in defensive formation: its order of march was dictated by the terrain. Much more likely than not, a medieval army went over a high pass in something like single file. One never knows how to judge medieval tactics; they depended too much on the particular combatants involved. But it cannot have been good to ignore the possibility of danger implied by the relatively defenseless posture of an army entering the high mountains, with undefeated enemies behind.

It is this context of potential danger that gives their full meaning to Charles's two sentences concerning the crossing of the pass:

> You see the defiles and the narrow passages.
> Choose now who shall be in my rear guard. (741–42)

It also makes clear why Roland speaks unstintingly of resistance and never of victory. Victory is not his assignment. It is not part of the context of Roncevaux. Neither does he require any orders. The nature of his job is clear on its face, and he sums it up himself. If an attack comes, when it comes, he must stand his ground between the attackers, with their advantage of surprise, and his comrades, and in the crudest of terms buy time for the army to cross the passes safely (as it does) even at the cost of his life.[14]

Roland promises nothing more, but the text underscores the urgency of his situation in various ways. Naimon knows that in this extremity things will be hard and that they cannot be changed: the rear guard is Roland's—no baron can or will change that—but send good men to make a stand with him! (778–81). And Gautier del Hum echoes, as compactly as possible, Roland's own words of commitment in the face of danger: "I am Roland's man, I must not fail him" (801). In an embedded replica of Charles's choice, Roland then does an obvious thing. He sends his vassal onto the high ground, with a detachment, "lest the emperor lose any man of his there." The narrator here adds the same qualification Roland used in his acceptance. Gautier will not come down, however rough the going, until many swords have been used (810–11). When his men are dead, and he has done all he can, Gautier still does not flee. Critics have wrongly accused him of cowardice, as they have been wrong to accuse his captain of heedlessness.[15] Instead, Gautier rides down into the thick of a hopeless battle, fights on, and is killed, one of the very last, at Roland's side.

I will not discuss Roland's speeches in the Second Horn Scene or the Council of Charlemagne in detail here; both are treated at length in the Commentary. Where the council in particular is concerned, it has now become commonplace to recognize that Roland, not Ganelon, has grasped the situation rightly and that his arguments from long experience of Marsile's perfidy are justified. Surely the analysis already given suffices to show that, despite our impressions, the exhibition of heedless pride is not Roland's function in the Oxford text. We must admit that Roland not only does not *do* the sort of thing we have ascribed to him without full study of the context; upon close examination it is clear that he does not *say* the sort of thing our criticism has implied. I do not doubt that it is beyond the power (and outside the

[14]The risks Charles and his men run in returning to Spain to answer the horn-call are not Roland's fault but Ganelon's.

[15]See the works cited in notes 72, 73, and 119 to the Commentary.

proper domain) of scholarship to prove that Roland never makes any statement that cannot conceivably be interpreted as prideful. But the textbook description of his character requires him to be consistently and blatantly prideful, and that I think the text does not allow. Primarily, he does not boast, at least if boasting means to proffer exaggerated statements of one's own prowess and importance. We may not like all the overtones of what Roland says, and the results may unsettle us, but what he says is true nonetheless, in the only context in which we can know him. From the very first he calls for vengeance and war, which is unpleasant of him, but he does so, and he is the only character to do so, on the basis of experience.

Roland is neither Hotspur nor Custer.[16] Despite the overtones of the adjectives applied to him in criticism, the intensity of his speeches is a response to the challenge of his situation and not to the excitement of bloodlust. His words are strong because he is using them (and his exemplary swordstrokes) to urge his men to their duty, in circumstances where hesitation means more than momentary embarrassment. The only irony in his speeches is the controlled irony of his grim jests—the reference to Oliver's broken lance (1360–62), perhaps his exclamation when the rash Saracen seizes him: "I don't think you are on our side!" (2286). It is a point of view he shares with those around him, with Oliver at first (1006–7) and with Turpin. This is no more and no less than the battlefield humor of any and all fighting men, who laugh as they set to work, and laugh ironically because they know only too well what is ahead.

In arguing that Roland's role in the *Song* is exemplary, I am of course also suggesting reevaluation of the roles of the characters who disagree with him or comment otherwise, by word or deed, on his acts. I have had occasion, in Chapter 2, to speak of Charlemagne in connection with the work's most significant and decisive scene, that of the hero's nomination to the rear guard, since Charles's situation and Roland's are closely bound in that scene. I will speak briefly of Aude and Gautier del Hum at the end of this chapter. But first a few words about two other major characters—Ganelon and Oliver—are in order.

I have described Ganelon's double betrayal in the Commentary. Ganelon's machinations have two sets of victims: the rear guard, and

[16]It is not without relevance to the present study that Rosenberg once chose Roland as metonym for the unfortunate cavalryman, see Bruce Rosenberg, *Custer and the Epic of Defeat* (University Park, Pa., 1974), xi (cf. 175–81), and Goldin, "Die Rolle Ganelons," 140–41. This may remind us that Custer actually *was* in command and on the offensive. For comparisons between Roland and Hotspur or Young Hal, see note 4 to Chapter 2.

the pagans who believed his claim that Charles was fighting only because Roland spurred him to it. ("Whoever betrays a man brings death to himself and to others" [3959], though the reference there is to Ganelon's compurgators; see the commentary to laisses 287–89). That turn of events naturally helps give us a sense of his character. But the most important thing from the point of view of the theme of duty and responsibility is surely the lie he tells Charlemagne upon his return from Saragossa (laisse 54). Not only does Ganelon avoid his mission in this particular as in others, but worse than that, his falsehood covers up the infidelity of the enemy. In the long run, he betrays even Naimon's good sense, by making it impossible for the Franks to know what the hostages really mean. It is therein that the larger significance of his character lies. As the *Song* shows him, he is not only a traitor in the mechanical or functional sense; above all, he serves as a constant reminder of the vulnerability of the feudal community of trust.

Yet the issue in describing Ganelon is not precisely that of individualism versus something else. Rather, through the figure of the traitor, the text shows how an individual's shortsightedness can do great harm, while simultaneously showing, through the example set by Roland, how the individual can further the general good by accepting necessary constraints. But Roland, with Charles, Turpin, Gautier, and his detachment solidly behind him, is no more isolated than any epic hero, and perhaps less so than many. Critics working deductively from the *démesure* theory have sought to assign something very like Ganelon's role to the hero instead and have parsed an unbridled individualism as the cause of the Roncevaux tragedy.[17] But that

[17]Among many others, Gérard, 445, 464–65; Hunt, "Structure," 306 (Roland's individuality versus Charles's); Pensom, 91 (Ganelon's versus Roland's), 92–93 (poet favors society); Waltz, e.g., 51–56, 61–65. Pensom, 131, also defines Roland's neurosis—a basic concept for him—as "the repressed conflict between his identity as a 'clan-member' and his identity as a servant of the state." Kirsch, 396, speaks of a tension in Roland between incompatible concepts of vassaldom and sovereignty. The ideas that Roland and Ganelon have the same individualistic ethos, are similarly heedless, and share the responsibility for Roncevaux appear in various forms; see, e.g., Hall, "Ganelon and Roland," 266; Sarah Kay, "Ethics and Heroics in the *Song of Roland*," *Neophilologus*, 62 (1978), 480; Mermier, 93–94 ("both Roland and Ganelon display a certain lack of responsibility"); Gérard, 452ff.; Halverson. But Calin, 18, no doubt following Waltz here, attributes two different, competing ethics to them. See also Battaglia, Stranges, and Robert Eisner, "In Search of the Real Theme of the *Song of Roland*," *Romance Notes*, 14 (1972–73), 179. To explain the author's apparent preference for Roland, Kay, 487–88, postulates a "transformation of ethics" that makes legitimate in Roland's case acts that would be unethical in real life. Roland fights for personal and family honor (Kibler, "Roland's Pride," 151, 154). Cf. Gaston Paris, *La Poésie du Moyen Age*, vol. 1, 2d ed. (Paris, 1887), 109 ("from personal pride, first of all, and from family pride, but also from a sense of national honor"); Mermier, 95; Burger, "Deux Scènes," 113.

role—the heedless pursuit of private ends and personal status—is the traitor's. Of the two, he is the one who uses his free choice from the beginning. In a major departure from the traditional procedure, Roger Pensom has provided a remarkably similar restatement of Ganelon's position relative to Roland in the poem: "Ganelon is dedicated to his own freedom, and Roland to the acknowledgement of the constraints that bind him and which order his life."[18] But despite his numerous remarks on the "common-sense" aspects of the narration, Pensom appears to share at least some of the mistrust of the story to which I have referred and to which I will return in the next chapter. He relies on analogies with the categories of psychoanalysis as warrants for his interpretation of this passage and others. Thus, further along, he classifies Roland's sense of responsibility as "neurotic."[19] I will continue to stick as closely as I can to the poem's events and words, which do not suggest to me the sort of internal conflict Pensom describes in the hero.

Roland is the first to speak in the Council Scene, but he names no names except Marsile's, and insults no one in particular (unless we make the large assumption that the unexpressed plural subject of the verb *loerent* in line 206 is Ganelon and not the plural *Franceis* from 205). The hero's argument is historical, and the necessities to which he refers have no personal dimension. Only a very strong extratextual hypothesis like *démesure* can invest his words with insulting qualities. Ganelon chooses to fling the first insult of the poem in response, and his counsel flies in the face of reality as established by the Franks' prior experience of Marsile. He chooses to make a cutting reply to a reasonable if energetic evocation of the situation as it stands. Following a principle discussed in Chapter 2, Ganelon's first choice then governs at least his own later choices, including the choice to betray, since his embassy is the logical but impractical result of the counsel he gave in his first speech. What happens to him is clear without our having to extrapolate, from his allusions when cornered, some idea of a long-standing quarrel between him and Roland. The quarrel that is in the text is enough.[20]

In general, then, our understanding of the text has little to gain by our injecting either great subtlety or lonely nobility into Ganelon's reactions in the Council Scene and the later actions that follow from them.[21] There is no longer much risk (as perhaps there once was)

[18]Pensom, esp. 84–95.

[19]Ibid., 133ff.

[20]The idea that something we never learn about must precede the Council Scene in order for it to possess coherence goes back at least to Petit de Julleville (in his 1878 ed., 67) and is still repeated with some regularity despite such arguments as Hall's.

[21]The "good Ganelon" motif in criticism is another very old one. Paulin Paris, 740:

that, if we decide Ganelon is wrong, critics unsympathetic to ancient narrative forms will mistake him for the mustache-twisting villain of some simplistic melodrama. Like the setting in which he appears, the character may be thought univocal without being considered simplistic. His initial insistence on treating with an untrustworthy enemy leads him into prolonged opposition to his society's best interests. He makes a mistake, and hews to it; there is, unfortunately, nothing unrealistic in that. We should not forget that Ganelon was created in an age when error had overtones of commitment to evil and that (much like the pagans) he cannot desist from perversity. But we do not have to take that fact as a starting point for discovering what he does in the text. There have been numerous apologias for him, but none has reconciled him with all the facets of his manifestation in the *Song*. Thus Moignet, for example, follows Ruggieri's lead in saying that Ganelon's challenge to Roland before leaving on his mission is legitimate because it is couched in technically valid terms; yet this fails to address a larger issue. No *desfi* is valid except as a response to sufficient provocation, as Ganshof implies.[22] Even without reference to the fact that both Roland and Ganelon are on campaign in Charles's service, even without recalling (as Ganelon does not) that he swore to aid an enemy, the pretext Ganelon uses is far from adequate. Roland's suggestion, followed by a procedurally correct ratification from the group, is nothing but the consequence of Ganelon's own arguments, and no provocation at all.

A certain body of secondary literature nonetheless argues that

---

"Even as a criminal, Ganelon possesses a sort of heroic grandeur: he has his reasons for wishing to include the entire council in his vengeance" (this passage also furnishes a typical example of affirmation without argument). On the Ganelon problem, see the works cited by Brault, *Song*, 1:378, nn. 539–40, and J. Thomas's summary, 91; Thomas suspects Ganelon's defenders among critics are more numerous than those who condemn him. For examples, see Le Gentil, *Song*, 82–87, 114–16; Eisner, 182–83 (his treason "unwitting"); Stranges, 334, 340–41, 343 (forced to betray by circumstances); Burger, "Rire," 9; Moignet, 45, 49; Waltz, 31–32; Halverson, 666; Ruggieri's study on the trial, cited in note 132 to the Commentary. Others find him partly good or ambiguous: Petit de Julleville, 66–69; Léon Gautier, "L'Epopée nationale," in Louis Petit de Julleville, ed., *Histoire de la langue et de la littérature française*, vol. 1, part 1 (Paris, 1896), 96 ("he is struggling with himself"); Owen, *Song of Roland*, 20–21; Marianne Cramer Vos, "Ganelon's *mortel rage*," *Olifant*, 2 (1974–75), 16; Horrent, *Chanson de Roland dans les littératures . . .*, 270–71. For another group of scholars, Ganelon is clearly evil (Robertson, *Preface to Chaucer*, 163–65; Golden, "Die Rolle Ganelons"; Pensom, 94ff.; Brault, *Song*, 1:100; Kellogg.

[22]Ganshof, 98–99, discusses only relationships between lord and vassal, not among equals, but the gravity of situations leading to *diffidatio* is unmistakable (cf. Lemarignier, 138–39).

Ganelon never committed treason and that an attack on Roland was (as Ganelon claims when on trial) a matter of private vengeance, not implying betrayal of Charles or the army. We have no way of knowing what Ganelon was thinking when he explained to Blancandrin and Marsile how to deprive Charles of his right arm (laisses 29–30, 41–45). But we can at least compare Ganelon's claims about the act with what the poem shows. His claim, made after we have seen the bloody consequences of what he did, is not at all compelling, even if we were to decide that conflict between king and "overmighty subject" is a generic attribute of heroic epic.[23] Let us grant that in reference to the much more tenuous relations of twelfth-century political life, with its multiple homages, treason is a difficult term to apply. Local laws in the eleventh or twelfth century may have been quite as complicated as the situations they had to resolve. But feudalism is the setting and not the theme of the *Song*. The theme is responsibility: the knight's duty to serve God and one suzerain as a knight. Like any trial, Ganelon's may bring to mind any number of potentially relevant analogies and arguments. But the Oxford poet's art is, once again, an art of reduction. As he settled the Spanish question on the battlefield, he proves by unanswerable violent device that the right can prevail even when men's prevarications hinder it. The issue in the Trial Scene is the power of Ganelon's family and friends to prevent or delay judgment—summed up in the threatening presence of Pinabel, who has sworn to champion Ganelon without any reference whatever to law. The barons do not acquit Ganelon; they fail to judge at all. They are *felun*, as Charles puts it, deficient in feudal morality, offering no *consilium*. It is their abdication and not any uncertainty about Ganelon's guilt that gives rise to the duel, making Thierry's confrontation with Pinabel every bit as necessary as the fight at Roncevaux, and (for much the same reasons) every bit as significant.

Oliver is not like Ganelon. He is clearly different from Roland, but not his opposite. However, a reaffirmation of the primacy of sacrifice as an ideal in the poem means a reevaluation of Oliver's stance, one that will be at least as thorough as the one to which Ganelon's must be subjected. The classic view of Oliver is that he embodies *sapientia*, thought, while Roland knows only action.[24] The deduction behind that opposition seems to be based on Oliver's pleas for release from what he says is an unnecessary combat. Critical tradition assumes,

[23]For such a claim, see Jackson, esp. 129.

[24]The idea that "Roland's behaviour may be dictated by an ethos which invests action with positive moral value" is expressed most recently in Kay, 483.

minimally, that because Oliver expresses concern with saving lives, Roland must be throwing them away. The hero does not answer Oliver because he is unable to.

But the famous, ink-drowned scenes of argument become clearer if we recognize that Roland and Oliver are not talking about the same things. They are not taking the opposing sides of a single argument; their premises are different.[25] Oliver is expressing the urgency of the immediate situation, while Roland looks beyond the circumstances to their consequences. Oliver may be concerned with saving lives, but Roland is concerned with why men may not care whether they die. If anyone were to blow the horn, it would have to be Roland, but that is not the same as saying that Oliver furnishes him good reasons to. As ever, the hero argues from principle, while his companion can, for the moment, see only the approaching Saracens and their unexpectedly vast numbers. As Ganelon's and Naimon's wills to peace strike a chord in us, so does Oliver's anxiety. It seems cruelly insufficient for Roland to say or imply that if only we do our duty everything will work out in the end. Yet what appears to be prudence, like what appears to be peace, may turn out to be something else in the long term. I repeat that the paradoxical nature of this idea may explain why the *Song of Roland* is ordered the way it is: not because the point it has to make is simplistic, but because it is a challenging idea and needs to be presented as strongly as possible. For within the *Song*, everything does work out. At the end, Spain is rid of the foes of Christendom, and Thierry at last sees to it that justice can be done.

Thus the consideration of how the principal characters are related brings us back to matters of structure. The traditional reading of the *Song*, in assigning to Oliver (if not to Ganelon) virtues as a soldier and counselor that Roland does not possess, furnishes a paradox that competes with the paradox of duty. It yields a complex arrangement of two heroic or exemplary protagonists. Their precise values have proven difficult to fix, but generally speaking, Oliver is said to be superior in wisdom and both are thought about equal in prowess.[26]

[25]J. M. Enders, "La Logique des débats dans la *Chanson de* Roland" (M.A. thesis, University of Virginia, 1979), shows that their forms of argumentation are significantly different also. As we might expect by now, Roland's is deductive, beginning with principles, and Oliver's is inductive, beginning with an immediate situation. Of course, inductive arguments are local, while deductive arguments are general in their applications.

[26]On the *proz-sage* dichotomy, see the commentary to laisse 87, and also Brault, *Song*, 1:11–15; Misrahi and Hendrickson, 359–61, 364–67; Uitti, 109–12; Wendt, 290–96; Jean Subrenat, ". . . e Oliver est proz," *Etudes de philologie romane et d'histoire littéraire offertes à Jules Horrent* (Liège, 1980), 461–67. The idea of Oliver's superiority is again

The present reading clarifies things in this area, as it does elsewhere, by placing Oliver on another level, giving him the role that Ganelon's defenders, by and large, have sought to assign the latter: that of a noble man who makes a mistake only under great pressure. The complexity is not entirely lost; only the emphasis changes. For this and other reasons, I have felt free to describe the poem as didactic and its hero as exemplary without any fear of diminishing its interest thereby. The attractive notion of a worthy but flawed knight who falters in his duty to a comrade is still in the work, but the poem's range has been extended. It still includes three types of protagonists, but at a greater remove from one another. Ganelon does ill, Roland does good, fairly consistently, but there is still room for the recognition that these are extremes. Roland is what has sometimes been called an *actor,* Ganelon is an *opposer,* but Oliver is a foil (*repoussoir*).[27]

Blind to the implications of what is happening, the hero's comrade lashes out verbally at him more than once. Later, when physically blinded, he will symbolically strike Roland an unjustified sword-blow and receive his forgiveness. A bit like Ganelon, he knows only one kind of danger. Yet he does not commit treason. He does not hear Roland's statement of principle well, but he knows his duty in spite of that.[28] That is why he is *esguaret,* disturbed, at the thought that he must stand his ground. But when Roland dies for duty's sake in a large sense, Oliver dies too, for the sake of that smaller duty of comradeship.

That is enough. As long as Roland knows his responsibility as lieutenant and leader and holds to his promises in the face of adversity, then Oliver will in fact follow him and meet his fate also. This could be pathetic, but only in another setting. Roland dies the death of knowledge. He has spoken of the danger and sworn to discount it,

---

both ancient and very well entrenched. Léon Gautier, "L'Epopée nationale," 89, spoke of his "tranquil valor, alongside [Roland's] frantic bravery"; Paulin Paris, 741, claimed that "Oliver seems to prevail, because he adds caution and calmness to [Roland's] warlike fearlessness." The idea can be traced down to Fox, 68–69: "The poet clearly expected his audience to admire Roland . . . but to approve rather of Oliver and his saner, more practical approach." Further examples may be found in Le Gentil, *Song,* 110–11 (our "secret preference" for Oliver); Mermier, 98–99; Pauphilet, *Legs,* 76; Faral, *Chanson,* 218; Siciliano, 346–47; Gérard, 448–49; Halverson, 664 (Roland "is not quick"; Oliver "thinks . . . in terms of the common good" and is "something of a new man"); Williamson, 557 (Roland is "selectively deaf" to Oliver's advice); Calin, 23 (Oliver is Roland's "better conscience").

[27]For a summary of this "modèle actantiel," energetically applied to the study of narrative about a decade ago, see Oswald Ducrot and Tzvetan Todorov, *Dictionnaire encyclopédique des sciences du langage* (Paris, 1972), 290–91. Ducrot and Todorov do not mention the term *foil;* its use here is a matter of induction.

[28]See Brault, *"Sapientia,"* 101; Crosland, 82; Uitti, 109, Del Monte, 234.

from the first. That is a form of *sapientia*—possibly the implication of the line that calls him *proz.*[29] Oliver's strength is in the fortitude of adherence in the face of doubt, and that could, just possibly, be a meaning of *sage.*

Roland can see what Oliver cannot. He speaks not of the moment, but of the potential effects of his actions in the future. If he fears *malvaises cançuns,* it is because his deeds will live after him in exemplary form (he is already inside an epic) and readers and hearers will learn from them. This is, by implication, one of the civilizing principles behind feudalism: that a promise can be held binding beyond the present; that a knight can describe a future for himself and then hold to it. Roland's death, then, implies the survival of his principles. That means we must consider the Baligant and Trial episodes, whatever their ultimate origins, as being at home in the poem we have. They do not merely prolong the battle of Roncevaux, but make its meaning explicit. They are, at least, clearly foreshadowed in Oliver's accusation: *Ja mais Karlun de nos n'avrat servise* ("Never again will Charles receive our service"; line 1727). That has been taken as a self-evident condemnation of Roland, but the text shows it to be as irrelevant in the mouth of the doubting Oliver as in the mouth of the boasting pagan Escremiz: *De bons vassals avrat Carles suffraite* ("Charles will be short of good men"; 939). The sequence may originally have been the result of historical accident. The Baligant episode may not be as old as the rest. But once we recognize the theme of sacrifice in the work, we will see that the army's victory over Baligant's men (see 3511–16, 3543–59), like that of Thierry over Pinabel, is meant to show the consequences of the sacrifice the poem advocates.

Finally, the death of Gautier del Hum and Aude's refusal to live after Roland's death are elegantly embedded echoes of the principal theme of responsible commitment, expressed through the same sense of hierarchy. Gautier's decision depends in the first instance on Roland's, and his story is set within the story of the rear guard. Aude dies because Roland has died, and beyond all sentimentality the thing she says is perfectly adequate to the situation. Roland was pledged to

[29]On *proz,* see also Brault's different arguments in his "*Sapientia,*" 105–8. Thomas Aquinas's later definition of *fortitudo* may include traditional elements. "For Saint Thomas Aquinas courage [la force, *fortitudo*] is . . . both firmness of mind in the accomplishment of a duty and, in consequence, the condition for all virtue. . . . Fortitude is *a kind of golden mean* [*conduite du juste milieu;* my trans., emphasis added; see original, p. 407], 'a virtue which moderates fear and boldness for the common good.'" (Contamine, 251.) Niles cites a definition of *fortitudo* that includes forbearance and patience, from the Anglo-Saxon Wulfstan; see John Niles, *Beowulf* (Cambridge, Mass., 1983), 224–25. On *sapientia,* see Brault, "*Sapientia,*" 108ff., and McCash, 143–44.

her, and whatever the pledge she made in her turn, she considers that situation purely and simply binding. "May it not please God, his saints, or his angels, / That I remain alive after Roland" (3718–19). Aude echoes Roland's refusal of the easier alternatives Charles offers, and her assent to duty is as straightforward as his. She does not die of a broken heart, but as Roland and Gautier died: in witness to a principle.

Thus even if the question had any bearing on interpretation, we would not need to agree that an exemplary *Song of Roland* lacks interest or even complexity of texture, where either structure or the relationships among characters are concerned. To bend a cliché, it is Romanesque in its way: a powerfully stark architectonics that sometimes stands alone and is sometimes highly decorated.[30] To be more direct, it is a straightforward story set in complicated circumstances, which is, perhaps, one of the ways we can distinguish moral art from naive propagandizing. It may even be to our advantage as humane critics to exchange the old Roland for the new. It may make Ganelon or Oliver seem more at the mercy of their fears and hesitations.[31] But in return, we get a poem in which numerous interlocking gestures are structurally decisive and are not obscure bits of byplay. Above all, we receive a hero of towering stature, exaggerated at times as Romanesque figures are, yet whose exaggerated traits are appropriate to the size of the challenge he faces. Time has tried, in its unsettling way, to diminish his stature, but the path he chooses leads to an authentically heroic destiny. Maybe the name of the narrow place where Roland's road ends can come to stand for something besides a grandiose debacle.

[30]On Romanesque aesthetics in the visual and literary arts, see Robertson, *Preface,* 138–71; Brault, *Song,* 1:44–47; Farnham; Nichols; Charles F. Altman, "Interpreting Romanesque Narrative: Conques and the *Roland,*" *Olifant,* 5 (1977–78), 4–28.

[31]I would not go so far as to endorse Van Emden's claim that Cartier's analysis "runs the risk . . . of turning Oliver, Charles and Naimon into imbeciles and cowards" ("Guarant," 26). Cf. note 9 to this chapter. Among the Christians there are not two systems at odds, but two ways of reacting to stress and challenge—*pace* Halverson.

[4]

Coherence and Ideology

Through the situations, characters, and contrasts described in the Commentary and the preceding chapters, the *Song of Roland* offers the picture of a heroism based in awareness and choice. Its place in early medieval society should not be difficult to recognize, for the heroism of choice is well suited to the freedoms and concomitant restraints of the feudal arrangement. By choosing freely (in principle) to follow a leader, and by doing a voluntary act of homage, feudal people participated in the fixing of their own futures.[1] But the personal promises of homage also imply that when theory and abstraction come to the test, then the person and the concept will be tested together. For heroism to mean anything under the homage bond, the hero must understand the ideal of commitment, the promise itself, and their relationship to what may happen in the future.

The *démesure* interpretation of the *Song of Roland* became standard at a time when critics and historians did not treat such concepts as coherent. In fact, their attitudes toward their subject in general can hardly have predisposed them to take feudal ideas in literature seriously. The most fruitful context in which to view the *Song* is not the spontaneous and "childlike" Middle Ages dear to Gaston Paris: "The men of that time were less inclined to reflect on things than we

[1]As Ganshof said (though he was speaking of the Carolingians): "*Fides,* faith, is fealty promised under oath; it is this which governs the conduct of a free man, while a slave is governed only by fear of the rod" (p. 29). It is true that R. H. Bloch has associated with the *Roland* and with Old French epic in general "a certain closure to its own posterity . . . a blindness to (repression of?) any possibility of the future" (R. H. Bloch, *Etymologies and Genealogies,* 103; Roland is "a terminal figure," 105); but cf. the studies cited in note 157 to the Commentary.

are. . . . They lived naively, like children, in whom the thoughtful life developed by civilization has not yet stifled the free growth of natural vitality."[2]

The *Song* is much easier to grasp if we remove it from the age of unthinking naïveté and set it instead in the age institutional historians inquire into: a Middle Ages actively (if unsystematically) working to create and maintain order among sometimes unruly adults. Post-medieval culture in general (not just literary historians and critics) has taken a pessimistic view of medieval concepts of social order. I will refer again shortly to the effect of that pessimism on criticism of the *Song of Roland*. Let it suffice to say here that it is not necessarily criticism's role to imply that literature can succeed only by showing the irrational side of such an arrangement as the feudal scheme.

Once again, this leads not so much to an argument for Roland, as a personality to be approved, as to the argument that his personality is at most a secondary issue. The poem presents above all the interaction between principle and situation. Different characters, we have seen, react to the situations portrayed in different ways, according to their lights. But the situations are the primary givens, not the characters, and the *Song of Roland* is a study in how each knight faces them.

That is one of the phenomena that give the work its universal interest. It is far too easy to distance oneself from the unpleasant man we have come to know as Roland, and to deny the immanence of dangerous choices like the one he makes. And it is risky to proceed as though we were sure feudal society was incapable of conceiving the immanence of personal responsibility in terms of its own. Yet numerous critical essays have sought a sense for the *Roland* in modern psychology, in Greek literary theory or the distantly related structures of classical French tragedy, in primitive myth, in timeless theology, and elsewhere, to the neglect of basic assumptions about warfare and politics current in the era of its composition and first diffusion.[3]

[2]Gaston Paris begins: "The Middle Ages are an essentially poetic period. By that I mean that everything in them is spontaneous, capricious, unexpected" (*La Poésie du Moyen Age*, 1:9).

[3]I have been led here, by a different conception of Roland's actions and also of feudal principle, to a conclusion much like that associated with the work of Erich Köhler, Matthias Waltz, and Karl-Heinz Bender. The *Song of Roland* is an idealizing work and can be viewed as implying a political program, requiring individual commitment to the ideal community, the *projektierte Gemeinschaft*. The authors just named appear, however, to associate feudalism with rampant individualism and even anarchy, in the tradition of Hegel or Marx. I prefer the historians' use of the name to evoke a system of relationships and duties not at all antithetical to stability or even monarchy. See also Waltz's important note: "In the contemporary mind, to be sure, this was certainly not a projected society, but rather something like the true society in contrast to

To study the logic of choices and their effects in the *Song of Roland* does not mean forgetting Gaston Paris's prestigious characterization of the narrative as a series of "successive explosions, constantly cut short, then suddenly bursting out again," nor can one ignore the strong interpretation Eugène Vinaver put on that remark of Gaston Paris's: "This brings us to the threshold of a world unaware of the art of transition, and grants the work the right to exist beyond any concern with continuity."[4] However we read the *Roland* globally, it may indeed appear locally disconnected to us at times. That does not mean we can assume that our uncertainty is always an effect of composition. It may instead stem simply from the historically conditioned fact that the *Song*'s events do not always have the results, and that its characters do not always exhibit the reactions, that we tend to expect. A denial of all concern for continuity in a traditional narrative (or its author or its world) on the grounds of apparent obscurity may well be a fundamental methodological signal. The denial might well have been the prelude to intense historical study and debate, not an occasion for enthroning *démesure* and ambiguity as keys to the ancient work. The commentary to laisses 69–88 should suffice to demonstrate that paratactic style and the self-contained laisse do not necessarily imply a breakdown of narrative sequence. The *Song* may be clear without being explicit, if we allow that juxtaposition of episodes and speeches can serve as a device of communication. And if we let one further probability guide us—the very strong likelihood that the public with which the *Song* communicated had certain knowledge and attitudes in common—then we will never need to argue from the major premise of incoherence to make a point about either its style or its meaning.[5]

How can a work be laconic and still be clear? I have suggested an answer. The *Song of Roland,* like other great medieval works, is *allusive.* The text involves experiences and concepts familiar to the intended audience without giving an explanation then and there. This allusive quality, when it exists, must not be confused with inherent mystery or contrived circularity. Sometimes an implied audience appears to be treated as if it is at home, yet the critic remains at sea.

---

the real existing one. Nonetheless, the term 'projected society' is preferable to a term such as 'ideal' or 'true' society, because it brings out a very important fact: *this society has no institutional reality as yet*" (Waltz, *Rolandslied,* 19, emphasis added; cf. 24, 36, 39, 49).

[4]Eugène Vinaver, *A la recherche d'une poétique médiévale* (Paris, 1970), 52–53; similar remarks in Vinaver, *The Rise of Romance* (New York, 1971), 4–14. On cause and effect in the *Song,* compare Hunt, "Character and Causality," 4, 30–33; Kay, 481; Bédier, *Légendes,* 3:418 (who says we understand, despite their absence).

[5]See the discussion in Chapter 1, and the works cited in note 20 to that chapter.

Then the suspicion arises that an intended or real audience may have been expected to respond to a cultural reference. Under those conditions, the critic's job is to seek and sketch the modes of thought and action to which the work is probably alluding.[6]

This is the step Erich Auerbach explicitly refused to take, and his refusal may be seen as symptomatic of a lacuna in mid- to late-twentieth-century criticism.[7] In his famous discussion of the scene in which Roland is nominated to lead the rear guard, Auerbach asks why Charlemagne does not do the things that a reader—*this* reader—expects him to do. Why does he accept the nomination without ratification by the army? How much does he know of Ganelon's plot? How can he be so angry and yet fail to put a halt to the betrayal?[8]

"It is possible to find various explanations for all this," said Auerbach briefly, invoking what he called the "weakness of the central power in the feudal order of society."[9] But then he halted at the brink of history. After having mentioned this parallel order of explanation, he did not investigate the possibility that it may indeed explain what is not explicit—that there may be strong constraints, part of public knowledge, at work in the unfolding of this scene. Instead, he moved directly into the wonderful stylistic analysis that has linked his name to the important notion of parataxis in the poem. He never again paused to consider that the uncertainties of which he spoke may have been temporary accidents, characterizing a particular state of a given reading, rather than being essential features of the poem's technique of narration, to which an original or intended audience would necessarily have responded as hesitatingly as he did.[10] On the other hand, the reader deferent to the effects of passing time suspects that the resonance between text and cultural context in the Nomination Scene may once have been so strong as to approach denotative status. We

[6]For the view that allusiveness precludes logic (e.g., in the Horn Scenes), see Brault, *Song*, 1:29–30. As Wilson makes clear, the relationship between intended and implied audience is more complex than my remarks here might imply.

[7]Auerbach's refusal (in *Mimesis*) to seek explanations that are both artistically plausible and historically probable is part of a long tradition, despite its obvious affinities with recent antihistorical trends on the theoretical level. It is echoed by Vance, *Reading*, 12–23, and Farnham, 152.

[8]Auerbach, *Mimesis*, 87–88.

[9]Ibid.

[10]For the reading itself, in summary form, see Erich Auerbach, *Introduction to Romance Languages and Literatures*, trans. from the French version by Guy Daniels (New York, 1961), 98. I repeat that sentence parataxis is not at issue here, only the idea that the juxtapositions analogous to parataxis on the level of narrative sequence necessarily preclude logic and clarity. Cf. Farnham, 153; R. H. Bloch, *Etymologies and Genealogies*, 101.

are crossing a mountain with an army on foot; we do not know whether we can trust the enemy behind us. What then? asks Charles. But do we really need to wonder, even after almost nine hundred years?

To claim that we can only wonder is to give the impression of a textual incoherence that it would be premature to affirm. After all, incoherence is one of those hypotheses that disable induction: in simple terms, if we assume it, then we will not search for coherence, and we may not see the latter even though it exists. Critics have a certain obligation to test the alternatives before making sweeping pronouncements about matters so essential to the reception of a poem. Here it is clear that we might do well to examine some of the possibilities inherent in the historical explanation that Auerbach so summarily rejected, both for completeness' sake and in order to see whether our renewed picture of the poem is easier to reconcile with the text. In the case of a poem long studied but rarely expounded in all its parts, we may also have to refer to certain tendencies of the secondary literature. That is a complicated procedure and a thankless one, but I think the example from Auerbach suggests that it is an essential element of orientation for anyone who wishes to distinguish clearly between the medieval context of the *Song of Roland* and the things most often said about the work in a modern context. Before going on with the discussion of how *démesure* can usefully be replaced, I will continue in that vein here. It is natural to think that the possibility of coherence in the *Song of Roland* has already been pursued to some conclusion and that Auerbach's assumption is not an assumption but the result of a failure to find coherence. That is not at all the case.

What needs to be noted first, then, is the (perhaps surprising) extent to which a certain discontinuity or incoherence of structure in the *Song of Roland* is an unexamined assumption. Like many ideas in our critical baggage, it has a pedigree. It has been part of the literature at least since the middle of the last century, and it appears in the work of some of the most influential of all the specialists in Old French epic. In 1852, Paulin Paris reported in the *Song* "an obscurity that is not easily dissipated," which he attributed to the scribe's ignorance.[11] He was reacting to Jean-Louis Bourdillon's description of the Oxford poem as "the greatest batch of foolishness to be found anywhere." In treating the *Song*, Gustav Gröber spoke at some length of its "te-

[11]Paulin Paris, 748–49. Paris, 749, cites the remark by J.-L. Bourdillon, quoted below.

diousness, the expansions . . . the epic formulas, the distorted sources, the anachronisms, which sow confusion in the logic of the narration, spoil its essential mood, and prevent any effect of unity."[12] (He was comparing the Oxford poem with an ideal, lost text then often thought to have preceded it.)

Léon Gautier's classic school edition includes an explicit recommendation to the secondary-school teacher who is expected to use it: the teacher is not to attempt to compare the composition of the *Song* to that of the *Iliad* or to Virgil. "He will demonstrate with ease that the ancient models are superior in form." The scribe who copied the Oxford text, "poor man," was "not up to his task, and far too often distracted" (*fort médiocre et sujet à de trop nombreuses distractions*). As for the text itself, Gautier follows Gaston Paris's lead (if Gaston Paris did not follow his) in evoking its spontaneous and childlike character ("*primitif et presque enfantin*"): "It is a sort of improvisation whose sincerity is truly unmatched."[13]

Gaston Paris is perhaps the clearest of all the early authorities in his condemnations of the poem's composition. In his own textbook, the *Extraits de la "Chanson de Roland,"* he describes the Oxford poem as Gröber was to do in the next generation. To Paris it was a poor copy of a finer (but lost) original, and its redactor, despite some good work, was unable or unwilling to bring it up to proper narrative standards. "In his work of adaptation and embellishment, he overlooked more than one contradiction. Marsile states at the outset that he has no army, and then fields an immense one; his uncle, the *algalife* (caliph) seems to play an important role at first, and scarcely appears afterward. . . . The character of Ganelon presents . . . striking inconsistencies."[14] The same textbook shows impatience with the arrangement of the opening episodes in the Oxford text. It is not "natural" for Marsile to send messengers to Charles rather than vice versa; the mission of Ganelon to Saragossa is "without any very clear function": "Our poet seems to have imitated here an episode belonging to an earlier part of the epic tradition concerning the Spanish campaign, and this

[12]Gröber, 2(1):463.

[13]Léon Gautier, *La Chanson de Roland,* "new ed." (Tours, n.d.), viii, xxx–xxxi; Gaston Paris's *Histoire poétique de Charlemagne* (1865; 2d ed., Paris, 1905) and the first edition of Gautier's *Epopées françaises* (Paris, 1865–68), the masterpieces of the two great nineteenth-century interpreters of the *Song of Roland,* are roughly contemporary. Both authors also published later works in which the poem is described, but it is not always possible to know whether they had influenced each other.

[14]Gaston Paris, *Extraits,* xxvi–xxvii. The same words appear in Gaston Paris's influential textbook, *La Littérature française au Moyen Age,* 61.

rather unfortunate innovation causes confusion throughout the entire first part of his presentation."[15] The invocation of a traditionalist doctrine of epic transmission to explain what is taken (on no compelling grounds) to be an inconsistency may be noted. But what is more important for the moment is the ease with which Gaston Paris dismisses the known poem in favor of an unattested ideal text—a dismissal undoubtedly made easier by his conviction (stated elsewhere) that the authors of the surviving medieval texts had no sense of literary art. More than once, Gaston Paris refers to the "limited amount of thought they devoted to their works" and to "their ignorance of . . . the conditions of their art."[16] These are the specialist advocates of medieval literature speaking; we will see further on that a nonmedievalist like Brunetière put his condemnations even more strongly.

To the mind of Gaston Paris, then, there was something obviously missing from the *Song of Roland*, something he expected to see in narrative literature and did not find here. Surely one of the missing elements was psychological motivation (Ganelon's, for example), the work's theme having long before been defined as psychological in nature.[17] And, of course, Gaston Paris and the other authors quoted were the lions in the path for the generations that followed and that tried to apply broader standards of literary success to medieval works—the generation of Auerbach and of Joseph Bédier (who was Paris's pupil) and that of Vinaver (who was Bédier's) and of Robert Guiette. We shall see that the logic Bédier defends in the *Song*, in reaction to criticisms of the sort just quoted, is a logic of psychological reactions. In all this, mountains, promises, and soldiering are mentioned only in passing.

Given the prestige of the pioneers, it is easy to understand why it is not rare today for the *Song of Roland* to be described, both openly and by implication, as a partly or totally incoherent sequence. "To understand the various decisions of our author is not an easy task," says Le Gentil.[18] The poem remains narrative, but the relationship of its parts is a mystery. We will recall that Zumthor speaks of "what appears, on the level of narrative causality, to be a lack of clarity, an ambiguity

[15]Gaston Paris, *Extraits*, xviii–xix.

[16]Gaston Paris, "Préface," in Petit de Julleville, ed., *Histoire de la langue et de la littérature française*, 1,1, pp. q [*sic*] ff.

[17]See note 23 to Chapter 1, above.

[18]Le Gentil, *Song*, 126.

deriving from the uncertainty into which the reader is plunged."[19] Whether we are partisans of the "clarity" loosely associated with French classicism, or else lovers of ambiguity and the *discontinu,* we will probably think of this mystery as an issue of aesthetics. Yet the pleasures and challenges of uncertainty may not be the only elements present: the presumption of incoherence is first and foremost a matter of interpretation, and the presumption here has been sustained specifically by the idea of Charles's and Roland's freedom from restraints of hierarchy and terrain—a notion necessary to the *démesure* hypothesis and thus one that has been in the back of nearly every medievalist's mind for a long time. It may be a habitual way of combining the aesthetics with the reading that "plunges the reader into uncertainty" here, and not the events of the text or their relationships.

This, then, is one of the places where a hermeneutic circle may turn static and even vicious by blocking the normal process of testing fuller explanations. From the very first, the pioneer medievalists displayed their confidence that reasons for certain elements and combinations in the *Song* need not be sought. Their insistence on a few key lines and scenes makes much of the narrative text appear to be peripheral or extraneous to the sense.[20] After all, both medieval poets and their audiences tended to pay little attention to how poems were constructed (I return to Gaston Paris's seminal work here): "Speaking to an audience which has neither any established ideas of literary perfec-

[19]Zumthor, *Essai,* 337; this is perhaps an echo of Auerbach's description of "a paratactic situation made up of theses which, extremely narrow as they are, are yet full of contradictions" (*Mimesis,* 88). "How do we explain the lack of logic in the central conflicts which propel the poem's action?" asked Vance in 1970 (*Reading,* 2). On incoherence, see further Gaston Paris, *Histoire poétique de Charlemagne,* 22; *Extraits,* xix, xxvi, xxvii, 94 ("It is a bizarre idea, if grandiose, to have Roland seek out the bodies of the eleven other peers"); Bédier's discussion, *Légendes,* 3:405ff.; Le Gentil, "A propos de la *démesure,*" 209; Ross, "Before *Roland,*" 176 ("muddle and confusion"); Halverson, 667 (Thierry's charge against Ganelon is a "gratuitous" introduction); Menéndez Pidal, frequently (e.g., 430: Charles does not act on dream evidence); Owen, "Secular Inspiration," 391 (on Roland's nomination of Ganelon); Julian Eugene White, "*La Chanson de Roland*: Secular or Religious Inspiration?" *Romania,* 84 (1963), 398–408 (Roland's manner of death is "manifestly ridiculous," 406).

[20]The atmosphere created by such pronouncements may help explain judgments on the text that we might otherwise find difficult to comprehend. "The poem is hardly cluttered with events; its story is easy to tell," says Petit de Julleville, *Histoire de la littérature française des origines à nos jours,* 10th ed. (Paris, 1895), 21; indeed, he recounts the opening scenes in fifteen lines. Gröber, 465, spoke of "contradictions in the narration." Crosland, 91, spoke of the poem's "digressions" and monotony; it is "saved from dreariness by the flashes of humanity which will keep breaking through" (despite the poet?). Menéndez Pidal, 125, ironizes on the Baligant episode: "As if the Almighty had not done enough, another battle is thought necessary."

tion, nor any serious concept of science, nor indeed a stable and regular way of life, the poet seeks only to amuse or to move his audience, giving no heed to verisimilitude, to artistic composition, or to formal refinements."[21] It is natural to conclude that seeking a story's logical underpinnings under such conditions is a waste of time. That attitude has had its effect on critics and interpreters who have regularly accepted incoherence in varying degrees even when they refuse the major premise of naïveté. Hence not only the easy dismissal of the Baligant episode, but also certain vexed critical reactions to the reappearance of Gautier del Hum or to Aude's death. And it is largely true that (in Auerbach's words) "the poet explains nothing," at least through sentences or *sententiae.* Yet local parataxis does not exclude global meaning. There may be no need for "explanatory connectives" on that level. The contradictions may exist only in the expectations of readers who have not yet explored the things to which the poem alludes.

It will now be easy to see that more recent criticism, such as Eugène Vinaver's subtle discussion of the death of Roland, may well rely on ideas about the poem that have long been current. The aesthetic attractiveness of Vinaver's remarks should not obscure the alternatives they do not present. More clearly than Auerbach, Vinaver takes a stand on the interpretation of the work as a whole, and (following a suggestion of Bédier's) he finds it ambiguous.

> What, finally, is the *Song of Roland* taken as a whole? Is it the triumph of a bold man, who is right, over a wise man, or the opposite? Roland or Oliver: which is the triumphant hero? "The poet," as Bédier so excellently put it, "does not choose; he was too human to choose." I would be tempted to say he was too much a man of the twelfth century to need to choose. . . . What, then, does it mean to be brave when one is not "wise"? Is it foolish pride, as Oliver thinks? Roland, it is said, hopes for victory; but if he does, it is not thanks to his ability as a leader to gauge the enemy's strength. . . . The poet does not say; he does not decide. He is not constrained by any desire for a reasoned solution, for any "unity of spirit," for any moral coherence. A profound and unresolved duality is what remains.[22]

And here we have the motif of incoherence in a resolutely modernist form.[23] Is it then surprising that Vinaver's defense and praise of the

[21]Gaston Paris, *La Poésie du Moyen Age,* 1:21.

[22]Vinaver, *A la recherche,* 73–74.

[23]For statements in the same vein, see Brault, "*Sapientia,*" 101–2; Siciliano, 355; Gérard, 445, 448, 450; Hunt, "Tragedy," 797.

work takes the form of an exposition on this very uncertainty, granting the *Song* (after Lanson) "a power superior to that of a sequential narration?" Of the period in which the poem was composed, he adds:

> We are purely and simply at a point in our literary history where the problematics of life, the reasoned motivation of human acts and gestures, is still outside the language of poetry. In the *Song of Roland,* nothing is clear in itself, and yet nothing is explained. At its deepest level, the poet places his work outside any relationship of cause and effect, in the expressive totality of juxtaposed themes which deny the moment of causation its role as moment of creation.[24]

The very encomium springs from a prior (and traditional) refusal to accept that the sequence can have a broad sense accessible by inference or induction, and there is no attempt to put it into a frame of reference (except for the allusion to what is and is not human). Yet, as in Auerbach's analysis (to which Vinaver refers), style does not speak for itself: "In the paratactic lines of the *Song of Roland,* the reader is never called upon to reconstitute, through thought, the underlying movement of causation."[25] The warrant of ambiguity is in fact a conception of the text as a whole without any basis in the study of its constituent parts: "One may see that this principle of composition [the reference here is to laisses of repetition] excludes any idea of continuity in the sense we have given the term since the seventeenth century, i.e., any subordination of the work's content to an autonomous, isolated, 'simple' condition controlling a vast ensemble."[26] This may indeed be good stylistics, but it does not follow that its extension into historical interpretation is justified. Vinaver's procedure, like Auerbach's, leaves little room for any comparison of content and historical context.

The assumption that makes this latter exclusion possible is not that it is somehow illegitimate to read the *Song of Roland* as a text whose parts are related to each other and to a theme—an obscure theme at first glance, perhaps, but one that is historically accessible. The assumption is, instead, that philology's work is already done and that the traditional claim of ambiguity is based on systematic investigation. I have argued above that such an assumption is dangerous. Its effect in muting curiosity and limiting the application of new observations may be measured in an affirmation of Ramon Menéndez Pidal's.

[24]Vinaver, *A la recherche,* 55–56.
[25]Ibid., 56.
[26]Ibid., 72–73.

Long before the recent controversy about the meaning of the words *proz* and *sage*, and about the sense of the too-famous line 1093, where both occur together, Menéndez Pidal had discovered that the "*proz-sage*" dichotomy long thought to characterize Roland and Oliver does not hold for the vocabulary of the text as a whole. Oliver himself is called *proz*, and so are several other characters including one Saracen. Inductively speaking, that information runs counter to the accepted characterizations based on the single line, and it might well have led to a thoroughgoing reexamination of the characters. But the induction was blocked. Rather than hew to the text and accept Oliver as *proz* (thus not exactly Roland's opposite), Menéndez Pidal in his turn invoked the doctrine of inconsistency to maintain the dichotomy as an important feature of the poem. Here again, his task was made easier by his hypothesis that the poem we have shares the features of "popular literature," which he took (in his particular formulation of the traditionalist theory of origins) as being inherently prone to confusion. "It is . . . the art of great collective achievements, in which one may well find contradictions, whose disconcerting depth is nothing but that of real life's own contradictions."[27]

This nexus of aesthetic and interpretive assumptions draws not only the external history of the text, but also its internal history, into its ambit. In a different application of similar premises, textual critics too were long eager to correct the Oxford text in order to reduce its apparent inconsistencies, which in practice meant positing an ideal whole before deciding whether its parts did or did not fit. Joseph Bédier then countered their arguments with a version of the *démesure* hypothesis, and a mass of arguments about specific passages, which give the appearance of establishing a reading when in reality the original hypothesis of meaning was still being used as evidence for an editorial philosophy.[28]

In what was perhaps the most striking example of editorial hypercorrection, Léon Gautier had appealed to other manuscript texts in the Roland tradition in an attempt to gloss over an element of Ganelon's embassy to Marsile, rather than see how it might fit the Oxford text if his hypothetical notion of the embassy were modified to match the Oxford version. Following the later Venice VII and Châteauroux manuscripts, Gautier inserted a new twenty-sixth laisse

[27]Menéndez Pidal, 347. Oliver is in fact called *proz* several times, though Roland is not called *sage*. For details, see Subrenat, ". . . e Oliver est proz."

[28]See Bédier, *Chanson de Roland commentée*, 99–101, 121–22, 131–32, 151–52, 163, etc., and cf. Bédier, "De l'édition princeps de la *Chanson de Roland* aux éditions les plus récentes," *Romania*, 63 (1937), 433–69; 64 (1938), 145–244, 489–521.

into his highly influential edition of the *Song*. In the new laisse, Charles, upon giving Ganelon his mission, orders him to say what the Oxford text has him say only after he is in Marsile's presence, far from Charles (see my commentary to laisses 33–37).[29] Ganelon tells the Saracen that he must cede half of Spain and accept Roland as his equal in the other half. Charles makes no such demand in the Oxford text, and the poem still makes sense (a suggestively different sense) without correction. Ganelon does not speak the truth to Marsile, and there is no reason to think he would; in stating bitterly harsh terms and naming Roland, he is playing his own game. There is no reference to any division of Spain anywhere outside Ganelon's speech and the *remaniements.* When Marsile says he has agreed to submit, the Franks do not occupy his territory, but leave, Roland with them. The letter read out in lines 488–94 is Charles's real message to his enemy, and the contrast between it and Ganelon's words has a strong claim to be part of the work's construction.

Bédier noted the editorial distortion without realizing the importance of the contrast between Ganelon's speech and Charles's letter (with its poignant references to Basan and Basile and to the *algalife* as supreme hostage). Bédier's defense of the Oxford reading thus falls short of recognizing the thematic importance of Charles's concerns. Charles's war is not a war of conquest: Spain will not be divided, but Basan and Basile cannot be forgotten, and any deal struck with Marsile must be guaranteed by a genuinely irreplaceable hostage—Charles's interpretation of Naimon's argument in laisse 16. It is Ganelon's false report of the *algalife*'s death that allows Marsile to appear at Roncevaux and attack Roland with some chance of success. This aspect of the poem's interlocking episodic structure is modified in V7 and Châteauroux, and though he intended to make that clear, even Bédier did not draw, on a higher level, the conclusions his observations suggested.[30]

There is more to be said about the passage. As often happens, the *remaniements*' emendation, medieval though it is in origin, actually introduces a new confusion. The Oxford text has a clear movement from event to consequence here. Marsile's son Jurfaleu, immediately upon hearing the letter read, compares the written word to the speech and realizes Ganelon has "spoken folly." But his angry reaction in turn would make little sense (and would perhaps call for emen-

[29]Edmund Stengel and Theodor Müller had made the same interpolation; see Horrent, *Chanson de Roland dans les littératures . . .* , 158–59.

[30]Bédier, *Chanson de Roland commentée,* 132–33.

dation itself) if Charles's message were taken to be the one Ganelon spoke and not the one in the letter. Adjustments of this sort, even when manifestly medieval, are part of the history of the *Roland* legend, not to be too quickly assimilated to the Oxford poem that is today our point of common reference in interpretation. Thus, incidentally, I have avoided citing those autonomous parallel versions even where they appear to strengthen my case.

This lengthy discussion permits us to situate and describe what is presently the dominant hypothesis of the *Song*'s meaning and construction. I mean, of course, Bédier's own presentation of the poem as a drama of personalities in conflict, each with its flaws, and with every characteristic contributing to the pathos of the result. This is the interpretation already latent in Francisque Michel and Petit de Julleville; it was accepted, cited, and sometimes slightly modified by T. A. Jenkins, Vinaver, Le Gentil, and many others. The foregoing arguments make it clear that Bédier's interpretation was part of an aesthetic defense of the work, in reaction to the doctrine of incoherence as embodied in the traditionalist theory of epic origins. As he was to do in his textual criticism, Bédier in essence chose to defend the *Song*'s unity on grounds chosen by his predecessors. He made his well-known analogy between the *Song* and French classical tragedy[31] at a time when "traditional" or "folk" art still lay under a shadow of opprobrium in academic and critical circles. True, Gaston Paris had briefly noted that the *Song* exhibited an artistry that was "essentially French, recalling, in many of its aspects, the way in which our classical tragedies are conceived." But, as Vinaver points out, logic of sequence was not one of those points.[32] The surface appearance of inadequate motivation in such a highly allusive poem fit in too well with the *cantilena* theory, with its bits of text like mismatched beads on a string. And the *cantilena* theory, at the time of its first application, was a handy justification of the *Song*'s form, through romantic archaizing on the macrostructural level, just as the appeal to parataxis and "explosions" tends to justify its form to modern readers, on a smaller scale.

Yet the result was not to everyone's liking; to individualists, the traditionalist theory made the medieval epic still seem too much like what Nabokov once called "the random thrum of a people."[33] Bédier's famous passages in the *Légendes épiques* succeeded in lifting that

[31]Foreshadowed in Gautier's contribution to Petit de Julleville's *Histoire de la langue et de la littérature française,* 1:96–97.

[32]See Vinaver, *A la recherche,* 51–53.

[33]Vladimir Nabokov, trans., *The Song of Igor's Campaign* (New York, 1960), 6.

cloud to such a degree that the far-reaching aesthetic implications of the traditionalist-individualist controversy are now sometimes forgotten.[34] Bédier chose, consciously or not, to save the *Song of Roland* from the possibly unfortunate implications of neotraditionalist theory by elevating it to equivalency with respected types of literature. That meant investing it with the psychological intensity that can be found in Corneille and the classics of novelistic fiction as well.

Thus the question of whether the text is in fact as incoherent as claimed was never addressed in any fundamental way. The characters were consistent within themselves, and if the text seemed to falter, their putative strengths and weaknesses would furnish explanations of what the work did not make clear. The applications made of that principle have been legion.[35] And yet Bédier's own words, including those reproduced by Vinaver and quoted above, reveal the hesitations of a scholar who had an unparalleled familiarity with the text. Roland must be wrong—our entrenched sense of his character demands it—and yet Oliver does not seem to be right either. In conclusion, Bédier fell back on a familiar universal. To be human, as a poet, means to write ambiguously. "Such is the dilemma Turold offered. Oliver resolved it in one way, Roland in the other. The poet approves them both, enfolds both in the same tender embrace. . . . Between the 'preux' and the 'sage,' he does not choose; he was too human to choose."[36] But the hermeneutic starting point was never subject to revision.

The *Song of Roland* no longer risks banishment from the canon. The work of Jean Rychner and of Joseph Duggan, for example, has established its formal qualities without linking them to any interpretation, and that will stand (whatever our attitude to the question of oral composition) as long as form is recognized as an essential feature of literary texts. We need not cling to an old description of *Roland*'s thematic greatness for fear the poem will seem weak or unlovely without it. Nor are we required to argue that a blind fool who leads better men to their annihilation is ipso facto one of early medieval literature's outstanding heroes. Thus we may solve a great problem of reading, since we no longer must struggle, with Le Gentil and others,

[34]But cf. Cerquiglini, 42–43.

[35]Cf. Del Monte, 225: "Not only is such an interpretation thought to be correct and coherent, but it is also taken to be proof of the poet's artistry that he created a human and complex character, endowed with positive traits but not immune from flaws, rather than an abstract symbol of exemplary perfection." See also the works cited in Duggan, *Guide*, nos. 348–83.

[36]Bédier, *Légendes*, 3:444; cf. Siciliano: "Oliver was right" (p. 348); "the madman [i.e., Roland] was right" (p. 355); cf. Cerquiglini, 55.

to justify vainglorious words, or identify humanity, with Bédier, as a refusal to express a commitment. If we long for a major character to exhibit that rounding we prize, to temper his audacity with the chimera of false security, mix his beauty with pride, or fix his gaze upon a fleeting present, there are Oliver and Ganelon. But at the end of the eleventh century, with the building of Europe only begun, they are not given the last word. Nevertheless, for lack of such a historical orientation, the textbooks and the great syntheses of medieval literary history picked up the notion that a great deal of what happens in the song is inexplicable, and it became a scholarly tradition to explain the text not by reference to how its sequences and juxtapositions work, but by reference to a limited number of selected lines and scenes. Long ago we lost our habit of close reading where the *Song of Roland* is concerned, and our approach to it as exegetes lost its cutting edge.

As my earlier discussion of Vinaver's theses suggests, now that literary criticism and aesthetics in general are more inclined to allow for certain kinds of incompleteness in poetry, the mysterious quality ascribed to the *Roland* is sometimes seen as a virtue. This eases the aesthetician's task, but not the historian's. It leaves the interpreter with the burden of describing a heroic narrative, admirable in style, perhaps, but not to be grasped as a memorable story—a tale full of loose ends, whose parts do not quite add up. Yet if it is an epic, and perhaps both a primary epic and an exemplary one, as we usually say, then it is not just anachronistic prejudice that leads us to expect an "overriding theme" and linkages among its narrative elements. The suspicion remains that the *Song of Roland* is not so much incoherent, or mysterious, as it is difficult to reconcile with the received hypotheses of Roland's character, of his place in the text, and of the text's place in the Middle Ages. I am convinced that the appeal to an aesthetics of obscurity in *Roland*'s original audience is unnecessary. We may accept that its medieval hearers followed it as a craftsman's story, clear in its references to what they knew as common beliefs and experience.

[5]

The Feudal–Christian Setting

Achronistic criticism is sometimes said to be a recent trend, but it has clear antecedents in nineteenth- and early-twentieth-century interpretations of the *Song of Roland.* There is nothing specifically eleventh-century about the *démesure* hypothesis of interpretation. The points of reference it assumes are (perhaps deliberately) analogical ones, chosen from outside early-medieval ideologies entirely—*hamartia,* Cornelianism, the primacy of the individual psyche. Achronism then tends, thanks to the specific analogies it uses, to become anachronism. I want, on the contrary, to show that the *Song*'s words and events make a specific kind of sense in a particular historical context. That can be recognized, I think, only if we admit that the *démesure* hypothesis is an incongruous principle of reading, bringing on claims of narrative inconsistency by virtue of its very application.[1] But that formal argument is not one that can be made in a vacuum. The bones of a story like this one are too easy to wire together in the shape of some fantastic creature to which they never belonged before. There is much to be gained by considering in more detail how its themes, its narrative arrangement, and its cultural context reinforce each other.

Roland sacrifices himself and his men to the ideal of the given word. Ultimately it would not even matter precisely what he promises,

[1]On some of the difficulties raised by the standard interpretations, see Waltz, 51–54. Inspired by Alfred Foulet, Crist, Brault, Mickel, Kibler, and others, I have posited a superficially paradoxical ethic of service in the Christian feudal mentality; this helps me avoid seeing the text's construction itself as paradoxical. For the attribution of other kinds of paradox to the *Song,* based on other presuppositions, see Kay, 487–88 on the transformation of ethics; Hunt, "Tragedy," 796 ("Roland and Charlemagne lose [in the active sense] those whom they love"); Calin, 24–25 (Roland humbled, contrite, and a conqueror), 33 (Roland both a scapegoat and guilty).

if it were not that we must know what he says if we are to know it is true. Structurally the thing that matters most is that his promise is finally accepted and that he carries it out despite the suffering, while his enemies cannot carry out theirs. The details of the promise count primarily for our understanding of how the theme of responsible sacrifice is clothed. Still, we cannot neglect the setting if we are to judge the text. We must consider what it was like to be concerned with the essentials of feudalism, and that is neither structure nor rhetoric but history, the discipline without which the others may even yet be thought inconclusive. Roland chooses, fights, and dies in specified circumstances. Only a medieval soldier, perhaps, could be placed in exactly those circumstances, but any medieval soldier might have had to face them. Any might have had to choose between sacrifice and temporizing in the form these things take for the rear guard at Roncevaux. That is one source of the *Song*'s striking effect: it conveys a generalization through the particular. This effect, in its turn, may be the real proof of greatness for any alien literature—not its ability to suggest whatever "universal" concepts we wish to talk about at the moment, but the strength of the bonds between specific themes and an original setting.

The analysis I have been carrying on in the preceding pages may therefore seem old-fashioned, but it is not redundant. To describe a work's theme as accessible through its content and to scrutinize its narrative structure as the vehicle of that theme, to seek in an ancient poem a deliberate attempt at communicating ideas amenable to elementary logic, may appear to be only a rehash of a tired method. I hope to forestall that impression through a presentation of the points of reference I have assumed. They are themselves traditionally associated with the *Song of Roland,* but their use as firm referents for interpretive studies is not traditional.

The reader will have seen that I distrust explanations based either on deductions from psychological generalities or on psychological inferences from Roland's words. Given the form of his speeches, such hypotheses can refer only to an equally hypothetical concept of his personality. It is no doubt equally clear that I prefer the context furnished by sets of religious or social ideas—simplified and generalized though they necessarily must be, if they are to orient our global reading of the poem.

For the things of which the *Song of Roland* speaks openly, the ideas it names by their names, elements of feudalism and medieval Christianity, are not hypothetical. They are not among the often-proclaimed "universals" of experience and literature—among which we must in any case choose each time we apply one of them. The contents of the *Song*, abstractions included, are "particulars" of history. We do not know as much about those ideologies as we would like, but we are not obliged to guess at their presence before we read the work. This is the hidden strength of the literary historian's occasional willingness to go "outside the work" in search of fuller information about elements to which the work alludes without explanation. The status of Christian or feudal ideas, then, is quite different from that of *démesure*. It is neither their natures nor the likelihood of their presence, but their precise functions in the text, that need to be established. In this chapter I will set forth some reasons for thinking that reference to the feudal concept of government, broadly defined, is essential to our ability to grasp the work's construction as a coherent text. Attention to its manifestations must supplant recourse to psychological hypotheses in our readings of the *Song*, as a matter not only of textual reference but also of strong historical probability.

Literary history is still sometimes described as only source and influence study, but as it applies to the *Song of Roland*, it is a form of history as complete as any other. Its subject taken generally is the expression of vital ideas and emotions by long-vanished writers in compelling forms. Its lesson, then, is a lesson of history, not one of aesthetics, but it can also teach the appreciation of literature, even literature that is initially strange and unpalatable, by broadening our concept of "compelling forms" to match the record of human achievement better. The faculty that allows this is roughly the one often called historical imagination: the insight into how things once worked, into why they are simultaneously foreign and coherent. Much of our historical schematization points the other way, robbing medieval people of their authenticity by implying, perhaps accidentally, that they must have experienced feudalism or Augustinian Catholicism from without, as the latter-day analyst does. But to the people who lived them as daily experience, they were not schemes at all, but expected and natural situations. The burden laid on us as historical readers is that laid on anyone who wishes to deal with the abstraction that is, for each one of us, another one's experience. That precludes taking the schemas per se as the ultimate objects of inquiry. It is not adequate to our task for us to say that we have difficulty understanding the elements of mental otherness. Seeing how cold scholasticism or rigid monastic rules or dry feudal law or dead allegory could possibly have held the attention of large numbers of people is indeed a challenge. But if we say that and stop, we have not done the job of confronting the art that is compounded of those things. We must take the concerns of medieval people as the established facts they are, and explain them, but if we are to explain their presence in major literary texts, we must admit their power to excite as well.[2]

References to "feudalism in the broad sense" or to "feudal society" or to the "feudal system" and its power to interest or excite the medieval audience, may remain difficult to accept. We often still perceive and even use *feudalism* as a faintly disagreeable school term; it is often enough by itself to put some distance between us and the people the *Roland* text was designed to reach.[3] But the situation the text treats is still understandable in general terms once we have paid sufficient attention to particulars. It is, however, necessary to consider what some of the ramifications of Roland's sacrifice were and are—why his response to what is asked of him must be inflexible if it is to mean anything in human terms.

The Old French epic is not a treatise on institutions, but it is about life in a society whose institutions, for its audiences, had none of the air of antiquarian triviality that discourages modern literary theorists. The hearers of the *Song of Roland* swam up to their necks in a history that is dry as dust to us; they may well have followed the cut-and-thrust of council and judgment with a passion like the one we think suffused their reaction to battle scenes.[4] Ancient institutions may be irrelevant to the way we conduct our lives now, but they are not irrelevant to our understanding of humanity, facing realities we no longer face.

This historicographic problem is one of the most difficult problems the medievalist has to solve, because as a matter of philology, medievalists have always associated feudalism with the *Song of Roland* without being obliged to integrate the feudal mentality into their readings. The forms of feudal government are familiar, but feudal habits of

[2]This is not meant as a "naive" statement, but it might well be one. With all our theoretical *getting* over the past twenty years, it is not certain that we have gotten understanding. For types of understanding that we seem to have a perennial tendency to neglect, see D. W. Robertson, "Some Observations on Method in Literary Studies," in Ralph Cohen, ed., *New Directions in Literary History* (Baltimore, 1974), 63–75; Cohen's introduction to the same volume, pp. 1–10; and Jacques Roger, "Lecture des textes et histoire des idées," in Georges Poulet, ed., *Les Chemins actuels de la critique* (Paris, 1968), 191–99.

[3]It is difficult to disagree with such critics of the terms "feudalism," "feudal society," etc., as Elizabeth Brown and the authors (including Bloch and Ganshof) whom she cites in "The Tyranny of a Construct: Feudalism and Historians of Medieval Europe," *American Historical Review*, 79 (1974), 1063–88. I have attempted, through explicit definition and a modicum of consistency, to limit the damage done by my use of the terms for my limited purposes, which are not comparative.

[4]Cf. Duggan, *Song*, 147–48.

thought are not. The passage I am about to quote deserves to appear here at length as an example. It offers the same kind of arguments I am making and takes a stance on historical context very similar to mine, and yet it is not interpretive in its use of these things. Like the commentaries of Bédier, it is full of hermeneutic implications but is not hermeneutic in intent or result.

> The entire *Song* . . . is studded with the terminology of feudal law. . . .
>
> But even more than with words, the *Song* is impregnated with feudal spirit. Charles is, of course, a feudal sovereign, but Marsile is also, and Baligant as well. Roland is a vassal of the emperor, and Ganelon is also, just as Marsile is the vassal of the emir Baligant. . . .
>
> This feudal world, this complex of vassals and lords, was united, as we know, by a mutual contract that placed obligations on both contracting parties, obligations that were defined and summarized notably in the often-quoted letter from Fulbert of Chartres to William the Fifth of Aquitaine, wherein it is stated that the vassal owes his lord faithfulness, aid, and counsel. As for the lord, his duties to the vassal present "a strong parallel with the nature of the vassalic obligation. . . ."
>
> [Roland] summarizes in very similar terms [the reference is to the "feudal credo" of lines 1010–12] the obligations of a vassal toward his lord. He fulfills these obligations to the last degree. . . . And the twelve Peers and the twenty thousand Francs de France who accompany them also affirm with their lives their fidelity and aid to their lord. All of them are aware of this sacrifice; all of them see their death approaching; they accept it with joy. But they also know that it will have its counterpart; they know they will be avenged.
>
> Our author . . . was so deeply immerged in the feudal ideas of his time, he possessed such a strong concept—a theoretical one, perhaps, but an ideal one and one profoundly felt—of the reciprocal rights and duties of lords and vassals, that he made of these legal concepts the very warp upon which he embroidered his admirable poem. . . . It is a song that glorifies a perfect, ideal, absolute relationship between vassal and lord; it is the poem of Roland, the good vassal.

This passage strikes me as both accurate and relevant. But it cannot be reconciled with the tragedy of Roland's pride and the resulting disaster. It states a conception of the global meaning of the poem that cannot be held simultaneously with the idea that Roland makes a horrible mistake, unless the poem of perfect vassality is itself a mistake, putting forth a theme that is accidentally but thoroughly undercut by the good vassal's error. It would seem inevitable that such a pervasively important frame of reference would have to be applied to the evaluation of the hero's temper. But the author of this passage is not in fact belaboring this point of literary history. Interpretation was, at the time, far from the forefront of his mind.

Some readers will perhaps have recognized the passages I am quoting, from the work of Paul Aebischer. They occur in an article in which interpretation is not an issue at all, in a "defense and illustration of the Baligant episode."[5] Aebischer's purpose was to use these observations to prove that the controversial episode was authentic. The article does not raise the crucial question of just how good a vassal the *bon vassal* is; feudalism appears in it as a supporting element in a philological argument. Yet, as Aebischer recognized, there *is* no other context for Roland's sacrifice, unless his words and deeds furnish one greater than society itself. That is, of course, what the psychological interpretation assumed about Roland's character: that it embodies a universal trait—a tragic flaw, an archetypal self-destructiveness, or a Freudian neurosis—whose exposition has no necessary link with specific constraints of circumstance.

Examples of the abortive application of historical context to the *Song of Roland* for various purposes could be cited to the point of excess, though not all show the same striking correspondence with the arguments I am making in these pages for reinterpreting the *Song* on precisely the grounds Aebischer gives for a completely different operation. I will mention only one other case here, because it *is* an interpretation and exhibits another procedure. I have in mind André Burger's *Turold poète de la fidélité,* whose title appears to presage a reexamination of attitudes toward heroism, duty, and disaster in the poem. Burger, in fact, makes little more than a passing bow to feudal concepts and atmosphere, speaking of homage, vassals, and the given word in a few brief paragraphs.[6] Significantly, to Burger vengeance and justice are religious terms only, invoked in reference to Ganelon and not the Saracens.[7] Burger does not forget his choice of title when he comes to interpretation, speaking of "Charles, faithful to God, fighting for Him seven years in Spain . . . all of his knights ready to give their lives for their king and for their God; Turpin exciting them by word and deed; Oliver, the faithful friend, obeying his leader and

[5]Aebischer, "Pour la défense," reprinted in *Rolandiana et Oliveriana,* 211–20, esp. 213–18.

[6]Burger, *Turold poète de la fidélité,* 63–64.

[7]Ibid., 65. Burger's decision to assign vengeance, as a concept, to the realm of religious values exclusively is supported by an appeal to Romans 12:19, which may also be read as excluding any earthly vengeance whatever: "Dearly beloved, avenge not yourselves, but rather give place unto wrath." For the distinction between ethics and Christian eschatology in the *Song,* see Chapter 6, below.

companion in arms even when he disapproves of what he is doing."[8] Yet this fidelity is not, for Burger, central to the poem; it furnishes only part of the background: "Fidelity is the backdrop against which the conflict between Ganelon and Roland stands out." In his interpretation, whose principal theme is pride, fidelity is in fact thwarted: "Ganelon himself, though blinded by jealousy and hatred, intends to remain faithful to his king while simultaneously taking revenge upon Roland, and Roland, equally blinded by this prideful conflict, refuses to see that his duty as a leader is to warn the emperor of the danger he is facing . . . [this] sin of pride will prevent God from intervening at Roncevaux to grant him victory."[9] In the cursory paraphrase that follows, Burger relies on the critical tradition, not on new structural or contextual arguments. He uses Roland's 'mauvais caractère" to explain the events he describes.[10] The result is in many places the opposite of the commentary I have given, as when Burger accepts as authentic Ganelon's oral message to Marsile and approves his conduct).[11] Thus even in a study of apparently historical orientation, feudal concepts have only ad hoc, temporary applicability and do not furnish firm points of reference. Whatever principles Roland may invoke, he is governed by an overriding theme of selfishness. Feudal commitments may matter in the analysis of secondary characters, even Gautier and Aude, but the major characters transcend their commitments by denying them.

These summary examples suggest that the social system in the *Song of Roland* has often been envisaged with something less than the sympathetic curiosity required to evaluate its function in the text. Feudalism's (sometimes latent) negative associations help explain our reluctance to begin our study of the poem in the way that might otherwise seem potentially most fruitful: by asking whether the movements of the Council, Nomination, and Trial scenes make narrative and aesthetic sense primarily in terms of early feudal conventions and a feudal ideal. Before I propose a positive reply to that question, I will consider briefly the conventions, as institutional historians describe them, and the ideal, as it derives from them. This use of one kind of history as a check upon another may seem circular at first glance, but upon reflection it is clear that institutional history depends on different kinds of inferences from those used to detect the ideologies al-

[8]Ibid., 111.
[9]Ibid.
[10]Ibid., e.g., 112–14, 118, 125, 127.
[11]Ibid., e.g., 119–21.

luded to in literature. The corpus available to Marc Bloch, F. L. Ganshof, and their successors is, to boot, both larger and more explicit than the corpus of imaginative literature.[12]

Feudalism is, in the first instance, no specific law or set of rules, but a principle of social organization, familiar in broad outline to practically anyone (including, if need be, churchmen) in France or England in the late eleventh or early twelfth century. Allowing that the social setting is inextricably bound up with the reasons for Roland's death means a general presupposition: that people living under a particular social (or religious) system will habitually involve that system in the expression of their thoughts. That starting point is sometimes labeled dangerous, but it is safer than claimed—much safer than its opposite—as long as we are careful to remember that we are dealing with a tendency rather than with some mechanism that dictates every detail of literary and artistic expression.[13] Not everything in every early medieval text is there because of feudalism, but whenever there is a clear and direct evocation of what we recognize as feudal attitudes and practices, as in Roland's famous "credo," we must accept it as a reference to social mores that the implied audience knew, perhaps shared, and surely responded to. This approach limits the autonomy of the critic, but the alternative makes a mockery of any literature that involves ideas.

The characters of the *Song of Roland* stand in relationships to one another that are unlike those obtaining among leading citizens of more recent societies—relationships that were coherent and logical in ways that are now widely recognized among institutional historians. The coherence these scholars describe is sufficiently strong to create uneasiness with the venerable tradition that makes feudalism a cant

[12]In other words, I accept the distinctions made by Robert Fossier, *Histoire sociale de l'Occident médiéval* (Paris, 1970), 10–12.

[13]That feudalism is a fluid, not static, concept is a conclusion of common sense, vigorously underscored in particular by Thomas Bisson, see "The Problem of Feudal Monarchy: Aragon, Catalonia, and France," *Speculum*, 53 (1978), 460–78. The variations in the judgment of characters in the *Song* are accompanied by a wide variety of claims about the role of feudalism in the text—in particular, that there is a tension or disjunction between "feudalism" and eleventh- or twelfth-century ideals of government. Feudalism is conceived for this purpose as the "old order" or "every man for himself" (as in Halverson, 661ff., also Eisner and Stranges), but cf. Ganshof, "The Feudal Bond as a Check on the Disintegration of the State," *Feudalism*, 60–61; M. Bloch is less sanguine, 408–20. Oppositions between feudalism (now defined as tending toward stability and centralization) and the society of clans are made by Jones, Bender, Gérard, Calin, and Pensom, among others. Feudalism and monarchy are sometimes also specifically opposed. I have tried to take an approach that will recognize the considerable degree of *a posteriori* analysis in such dichotomies. See also note 8 to Chapter 6; Brault, *Chanson*, xx–xxi.

term for backwardness. As Fossier puts it, "I think the time has come to repudiate the traditional cliché of feudal anarchy."[14] This adjustment may help counter the tendency among critics to acknowledge the presence of "feudal elements" in works without ever seriously considering that medieval poets may have used those elements as the very stuff of great art. We may no longer accept Brunetière's claim that a "relative impotence of the spirit" and a "sterility of thought" are natural by-products of "the very constitution of society in the Middle Ages." Our suspicion ought to be aroused by any judgment whose implications match the polemical dicta of influential proto-specialists such as Michelet: "This art [Gothic], whose form is subject to criticism, was also deficient in its social principles. The society from which it sprang was too unequal and too unjust."[15] Yet the rehabilitation of medieval institutions has not affected literary study to the degree desirable. We cannot help noticing that our Rolands, our Lancelots, and our Eliducs move in a particular kind of society, but we avoid its vitality. If we hope to keep our historical curiosity alive, we will do well to remind ourselves that the game of politics is not abstract in medieval French epics. It is seen through the eyes of the players. Thus, once again, the term "politics" is inadequate if it fails to convey the potential excitement of participation in a form of government in which each participant commits himself as an individual and is not represented by anyone else.[16]

That feudalism was a practical method of participatory government, and not just a pretext for privilege, is therefore one of the more important ideas behind twentieth-century historical scholarship on the medieval period. To cite Joseph Strayer's succinct definition will not do that scholarship justice, but for present purposes it is difficult to improve upon it:

> To sum up, the basic characteristics of feudalism in Western Europe are a fragmentation of political authority, public power in private hands, and a military system in which an essential part of the armed forces is

[14]Fossier's remarks on anarchy and "stabilité" will be found in his *Moyen Age,* vol. 2 (Paris, 1982), 14.

[15]Ferdinand Brunetière, "L'Erudition contemporaine et la littérature française du Moyen Age," in *Etudes critiques sur l'histoire de la littérature française,* 4th ed. (Paris, 1896), 1:21. In the same vein, Michelet, Renan, and Taine are cited by Janine Dakyns, *The Middle Ages in French Literature, 1850–1900* (Oxford, 1973), 45 (Michelet, quoted here), 66, 72.

[16]Compare, however, the form of the distinction Owen (*Song,* 23) makes: "More than the political questions it was surely the human ones that most fascinated and inspired [the *Song*'s] author."

> secured through private contracts. *Feudalism is a method of government,* and a way of securing the forces necessary to preserve that method of government.
>
> This is not as narrow a definition as it seems. The possessors of political and military power will naturally mold their society to fit their own needs. They will manipulate the economy so that they get the greatest share of production; they will, as wealthy consumers, influence writers and artists; they will establish standards to which their society must conform. Thus, it is perfectly legitimate to speak of feudal society, or a feudal age, if we remember that it was the political-military structure that made the society and the age feudal.[17]

This approach has come to be widely accepted. However, it has proved difficult to make the transition from the manipulations, influence, and molding mentioned in the second paragraph, with their overtones of direct force and potential abuse, to the idea that many medieval artists may have seen such a "method of government" as both natural and beneficial and given it their assent without being forced. We tend to associate greatness in art with resistance to the "dictates" of society, but the universality of that resistance is not assumed in these pages. We should recognize instead that any desire for peace, stability, and their concomitant benefits to humanity may appear in early medieval literature as an idealization of a firmly established system of relationships among vassals and lords. The force of the *Song of Roland,* then, can be said to lie in what John Benton has so cogently described as "the power to move men to re-think their self-interest in terms of higher ideals, to the point that in real life as in epic imagination they might actually prefer honorable death to shameful flight, group loyalty to limited personal advantage, and in the process build stronger governments and assure peace and stability."[18] It may seem odd to refer to the denizens of frontier Europe as champions of order and enemies of the arbitrary. And yet it is true that the age that produced the *Song of Roland* was the prelude to a period of relative stability, and that may not be an accident. Without the impulsion given by people of the late eleventh and early twelfth centuries, those of the later twelfth and the thirteenth could not have known their

[17]Joseph Strayer, *Feudalism* (New York, 1965), 13; emphasis added.

[18]Benton, "Nostre franceis n'unt talent de fuïr," 248–49; cf. 246. The consciousness of class or subclass invoked by Waltz (*Rolandslied,* 64, 105–7, 128ff.) and Bender ("Un Aspect de la stylisation épique: L'Exclusivisme de la haute noblesse dans les chansons de geste du XIIe siècle," *Société Rencesvals: IVe Congrès,* 95–105) is wisely denied by Benton: "The *Chanson de Roland* can be considered an enculturative instrument for an entire warrior class, from the most aristocratic . . . to the lowest *milites* with pretensions to chivalric honor" (246–47, n. 51).

flowering of organized forms: the codification of law, the Gothic achievement, the universities, the cyclical arrangement in literature. Is it too early to admit that feudalism, as a method of government (not an ethos) was both potentially and sometimes actually a successful bar to confusion and anarchy, that the author of the *Song* and his contemporaries may genuinely have thought the rules of society, and the attainments they promised, were ideals worth dying for? Or do we still prefer the Enlightenment analogy between feudalism and the unReason of the Ancien Régime? Do we still think of "chaos" and unrest as welcome to "feudal" people and conceive of their heroes as living only for the short term?

If the principles of hierarchy, obedience, and service that have seemed so paradoxical in the *Roland* were accepted ideals for many people in the Middle Ages, that was partly because they had become established traditions in a time when the risks of innovation were staggering, but also partly because as principles they are indeed coherent.[19] In the ideal scheme, benefits flow two ways, with the farmer, the artisan, and eventually the lesser warrior offering produce, labor, and service to the chieftain who is freed thereby to take on responsibility for his suppliers' security. The noncombatants are protected, the combatants and organizers are maintained, and everyone's interest is served, as long as the machinery runs steadily. If anything, the system may in some ways favor the "lower orders," those who are protected without any immediate personal risk. That may be why the warriors needed encouragement to induce them to risk their lives, equipment, and health in the short term, for the sake of general long-term benefit—to themselves if they survived, but to the principles that assured protection even if they did not. Hence the *Song of Roland* as incitement to courageous action in the defense of one's comrades.

Thus I may seem to neglect, with Strayer and Ganshof, the economic side of the question, which has led Marxist historians in particular to insist, for example, on the coercive aspect of feudal rent.[20] If I do so, it is because I strongly suspect that, in many minds, the promise of relative security was a sufficient incentive. As Herlihy says, "The need for protection would usually have been, for the vassal, the strongest consideration in entering the feudal partnership."[21] Much the same might be said of anyone, even a peasant, who simply accepted life under a lord's protection as a foregone conclusion: the needs

[19]Giving up (or not asserting) certain rights in return for group identity and protection is not an irrational act.

[20]See Herlihy, xvii–xix.

[21]Ibid., 74.

were similar, if not the nature of the choice. Or perhaps I am only following the common suggestion that the *Roland* idealizes feudalism as it might have been in the century or so preceding the growth of towns and the expansion of the money supply.

That distinction raises another question. To which of the two loosely distinguished "feudal ages" should we think the *Roland* belongs? Whether it stems from the atmosphere of the "first feudal age," an age of traditional institutions long unexamined, or from the "second," when princes and magnates began to manipulate those traditions to their own ends, is difficult to establish with certainty. The poem is often studied as though it were firmly rooted in the second (though precise dates cannot be established either for the epic or for the "ages"). It has been described both as propaganda for Capetian centralization and as a manifesto for baronial autonomy. Yet its mentality of reference is apparently that of the first age—of, say, the eleventh century, to which Bédier attributed it.[22] It describes not localized, temporally limited, and manipulable institutions, but rules that are thought of as immutable and more-or-less God-given, rules that it is the right-thinking man or woman's grace to follow, and the evil man's curse to flout. The fighting in it is between those who adhere to the rules and those who do not; the only way to manipulate the rules is through treachery.

It is equally possible that the *Song of Roland* is in these terms a transitional document, mustering some of the emotions and instincts of the first age in the service of that increasing desire for order often said to characterize the second. Since the whole period from the year 1050 to 1150 is a transitional period in one sense or another, there is nothing surprising here. We may note that the work, in surviving its original period, presumably became like the institutions it preents, and could have been mined for specific propagandistic value by the princes to whom it was available around the year 1175, without having been first created to serve those ends. This distinction is another aspect of "reception history"; it may cast light on the disagreement between Hans-Erich Keller and John Benton about the author's own intentions.[23]

These paragraphs imply that specific military and legal customs of early medieval Europe should not be applied to the *Song* too narrowly, lest they descend from the level of history to that of special

[22]Bédier, *Légendes*, 3:448, 451.

[23]Compare Benton's opinion (pp. 242–44, 248, 254–55) with Hans-Erich Keller, "The *Song of Roland* and Its Audience," *Olifant*, 6 (1979), 259–74.

pleading. The respect given tradition—the custom of customary law—serves as an entirely adequate, if broad index of early medieval distrust of arbitrary authority. We need not insist that only certain barons, in a certain period, would sponsor the literary expression of such distrust. Furthermore, if Charles is restrained by custom from rejecting Ganelon's proposals or hanging him on suspicion, then he is also constrained by common sense. There is no rigid doctrine of kingship here, but there is a rough division of powers with implications for the character of the emperor. Charles exercises what I have called, for the nonce, the executive power, but not the legislative. He cannot decide policy alone, but calls on the barons, consulting the group around him at nearly every important turn. On the other hand, both he and Marsile have the task of deciding how a policy, once settled upon, will be carried out.

We can derive a sense of where this division falls from observation of what the chieftains actually do in the poem. It is well known that we must resist the traditional temptation to compare Charles, in his majesty, with the absolute monarchs of later times, those who could impose at will a tithe on their "subjects" or require a month's stay in a garret at Versailles. What is less obvious, perhaps, is that the Charles of the *Song of Roland* may not be too hastily judged with respect to details of the emerging ideology of medieval kingship. No matter how sophisticated the history behind them, *a priori* insistences on how well or how poorly the undated poem matches some documented practice of some specific time are ultimately misleading. Charles's power is not a mere abstraction: it depends on the people around him, as in global feudal theory it rightly should. He rules freely only insofar as he recognizes the source of his power to rule, and his procedures of consultation make that recognition explicit. Not only does he want to act in concert with the "men of France" (167), but he has no other choice in the last analysis, for his men are his court, his army, his administration, and his police. Here, as in matters of warfare, a strong strain of practicality enters into interpretation. Charles rules according to need and not only by right.[24]

To focus the study much more narrowly than this would be to assume too much.[25] In the nature of things, any attempt to tie the

[24]See Bisson's distinction between feudalism and feudal monarchy; the latter, he argues, is in France largely the creation of Philip Augustus (Bisson, "The Problem of Feudal Monarchy," 470–78).

[25]Invoking a precise difference between *consilium* and *judicium* under the blanket term of "feudal law" means applying details of institutional history in ways that historians might well hesitate to accept. See Köhler, *"Conseil des barons" und "jugement des*

Oxford text to a particular domain (much less a county or two) and a particular quarter-century (much less a decade or year) is more than likely to fall through. And though they changed slowly with time, the rules of law sometimes changed sharply with place in the Middle Ages.[26] We must remain on a general plane when dealing with a work that might have been created, or could have coalesced, in France around the year 1065 or in England around 1120 (and these are not the extreme dates). Finally, its text may contain both traditional and innovative details at once, without our being able to tell them apart in the absence of further information.

---

barons": Epische Fatalität und Feudalrecht im altfranzösischen Rolandslied (Heidelberg, 1968), e.g. 29: "The scene of the embassy [Council] is presented as a legal procedure following set rules, as a *jugement selonc touz erremanz, as the customary collections put it later*" (emphasis added).

[26]Whence the procedural question, *sub qua lege vives?* See Delort, 114, and M. Bloch, 111–12.

[6]

The Feudal-Christian Ethos

I have described a scholarly tradition of reading in which the practical and emotional needs of a warrior society are given short shrift. The transcendent psychologies of the characters, and not any necessity outside them, have long been taken to be the principal motors of action and reaction in the Roland story and thus as the inevitable points of reference that furnish its themes their context—when they have a recognizable context at all. Feudal principles and Christian eschatology are widely acknowledged as important to understanding the *Song,* but they are not expected to explain it themselves.

The classic statement of the psychological interpretation, that of Joseph Bédier, has already been mentioned. Bédier said:

> In this poem Roland and his companions, far from submitting to their fates, are rather the makers and masters of their destinies, quite as much as any characters in Corneille. Their personalities give rise to events and determine them; better yet, it is Roland's personality alone. . . . The only fate that dominates them is the nobility of their own hearts. To invent circumstances such that the valiant men destined to be ambushed suspect it, half guess it will happen; to lend them feelings such that, while forseeing the danger, while in a position to avoid it, they still prefer to run the risk; to keep us in suspense . . . in a word, to shift the action from the factual world of fate to the universe of free will—that is Turold's achievement.[1]

This statement has been given wider currency and application in Pierre Le Gentil's chapter on the *Song*'s significance: "No one will miss

[1]Bédier, *Légendes,* 3:426–27.

the rendezvous at Roncevaux, and no one will be there who is not compelled by the diabolical lucidity of the traitor or by the splendid folly of the victim. As Bédier said, Roncevaux is inevitable. But fate acts in accord with the nature of the characters and becomes an expression of their free will."[2] Likewise, more recently, Eugene Vance has said:

> Obviously, [the] characters . . . bring into the poem with them a basic framework of causality from which the action must derive. The mere mention of their names together is evidently enough by this time to guarantee a tale of tragedy. . . . The extent to which the design of the *Song of Roland* is contingent upon traits of human character (which may simultaneously be viewed as aspects of destiny) becomes more apparent as Ganelon plots his treason with Blancandrin during their journey to Marsile's court. . . . Roland's pride will force him to accept the [rear guard]. Honor dictates the forward motion of the poem.[3]

Even those scholars who argue that Roland is a positive character seem obliged to concentrate, as the *démesure* theory bids, on individual honor and personal traits as the forces behind the narrative. At the very least, they concede some unpleasantness in Roland's character. Thus Gerard Brault: "Anyone endeavoring to justify Roland's behavior has to contend with a number of ambivalent character traits, in particular his boasting and his apparent indifference to the fate of his men at Roncevaux. . . . It is difficult for the modern mind to apprehend the medieval ideal embodied by Roland. However, an illuminating parallel is to be found in the stubborn and imprudent conduct of Thomas Becket."[4] Or William Kibler: "Roland is a warrior for his time: a bold, brave, often rash, headstrong lord. He is a feudal knight, not a courtly lover. He is a product of the 'Golden Age of Feudalism': a warrior knight, courageous and *preux.* He fights for God and Country, but never forgets his personal honor and glory, his family's. He reflects an era in which a knight was expected to be brave to the point of foolhardiness."[5]

The terms of these descriptions must be modified, not only by

[2]Le Gentil, *Song,* 87.

[3]Vance, *Reading,* 10, 19.

[4]Brault, *Song,* 1:42–43.

[5]Kibler, "Roland's Pride," 152; for other examples of lack of sympathy with Roland's presumed character among his defenders, see the works cited in note 11 to Chapter 2, above, and also, Gerard Brault, "The *Song of Roland,* 778–1978," *Olifant,* 6 (1979), 208 ("we find it difficult to tolerate self-righteous individuals like Roland who act in the name of a higher imperative"); Uitti, 107; Misrahi and Hendrickson, 364.

addition or exclusion, but also by refinement and reordering. We will not be able to realize fully that Roland is an exemplary character until we have learned to put his actions into both their relevant contexts—the poem's sequence and the larger framework of a particular society. The poet or singer was concerned, then, with individual attributes primarily as they served as means to tell a tale about something else. The theme of responsibility in the *Song of Roland* is a matter of primary public concern, such as an epic might be expected to set before its audience. In abstract terms, that theme is the relationship between theory and practice in organized society. The duty involved is a duty to one's fellows, and the courage is that required by a sense of duty.

Brault goes on to make a similar point about the notion of Christian sacrifice,[6] but I will explore first, instead, the problem Charles and his knights face in the context of the social organization that suffuses the poem quite as much as Christianity does, that is, in terms of promises kept and broken, and of what promises imply in a world made rational by homage and other oral commitments. These considerations of individual and group seem to me to offer modern readers the most efficacious entry into a poem that presents God's victory as assured but shows men's contributions to it as uncertain. It is the context of these great deeds that most needs elucidation. By giving it most of my attention in the Commentary and in these chapters, I do not mean to imply anything like acceptance of the rigid distinction between "secular" readings and "sacred" readings.

Behind my discussion, then, lies the idea that the maker of the Oxford *Song of Roland* set out to make a point through his restatement of heroic legend. Like the preceding assumptions about society, this assumption of the intent to communicate is often decried, yet it is not a pure assumption, and not especially risky here, though it is less obvious on its face than the notion that the *Song* was made in and for a different age. The *Song of Roland* does not place its exposition inside men's minds, but shows their actions and what they win or lose thereby. That is why an analysis of what happens and what is said can in large measure supplant our hallowed trick of leaping to what is *behind* the *Song*'s events—unstated motives, old quarrels, Freudian categories, latent paganism. There will always be room for guesswork, but of the historical kind, made necessary by the loss of codes and information once commonly available, not the result of fundamental ambiguity or "surplus of meaning."

Indeed, the *Song of Roland* cannot be ambiguous even in the way

[6]Brault, *Song*, 1:43–44.

myths are in the abstract. It is a developed text, a mediation of the myth, and it needs to be studied as a separate entity.[7] Though a myth can be compared, in its general outlines, with a constructed text, it does not replace or explain the text any more than its sources do. We are dealing with a great didactic poem rather than with an exercise in pure form. Like much medieval work (perhaps most actualizations of myth), it bends heroism to specific ends. The corollary notion is that the poem has its primary intended audience among the members of the military caste, knights and sergeants. The link implies that it has a teaching function. At the same time, its maker did not anticipate the need to show, for our edification, that maintaining organized society as he conceived it was a vitally important matter. He does not himself become an apologist, supplying an explicit commentary that might never have been missed in fiction with a more familiar setting.

It is not immediately necessary to consider whether the author had been to school or not, or, more precisely, whether he was familiar with classical motifs, formal rhetoric, the works of other authors, iconography, logic, or philosophy even if he had not studied such things systematically. These important questions have been raised and are being pursued vigorously elsewhere. All we need to consider for the moment is that anyone who would have chosen the content of the *Song of Roland* would also have known a few basic things about his own surroundings: that society was organized as a hierarchy with the king as nominal head; that knights were bound to their status and functions by personal promises made all the more solemn by the fact that they were not documented and could not be enforced by the law of written contracts; and finally, that the West was Christian in confession. These old principles of description—so broad that few qualified medievalists, or none, would disagree with them—in fact orient us toward a new understanding of the *Song*.

Neither does it matter precisely who the Saracens were, or that the Arabs of Spain were not all Charles's enemies in the eighth century. The poem was written about soldiers, and for better or worse, soldiers are not concerned with the ultimate origins of evil. It is enough to know that Marsile and his men are the opposites, the arbitrary enemies of Christendom. The latter term, however, must be understood exactly. It is a realm where lies and treachery, though they occur, are not condoned. The reasons for that are not just moral in the abstract; they have pragmatic overtones. The Saracens are sometimes de-

[7]For a similar distinction, see Uitti, 18–19 (though he speaks of *legend* rather than myth), 26–27.

scribed as being "feudal" in the same way the Franco-Christians are, but there is an essential difference. The forms of feudal government—councils, chieftains, and fiefs—are empty without their underpinnings of true speech and trustworthiness. What is in danger of destruction, if the enemy prevails, is a society ruled by a concern for order, for solidarity, and, beyond its bellicosity, for the only peace it can envisage this side of the grave, the peace that is won by holding the arbitrary at bay.

Christendom, then, is not precisely Christian religion. A great deal of ink has been spilled over the question of whether the *Song* is a "secular" or a "Christian" work. This is to a large degree a false problem, or at most a problem of definition.[8] Historically speaking, the poem may with no difficulty be both; or, more precisely, in the terms of the debate as we encounter them, it must be neither, because it cannot be made one or the other exclusively. The two terms are too broad to represent a universal dichotomy of experience or of literature. On the contrary, in Brinton's words, they represent the familiar phenomenon of "faiths that live together in actual if illogical partnership in [the] heart and mind (illogical in the sense that some of these faiths, say Christianity and national patriotism, may have mutually incompatible ethical ideals)."[9] It is to our advantage to include in any discussion of the *Song*'s ideology the more precise distinction between ethics and eschatology.

The culture of early medieval France is noted for its adherence to Christian eschatology, and in my Commentary on the *Song* I have tried not to neglect the possibility that its meaning is best construed with the help of some elements of Christian doctrine. There is undoubtedly little to be gained by applying the premise that the author

[8]"A Christian Germanic hero is not quite the contradiction in terms some commentators seem to assume" (Hieatt, 425; cf. Niles, *Beowulf*, 251–53). "Judged by their own lights, the barons of the *Song of Roland* are surely 'true Christians'" (Jones, *Ethos*, 156). Jones nevertheless arbitrarily insists on a conflict between earthly glory and God's service (ibid., 80, 82, 126) and speaks of a "conscious defiance of Christian dogma" characterizing the Middle Ages specifically (p. 151). Concerning this presumed dichotomy and its reality or lack thereof, see Brault, *Song*, 1:10, *Chanson*, xxiv; Kibler, "Roland's Pride," 156; Owen, "Secular Inspiration"; Boatner, 574ff.; Van Emden, "Guarant," 27, 30; Halverson, 663; White, "Secular or Religious Inspiration?" I have mentioned the tendency among critics to place "feudalism" into a dialectical relationship with other medieval tendencies of thought (see Chapter 5, note 13).

[9]Crane Brinton, *The Shaping of Modern Thought* (Englewood Cliffs, N.J., 1963), 146; cf. Ariès, "Histoire des mentalités," 402–3. Uitti is certainly right to include this combination in his treatment of what he calls *epic binarism*. In a text like the *Song*, human beings and their secular institutions are shown as working for the glory of God as a natural matter (Uitti, esp. 79–80, 99–100; cf. the broader structural orientation of pp. 236–37, recalling Zumthor's system of oppositions plotted on the logical square).

of the *Song* was working at odds with some of the most striking aspects of the content he chose. His attitude toward death and martyrdom is, superficially (that is, on the level of conscious literary expression), that of the Christian who believes Paradise awaits us after our deaths, if we know how to attain it. That, at the very least, is what he shows when he recounts Roland's death.

The expression of such beliefs in medieval literature has occasionally been slighted and even denigrated, but that is often only another sign of our occasional lack of instinctive trust in our ancestors' creative capacity. It is not uncommon for medievalists to posit some incongruity between Christian world-views (taken broadly, as the diversity of the period suggests they must be) and the structures and meanings of the works that imply them. But a medieval author deserves to have his full range of artistic devices taken into account, even if one of his tools of composition was the evocation of an eschatology no longer taken for granted. Of course we have no way of proving that a Turold personally shared the religious beliefs known to have been predominant in his time, but (at the risk of repeating what I have already said about ideas in the work) we take on a considerable burden of proof when we claim that he did not rely on them, or sought to undercut them, in communicating with an audience of his contemporaries. The vastly more probable hypothesis is that the *Roland* redactor built the arguments between Roland and Oliver, and the scenes that show their last moments, into the framework of Christian attitudes toward death.

In this connection, readers are well advised to consult the detailed notes and commentary of Gerard Brault. They contain a great deal of information, both general and specific, that I have not attempted to include, and much of the information is of particular interest to anyone who wishes to understand how numerous medieval readers would have applied their knowledge of biblical and patristic materials and of typological techniques of reading to the *Song*. Readers today will not be able to understand everything the *Song of Roland* has meant to our fellow humans unless we understand what it was like to read as many of them did, with simultaneous attention to a work's overt story line and to the typological or "allegorical" networks that are relevant to it. There may be some disagreement about the role higher religious and intellectual culture had in the *Song*'s elaboration, but there can be little doubt about how educated medievals (wherever they had studied) would often have received it.

The status of religion in the work has been hotly debated, to a large extent, because the checkered ethical history of Christianity lends itself to arguments that reduce the entire religion to specific and limited ethical components.[10] Failure to take Christianity's ethical instability into account has clouded the controversy aroused by George Fenwick Jones's assertions concerning the paganism of the work's ethos. Perfunctory Christianity is perhaps more a norm than an aberration in the history of Western civilization. In any case, not every professing Christian could have lived by all the tenets to which professing Christians have subscribed at one time or another, because they conflict. Furthermore, it is true that many Christians do not live by the tenets they themselves profess. But we will never accomplish even a superficial reading of the rear guard's last stand if we insist that the violence of these men means they are unbelievers.

As with feudal theory, then, so with Christian doctrine. My Commentary avoids dependence on any detailed interpretation of what Christian life and action are, for it would be difficult to prove that a given anonymous eleventh- or twelfth-century author somewhere in northern Francophonia understood my terms exactly as I do. More important, however, I have tried not to neglect certain eschatological beliefs that any Christian must profess, short of apostasy. These differ from the ethical tenets Jones uses to test the poem, but I think Jones's version of the distinction between ethics and the "Christian myth" does not quite account for the role that basic Christian beliefs play in this narrative.[11]

For Christians, the soul is immortal, and the body is not. The afterlife (whatever its precise form) is inevitable and eternal. Thus the afterlife is what counts, and not the transitory life of the body. The believer, in principle, does not fear death, for it frees the soul. The author of the *Song* in the Oxford version does not speak of grace, mercy, forgiveness, or infinite love, and he does not portray his warriors as men of compassion. But while he does not express these

[10]Scholars have at times been all too eager to classify as "pagan" or "Germanic" (and hence, in some formulations, as "feudal") the "primitive and warped view of Christianity" that Jones (*Ethos,* 146) attributed to Turold. Some of the attitudes and assumptions thus identified can in fact be found not only in the Old Testament but also in chronicles, essays, correspondence, proclamations, newspaper articles, and television shows from time immemorial to the present, whatever the society. The fact that today these truculent and even violent notions are not shared by certain intellectual communities is discussed in Chapter 7, below.

[11]"Humility is better than pride, . . . love is better than hate, and . . . forgiveness is better than vengeance" (Jones, *Ethos,* 101). Jones insists on ethics (thus defined) as essential to Christianity, but the basic idea of separating ethics and eschatology is his: "Roland and his men accept Christian dogma without Christian ethics" (ibid., 157); "In embracing Christianity, they had accepted its mythos but not its ethos" (ibid., 151). It does not follow that the ethic they do accept is strictly personal: cf. Owen, "Secular Inspiration," 400.

ethical concerns of Christianity, he certainly does share both the eschatology and the cosmology of the Christian tradition, presenting life after death, the presence of angels, and the intervention of God in the affairs of men (as he presents the ultimate triumph of God's cause) as received truths. It is this eschatology—reinforced by Turpin's ritual and vindicated by the descent of angels (presented in the same style as the battle scenes)—that is Roland's reward and his ultimate help in time of trouble.[12]

The *Song of Roland* refers, then, not precisely to a code, but to a right understanding of civilized behavior in the feudal Christian matrix.[13] That is clear from what happens to the central Christian characters, from the sanctions applied to Ganelon, and from Roland's apotheosis. Ganelon's pledges and Pinabel also meet their deaths because they have sworn falsely, not because of what they worship. It might also be argued that the punishment of the pagans at Roncevaux is the result of their treachery and their alliance with a traitor. Personal honesty and truthfulness are themselves traditionally Christian ethical concerns. Here is where the strong link between personal and public morality characteristic of feudalism comes into play again, for the ethic of honesty in the *Song of Roland* is also a public and practical one. In all the instances just cited, supernatural intervention is a sign of right behavior in a natural context. The idea that "feudalism" itself is a more or less coherent system of government implies that feudalism necessarily has ethical components; for all the reasons suggested above, and developed further in the following chapters, I think it is impossible to give an adequate account of what Roland says and does unless we perceive his behavior as coherent also, and as ethically consistent.

Yet there is no reason to circumscribe the poem within these limits. Feudal ethics and Christian eschatology are two orders of fact, not rivals, one of which must exclude or even necessarily diminish the other.[14] The work illustrates this clearly (even without reference to

[12]Hence the irrelevance of Menéndez Pidal's claim (p. 243) that the *Song* is not Christian because its characters do not invoke the names of God and Christ with any great frequency, which seems to imply that Christian literature is defined by density of sacred references. For Owen, in contrast, religion is "a rich backcloth," though it remains "irrelevant to the actual plot" (Owen, "Secular Inspiration," 390).

[13]"A feudalism transposed into an ideal *communitas*" (Uitti, 79; cf. 86–88); "a unity transcending divisions of clan or region" (Pensom, 97). See also the remarks on the *projektierte Gemeinschaft* in note 3 to Chapter 4, above.

[14]"God's cause, that of Christian against pagan, is still a feudal cause and a cause of honor, as the poet envisages and presents it" (Farnham, 162). Cf. Contamine, 270: "Intimately engaged in the wars of the period, the church hierarchy experienced at the same time an inevitable secularisation of its habits, training and even appearance. In parallel, it was led to sacralize and sublimate warrior values."

the religious import of the Baligant episode) through its use of divine approbation and the heavenly afterlife as forms of ultimate recompense. Roland, Oliver, and the members of the rear guard are, among other things, holy martyrs.[15] Emissary angels join in the poem's action and determine its import in ways that are familiar to every reader—guiding Thierry's stroke when he defends Charles against *felonie,* and lifting Roland to Heaven when he has carried out his worldly vows.

It is, then, too simple to say that feudalism is a rational system and Christianity a faith, and that hence the poem is feudal in its ethics and Christian in its eschatology, and leave it at that—"the Germanic spirit in a Romance form," to borrow Gaston Paris's phrase. But history offers no warrant for calling a work "secular" because it does not show the full panoply of Christian mythology and beliefs simultaneously. I prefer a term that better evokes the intertwining of eternal eschatology and cosmology with the social ideals of a time and place. Hence I have spoken of Christendom, or feudal Christian society, as the realm of divinely sanctioned right behavior, the realm Roland and his comrades are sworn—and determined—to protect.

In this view, the *Song of Roland* is not an ambiguous text, but it does not follow that it must be everywhere self-explanatory. It is an epic of action and reaction, and while its structure suggests a moral, its rhetorical scheme does not involve moralizing. Of course, great art is not necessarily the vehicle of its own explanation, but that does not mean its points of reference cannot be discovered. Such matters as vengeance, vows, fidelity, and consistency belong simultaneously to medieval Christendom and to the effect the text achieves, being part and parcel of the construction of both. To grasp that requires only a general, functional understanding of basic feudal and religious notions, but that understanding is difficult in itself, and not the least for one final reason.

The poem's names for the elements of feudal Christian ethics are familiar in form, whether we translate them or not. But the words of the text—honor (or better *los,* "earned reputation"), shame (or *huntage*), pledge (*plevir*), aid, betrayal (*traïsun*), the good (*prod*), faith and constancy (*amur, fei*)—clothe values and arouse associations that nearly nine hundred years later we must strive to discern. The effect of this foreignness on criticism can be even more subtle than the general debilitation brought on by lack of sympathy with feudal ideals. Still,

[15]At least in the vocabulary of the text; they are not given a direct choice between death and abjuration. To die for one's overlord was sometimes called martyrdom; see M. Bloch, 232. A contemporary tendency of thought not only made the emperor or king a vicar of Christ, but also identified him as "God and Christ through grace" (Brault, "*Sapientia,*" 102).

we cannot see what is vital in the issues Roncevaux raises unless we see that feudal terminology is not being used in the *Song* in a trivial way. The fate of Ganelon may indeed be seen as meaning precisely that: that feud and vengeance are instruments of leadership and not personal privileges, that they are not to be applied lightly.

Readers conversant with studies on the *Roland*'s lexicon will recognize the debt my Commentary owes, in this area, to George Fenwick Jones's highly detailed pioneering study, and of course to G. S. Burgess's broader *Contribution à l 'étude du vocabulaire pré-courtois.*[16] If our conclusions differ at times, it is usually because for some key term I have tried one of the meanings these authors attest and accept, but in a place where traditional ideas about the poem did not invite them to try it. In some places I am convinced that Jones's insights into the values of terms have implications that Jones did not himself recognize. Thus when Ganelon says to Roland, "*Jo ne vus aim nïent*" (306), he is indeed doing as Jones said: "He means that he is changing from 'friendly' to 'hostile,' and therefore he must also defy the twelve peers because they are Roland's *ami,* in the sense of allies. . . . To be sure, Ganelon will hate his stepson, but that is not the crux of the matter. More important is the legal notice that he is proclaiming a state of hostility."[17] But, like Oliver's later *desfi,* this is not byplay. It is an act of great resonance for the reasons Jones gives, and the interpretation of the work must take that into account. Through this ill-justified and untimely challenge, Ganelon introduces into the plot, early on, that destructive disdain for the warriors' bond that Roland, instead, is sometimes accused of harboring.[18]

Similar things may be said about the adjective *proz,* which at last has been thoroughly studied after a good century's time, during which it was confused with, and even purely and simply translated by, its Modern French false cognate *preux.* "Roland is bold, but Oliver is wise. That is all [our author] needs to define his characters"—so, we remember, ran the dictum of Lanson's influential handbook. But the word turns out, upon delayed examination, to involve *consilium* as well as *auxilium,* the inseparable duties of knighthood defined by Fulbert of Chartres.[19]

[16]See note 3 to the Commentary. Jones's definition of Christianity has been criticized as too narrow (cf. notes 8–11 to this chapter), but that does not affect his major point about semantics: many of the words in the *Song of Roland* have false cognates in modern French and English.

[17]Jones, *Ethos,* 36.

[18]Vance, *Reading,* 52–53; Hunt, "Tragedy," 796; cf. Renoir, "Roland's Lament," 574–75.

[19]The quotation from Lanson's handbook is from p. 30. See note 10 to the Preface, note 26 to Chapter 3, commentary on laisse 87, and note 87 to the Commentary, above.

The term *vengeance,* however, deserves a word or two here. The imperative *vengez* is one of the first words Roland uses, and it may be taken as summing up the counsel he gives Charles and the army in his speech in council (210–13). It can hardly be doubted that its presence is one of the textual phenomena that have contributed to our view of Roland as an impetuous, combat-hungry warrior. Like *feud* and *feudal* themselves, the term has for us the overtones of vendetta. It also squares better with the harshness of the Old Testament than with the ethos of the Prince of Peace. These associations have probably contributed to a general reluctance to speak of the theme of vengeance as a major theme in the work, despite the frequency with which it occurs (e.g., lines 213, 1149, 1505, 1744, 3109, 3411).[20] But the hero's remarks may appear sensible in the context of feudal commitments. Vengeance is implied in the overlord's sworn duty of protection, which by an obvious mechanism extends to protect the living only if the enemy or potential turncoat knows that even a successful attack on a vassal means his own destruction afterward. Striking back is in fact conceivable as a sociopolitical imperative, and as the logical ex post facto reaction to the murder of someone a suzerain has given his word to protect. Like the other values Turold's soldiers neglect to their peril, the value of retribution contributes to the efficacy of the feudal bond. It was a mistake for them not to have shown by immediate action, when Basan and Basile died, that such obvious treachery as Marsile's is always punished. The second Saracen treachery, and Ganelon's, may even imply that Roland and the rear guard would not have died if the Franks had done their duty from the first.

Thus it is surely misleading simply to equate the ideal notion of revenge, a necessary act of leadership in some circumstances, with the blindness that our contemporary idea of feud implies—which the feud as a concept indeed came to imply in the Middle Ages.[21] Yet the duty of vengeance carries a potential for dangerous misapplication. That risk is in fact dealt with openly in the *Song*: it is Ganelon who undertakes, without any known cause, what he calls vengeance (3778), though Roland never wronged him—at least not by suggesting his name in a meeting where the decisions are not made by individual knights, and where, indeed, Roland's only other suggestion was rejected by the group. Like the imperative of trust, the duty of

[20]"The theme of vengeance shapes the plot," says Halverson, 661, but he means vendetta. Jones associated vengeance with paganism (*Ethos,* 184). But cf. note 13 to the Commentary, above.

[21]See the commentary on laisse 14; M. Bloch, 411; R. H. Bloch, *Medieval French Literature and Law,* 63ff.

vengeance is seen from both sides through the events of the text, but to show both sides is not to refuse all choice.

Njal's Saga, many decades later in another place, seems to protest the grim mechanics of such symbolic killings. But in the *Saga,* the feuds are blood feuds, and there is always a relative ready to strike back automatically, with no thought for logic or justice. The *Roland* poet knows the fighting will never stop, but his explanation is different. The cause of all this suffering is not the frailty of institutions, but the presence of evil in Creation. That evil manifests itself as a concrete force outside the characters, even beyond Ganelon's lies. It is imperial paganism, and it must be combated because its ultimate victory is unthinkable. In the aggrandizing way authors sometimes have, the poet uses an eschatology of good and unredeemed evil both as one of the narrative causes and as a referent, justifying horror and suffering by his beliefs, and insisting the victory will inevitably belong to his civilization. We may or may not accept the premises, but the poem is consistent. There is a king in the *Song of Roland,* and his job is a necessary one. We may say that *Njal's Saga* and the *Roland* express the concerns of different ages, or we may prefer to think that both ways of facing the tragic elusiveness of peace have coexisted throughout history. What we may not do is allow our sense of other perspectives to overcome the eschatological force of the *Roland* text.

In sum, the *Roland* problem is a form of the problem of dealing with alien cultures. One of the most important tasks facing the medievalist—one we have barely begun to tackle—is the task of understanding and describing the humanity inherent in literary monuments that seem at first to express inane or fanatical ideas. That is *our* paradox: to accept that fellow humans may have counseled apparent inhumanity in forms that have great aesthetic and emotional power. In this precise sense, literary history transcends the history of ideas. Roland and his maker, the creation and the creator, are dead, and we cannot make them live again. But that also means we need not fear what we take for excesses in them. If we react to their ideas and acts as though they had direct consequences for us, then we will condemn or extol them exactly as we would living ideas and living men, and the lessons we might learn from them indirectly will go unlearned.

The final chapters of this book are devoted to the question of likes and dislikes, but first there remains the important task of setting forth the broad principles to which Roland adheres. They are basically a set of limits, for understanding cause and effect in the *Song*'s narrative means understanding the limits the characters accept as part of their roles in the given situation and in the poem's world.

In the feudal nexus of duties, a poem about how to lead will also be a poem about how to follow. The *Song of Roland* and its hero exude not a hunger for victory or a thirst for glory, but a longing for the bedrock of trust, a desire for knights to perform what they promise. Glory in the *Song of Roland* crowns the steadfast. The importance of this principle flows from the historical considerations already mentioned. In our time the security of the given word is often guaranteed by our institutions. In the poem, instead, the personal oaths of reliable men guarantee the survival of social structure. Yet we may still discern the courage (even in the face of reproof) that Roland deploys in response to a challenge that puts his sworn word at risk.

In the *Song,* Roland, Oliver, Gautier del Hum, and the peers all die because they act as though they trusted Ganelon. It has made them, or at least Roland, seem stupid to generations of commentators. But early medieval knights often had little choice but to rely on trust, not as a matter of abstract adherence to a "chivalric code," but because they had no more practical way of doing business, dispensing justice, or keeping the peace. (It has been said that the detailed code of knighthood comes into being as the need for it becomes less obvious.) Honor in the early feudal context thus shares the strong practical aspect of the system. A ruler who wished to carry out a policy through strength, or one who needed to defend himself and his people, relied on the prior oral promises of homage when the time came to raise troops and constitute a tactical staff. Either the men who had sworn to help him would come when called, or his cause, good or bad, was doomed. A prince could not assemble or retain a court, or send men to treat with another court, without such assumptions. Charles at first seems weak because he submits to the resulting mechanisms and does not put them aside even at great need, but his forbearance is part of the ideal by implication. He is in fact so strong that he can deal even with Ganelon as the principle of trust requires.

For centuries the men and women charged with the government of Western Europe had a principle of contract but no written standard code of law. There was no central authority that could enforce compliance in matters of public responsibility, or demand attention to questions of common interest. The scattered counts and barons were often autarchic in such matters, thrown upon their own resources as they were in economic affairs. In fact, they often chose to stay at home when called, but in the realm of the ideal, where the *Song of Roland* situates its exhortation, they must be present when needed. In that, they differ little from the leaders and defenders of any society or institution, but we must know the form the call takes for them, and on the Spanish campaign its form is especially harsh. Our reading of the text will not be adequate until we have realized the importance of an atmosphere in which a simple promise establishes such rigorous expectations. We need not approve of this rigor, or share any of its specific elements ourselves. We need only allow that it mattered supremely to some of our forebears and that they could sing with energy and even passion about the community of trust, even though at first glance its associations do not move us.

Critics speak up occasionally in priase of Ganelon or even an imaginary Roland as individualists and rebels, or imply that we cannot take the *Song of Roland* seriously if it is "monarchical propaganda," but those are not the issues it treats. The issue is the real danger that men will never see any point in concerted action.[22] The *Song of Roland* called for foresight in a time when such notions as the public good and the common weal were not yet safe clichés of political science. It is not helpful to propose that Ganelon does not need to pay any heed to the doomed institutions of bygone days. The traitor is not Roland's rival, he is everyone's foe, and the threat he poses goes well beyond personal enmities.

I have said that feudal institutions are not themselves the themes of the *Song,* however. They are the setting, which gives force to the theme of responsibility, that personal responsibility that the feudal system required of its public officials. Hence the setting and theme are complementary. One may stop short of a balanced presentation of such interdependent phenomena, but the fact that some scholars stop early is no justification for avoiding an inquiry of this type altogether. On the other hand, linking feudal habits of thought with what happens in the *Song of Roland* is not just a matter of detail. Those habits are part of the maker's panoply of constructional devices.

To take a fresh example: when Oliver strikes Roland blindly, and nearly kills him by mistake, the hero's response seems flat at first glance. "You gave me no challenge," says Roland, using the verb *desfier* (2002). That may remind us that at various times and in various places the *desfi* was a term wound about with precise (though differing) rules of application, concerning whom one could challenge, in what form, and to what purpose. But in the final exchange between Roland and Oliver, it is simultaneously a technical term and a literary device of considerable resonance. It refers not to some momentary

[22] I refer to Contamine's suggestive discussion of political disintegration (pp. 43–44); compare C. W. C. Oman's remarks on the Great Moot of Salisbury in *The Art of War in the Middle Ages* (Boston, 1924), 1:365; Benton, 242 and his n. 31.

lapse of etiquette, but to the structure of the relationship between the two men. The negative *desfïer* here is a typical Rolandian literalism. It actually goes without saying that Oliver has not given Roland any challenge, for he has no reason to strike him, just as he had no reason to chide him earlier. If Oliver issues no *desfi,* it is because his conduct is not rational: nothing makes him Roland's opponent except blindness. It is not the details of law, but the machinery of the poem, that is being evoked.

Similarly, one might easily claim that in various passages (let us say the Nomination Scenes) feudal procedure as it was somewhere codified is not being followed and that the obligations involved are therefore somehow less real. As I have noted in the Commentary, such technicalities have been applied to Ganelon's defense against the accusation of treason. It seems absurd to claim that settling a private account with Roland means having the Saracens come and wipe out twenty thousand men and more, under cover of a spurious treaty. Further, Roland's *a majori* argument that he must accept suffering as part of his condition can hardly be negated by some failure to touch all the bases, even assuming that we know where all these are located. Yet beyond this lies the question of how we are to apply our knowledge of the past to the elucidation of a formidable poem. I have tried to do this by taking feudal and knightly culture in a broad sense.

The warrior ethos that derives from feudal organization involves courageous devotion to duty, in the service of a sense of order. It is exemplified by the grim readiness of Roland and his men to fight to the end in defense of their comrades when duty comes upon them in a narrow, bitter place. Roland is a man whose tenacious and simple bravery stands as an example to his fellow soldiers in the text, just as his steadfast adherence to the rules of an imperfect but workable feudal system could have shown medieval people the need for strength of will if a stable society, with all its benefits, is to be maintained.

Thus the *Song of Roland* is hortatory, not meliorative. It exalts a norm as the means of progress, rather than a vision of new goals. The norm is harsh, and without clear reference to the circumstances Roland's adherence to it has seemed exaggerated. But the replacement of the norm is not one of the ideas in the poem, for the circumstances do not call for it. The work's excitement does not come from the struggle of two ideals—fortitude and sapience, or restraint and freedom. It comes from the fight men must wage against pain and fear if they are to match a single ideal. We could call that ideal "the chivalric code" or "knightly" behavior, if those terms were not at once anachronistic—the eleventh century is not an age of chivalry as we know or imagine it—and too easily sentimentalized. Roland's code is a soldier's code, an inevitable code where it is appropriate, because it is appropriate only where the need is extreme. We may find an epic incomplete if it presents no alternative to such a code, but art is, after all, incomplete by definition. The art of the *Roland* poet consists first and foremost in such a reduction. Whoever he was, he seems to have accepted Augustine's reconciliation of the just war with Christian ethics.[23] His trim sketch of council and combat shows that the war in which Roland dies is an obvious necessity.

[23]Reflection on the *causes* of war seems to have grown up first in Scholastic thought; see Contamine, 280–82. On the general concept of the "just war" and its Augustinian form, see, e.g., *New Catholic Encyclopedia,* vol. 14, 802–7, vol. 11, 39; R. H. Barrow, *Introduction to Saint Augustine, "The City of God"* (London, 1950), 206–7.

[7]

The Aesthetics of Heroism

Thus far my principal subject has been the necessary and primordial practicalities of reading the *Song of Roland,* and hence I have concentrated on matters of history, with only passing references to thematic categories of the sort that are sometimes conceived as timeless. I have devoted several chapters to particular aspects of the *Song*—its structure and the relations among its characters, its Christian eschatology and feudal context—and to some of the critical reactions to them. Now it is time for me to meet the implied challenge of those terms and to move from the particular toward a general concept of heroism.

The task is both delicate and necessary. It is delicate because it involves evaluation and analogy; it is necessary because heroism does not disappear from the record of human affairs when we pay it no heed, any more than pride and stupidity do. Heroism is not exactly timeless; its aesthetic appeal, the enthusiasm it generates as an ideal, waxes and wanes. But as a theme of literature and a model or type of behavior, it resurfaces regularly enough to qualify as a traditional concept in the cultures that are heirs to the medieval.

One difficulty in treating the concept becomes clear when we consider the ambiguity not of the text but of some of our terms. Thus it is with the slippery adjective "human," which is understandably common in scholarly writing about the *Song* and which indeed has appeared several times in passages quoted in the preceding chapters. In *Roland* criticism, "human" is not in fact a generic or descriptive term, but an emotional term or a universalizing term of value. Moreover, while usually positive, it can be negative in implication when applied to Charles's so-called weakness or Oliver's putative common sense. Surely that is why the adjective "human" has received such divergent applications, laudative and pejorative, in critical judgments on Roland's acts, while at the same time he is never called a villain but is regularly designated by the term "hero." That raises the problem of *our* intention and motivation in the application of such terms. The term "human," for all its overtones of warmth or pity, may just as correctly be used to evoke the widely varying particulars of cultures and individuals. Then it reverts to history's side of the coin, where the universal and the general take on palpable shape. The term "hero," though not usually thought of as pejorative, proves to raise similar problems.

Stating the challenge simply, if we agree to undertake the sort of reading that integrates the text's content with the historical context in which it was heard, if we put forth an interpretation for a heroic song of deeds that its early hearers would have accepted and perhaps enjoyed, do we, despite ourselves, set the stage for rejection of the work by our contemporaries? If we try to grasp how a medieval interpretive community would have understood its *Roland,* then our reaction will vary, not merely with changes in ourselves but also with changes in our concept of the implied audience. There is a danger that we will find some characteristics of that implied community distasteful. The intertwining of principle and death in the *Song of Roland* lacks the subtlety to be found in Racine's *Bérénice,* Anouilh's *Antigone,* and elsewhere. The *Song* was written with a bluntness that many of us would not have chosen to use. Heroism is out of style now in some intellectual circles—enough to lead critics to overlay Roland's heroism with psychological, anthropological, and structural analogies that seem to make it more palatable. Yet if we are able to accept its presence, the bluntness may remind us of the irreducibility of heroic choice in a way that cannot be supplanted by forms we find more sophisticated, or conveyed to the reader by the multiplication of metaphoric schemes.

In this chapter and the next, I intend to consider some of the potential responses of readers to the qualities that make Roland a hero. By that general term "hero" I mean a literary character who is given exceptional strength and who deploys it to a purpose. The hero's striving does not go unremarked; in fact, it is part of the epic's function to emphasize it. Thus, whether or not Roland ever lived, his story touches the world outside literature. Its existence and his imply a standard, a measurement, even values, to which living humans can compare themselves and the actions they see around them.[1]

[1]I note that this paragraph includes all the elements of the "dictionary definition" of the hero, as it occurs, for example, in the *Oxford [New] English Dictionary* (5:245–46), although the OED does not distinguish between literary characters and living persons in the same way. Compare the narrower definition summarized by Jackson: "physical courage which often borders on rashness"; near-invincible strength; and "a near-obsession with fame and reputation which is the hero's prime motivation" (Jackson, *The Hero and the King,* 120). On the poem's values, see Uitti, 79, 106; Owen, "Secular Inspira-

That these considerations are distant from many important concerns of latter-day literary criticism, especially aesthetic ones, is not disabling to the discussion. We are learning that every style of evaluative criticism has both an appropriate corpus and limitations outside that corpus. Canons of evaluation that favor highly ramified, metaphoric, ironic, mimetic (or perhaps covertly didactic) texts will tend either to depreciate or to caricature the unambiguously heroic narrative. Yet, as William Calin has recently reminded us, such canons of choice and rejection do not suffice to enfold all that is and has been moving in literature, nor do they define all that gives pause in famous texts.[2] Constance Hieatt characterized Roland as a "Germanic" hero and compared him with Beowulf, Hagen, Gunnar, Skarphedin, and Njal, and yet her definition is a general one. The hero is "a brave warrior who proves his valor in the ultimate way, facing, with undaunted courage and resolution, certain or almost certain death and destruction."[3] Centuries after Turold, Claude Mauriac could still say: "To choose the lesser chance of survival is a particularly acute way of being alive."[4] Not only Saint-John Perse, Aragon, and Pierre Emmanuel, but also Saint-Exupéry, Malraux, Camus, and perhaps dozens of other authors of narrative in the twentieth century propose models of heroic behavior. We may or may not embrace such models ourselves, but we need not deny the reality of their appeal. Indeed, the creation of antiheroes is a form of commentary on the ideal. To the extent that the cultural tenets of deconstructionism apply, it may even be thought to affirm it.

Part of the study of the *Song of Roland,* therefore, is the task of facing up to themes that are out of fashion both aesthetically and

---

tion," 398; Kirsch, 396–97; Gérard, 461–63 (though he dissociates Roland from them). Niles has recently reached conclusions about *Beowulf* that are strikingly similar to mine about *Roland;* see esp. his reevaluation of the notions of public responsibility and of Beowulf's character and achievements (John D. Niles, *Beowulf* [Cambridge, Mass., 1983], 224–54).

[2]See esp. the conclusion to Calin, 424–45. To the idea of a steady decline in the prestige of the hero (cf. Jauss's discussion of Frye's theses in his "Levels of Identification"), I prefer Bloomfield's more sophisticated idea that sympathy for heroic figures comes and goes; see Morton Bloomfield, "The Problem of the Hero in the Later Middle Ages," in Burns and Reagan, *Concepts of the Hero,* 27–48, and cf. note 5, below. It is not my purpose to discuss aesthetic theory here in detail, but only to suggest that neither our desires nor our expectations in this realm can lead to solid readings by themselves. Our business is not to remake the text for fear we will not like the one we have. Historical aesthetics can proceed only in the other direction, from interpretation toward evaluation. A good part of Gadamer's *Truth and Method* is occupied with this question ("Aesthetics has to be absorbed into hermeneutics," p. 146).

[3]Hieatt, 424.

[4]Claude Mauriac, *Malraux ou le mal du héros* (Paris, 1946), 12.

intellectually and that—perhaps partly for that reason—are often distorted or cheapened in popular culture.[5] Not that we do not still respond to them in our way, but like our response to the work's content, our hesitant response to its themes is strange by likely medieval standards. Though concern for clarity might suggest that I avoid the aesthetics and the ethics of Roland's heroism and limit myself to interpreting the poem, I have found that to be a misleading approach in the last analysis. The following essays refer from each of the three aspects to the others. The result is speculative as well as analytical, but the importance of such a study is beyond doubt. We cannot know what criteria, if any, make actions and choices admirable in our own time and place unless we have something to compare them with. The past, approached through its particulars, is nearly the only context *we* have outside myth and the imagination. That, at least, is not a "larger question" than the interpretation of the *Roland;* each is a part of the other.

I suggest that the heroic ethic of the old poem is, in its starkness, something of an embarrassment to the modern academic critic. Our response to the work is affected by that embarrassment. Even medievalists, with the successes of Romanesque art to guide them (and its reputation to reassure them), sometimes hesitate to grant full artistic status to didactic works. In the *Song of Roland* we have not only a text bearing ideas, but also some ideas with quite unpleasant modern associations. In the end, our desire to serve the poem and ensure its acceptance through an honest enthusiasm may lead us to mask its power as an exemplary story, through interpretations that seem to us more humane, and thus more appealing, than the humanity of its maker and its earliest audiences. The dilemma, for the medievalist critic, is quite real. In our understandable desire not to condescend to medieval authors by denying their work the potential for richness, we may risk condescending to them in a more fundamental way: by denying that they could have pursued aesthetic goals of their own that are not compatible with the notions of poetic richness dominant in recent times.

That the risk is real may be seen in the ways the *Song of Roland* has been described in the not-too-distant past. Both its themes and its way of expressing them have sometimes been condemned on ostensibly aesthetic grounds. Ferdinand Brunetière's baldly polemical denigra-

[5]The historical implication of Northrop Frye's discussion seems to be that the progression by stages from godlike hero to antihero has been linear (*Anatomy of Criticism* [Princeton, 1957], 34–35). Jauss (e.g., 314) seems to suggest the sort of cyclical or irregular movement I have in mind.

tion of the work's aesthetic of character may seem to carry this amalgamation almost to absurdity, but it is nevertheless revealing:

> The characters [of the *Song*] have no life. Only their names differentiate its Olivers and its Turpins from its Estorgants and its Estramarins. The ones swear by Mahon and Tervagan, the others by Diex l'Espirital: that is their only distinguishing feature. It is strictly formal. At bottom, they all exude the same ferocious and brutal valor, they are all equally insulting and blustering. . . . *And nothing human beats behind that thick armor,* nothing but the intractable and silly pride of the barbarian, with his arrogant confidence in the strength of his arm.[6]

This unsympathetic reading seems to stem from some deep repulsion. The modern critic—especially the medievalist—may reject it automatically, without a thought for the amount of patient work that has gone into convincing a relatively small number of educated readers of its inadequacy. But we should also consider textbook judgments like Buckner Trawick's, which are not apparently polemical in intent, and thus exhibit a greater surface plausibility. Trawick says that the *Song of Roland* "is marred by exaggeration, dull cataloguing, and repetition. Character portrayal is crude: each person is either almost entirely good or entirely bad."[7] Anyone interested in the Middle Ages or in epics is likely to find this as supremely wrongheaded as Brunetière (to whom I shall return shortly). But the point about this uninspiring statement is not that it is wrong. It occurs in the wrong sort of book, no doubt, since it is difficult to imagine any reader of Trawick's manual wishing to pursue any further study of the *Song*. But Trawick's observations are correct. The poem is indeed characterized by exaggerations, lists, and a certain kind of repetition, and I have previously argued that one of its salient features is the portrayal of characters as representing some single moral stance.

There is more involved, however. To raise a point that is not very often considered in the philological tradition, Trawick's aesthetic judgment—conveyed by the words "marred" and "crude"—though it is based on anachronistic standards not widely applied to Old French

[6]Brunetière, 23. Emphasis in the original. It is not surprising that Brunetière disapproved not only of the way the work portrays character, but also of its composition, as noted in Chapter 5. "The poem is rather badly composed." To get the full effect of Brunetière's indignation, one must read the essay in its entirety.

[7]Buckner Trawick, *World Literature,* vol. 1: *Greek, Roman, Oriental, and Medieval Classics* (New York, 1953), 188–89. The influence of Brunetière may be traced here, or perhaps it is that of Lanson, before his "11e édition" (see Lanson, *Histoire,* 30, n. 1). For a mid-twentieth-century French form of the same disparagement, see Kléber Haedens, *Une Histoire de la littérature française,* 2d ed. (Paris, 1954), 20–21.

literature these days, is not wrong either. Statements of aesthetic reaction are not "falsifiable"; that is I. A. Richards's paradox, which the New Criticisms have solved after the manner of Pandora. But such statements are sometimes irresponsible. If their hidden presuppositions about what is *crude* were actually expressed, they would be incommensurate with their object. Remarks like Trawick's are not useful for understanding why the poem ever interested any (*human*) reader, or studying just how it *does* function as a piece of literature. After all, we do not have much to gain by trying to invest the *Song* with the (presumably neoclassical) characteristics Trawick apparently would have liked to see in it; it is manifestly crude in all the ways he says, in the ways many medieval works of art are, which is ultimately to say only that it and they do not correspond to Trawick's or my "horizon of expectations" as shaped by teachers and by other texts. That, in the perspective I have tried constantly to adopt, is a feature of Trawick's and my present horizons and not an inevitable way of grasping the *Song of Roland.* Surface strangeness has overwhelmed us, and like Victor Hugo at Reims in 1825, we express only our preference for the effect we already know: "And so I went yesterday to see the cathedral. It is an admirable monument of Gothic architecture. . . . The interior, as it is now, is much less beautiful than it was in its age-old nudity. Its old granite has been painted blue, its severe sculptures have been overlaid with gold and glitter."[8] And yet it is well established that cathedrals were often brightly painted in the Middle Ages. The sense of gaudiness comes from a comparison with the ideal of severity and is not identical with medieval experience.

These principles of evaluation and history are well known and are now being given fresh life through the insights of reception history. There would be no point in insisting on them here if it were not for the fact that, taken in a general sense, they conflict with strong tendencies in *Roland* criticism. If we intend to practice the kind of history in which "the past and the present shed light on each other mutually,"[9] we must apply a less-familiar corollary to the principles of aesthetic shift made familiar by summaries of reception aesthetics. The corollary is this: Praise is a two-edged sword, just as denunciations are; if we may denounce a medieval work for failure to match

[8]Cited in Patricia Ward, *The Medievalism of Victor Hugo* (University Park, Pa., 1975), 22.

[9]This is Jacques Le Goff's formulation of the ideal of New History, *La Nouvelle Histoire,* 220, deriving from Marc Bloch, *Apologie pour l'histoire ou le métier d'historien* (Paris, 1952), 11–16.

some set of irrelevant standards, then we may also risk praising it for reasons that are misleading, despite appearances.

Some defenses of the *Song*'s greatness do not differ greatly in their degree of historical penetration from Trawick's denunciation. We have encountered something like its dialectical opposite in Zumthor's "the text can be understood only imperfectly, or not at all." When Bédier refused to reduce the treason plot behind the Roncevaux story to a "crude melodrama," he was doing little except claiming the opposite of what Trawick (and Brunetière) claim, by saying that the important features they missed (especially complexity of characters) are there after all. Neither critic seems to have considered positing a narrative strain in which none of those things was primordial, in which the concern was not for verisimilitude but for other kinds of effect—exemplary or moral.

There is some reason to think that we still do not quite dare to face the question of didactic literary values, that we remain under the influence of Mallarmé, Valéry, or Croce despite the serious examination of medieval literature's teaching function in the work of Robertson, Nichols, R. H. Bloch, Uitti, and others. At least specialist treatments of the *Song of Roland* continue to offer similar attitudes about what makes it aesthetically important and about how it must be read if we are to recognize its importance. The tradition already discussed in Chapter 4, that of equating literary success with ambiguous complexity, remains present in Calin's remark that "*La Chanson de Roland* is . . . on the political and psychological levels, a far more sophisticated, ambivalent work than, say, Auerbach would want us to believe."[10] And Roger Pensom affirms that "Roland is a man and a real one" (this indeed appears to be one of the major premises behind his interpretive paraphrase of the *Song*), adding that "systematic interpretations, whether they be Christian or secular, have the regrettable effect of diminishing the very humanity that makes him so irresistibly fascinating."[11] There can be no doubt that, along with humanity (already discussed), reality and irresistibility are very positive traits, and so, within our natural horizon of expectations, the claim, though opposed to Trawick's, bears the same sort of plausibility. Yet the statement bypasses the fundamental questions raised at the beginning of this chapter. What if our medieval ancestors found aesthetic power in

[10]Calin, 437.

[11]Pensom, 141; both the opposition of *fortitudo* and *sapientia* (pp. 84–85) and the attribution of psychological motives to characters (or "the apodeixis of mental states," p. 133) are basic to Pensom's interpretive paraphrase (pp. 79ff.).

systematic thought (as there is considerable evidence they did)? Are we to reject their feudal or Christian systematizations of experience? When we think of modern psychology as rooted in diversity, we forget the senses in which it too is a systematization; Freudian psychiatry is capable of being downright schematic. Might not medieval people have thought their schemas humane and realistic, as we do ours? And if we come to view our ancestors in that way, can we come to sense the aesthetic powers that once resided in those systems?

It is not until we proceed in the direction these questions suggest, until we look at the text to see whether its narrative features do not, in fact, require set historical referents, that we realize that fixed ideals are also part of both human creative experience and the history of response. Literature can be both systematic and fascinating, but this means distinguishing between elements of "reality" in the literary character Roland and elements of reality and humanity in authors and audiences who actually lived. Pensom later adds, "The poem is famous because it is intensely moving, not because it is morally instructive or historically accurate,"[12] and here, perhaps, the pattern emerges even more clearly than before. What is true of form (cf. Chapter 4) is also true of themes: Pensom's statement may, as ever, be true in itself, but the apparent aesthetic bias of its negations does not necessarily control interpretation. The question of why the poem is (now) famous is answered, but not the question of why it is (at various times) moving. It may be moving for any of a number of reasons, from which moral application (for some readers or hearers, if not all) cannot be excluded by generalizing one reader's reaction, one "tradition's", or one "community's."

If, then, we replace verisimilitude with ambiguity, pathos, tragedy, or some other term positively intended, we may not escape the problem caused by an entanglement between our preferences and our sense of literary prestige, on the one hand, and the way we read the text, on the other hand. To take an obvious example this time, Roland's alleged heedlessness, his concern with action and glory, and the consequences often ascribed to them, may seem to give the work great poignancy,[13] but that labeling is not the whole of the critic's job. We have not finished our task until we ask whether the construction of the work, or even its author's intent, is consonant with the poignancy we see in *démesure*. If the *Song* is organized about something else entirely, then for better or worse its effect (once we give it free rein)

[12]Ibid., 155.
[13]See Le Gentil, *Song*, 32; cf. Le Gentil, *Chanson* (1st ed.), 42, or Sicilano, 339.

may be different. With Tony Hunt, I have argued (see Chapter 2) that *démesure* is not a flaw that automatically qualifies as tragic, and that the fight at Roncevaux is not a tragic situation as the work shows it. Critics have sometimes argued as though the tragic label, once applied to the *Song of Roland,* cannot be removed without great risk. Still, pathos is not tragedy, and neither is the only way to be touched by literature.

On the other hand, an "Aristotelian reading" of the *Song of Roland* is not irrelevant or wrong merely because Aristotle was Greek and not early medieval. It is irrelevant if it leads us to confuse Roland's moral triumph with error, and it is wrong if it must be taken to mean that martyrdom is to be assimilated to Aristotelian tragedy—I repeat that this, significantly, is not Hunt's position.[14] If an invocation of Aristotle carries greater weight in some intellectual circles than a reference to medieval ways of organizing things, that development can nevertheless have no retroactive force, either on the constitution of the text or on the reactions its maker expected his subject to elicit from an audience. If a Christian or feudal reading (or one that seeks to avoid contradicting Christian and feudal principles) is preferable, then it is preferable not only because Turold was *not* Greek but also because it permits of a coherent and balanced account of the text's contents, sequence, and emphases.[15]

What, then, are some of the things we miss when we let our response to the poem hinge on our ability to detect familiar forms of verisimilitude, ambiguity, or pathos in the actions of its characters? I would like to consider briefly one of the traditional notions about the Council of Charlemagne and its implications for the narrative of Ron-

[14]Some concept of Aristotelian tragedy has, one suspects, underlain most or all of the offhand references to the work as tragic from Gaston Paris on, but the notion was never properly analyzed until Hunt's thorough study, "Tragedy." I recall that, for *hubris,* Hunt substitutes the idea of *hamartia* as a tragic error with unintended consequences (see also Hunt, "Character and Causality," 4). This requires the assumption that Roland does not act deliberately, which implies that he does not understand the promises constituted by his own speeches (Hunt, "Tragedy," 796, 798, 800–801; cf. Owen, "Secular Inspiration," 397–98). As noted above, Hunt concludes that the poem still does not qualify as tragic and is thereby weakened (pp. 803–5).

[15]Much the same can be said of Pensom's attempt to describe Roland's "personality" in Jungian terms. Pensom, 152, faces the issue squarely when he says, "The Jungian view presents the most useful modern paradigm for the exposition of the poet's underlying scheme." But before proceeding to speak of "personality-integration," "conflict and repression," "trauma and disintegration," or a "persona of reconciled opposites," we must decide on the elements that are to make up, as it were, our "case report" on Roland. It is far from self-evident, for example, that Roland's use of the plural or the interrogative in laisse 128 is adequate proof that he is "weak, confused and overcome by fear" (Pensom, 153).

cevaux. The literature contains a certain number of claims that Roland must be wrong, and Ganelon right, when the one champions conflict and the other champions compromise (cf. Chapter 3). The psychological bases of our sympathy for the would-be peacemaker are clear, but our taste for psychological exposition and realistic character development should not be allowed to play us false. Only if we recall that we are dealing with a constructed narrative, and not a slice of reality, will we be able to interpret the entire sequence of events cogently from the council to the blowing of the horn.

Real-life warriors and Christians do indeed often have the chance to make peace through negotiation. The creations of Turold do not. The opening scenes of the poem, and its very last scene, are designed, without a doubt, to show the necessity of war. The Franco-Christians are not the initiators of hostilities but the defenders of Christendom, against Marsile, against the aggressive invader Marsile represented, his suzerain Baligant, and ultimately against the besiegers of Imphe. If the Franks do not fight, they will be cheated, betrayed, and trampled. Sometimes real life is like this, and sometimes not. Charlemagne is one of history's most famous empire builders, but the Charles we see in action in the *Song* is defending his home and his civilization against invaders from another world, who swear they will overrun his land. The characters of the *Song of Roland,* as literary characters, do not have our burden of distinguishing when war is and is not justified, any more than they have our freedom to listen to Ganelon.

All this implies what E. D. Hirsch calls a rule of thumb in the task of understanding ancient works. "The esthetic" may be, as Peter Hoy puts it (after Gadamer), "a moment of the hermeneutic awareness,"[16] but it is only one of its moments, not the controlling one and not a point of departure for it. Before assigning aesthetic values, positive or negative, to the *Song of Roland*'s narrative features, we must first establish what those features are. They cannot be deduced from aesthetic categories.[17] If having a flawless hero does make the work a failure somehow, and there is nevertheless strong evidence to the effect that it does have such a hero, then we must accept the "somehow failure."[18] But both the origins and the limitations of the "some-

[16]Hoy, *Critical Circle,* 107; cf. note 2 to this chapter. "Rules of thumb" is Hirsch's term for the axioms of probability that guide "local hermeneutics," of which I take this reading to be an example (see Hirsch, 18).

[17]The *Song* challenges "the very notion of esthetic interpretation" (Cerquiglini, 40). I would not refuse to consider that the use of modern psychology as a substitute for medieval (or to make up what is perceived as a lack of any equivalent) is an aesthetically motivated use; see the following note.

[18]On the aesthetic superiority of ambiguous or tragic readings of the *Song* and its characters, see, e.g., Pauphilet, *Legs,* 80 ("An astonishingly good sense of decorum led

how" will at the same time become clear. If we agree to speak of the *Song of Roland* as coming to us from the past, then it simply does not matter whether, at first blush, it appears successful or not. That is one of the glorious and neglected strengths of the discipline of critical interpretation applied historically: it teaches us to see why works we do not immediately like were written anyway. This is true of Shakespeare, as it is true of Donne, or Racine, or even (as it turns out) Valéry, Mallarmé, and Eliot. The works of these great writers are in some sense (an obvious sense, to anyone who teaches them in university courses) inculcated preferences and acquired tastes, and where we assume our responses to them to be "somehow" natural or innate is precisely where we need more information and training to avoid confusions whose roots are in anachronism.

Thus there is no reason to conclude that the treatment of character in the *Song,* as both Buckner Trawick and I have described it, is ineffective. Here I will shift my ground slightly, in order to come to grips with Brunetière's polemical attack on the barbarism of the work's protagonists. Precisely because it is polemical, Brunetière's judgment suggests something that Trawick's does not: in the case of the *Roland* it is not necessary to show only that it is our duty to past humanity to read and praise the work even if it appears dull. One of the most problematic things about the *Song* is precisely that it does not appear dull. Its themes, once we recognize them, are almost too compelling.

Whence, I suspect, Brunetière's energetic denunciation of *l'intraitable et risible orgueil du barbare* ("the intractable and silly pride of the barbarian") which is not the reaction of someone insensitive to the text's own energy. It is difficult to know exactly what positive values Brunetière was intending to contrast with the "inhumanity," the ferocity, the valor, the pitiful pride he decried in Oliver and Turpin—magnanimity? humility? equanimity? But apparently he was so affected by the characters' bellicosity that he never asked whether their

the poet to avoid the error of making his traitor entirely evil and perfectly odious"); Brault, *Song,* 1:180 ("To justify only Roland is to neglect the poignant human tragedy"); Van Emden, "Pro Karolo Magno," 182 ("The *Roland,* like any work of literature, gains in stature if the outcome evolves ineluctably from a situation in which the rights and wrongs are shared"); Vance, *Reading,* 51 ("Roland is at last wise and Oliver is at last bold. . . . I believe that the inversion of roles is an attempt on the poet's part to ennoble his characters by allowing each to share the virtue of the other"). Siciliano, 353, also 333–34, quotes in this connection a maxim of La Rochefoucauld's: "Vice is part of the very composition of virtue." Despite all this, the question Jacques Thomas, 92, asks about Ganelon can be extended to all the characters: "Is it not prejudicial to believe that a schematic and static psychology must derive from clumsiness or bad taste?" Cf. Battaglia, 356.

literary context justified the attitudes the text lends them. To argue that Brunetière was mistaken about the bellicosity itself, to defend the work's characterizations as subtle and complex, is to beg the same question.

The thing Roland illustrates is a paradox, and that is why his tenacity and the obviousness of his triumph correspond to often unrecognized rules of textual decorum. The defense of society as a whole—its people and also the rules that give it definition—requires sacrifice, even stubborn insistence on sacrifice, from some of the individuals who are in the society. That is an uncomfortable truth, with many degrees of application in real life. It is not difficult to imagine that a poet might think its literary illustration must be very clear if it is to illustrate at all: the paradox must be fully visible, with the happy results of the sacrifice immediately at hand. And so the *Song of Roland* makes Roland's situation explicit in the interest of cohesion. He suffers and dies so that an ideal may live, and he is fully vindicated. That is the way the human condition often is presented in developing societies, developing religions, or anywhere the ground will support the structure of martyrdom.

Thus Brunetière's reaction is like Trawick's: unfalsifiable and inappropriate. But if we seek to replace the easy assumption of aesthetic universals with an account of historical particulars, we may encounter fresh difficulties. If the characters of the *Song* are potentially compelling, their words are also uncomfortably like what we hear around us. At first glance, the implied community discernible behind them may remind us (as perhaps it did Brunetière) of aspects of our own experience. To take a painful example, it is difficult for a contemporary American critic to discuss the *Song of Roland* without thinking of Vietnam and the decade and more of American involvement there. No one who was touched by that wrenching time can escape a twinge of uneasiness on hearing Roland say that his duty is to accept death regardless of the situation. After all, the unwavering commitment to principle that I have ascribed to Roland, and the foolish unwillingness to face facts that is commonly attributed to him, are opposite sides of the same coin. In the abstract, we may describe a heroic action either way. But the concrete text points us toward the first notion, that of meaningful sacrifice, and it leaves no room for the sin of pride, which is a corollary to the second notion. We may describe Roland as a flawed hero and a failed leader, but only by ignoring the shape a fellow being once gave his agon.

This may well recall one of the more important principles of modern hermeneutics: our recognizing what Turold has to say does not mean we agree.[19] We can allow a clear moral stance in art without having to allow that our lives are always arranged as the art is. The distinction between the two may even help explain why the *Song*'s creator made the circumstances of Roland's sacrifice so clear-cut. It was claimed, on uncertain evidence, that in Vietnam we knew who the good guys were, and what were the intentions of the bad. Roland the character actually does know those things, in a way that real life rarely allows for. We may claim that his creator was begging the most essential questions about warfare, when he portrayed it as the unavoidable and unique response to omnipresent evil. Still, if war is not always and everywhere perfectly just, we must nevertheless consider that it has not always been avoidable. Then, if it has not done so yet, the Allied response to Hitler may come to mind, and we may wonder whether every soldier who stood his ground in that fight was not in some palpable sense a hero.[20] Yet World War Two also had its impurities, its misdirected artillery, its Anzios and Dresdens. That brings us back to Roland's insistence on the larger picture—family, France, *la geste, los*—and to the notion that unhesitating sacrifice is not always mindless. That principle cannot stand much abuse, of course, and its fragility is proven whenever it is cheapened by insisting on it when it is not appropriate or needed. Near the end, a Vietnam infantryman could state Roland's heroic principle in résumé and mean it as a definition of insanity: "All heroes do is die good."[21] Such are the issues Roland's moral victory raises, and the more distasteful we may find them, the less right we have to dismiss the *Song* as the creation of barbarians.[22]

Roland's agon, then, takes place inside limits narrower than we might choose. The problem in the *Song* is not whether the war against Marsile and Baligant is to be fought, but how, and at what cost. As aesthetes and readers-for-pleasure, therefore, we may reject the poem as being a nasty, bloody little tale whose known virtues cannot redeem its subject. There, at last, we would join Brunetière and Trawick on firm aesthetic ground, for we would no longer be claiming that our aesthetic response must be predicated on some subject or

[19]See Gadamer, *Truth and Method*, 237–38, 259–60; Hirsch, 6.

[20]For a recent "nonliterary" expression of this idea, see Lance Morrow, "June 6, 1944," *Time*, May 28, 1984, 11–12. For the participants' view of fear and soldiering, one may consult the memoirs they wrote, e.g., Guthrie Wilson, *Brave Company* (New York, 1950), 215. I am indebted for this reference to Frank E. Williams, Esq.

[21]George Stover, as quoted in *Newsweek*, December 14, 1981, 69.

[22]"When people are at their silliest or most vicious they always claim to be 'representing' something" (Boatner, 578). The converse is, however, not necessarily true. On the historical concept of the "just war," one may begin with the works briefly mentioned in Chapter 6, note 23, above.

set of contents we prefer to the one in the text. But then the history of reception raises its head once more, to assert a truth that is not among the prolegomena to a humane criticism, but part of its essence. The *Song of Roland,* with its violence and its creed of struggle, is arguably one of the major creations of earlier Western culture. Its craftsmanship on the "microstructural" level, its effective use of formula, motif, exoticism, and accumulation, its spellbinding, cascading laisses, are increasingly accepted as fine art. But if it was made with skill, it was also imitated with ardor, and we may infer that it was recited with energy and heard with interest and even excitement. Much of its content was preserved, rewritten, for centuries, in the self-assertive way our ancestors had of preserving things. It has since been both attacked and defended with enthusiasm. It has obviously been moving for others besides just ourselves, and it behooves us to ask why the story of Roland captured the attention of medieval people to begin with, if we are indeed to speak of literature in the full sense.

To turn briefly from war to religion, at first blush it might seem impossible to speak of a Christianized presentation of death as being great literature. The issue seems to have only one possible solution by definition, and thus to lack any potential for depth of presentation. The Good News of Christianity, after all, specifically transcends death, negates it, or, better, turns it into a blessed event. Medieval people, much more likely than not, believed firmly in Heaven and may even have looked forward to it in all seriousness as a reward for a Christian life. More to the point, whatever they actually believed, they *claimed* to adhere to the Christian eschatology of salvation, and the *Song of Roland* is literature and not the heart's deepest confession. So the risk Roland takes at Roncevaux is a sham. All he and his men need to do is grit their teeth for a time, and they will win eternal life.

And yet the *Song of Roland* treats the theme of death and sacrifice in anything but superficial fashion. It is Oliver's presence that reminds us that we are not all single-minded heroes and that fear can temporarily obscure our strongest beliefs. Oliver is no less Christian than Roland, surely, and no less a martyr, as it turns out. But when he hears the whistle of death's blade, he flinches. Any Christian might do the same; that is the crux of the issue and the drama of the Horn Scenes, for if the hope of salvation is inbred in us, the fear of death is innate. And yet Roland himself does not even know Gethsemane.

It should by now be clear why I began by citing a nonmedievalist such as Ferdinand Brunetière or Buckner Trawick. Of course no one of any scholarly authority today would say the sort of thing I have quoted from their work. Medievalists nowadays are expected to take epic exaggeration, allusive exposition, parallel laisses, and other formal features of an alien literary style for granted. But the implications of aesthetic judgments about thematics and ideology have not always been recognized, and this may be especially true of those that are intended to be positive judgments. When, with Bédier, we assert the *Song of Roland*'s artistry, we speak as a medievalist community. And yet it is not the outsiders' lack of specialized knowledge—of all that Rychner, Duggan, Uitti, and others have had to say about the *Song*'s poetics—that raises the problem. It is the incongruity of the outsiders' condemnations with the text; and specialists do not make themselves safe from that merely by referring to the aesthetic defenses that are already in the literature of the subject.

It is, however, safe method (as safe as the affirmation and defense of difference ever is) to let Roland be entirely right and Oliver generally wrong. We need only accept that our initial discomfort is a matter of habit. Looking for the pathetic grandeur of *hamartia* or for a condemnation of aggressiveness in the *Song of Roland* is like looking for revolutionary fervor in the *fabliaux* or genteel dalliance in the *Roman de la Rose:* a natural initial reaction. But there is no reason why such a reaction should become a permanent habit, if we are persuaded that the text is not congruent with it.

Confusion between the *démesure* theory, with its various attractive features, and the *Roland* text is so widespread that anyone reading the secondary literature on the poem can find numerous examples by merely comparing the criticism and the text. The scattered illustrations I have given in earlier chapters may be fairly taken as representative of a large body of phenomena. They are not aberrations, but reactions to the complex of pressures that bear on our readings. Still, once we become aware of those pressures we are required to ask ourselves whether we have not attempted to establish the *Song of Roland* as canonical great literature by altering it, through the logic of *démesure,* away from its original heroic status. In the simplest terms, before we can decide whether or not the sacrifice of life is heroic and inspiring, we must consider what principle or purpose might be thought more important than life.

[8]

Roland's Simple Heroism

In his *Légendes épiques,* Joseph Bédier argued brilliantly that the *Song of Roland* is a unified and planned sequence. But by the time Bédier set out to establish that the *Song of Roland* was made by a medieval Frenchman and was not a patchwork of eighth-century relics, the interpretation of the epic through an internalized psychology of the individual, without reference to the moral prerequisites of feudal soldiering, was a scholarly cliché. Its application appeared to cause no difficulty. Hence Bédier lent his prestige to an interpretation that was compatible with the very notions he was combating and never looked for the little pieces of grit in its mechanism, the bits of text that the standard hypothesis of *démesure* did not address.[1] Neither, it seems, have many of his successors.

It is as clear as ever that the Oxford *Roland* is not a cantilena but a complex work of literary art. Bédier's famous argument for its unity did not (as we have seen) forestall renewed affirmations of its ambiguity. But to contest Bédier's explanation of the work's structure does not jeopardize its status; rather, it reveals real solidity of organization. As I have argued, the context of Roland's actions includes a feudal bond that must be maintained, for it is interwoven with the very fabric of society. The challenge facing Roland must be met on the battlefield, but also in the realm of principle. If we read the textbook descriptions of his unruly pride, we may conclude that the best thing medieval Europe could have done with a Roland was to send him away on a Crusade.[2] But that is a false vision. In fact his primary characteristic, from the first, is acquiescence in the procedures that keep his society whole. The *Song of Roland* has been called "Diony-

[1]Similarly, Menéndez Pidal's competing critique of the Oxford poem as lacking unity (pp. 121–46), like those of his predecessors, derives from considerations about usefulness, simplicity, and the like. Further discussion in Riquer, 85–105.

[2]Cf. Vance on Roland's "destructive individualism" (*Reading,* 62–63).

sian" (the allusion is to Saint-Denis) or Capetian in reference to the consolidation of the French monarchy during the twelfth century. Yet it is far more than that; it involves the aspirations of an entire age. Here is how Joan Evans describes the times in which the *Song* was first copied and circulated:

> Somewhere about 1100 it seems as if Europe settled on an even keel. In England the Norman dynasty had established itself militarily and administratively. In France Philip I had established a rival kingdom, the Cluniac reform had revivified religious life, and the Crusades had started on their way. In Germany Henry IV was establishing the Empire on a firmer basis. In Italy Pope Gregory VII had lost his fight against the Emperor, but had gained new spiritual force for Rome. In Spain Alfonso VI of Castile had made Toledo the capital of Christian Spain, and the Cid had conquered Valencia. In the Eastern Empire the Comneni had suffered the inroads first of the Normans and then of the Crusaders; the weight of power was shifting westward. In Europe it is fair to say that a measure of stability had been achieved, in which the forces of feudalism, monasticism, scholastic philosophy and civic growth could work together to make the history of the Middle Ages.[3]

And yet this is a referential context that is not only medieval. Beyond the contrasts of fear and misapprehension, courage and vision, which the epic makes visible through Oliver's hesitation, Ganelon's bitterness, and Turpin's or Gautier's stout affirmations, we glimpse the society for which the battle was fought. Still further beyond is the feudal and Christian world to which the *Song* as exemplary and hortatory literature was addressed. But the widening circle of the poem's significations does not end there.[4] It places the battles of Spain in a wider framework, using the risks of war and the strengths of great leaders to express a broad concept of commitment. It stretches to cover every field on which soldiers by whatever name have stood their ground.

"If people are to have reasons to live, they must be given false ones," Montherlant once wrote.[5] *A fortiori,* if the task is to kill or be

[3]Joan Evans, ed., *The Flowering of the Middle Ages* (New York, 1966), 9. Fossier (*Le Moyen Age,* 2:6) also speaks of "the undoubted 'century of major progress' which we situate between 1010/30 and 1150."

[4]Though a complete analysis of combat ethics in the *Song of Roland* cannot neglect the context of the combat. The war in the *Song* is not a war against Christians; it is a feudal war in the proper sense, "large-scale warfare (*bellum* properly so called), undertaken on the authority of public powers with the aid of vassals owing host and riding services" (Contamine, 272), not a raid or private quarrel, and (at least where Baligant is concerned) it is a defensive war, not an offensive one. For the importance of these distinctions throughout the early Middle Ages, see Contamine, 260–80.

[5]Henry de Montherlant, *La Marée du soir* (Paris, 1972), 103.

killed, society must give reasons for that terrible risk, and the reasons, whatever their merits for that purpose, may not seem good to literature professors.[6] The motives for fighting and dying in early French epics are not like those we usually assign for the casting of feelings into poetry. The winning of glory is one such motive, the gaining of Paradise is another; but the *Roland* author adds a third: defense of one's homeland and culture. The stakes at Roncevaux are higher than we sometimes admit; the courage Roland and the men around him show is also greater, and it is physical as well as moral.

I have saved one of the most important elements of a sympathetic reading of the *Song of Roland* for this concluding chapter: the battles on which the text lavishes so many lines and that nonetheless tend to be taken for granted in our concentration on mores and sequence. It would be a serious mistake to reduce the *Song of Roland* to its forms and thematics. In the last analysis, we cannot grasp it fully as a literary achievement until we have come to terms with its most obvious element of content: combat itself. Its ramifications are in ethics, politics, and myth, but its roots run deeply into the physical universe of battle. It is no place for the squeamish, we might well think, when we imagine Turpin's intestines tumbling through the sort of gash that the bright swords actually could make (2247). However beautiful a weapon is, it is still a weapon, and a threat.

On its surface, the *Song* is primarily about fighting. It describes a war; prominent among its events are military engagements and their preliminaries. It is first and foremost literal about these things: they need not stand for anything else.[7] The reason is that battle itself is one of humankind's extreme experiences, and the test of will and courage that is armed combat is one of humanity's most severe tests. It is here, if anywhere, that we should speak of psychology in the work—a simple psychology of resistance to physical threat and shock. The literary critic who fails to admit that wars are fought by people (humans), or

[6]"Scholars are happy in being, on the whole, sheltered from the harsher realities of life; this on occasion has its drawbacks, in that it encourages them to seek literary or mythological or philosophical explanations for details that may well be rooted in the conditions of daily life and the universal instinct for survival in a dangerous environment" (Sargent-Baur, 419, n. 44). I see no reason why this valuable reminder should not apply to themes, structure, and ideas as well as to details. Compare Farnham, 163: "In the twentieth century we have moved so far away from Christian martyrdom . . . that the stark simplicity of the martyr's death is hard to grasp"; see also Brault, *Song*, 1:185ff.

[7]I recall here Rosemond Tuve's distinction between allegorical writing and imposed allegory (*Allegorical Imagery* [Princeton, 1966], 219–33, esp. 219–22). This is related to the question of the implied audience, discussed in Chapter 1. Any battle may—legitimately in certain medieval terms—be read allegorically.

who cannot see that epics present characters in an extraordinarily revealing situation, as much a fit subject for great literature as are love, religion, and individuality, will be forever crippled in dealing with any poem remotely like the *Roland.* The poem speaks directly or indirectly of many things: society, comradeship, duty, courage. Its context is the kind of world we call feudal. But none of these things furnishes its narrative warp; warfare is their vehicle.

The long insistence on national patriotism and dramas of personality in the *Song of Roland* has drawn a veil between its readers and the horrible pageant of armed combat. Ours is, after all, a pacifist age by historical standards. We have largely succumbed to the occupational disease of generalship, and we mask the face of battle with jargon and abstractions. We would like for machines to wage war without us, and even without the enemy. But the institution of war cannot be made to exclude humans. In its structure, it is a ghastly test of sinew, skill, and doggedness.[8]

Thus we will fail to see the power in the *Song of Roland* if we forget that it shows men facing combat and doing battle. If we agree that experience and imagination are prime ingredients of literature, then for a medieval author the battlefield—what it asked of men and told about them—was surely a locus of high literature. And indeed, the challenges of warfare and the necessity of right behavior in combat were the stuff of literature for many centuries. Any disgust we feel for the irrational aspects of war should not incite us to erase or belittle that literature. With that caveat in mind, we may move from particulars to universals and reunite the ethics and the aesthetics of the *Song of Roland.*

Though the formal study of battlefield behavior is in its infancy, some starting points are available even now. John Keegan's work suggests that if we genuinely intend to read the *Roland* as a study in humanity, we must think what a medieval military engagement was like as an experience, and understand what that experience has had in common with the experience of warriors generally. No image of armies as well-drilled, well-oiled, and eager machines should obscure the fact that when men en masse have come to blows, some have

[8]"Above all, we dislike war, nor do we exalt warlike virtues" (Misrahi and Hendrickson, 367). Halverson, 664, cites a phrase from C. S. Lewis's preface to *Paradise Lost:* "the terrible phenomenon called a Heroic Age." This paragraph, and some later ones, describe an influential and widespread view; it is, of course, not a unanimous one. Compare Guthrie Wilson, writing a generation ago: "Two things are of the greatest moment to men—women, and war. And the greater, because of its demands upon fortitude, because of its nightmare quality, is war" (*Brave Company,* 227).

struck, some have stood, and others have run. Keegan's definition of battle deserves quotation at length, for it reminds us that humans do not stop being humans when they start to fight.

> What battles have in common is human: the behavior of men struggling to reconcile their instinct for self-preservation, their sense of honour and the achievement of some aim over which other men are ready to kill them. The study of battle is therefore always a study of fear and usually of courage; always of leadership, usually of obedience; always of compulsion, sometimes of insubordination; always of anxiety, sometimes of elation or catharsis; always of uncertainty and doubt, misinformation and misapprehension, usually also of faith and sometimes of vision; always of violence, sometimes also of cruelty, self-sacrifice, compassion; above all, it is always a study of solidarity and usually also of disintegration—for it is towards the disintegration of human groups that battle is directed. It is necessarily a social and psychological study. But it is not a study only for the sociologist or the psychologist, and indeed ought not perhaps to be properly a study for either. For the human group in battle, and the quality and source of the stress it undergoes, are drained of life and meaning by the laboratory approach which social scientists practise. Battles belong to finite moments in history, to the societies which raise the armies which fight them, to the economies and technologies which those societies sustain. Battle is a historical subject, whose nature and trend of development can only be understood down a long historical perspective.[9]

Roland wins the battle of Roncevaux in these realistic psychological and moral senses. I have quoted Keegan extensively primarily to show how a military historian sums up the true core of the Roncevaux epic as a matter of universal experience. Roland's victory is a victory for solidarity and a victory over fear. It is an ideal topic for a heroic epic to commemorate, to keep in public memory just as the public vows of vassals were kept. Keegan is writing about Waterloo and the Somme as well as Agincourt, but his terms enfold our medieval *chanson de geste,* its content and its likely purpose for existence, almost perfectly. If the *Song of Roland* has long remained partially obscure to critics, it is in large part because we have failed to respect the act of will (with its concomitants, faith and courage) that Roland's stubborn refusal to sound the horn represents.

To keep this magnificent response to the stress of battle in mind is to keep our reading near the heart of the text. As important as social

[9]Keegan, *The Face of Battle,* 296–98; cf. the French army field regulations of November 1913: "Battles are moral struggles" (cited in Benton, 238).

considerations are, to bound our concept of Roland by them would be to give an imperfect account of his character and his importance as a literary figure. He is more than a figure of discourse: he is a Hero writ large because he is given the chance to bear witness to the essential nature of heroism itself. It is the manner of his sacrifice that makes Roland a hero for all times. His heroic qualities, put simply, are steadfastness and personal courage. These are exemplary attributes in any society in Western tradition. They can degenerate into mere stubbornness and bravura, but a close analysis of the hero of Roncevaux shows that in him they are positive.

Through *a posteriori* surmise, we may invoke the lurking risks of fanaticism in Turold's attitudes or in those of his characters. The text is like a map: to its highroads of meaning, we can always associate byways, hillocks, and swamps of significance. We can draw in the monsters beyond its borders. But none of this accretion undoes Turold's cartography. If we but yield to the fascination of the original, we may descry, in spite of ourselves, something our scrawls have only obscured. That, at least, is the hope born of historical curiosity, for there can be no epic without a time and a society.

Nor can we speak of epic without a certain kind of text before us. The impressive permanence of the epic character is not an abstraction to be applied indiscriminately; like all such notions, without the particulars of texts, it loses all substance and conviction. Its terms are misapplied (to the wrong character, for instance) or even contradicted (by the pettiness of *démesure* in action, or what Bédier called the "point d'honneur suspect"),[10] without close reference to the narrative from which the generalization derives.

But on the other hand, if impatience with foolishness as a would-be heroic principle leads us to induce a reading of the *Song of Roland* without using that principle, and if the resulting text often matches the concerns of its time in a broad sense, then we are well on the way to solving the *Roland* problem in terms of many human things as the feudal age put them. Duty, trust, lies and truth, sacrifice, fear, fatigue, frustration, and the courage that serves as touchstone and makes all these things clear: of such is the *Song* made. They yield to no other theme in universality simply because their expression is specifically early feudal. *Homines mulieresque sumus;* there is no surprise that the past can speak to us, once we have stopped talking to ourselves.

[10]Menéndez Pidal speaks of "a point of honor so subtle that it is incomprehensible even for Oliver himself" (introduction to the *Poema de mio Cid,* cited in Burger, "Deux Scènes," 105).

Some readers of skeptical bent will object that it is all a chimera, as all successful observations ultimately are in some sense.[11] But at some point we must leave epistemology and take up the poem, and close textual analysis remains the obvious place to start. Then we can pull and tug at our interpretation until it sits at ease with the information we have and with probability. The surprise, then, is not that the new reading of Roland's heroism is capable of satisfying us in the end. It is intuitively more surprising that such a satisfactory reading is reached through such superficially alien considerations as the feudal system, a transcendent Christian eschatology, or the rigors of battle.

The conclusions I draw are, then, new, as only the thorough application of basic principles can make them. Once put into context, the words and deeds of the hero Roland can be seen as reasonable, correct, and even measured, to a degree not fully recognized even by his staunchest defenders among recent critics, and to an extent entirely incompatible with the theme of exaggerated pride on which nearly all commentary on the *Song* has depended in the past.[12] Thus divested of a misleading (and textually questionable) insistence on a tragic flaw in its determined and principled hero, the *Song of Roland* appears as a powerful statement of its age's deep concern with unique methods of creating and defending stability and order in human affairs. We have failed to understand Roland for the same reasons his fellows fail in the poem: because we forget to consider that in the life of every culture there may come a time when its defenders must stand their ground at whatever cost, or because we cannot agree when the time has come for such a sacrifice.

The *Song of Roland*, then, is not about a man who fights when he should not. It is about a group of men who do not fight when it is necessary. The work is not a paean to mindless violence. In it, the Franco-Christian armies must strive to defeat a fully armed host that the imperialist emir Baligant throws at them, and of course Roland

[11]A deconstructionist might point out that the exemplary text has to exist precisely because it does *not* match human experience: it is not the case that *all* the Saracens flee and that *all* the Franks stand fast. But historical mediation must accept the constructed text.

[12]The immense personal dimensions of feudal responsibility make the very applicability of the concept of "pride" to Roland problematic, even if we conceive it as a good quality. The original audience may well have conceived of pride as neither *orgueil* nor *fierté*, but as the intellectual concept of *superbia* proper, which to many early medieval people was not a mere "tragic flaw" but the chief sin and the fountainhead of all others (as in Gregory the Great, *Moralia in Iob*, 31.45.89). Wendt, 275, adds, "Bernard of Clairvaux called *superbia* a sign of paganism." On the other hand, excessive individualism was sometimes equated with the sin of pride; see Morton Bloomfield, *The Seven Deadly Sins* (1952; reprint, East Lansing, Mich., 1967), 69–84, esp. 75.

and his men succumb to vastly superior numbers after a bitter struggle. That is not genocide or the incitement to it, whatever the implications of the uses made of the poem in French schools early in this century.[13] The *Song* is not a particularly primitive work in its presentation of its ideal of soldierly necessity. Though schematic in its rhetoric and narrow in its ways of presenting character, the *Song* nevertheless clearly shows why the Franks should fight, why they do not, and what the results are, with enough sophistication that generations of critics could make it a study in psychological conflict between individuals when there is no such theme in it to speak of: its narrative is that dense.

Roland does not boast, nor does he misunderstand his duty, nor does he fail to grasp the situation in which he finds himself.[14] He is the type of exemplary hero we expect to find in an ancient epic. Neither pride nor folly is a feature necessary for the explanation and understanding of the Oxford text. Roland is a warrior of the sort any society may need whatever its popular images of war: steadfast, courageous, and alert, a leader by example.[15] It is in that broadest of senses—a challenging one to treat in a time of disillusionment—that Roland is a hero for the ages. We do not stand in his place, but we can glimpse how his sacrifice matters. His deeds, though they may seem obscure at first glance, can be shown to be worthy of the fame his epic has lent him. We do not have to qualify his heroism: it speaks to us directly, once we have accepted the validity, as a literary device, of the

[13]For "mindless violence" as characteristic of the *Song*, see Payen, "Poétique du génocide," 233; this is undercut by Payen's own references to Christendom under siege. The eleventh-century West may not have been as sure as we are that the "Saracen" menace was a thing of the past; see Duggan, "Generation of the Episode of Baligant," 64–74. That the *Song* is an imperialistic or nationalistic work is an idea traceable to Gaston Paris; it is the subject, in large part, of his December 1870 lecture printed under the title "La *Chanson de Roland* et la nationalité française," in *La Poésie du Moyen Age*, 1:87–118, see esp. 104–7.

[14]It is natural to wonder where the idea of Roland's boasting *did* come from. It seems likely that it is older than Bédier's formulation of the tragic-flaw theory, though it has become inseparable from it. Larry Crist and others have suggested that the concept of honor it entails may be associated with the generation of French scholars affected by Sedan, the fall of the Second Empire, and the siege of Paris—a generation perhaps understandably inclined to seek what it took to be parallels to the great national disaster to which incompetent, vainglorious leadership had led it. The phenomenon is not isolated; the Romantics, who sought somber precedents for melancholy in the late Middle Ages, left us an image of decline and *tristesse* that is still part of the standard description of the period (though filtered by the Symbolists and Huizinga); see Dakyns, 15–17, 195–220, 247–52. To grasp the importance of these phenomena is not to "rewrite history" but to recognize the relationship between history and cultural myth.

[15]"Medieval societies . . . made bravery in battle one of their essential values" (Contamine, 259; but Contamine also quotes from Duby, 253: "Courage, this novelty of the twelfth century").

war he wages. His heroism is that of the man who, without stopping to explain himself in detail, insists on plunging into the horrible. There is no need to evoke obscure motifs or archetypal behavior patterns lurking behind what he does, as though his words and deeds did not quite add up. What Roland does makes sense.

But his heroism is the heroism of obedience and conformity. He goes to Heaven—directly—because he does what he is expected to do and is not afraid of the paradox of duty. He acts as though fulfilling what is expected of him is the reasonable thing to do, no matter what strangeness other men may find in the situation. The attitude was slow dying, but in our literary culture, for better or worse, it is at a low ebb. Though popular culture, at least in the United States, still glorifies the brave without a second thought, higher culture has long pondered the dark side of regimentation and firepower. The knights are gone from literature, and have indeed been going since perhaps the turn of the twelfth century. In their place we find inefficient condottieri, or hapless Custers. We no longer think doing our best in God's cause means sure victory despite all appearances. Mighty men in our age have no such appeal from verdicts of Fate. They may break themselves in tasks beyond their strength, but it is for no reason, and with no guarantees. Michael, the Angel of Strife and Peril, will not come for them. They are gone when they are dead, they are "wasted," and since they are unique, they cannot be replaced.

But Roland's greatness is not in his unique prowess alone. It is in his willingness to trust God and scorn his fate. He does not even have to be a Christ-figure to fit a general pattern of knowing sacrifice. The paradox is still with us: on occasion, even now, human beings think they have the chance to change things by sacrifice, so that sacrifice becomes a joy. Without the certain comfort of Heaven's nearness, we may still be able to imagine a death that is a legacy.[16] Like all paradoxes, it is a difficult one to state and to tame. It has been called absurdity in more than one age. And that is surely part of Turold's motivation: to state that the paradox can be resolved, if we have the strength of will Roland has. Martyrdom is the ultimate exemplum.

In the last analysis, summing up heroism is not a matter for which discursive academic prose is designed. When the heroism is real (and it is real sometimes), scholars surely do well to leave its evocation to

[16]For example, Farnham, 163, mentions the assassination of John F. Kennedy in connection with Roland's martyrdom.

the makers of epics, with a pious hope that the singers' words will have something in them that tells the real heroes from the false.

When the heroism is in an epic already, it may appear to be both true and false at once, and the scholar who wants to speak of the former aspect has a doubly difficult job. I have given some examples from *Roland* criticism.[17] The adjectives grow shrill, extreme, absolute. The prose thickens and clogs. The simplicity of the last stand made by the best men, who cannot win but who cannot be beaten down, is overlaid by the transitory claims of nationalism, ideology, and even shifting aesthetics.

With Le Gentil and Payen, we tend to call that simplicity a "splendid folly." Yet the folly of heroism, like the folly of the Cross, is a metonym, a renaming. The very point of those figures of speech lies in their implied claim that sacrifice and abnegation are not in fact foolish. They appear so only when seen in the most limited perspective available: local, and immediate in time.

Who among us would not agree that under some circumstances valor should be tempered by consideration? The maker of the *Roland* can hardly be assumed to have thought the opposite. Yet when he told his tale, he gave Roland the honor of the field and the glory of martyrdom. We struggle, then, to learn what Turold's religion and ideas were so that in the end we may give them their share in the work, and no more. If we pay them no heed whatever, we are left with a blustering Roland who is too thoughtless to raise any issue of courage, sacrifice, or responsibility at all. But if we try, experimentally, to raise a prism like Turold's between ourselves and Roncevaux, then we will learn from that act and that vision what of its shape and colors change, and what parts our prisms do not disturb.

The final paradox of the *Song of Roland* is there. We may ask the brave and the resolute to stand and face terrifying enemies for the sake of any abstraction we choose. We can teach slogans to children and make robots of our infantries. We can drench people with the

[17]And here, for anyone who might still hesitate, are yet more: "blameworthy pride" (Van Emden, "Guarant," 30); "egotism . . . braggartry . . . blindness" (Le Gentil, "A propos de la *démesure*," 204); *haughty, obstinate, scornful* (Siciliano, 354); *adolescen[t]* (Brook, 122); *haughty*, "empty bravado" (Donohoe, 254–55); "insanely brave and too attentive to his glory" (Petit de Julleville, *Histoire*, 27); "rash, proud, and inconsiderate" (Renoir, "Roland's Lament," 575); "proud, rigid man" ["intraitable orgueilleux"] (Le Gentil, *Song*, 81). Nor do we need to limit ourselves to criticism: "[Lord Peter] Wimsey was the Roland of the combination—quick, impulsive, careless, and an artistic jack-of-all-trades. Parker was the Oliver—cautious, solid, painstaking" (Dorothy Sayers, *The Unpleasantness at the Bellona Club* [1928; reprint, New York, 1963], 63).

claim that there is no death. None of these things can wipe out the terror itself. The hero's victory is not won by the sword, it is won by mastery and the refusal to yield to terror. Robots are not heroes. Heroes know and choose, and beyond the bishops' exhortations and the slogans and the false heroes' claims that some abstraction is in control, they choose, most simply, to affirm that terror is not their master. If they live, they cannot quite explain. They say they were doing their duty; they say "somebody has to go." If they die, the epic says those things for them. The epic speaks false if it burdens their simplicity with the exposition of ideas. There is no fight without reasons and a setting, but the *Song of Roland* speaks true when it strips away all arguments and, through context and action, through Oliver's stumbling and Roland's tenacity, Ganelon's cheating and the army's prevarication, it shows that the hero's condition is as clear as it is harsh.

Works Cited

Aebischer, Paul. "Pour la défense et l'illustration de l'épisode de Baligant." In *Mélanges de philologie romane . . . offerts à Ernest Hoepffner.* Paris: Les Belles Lettres, 1949. Pp. 173–82. Reprinted in *Rolandiana et Oliveriana.* Geneva: Droz, 1967. Pp. 211–20.

Altman, Charles F. "Interpreting Romanesque Narrative: Conques and the *Roland.*" *Olifant,* 5 (1977–78), 4–28.

Ariès, Philippe. "L'Histoire des mentalités." In Jacques Le Goff, ed., *La Nouvelle Histoire.* Paris: CEPL, 1978. Pp. 402–23.

———. *The Hour of Our Death.* Trans. Helen Weaver. New York: Knopf, 1981.

Aristotle. *On the Art of Poetry.* Trans. T. S. Dorsch. In *Classical Literary Criticism.* Harmondsworth: Penguin, 1965.

Armstrong, Paul B. "The Conflict of Interpretations and the Limits of Pluralism." *PMLA,* 98 (1983), 341–52.

Aspland, C. W. *Medieval French Reader.* Oxford: Clarendon Press, 1979.

Atkinson, James C. "Laisses 169–70 of the *Chanson de Roland.*" *Modern Language Notes,* 82 (1967), 271–84.

Auerbach, Erich. *Introduction to Romance Languages and Literatures.* New York: Capricorn, 1961.

———. *Mimesis.* Trans. Willard Trask. Garden City, N.Y.: Doubleday, 1957.

Bancourt, Paul. "'Sen' et 'chevalerie': Réflexions sur la tactique des chevaliers dans plusieurs chansons de geste des XIIe–XIIIe siècles." In *Société Rencesvals, VIe Congrès International: Actes.* Aix-en-Provence: Université de Provence; Paris: Champion, 1974. Pp. 621–37.

Barrow, R. H. *Introduction to Saint Augustine, The City of God.* London: Faber, 1950.

Barzun, Jacques, and Henry F. Graff. *The Modern Researcher.* 3d ed. New York: Harcourt, 1977.

Battaglia, Salvatore. "La Glorificazione di Orlando." In *La Formazione della lingua francese.* Rome: Perella, 1945. Pp. 126–40. Reprinted in *Filologia e letteratura,* 17 (1971), 355–67.

Beck, Jonathan. "Prist l'olifan, que reproce n'en ait." *Olifant,* 9 (1981), 49–52.

Bédier, Joseph. *La Chanson de Roland commentée.* Paris: Piazza, 1927.

———. "De l'édition princeps de la *Chanson de Roland* aux éditions les plus récentes." *Romania*, 63 (1937), 433–69; 64 (1938), 145–244, 489–521.
———. *Les Légendes épiques*. 2d ed. 4 vols. Paris: Champion, 1914–21.
Bédier, Joseph, ed. *La Chanson de Roland*. Paris: Piazza, 1921; rev. ed. 1937.
Beeler, John. *Warfare in Feudal Europe*. Ithaca, N.Y.: Cornell University Press, 1971.
Beichman, Anthony. "Ganelon and Duke Naimon." *Romance Notes*, 13 (1971–72), 358–62.
Bender, Karl-Heinz. "Un Aspect de la stylisation épique: L'Exclusivisme de la haute noblesse dans les chansons de geste du douzième siècle." In *Société Rencesvals: IVe Congrès International*. Heidelberg: Carl Winter, 1969. Pp. 95–105.
———. *König und Vassal: Untersuchungen zur Chanson de geste des 12. Jahrhunderts*. Heidelberg: Carl Winter, 1967.
Benton, John. "Nostre franceis n'unt talent de fuïr: The *Song of Roland* and the Enculturation of a Warrior Class." *Olifant*, 6 (1979), 237–58.
Bisson, Thomas N. "The Problem of Feudal Monarchy: Aragon, Catalonia, and France." *Speculum*, 53 (1978), 460–78.
Bloch, Marc. *Apologie pour l'histoire ou le métier d'historien*. Paris: Colin, 1952.
———. *Feudal Society*. Trans. L. A. Manyon. Chicago: University of Chicago Press, 1964.
Bloch, R. H. *Etymologies and Genealogies: A Literary Anthropology of the French Middle Ages*. Chicago: University of Chicago Press, 1983.
———. *Medieval French Literature and Law*. Berkeley and Los Angeles: University of California Press, 1977.
Bloomfield, Morton W. "The Problem of the Hero in the Later Middle Ages." In Norman T. Burns and Christopher Reagan, eds., *Concepts of the Hero in the Middle Ages and the Renaissance*. Albany: State University of New York Press, 1975. Pp. 27–48.
———. *The Seven Deadly Sins*. East Lansing, Mich.: Michigan State College Press, 1952. Reprint, 1967.
Boatner, Janet W. "The Misunderstood Ordeal: A Re-Examination of the *Chanson de Roland*." *Studies in Philology*, 66 (1969), 571–83.
Bonnefoy, Yves. "Sur la *Chanson de Roland*." *L'Ephémère*, 4 (1967), 55–65.
Boutruche, Robert. *Seigneurie et féodalité*. 2d ed. 2 vols. Paris: Aubier, 1968–70.
Bowra, C. M. *Heroic Poetry*. London: Macmillan, 1952; 2d ed. 1966.
Braet, Herman. "Réflexions sur les rêves dans les chansons de geste." In *Société Rencesvals: Proceedings of the Fifth International Conference*. Salford, Eng.: University of Salford, 1977. Pp. 211–24.
Brault, Gerard J. *La Chanson de Roland: Student Edition*. University Park, Pa.: Pennsylvania State University Press, 1984.
———. "Ganelon et Roland: Deux anecdotes du traître concernant le héros." *Romania*, 92 (1971), 392–405.
———. Letter to the editor. *Olifant*, 3 (1975–76), 132–33.

______. "*Sapientia* dans la *Chanson de Roland.*" *French Forum,* 1 (1976), 99–118. Also in *Société Rencesvals: Proceedings of the Fifth International Conference.* Salford, Eng.: University of Salford, 1977. Pp. 85–104.

______. *The Song of Roland: An Analytical Edition.* 2 vols. University Park, Pa.: Pennsylvania State University Press, 1978.

______. "The *Song of Roland,* 778–1978." *Olifant,* 6 (1979), 201–8.

______. "Structure et sens de la *Chanson de Roland.*" *French Review,* 45, Special Issue No. 3 (1971), 1–12.

Brinton, Crane. *The Shaping of Modern Thought.* Englewood Cliffs, N.J.: Prentice-Hall, 1963.

Brook, Leslie C. "Le Forfait de Roland dans le procès de Ganelon: Encore sur un vers obscur de la *Chanson de Roland.*" In *Société Rencesvals: IVe Congrès International.* Heidelberg: Carl Winter, 1969. Pp. 120–28.

Brown, Elizabeth. "The Tyranny of a Construct: Feudalism and Historians of Medieval Europe." *American Historical Review,* 79 (1974), 1063–88.

Brunetière, Ferdinand. "L'Erudition contemporaine et la littérature française du Moyen Age." In *Etudes critiques sur l'histoire de la littérature française.* 4th ed. Paris: Hachette, 1896. 1:1–61.

Burger, André. "Les Deux Scènes du cor dans la *Chanson de Roland.*" In *La Technique littéraire des chansons de geste.* Paris: Belles Lettres, 1959. Pp. 105–25.

______. "La légende de Roncevaux avant la *Chanson de Roland.*" *Romania,* 70 (1948–49), 453–73.

______. "Le Rire de Roland." *Cahiers de civilisation médiévale,* 3 (1960), 2–11.

______. *Turold poète de la fidélité: Essai d'explication de la Chanson de Roland.* Geneva: Droz, 1977.

Burgess, Glyn S. "*La Chanson de Roland,* Line 400." *Romance Notes,* 13 (1971–72), 165–67.

______. *Contribution à l'étude du vocabulaire pré-courtois.* Geneva: Droz, 1970.

______. "Old French *contenance* and *contenant.*" In Raymond Cormier, ed., *Voices of Conscience.* Philadelphia: Temple University Press, 1977. Pp. 21–41.

______. "*Orgueil* and *fierté* in Twelfth-Century French." *Zeitschrift für romanische Philologie,* 89 (1972), 103–22.

______. "Remarques sur deux vers de la *Chanson de Roland* (vv. 3796–7)." *Société Rencesvals: Actes du VIe Congrès.* Aix-en-Provence: Université de Provence, 1974. Pp. 63–78.

______. "*Talent* in Early Old French." *Romania,* 95 (1974), 443–66.

Burrell, Margaret. "Ganelon's Act of Treason." *Olifant,* 4 (1977), 85–86.

Calin, William C. *A Muse for Heroes: Nine Centuries of the Epic in France.* Toronto: University of Toronto Press, 1983.

Capels, Kathleen M. "The Apple Incident in Laisse XXIX of the *Song of Roland.*" *Romance Notes,* 14 (1972–73), 599–605.

Cartier, Norman R. "La Sagesse de Roland." *Aquileia: Chestnut Hill Studies in Modern Languages and Literatures,* 1 (1969), 33–63.

Celletti, Maria Chiara. "Santi Rolando, Olivero e compagni." In *Bibliotheca sanctorum.* Rome: Inst. Giovanni XXIII della Pontif. Univ. Lateranense. Vol. 11 (1968), pp. 303–6.

Cerquiglini, Bernard. "Roland à Roncevaux, ou la trahison des clercs." *Littérature,* 42 (May 1981), 40–56.

Cherchi, Paolo. "Un Dovere della 'pietas' regia: l'uccisione del nemico." *Modern Philology,* 73 (1976), 244–56. Reprinted in *Andrea Capellano, i trovatori, e altri temi romanzi.* Rome: Bulzoni, 1979. Pp. 126–43.

Christmann, Hans-Helmut. "'Le Cunseill que mal prist': Zur ersten kaiserlichen Ratsszene des *Rolandsliedes.*" In Dieter Messner and Wolfgang Pöckl, eds., *Romanisches Mittelalter: Festschrift . . . Rudolf Baehr.* Göppingen: Kümmerle, 1981. Pp. 45–63.

Cohen, Ralph, ed. *New Directions in Literary History.* Baltimore: Johns Hopkins University Press, 1974.

Contamine, Philippe. *War in the Middle Ages.* Trans. Michael Jones. Oxford: Blackwell, 1984.

Cook, Robert Francis. "Roncevaux symbole de la nécessité." *Olifant,* 8 (1981), 352–66.

———. "Translators and Traducers: Some English Versions of the *Song of Roland,* Stanzas 83–85." *Olifant,* 7 (1980), 327–42.

Crane, R. S. *Critical and Historical Principles of Literary History.* Chicago: University of Chicago Press, 1971.

Crist, Larry S. "A propos de la *desmesure* dans la *Chanson de Roland:* Quelques propos (démesurés?)." *Olifant,* 1 (1974), 10–20. Also in *Société Rencesvals: Proceedings of the Fifth International Conference.* Salford, Eng.: University of Salford, 1977. Pp. 143–55.

Crosland, Jessie. *The Old French Epic.* Oxford: Blackwell, 1951.

Curtius, Ernst Robert. *European Literature and the Latin Middle Ages.* Trans. Willard Trask. New York: Pantheon, 1953. Reprint. New York: Harper and Row, 1963.

———. "Uber die altfranzösische Epik." *Zeitschrift für romanische Philologie* 64 (1944), 233–320.

———. "Zur Literarästhetik des Mittelalters." *Zeitschrift für romanische Philologie,* 58 (1938), 1–50, 129–232, 433–79.

Dakyns, Janine. *The Middle Ages in French Literature, 1850–1900.* Oxford: Oxford University Press, 1973.

Daniel, Norman A. *Heroes and Saracens: A Reinterpretation of the Chansons de Geste.* Edinburgh: Edinburgh University Press, 1984.

Del Monte, Alberto. "Apologia di Orlando." *Filologia romanza,* 4 (1957), 225–34.

Delort, Robert. *La Vie au Moyen Age.* Paris: Seuil, 1982.

Demoulin, Auguste. "Charlemagne, la légende de son péché, et le choix de Ganelon pour l'ambassade." *Marche romane,* 25 (1975), 105–26.

———. "Ganelon désigné pour l'ambassade." *Les Etudes classiques,* 45 (1977), 227–46, 377–89.

Donohoe, Joseph. "Ambivalence and Anger: The Human Center of the *Chanson de Roland.*" *Romanic Review,* 67 (1971), 251–61.

Duby, Georges. *The Age of the Cathedrals.* Trans. Eleanor Levieux and Barbara Thompson. Chicago: University of Chicago Press, 1981.

———. "Dans la France du Nord-ouest au XIIe siècle: Les 'jeunes' dans la société aristocratique." *Annales,* 19 (1964), 835–46.

———. "L'Histoire des mentalités." In Charles Samaran, ed., *L'Histoire et ses méthodes.* Paris: Gallimard, 1961. Pp. 937–66.

Ducrot, Oswald, and Tzvetan Todorov. *Dictionnaire encyclopédique des sciences du langage.* Paris: Seuil, 1972.

Dufournet, Jean. *Cours sur la Chanson de Roland.* Paris: Centre de Documentation Universitaire, 1972.

Duggan, Joseph J. "The Generation of the Episode of Baligant: Charlemagne's Dreams and the Normans at Manzikert." *Romance Philology,* 30 (1976–77), 59–82.

———. *A Guide to Studies on the Chanson de Roland.* London: Grant and Cutler, 1976.

———. *The Song of Roland: Formulaic Style and Poetic Craft.* Berkeley and Los Angeles: University of California Press, 1973.

Duval, Amaury. "Turold, auteur du poème de la bataille de Roncevaux." *Histoire littéraire de la France,* 18 (1835), 714–20.

Eisner, Robert A. "In Search of the Real Theme of the *Song of Roland.*" *Romance Notes,* 14 (1972–73), 179–83.

Elton, G. R. *The Practice of History.* New York: Crowell, 1967.

Enders, Jody May. "La Logique des débats dans la *Chanson de Roland.*" M.A. thesis, University of Virginia, 1979.

Evans, Joan, ed. *The Flowering of the Middle Ages.* New York: McGraw-Hill, 1966.

Faral, Edmond. "A propos de la *Chanson de Roland:* Genèse et signification du personnage de Turpin." In *La Technique littéraire des chansons de geste.* Paris: Belles Lettres, 1959. Pp. 271–80.

———. *La Chanson de Roland: Etude et analyse.* Paris: Mellottée, [1934].

Farnham, Fern. "Romanesque Design in the *Chanson de Roland.*" *Romance Philology,* 18 (1964), 143–64.

Fish, Stanley. *Is There a Text in This Class?* Cambridge, Mass.: Harvard University Press, 1980.

Fossier, Robert. *Histoire sociale de l'occident médiéval.* Paris: Colin, 1970.

Fossier, Robert, ed. *Le Moyen Age.* 3 vols. Paris: Colin, 1982–83.

Foulet, Alfred. "Is Roland Guilty of *desmesure?*" *Romance Philology,* 10 (1956–57), 145–48.

Fox, John. *A Literary History of France: The Middle Ages.* London: Benn; New York: Barnes and Noble, 1974.

Frye, Northrop. *Anatomy of Criticism.* Princeton: Princeton University Press, 1957.

Gadamer, Hans-Georg. *Philosophical Hermeneutics.* Trans. David Linge. Berkeley and Los Angeles: University of California Press, 1976.

———. *Truth and Method.* New York: Crossroad Press, 1984.

Ganshof, Frédéric L. *Feudalism.* Trans. Philip Grierson. 3d ed. New York: Harper and Row, 1964.

Gautier, Léon. *La Chanson de Roland.* "New ed." Tours: Mame, n.d.

———. "L'Epopée nationale: La *Chanson de Roland.*" In Louis Petit de Julleville, ed., *Histoire de la langue et de la littérature françaises des origines à 1900.* Vol. 1: *Moyen Age,* part 1. Paris: Colin, 1896. Pp. 80–98.

———. *Les Epopées Françaises.* 3 vols. Paris: Palmé, 1865–68. Second edition in 4 vols. Paris: Société générale de la librairie catholique-Welter, 1878–94.

Gellinek, Christian. "A propos du système de pouvoir dans la *Chanson de Roland.*" *Cahiers de civilisation médiévale,* 19 (1977), 39–46.

Gérard, Albert. "L'Axe Roland-Ganelon: Valeurs en conflit dans la *Chanson de Roland.*" *Le Moyen Age,* 75 (1969), 445–66.

Gibellini, Pietro. "Droit et philologie: l'ordre des laisses dans l'épisode de la colère de Ganelon dans la *Chanson de Roland.*" *Revue romane,* 7 (1972), 233–47.

Goldin, Frederick R. "Die Rolle Ganelons und das Motiv der Worte." In Kurt Baldinger, ed., *Beiträge zum romanischen Mittelalter.* Tübingen: Niemeyer, 1977. Pp. 128–55.

Goldin, Frederick R., trans. *The Song of Roland.* New York: Norton, 1978.

Goulemot, Jean-Marie. "Histoire littéraire." In Jacques Le Goff, ed., *La Nouvelle Histoire.* Paris: CEPL, 1978. Pp. 308–13.

Gröber, Gustav. *Grundriss der romanischen Philologie.* 2 vols. Strasbourg: Trübner, 1893–1906.

Guiette, Robert. "Les Deux Scènes du cor dans la *Chanson de Roland* et dans les *Conquestes de Charlemagne.*" *Le Moyen Age,* 69 (1963), 845–55. Reprinted in *Forme et senefiance.* Geneva: Droz, 1978. Pp. 172–80.

Hackett, Winifred Mary. "Le Gant de Roland." *Romania,* 89 (1968), 253–56.

Haedens, Kléber. *Une Histoire de la littérature française.* 2d ed. Paris: Gallimard, 1954.

Hall, Robert A., Jr. "Ganelon and Roland." *Modern Language Quarterly,* 6 (1945), 263–70.

———. "The Individual in Relation to His Society: The *Chanson de Roland.*" *Cultural Symbolism in Literature.* Ithaca, N.Y.: Linguistica, 1963. Pp. 17–32.

Halverson, John. "Ganelon's Trial." *Speculum,* 42 (1967), 661–69.

Hardison, O. B. "Tragic Flaw." In *Princeton Encyclopedia of Poetry and Poetics.* 2d ed. Princeton: Princeton University Press, 1974. Pp. 864–65.

Harris, Julian. "How Old Was Charlemagne in the *Chanson de Roland?*" *Romance Philology,* 25 (1971–72), 183–88.

Harrison, Robert, trans. *The Song of Roland.* New York: New American Library, 1970.

Hendrickson, William L., and Jean Misrahi. "L'Idéal du héros épique: Prouesse et sagesse." *VIII Congreso de la Société Rencesvals.* Pamplona: Institución Principe de Viana, 1981. Pp. 223–31. See also Misrahi and Hendrickson.

Herlihy, David, ed. *The History of Feudalism.* New York: Harper and Row, 1970.

Hieatt, Constance. "Roland's Christian Heroism." *Traditio,* 24 (1968), 420–29.

Hindley, Alan, and Brian J. Levy. *The Old French Epic: An Introduction.* Louvain: Peeters, 1983.

Hirsch, E. D. *The Aims of Interpretation.* Chicago: University of Chicago Press, 1976.

Horrent, Jules. *Chanson de Roland et geste de Charlemagne.* In Hans Robert Jauss et al., eds., *Grundriss der Literaturen des romanischen Mittelalters,* Vol. 3, tome 1, fascicle 2.A.I.1. Heidelberg: Carl Winter, 1981. Pp. 5–12.

———. *La Chanson de Roland dans les littératures française et espagnole au Moyen Age.* Paris: Belles Lettres, 1951.

Hoy, David C. *The Critical Circle.* Berkeley and Los Angeles: University of California Press, 1978.

Hunt, Tony. "Character and Causality in the Oxford *Roland.*" *Medioevo romanzo,* 5 (1978), 3–33.

———. "Roland's 'vermeille pume.'" *Olifant,* 7 (1980), 203–11.

———. "The Structure of Medieval Narrative." *Journal of European Studies,* 3 (1973), 295–328.

———. "The Tragedy of Roland: An Aristotelian View." *Modern Language Review,* 74 (1979), 791–805.

Huppé, Bernard F. "The Concept of the Hero in the Early Middle Ages." In Norman T. Burns and Christopher Reagan, eds., *Concepts of the Hero in the Middle Ages and the Renaissance.* Albany: State University of New York Press, 1975. Pp. 1–26.

Jackson, William T. H. *The Hero and the King.* New York: Columbia University Press, 1982.

Jauss, Hans Robert. "Levels of Identification of Hero and Audience." *New Literary History,* 5 (1974), 283–317.

Jenkins, T. Atkinson, ed. *La Chanson de Roland: Oxford Version.* 2d ed. Boston: Heath, 1924.

Jones, George Fenwick. *The Ethos of the Song of Roland.* Baltimore: Johns Hopkins University Press, 1963.

———. "Roland's Lament: A Divergent Interpretation." *Romanic Review,* 53 (1962), 3–15. Cf. "La Complainte de Roland: Une Interprétation divergente." *Cultura neolatina,* 21 (1961), 34–47.

Kay, Sarah. "Ethics and Heroics in the *Song of Roland.*" *Neophilologus,* 62 (1978), 480–91.

Keegan, John. *The Face of Battle.* New York: Viking, 1976.

Keller, Hans–Erich. "The *Song of Roland:* A Mid-Twelfth Century Song of Propaganda for the Capetian Kingdom." *Olifant,* 3 (1979), 242–58. Cf. "*La Chanson de Roland:* Poème de propagande pour le royaume capétien du milieu du douzième siècle," in *Travaux de linquistique et de littérature* (Strasbourg), 14, no. 1 (1976), 229–41; "La Chanson de geste et son public," in *Mélanges de philologie et de littératures romanes offerts à Jeanne Wathelet-Willem* (Liège: Marche Romane, 1978), 257–85; and "La Version dionysienne de la *Chanson de Roland,*" in Manfred Bambeck and Hans Helmut Christmann, eds., *Philologica romanica Erhard Lommatzsch gewidmet* (Munich: Fink, 1975, 257–88).

———. "The *Song of Roland* and Its Audience." *Olifant,* 6 (1979), 259–74.

Kellogg, Judith L. "Ganelon: The Poetics of Guile and Greed." *Olifant,* 8 (1980), 161–79.

Works Cited

Kibler, William W. "Again *La Chanson de Roland,* Verse 400." *Romance Notes,* 14 (1972–73), 621–23.

______. "Roland and Tierri." *Olifant,* 2 (1974–75), 27–32.

______. "Roland's Pride." *Symposium,* 26 (1972), 147–60.

______. "Roland versus the Barons." In Raymond Cormier, ed., *Voices of Conscience.* Philadelphia: Temple University Press, 1977. Pp. 53–60.

Kirsch, P. "La Condition du héros dans la *Chanson de Roland.*" In *Mélanges de philologie romane offerts à Charles Camproux.* Montpellier, France: Centre d'Estudis occitans, 1978. Pp. 385–99.

Kleiber, Georges. *Le Mot "Ire" en ancien français.* Paris: Klincksieck, 1978.

Klein, Hans-Wilhelm. "Was bedeutet 'Cum en Espaigne venis a mal seignur,' *Chanson de Roland,* 2900?" In Manfred Hofer et al., eds., *Festschrift Karl Baldinger zum sechzigsten Geburtstag.* 2 vols. Tübingen: Niemeyer, 1979. Pp. 258–65.

Knudson, Charles A. "The Problem of the *Chanson de Roland.*" *Romance Philology,* 4 (1950–51), 1–15.

Köhler, Erich. *"Conseil des barons" und "jugement des barons": Epische Fatalität und Feudalrecht im altfranzösischen Rolandslied.* Heidelberg: Carl Winter, 1968. Also in Henning Krauss, ed., *Alfranzösiche Epik* (Darmstadt: Wissenschaftliche Buchgesellschaft, 1978), 368–412.

______. "Observations historiques et sociologiques sur la poésie des troubadours." *Cahiers de civilisation médiévale,* 7 (1962), 27–51.

Lanson, Gustave. *Histoire de la littérature française.* 1894. Revised edition by Paul Tuffrau. Paris: Hachette, 1952.

Le Gentil, Pierre. "A propos de la démesure de Roland." *Cahiers de civilisation médiévale,* 11 (1968), 203–9.

______. *La Chanson de Roland.* Paris: Hatier, 1955; 2d ed. 1967. Translated by Frances Beer under the title *The Song of Roland.* Cambridge, Mass.: Harvard University Press, 1969.

Le Goff, Jacques. "Les Mentalités: Une histoire ambigüe." In Jacques Le Goff and Pierre Nora, eds., *Faire de l'histoire.* 3 vols. Paris: Gallimard, 1974. 3:76–94.

Le Goff, Jacques, ed. *La Nouvelle Histoire.* Paris: CEPL, 1978.

Lejeune, Rita. "Le Caractère de l'archevêque Turpin et les événements contemporains de la *Chanson de Roland.*" In *Société Rencesvals: IVe Congrès International.* Heidelberg: Carl Winter, 1969. Pp. 9–21.

______. "La Composition de Gautier de l'Hum dans la *Chanson de Roland.*" In *La Technique littéraire des chansons de geste.* Paris: Belles Lettres, 1959. Pp. 237–70.

Lemarignier, Jean-François. *La France médiévale: Institutions et société.* Paris: Colin, 1970.

Lonigan, Paul R. "Ganelon before Marsile." *Studi francesi,* 14 (1970), 276–80.

Lubbock, Percy. *The Craft of Fiction.* London: Cape, 1954.

Lyons, Faith. "More about Roland's Glove." *Société Rencesvals: Proceedings of the Fifth International Conference.* Salford, Eng.: University of Salford, 1977. Pp. 156–66.

Works Cited

McCash, June Hall Martin, "*Scientia* and *Sapientia* in the *Chanson de Roland*." *Medievalia et Humanistica*, n.s. 11 (1982), 131–47.

Maddox, Donald. "*E Baldewin mun filz:* La Parenté dans la *Chanson de Roland*." In *VIII Congreso de la Société Rencesvals*. Pamplona: Institución Principe de Viana, 1981. Pp. 299–304.

Mauriac, Claude. *Malraux ou le mal du héros*. Paris: Grasset, 1946.

Menéndez Pidal, Ramon. *La Chanson de Roland et la tradition épique des Francs*. 2d ed. Trans. Irénée Cluzel. Paris: Picard, 1960.

Mermier, Guy: "More about Unity in the *Song of Roland*." *Olifant*, 2 (1974–75), 91–108.

Merwin, W. S., trans. *The Song of Roland*. New York: Vintage, 1963.

Michel, Francisque. *La Chanson de Roland ou de Roncevaux*. Paris: Silvestre, 1837.

Mickel, Emanuel J. "Christian Duty and the Structure of the *Roland*." *Romance Notes*, 9 (1967), 126–33.

———. "Parallels in Prudentius' *Psychomachia* and *La Chanson de Roland*." *Studies in Philology*, 67 (1970), 439–52.

———. "The Thirty *pleges* for Ganelon." *Olifant*, 6 (1979), 293–304.

Misrahi, Jean, and William L. Hendrickson. "Roland and Oliver: Prowess and Wisdom, the Ideal of the Epic Hero." *Romance Philology*, 33 (1979–80), 357–72. See also Hendrickson.

Moignet, Gérard, ed. *La Chanson de Roland: Texte original et traduction*. Paris: Bordas, 1969. Cf. *La Chanson de Roland: Extraits*. Paris: Bordas, 1970.

Montherlant, Henry de. *La Marée du soir*. Paris: Gallimard, 1972.

Morrow, Lance. "June 6, 1944." *Time*, May 28, 1984, 11–12.

Muecke, D. C. *Irony and the Ironic*. 2d ed. New York: Methuen, 1982.

Nabokov, Vladimir, trans. *The Song of Igor's Campaign*. New York: Vintage, 1960.

Nagler, Michael. "Toward a Generative View of the Oral Formula." *Transactions and Proceedings of the American Philological Society*, 98 (1967), 269–311.

Nichols, Stephen G. *Romanesque Signs: Early Medieval Narrative and Iconography*. New Haven: Yale University Press, 1983.

Niles, John D. *Beowulf*. Cambridge, Mass.: Harvard University Press, 1983.

———. "The Ideal Depiction of Charlemagne in *La Chanson de Roland*." *Viator*, 7 (1976), 123–29.

Nykrog, Per. "La Composition du *Roland* d'Oxford." *Romania*, 88 (1967), 509–26.

Oman, C. W. C. *The Art of War in the Middle Ages*. 2 vols. Boston: Houghton Mifflin, 1924.

Owen, D. D. R. "The Secular Inspiration of the *Chanson de Roland*." *Speculum*, 37 (1962), 390–400.

Owen, D. D. R., trans. *The Song of Roland: The Oxford Text*. London: Allen and Unwin, 1972.

Paris, Gaston. *Extraits de la Chanson de Roland*. 3d ed. Paris: Hachette, 1891.

———. *Histoire poétique de Charlemagne*. 1865. 2d ed. Paris: Bouillon, 1905.

———. *La Littérature française au Moyen Age*. 4th ed. Paris: Hachette, 1909.

______. *La Poésie du Moyen Age: Leçons et lectures.* 2 vols. 2d ed. Paris: Hachette, 1887.

Paris, Paulin. "Roncevaux." *Histoire littéraire de la France,* 22 (1852), 727–55.

Pauphilet, Albert. *Le Legs du Moyen Age: Etudes de littérature médiévale.* Melun, France: D'Argences, 1950.

______. "Sur la *Chanson de Roland.*" *Romania,* 59 (1933), 161–98.

Payen, Jean-Charles. "Encore le rire de Roland." In *VIII Congreso de la Société Rencesvals.* Pamplona: Institución Principe de Viana, 1981. Pp. 387–91.

______. *Le Motif du repentir dans la littérature française médiévale.* Geneva: Droz, 1968.

______. "Une Poétique du génocide joyeux: Devoir de violence et plaisir de tuer dans la *Chanson de Roland.*" *Olifant,* 6 (1979), 226–36.

Peeters, Léopold. "Le 'Faire' et le 'dire' dans la *Chanson de Roland.*" *Revue des langues romanes,* 81 (1975), 376–93.

Pensom, Roger. *Literary Technique in the Chanson de Roland.* Geneva: Droz, 1982.

Petit de Julleville, Louis. *Histoire de la littérature française des origines à nos jours.* 10th ed. (1st in one vol.). Paris: Masson, 1895.

Petit de Julleville, Louis, ed. *La Chanson de Roland.* Paris: Lemerre, 1878.

Picherit, Jean-Louis. "Le Silence de Ganelon." *Cahiers de civilisation médiévale,* 21 (1978), 265–74.

Planche, Alice. "Roland fils de personne." In *Charlemagne et l'épopée romane: Actes du VIIe Congrès de la Société Rencesvals.* Paris: Belles Lettres, 1978. Pp. 595–604.

Poirion, Daniel, et al. *Précis de littérature française du Moyen Age.* Paris: Presses Universitaires de France, 1983.

Pound, Ezra. *The Spirit of Romance.* London: Dent; New York: Dutton, 1910.

Randall, J. R. *The Making of the Modern Mind.* 2d ed. Boston and New York: Houghton Mifflin, 1940. Reprint. New York: Columbia University Press, 1976.

Renoir, Alain. "The Heroic Oath in *Beowulf,* the *Chanson de Roland,* and the *Nibelungenlied.*" In Stanley B. Greenfield, ed., *Studies in Old English Literature in Honor of Arthur G. Brodeur.* Eugene, Ore.: University of Oregon Press, 1963. Reprint. New York: Russell and Russell, 1973.

______. "Roland's Lament: Its Meaning and Function in the *Chanson de Roland.*" *Speculum,* 35 (1960), 572–83.

Ribard, Jacques. "Y a-t-il du 'pacifisme' dans la *Chanson de Roland?*" In *Charlemagne et l'épopée romane: Actes du VIIe Congrès de la Société Rencesvals.* Paris: Belles Lettres, 1978. Pp. 529–38.

Riquer, Martin de. *Les Chansons de geste françaises.* 2d rev. ed. Trans. Irénée Cluzel. Paris: Nizet, 1957.

Robertson, D. W. *A Preface to Chaucer.* Princeton: Princeton University Press, 1962.

______. "Some Observations on Method in Literary Studies." In Ralph Cohen, ed., *New Directions in Literary History.* Baltimore: Johns Hopkins University Press, 1974. Pp. 63–75.

Roger, Jacques. "Lecture des textes et histoire des idées." In Georges Poulet, ed., *Les Chemins actuels de la critique.* Paris: Union Générale d'Editions, 1968. Pp. 191–99.

Rosenberg, Bruce A. *Custer and the Epic of Defeat.* University Park, Pa.: Pennsylvania State University Press, 1974.

Ross, D. J. A. "Before *Roland:* What Happened 1200 Years Ago Next August 15?" *Olifant,* 5 (1977–78), 171–90.

———. "Gautier del Hum: An Historical Element in the *Chanson de Roland*?" *Modern Language Review,* 61 (1966), 409–15.

Ruggieri, Ruggero M. *Il Processo di Gano nella Chanson de Roland.* Florence: Sansoni, 1936.

Rütten, Raimund. *Symbol and Mythus im altfranzösischen Rolandslied.* Braunschweig: Westermann, 1970.

Rychner, Jean. *La Chanson de geste.* Geneva: Droz, 1955.

Sargent, Barbara N. "Medieval *rire, ridere:* A Laughing Matter?" *Medium Aevum,* 43 (1974), 116–32.

Sargent-Baur, Barbara N. "Truth, Half-Truth, Untruth: Béroul's Telling of the Tristan Story." In Leigh Arrathoon, ed., *The Craft of Fiction: Essays in Medieval Poetics.* Rochester, Mich.: Solaris Press, 1984. Pp. 393–421.

Sayers, Dorothy L. *The Unpleasantness at the Bellona Club.* 1928. Reprint. New York: Avon, 1963.

Scully, Terence. "The Ordeal at Roncesvalles: 'Francs e paiens, as les vus ajustez.'" *Olifant,* 7 (1980), 213–34.

Segre, Cesare. *La Tradizione della Chanson de Roland.* Milan and Naples: Ricciardi, 1974.

Short, Ian. "Reinterpreting the *Roland:* Per Litteram, Sensum et Sententiam." *Romance Philology,* 34, Special Issue (February 1981), *46–*63.

Siciliano, Italo. *Les Chansons de geste et l'épopée: Mythes, histoire, poèmes.* Turin: Società Editrice Internazionale; Paris: Picard, 1970.

Smail, R. C. *Crusading Warfare, 1097–1193.* Cambridge, Eng.: Cambridge University Press, 1956.

Steinmann, Martin, Jr. "What's the Point of Professional Interpretation of Literature?" *Philosophy and Literature,* 8 (1984), 266–70.

Stock, Brian. *The Implications of Literacy.* Princeton: Princeton University Press, 1983.

Stranges, John A. "The Character and the Trial of Ganelon: A New Appraisal." *Romania,* 96 (1975), 333–67.

Strayer, Joseph. *Feudalism.* New York: Van Nostrand, 1965.

Subrenat, Jean. ". . . e Oliver est proz." *Etudes de philologie romane et d'histoire littéraire offertes à Jules Horrent.* Liège: n.p., 1980.

Thomas, Jacques. "La Traitrise de Ganelon." *Romanica Gandensia,* 16 (1976), 91–117.

Thomas, P. Aloysius. "The Structural and Aesthetic Heroes in the *Song of Roland.*" *Neuphilologische Mitteilungen,* 81 (1980), 1–6.

Trawick, Buckner. *World Literature,* vol. 1: *Greek, Roman, Oriental, and Medieval Classics.* New York: Barnes and Noble, 1953.

Tuve, Rosemond. *Allegorical Imagery.* Princeton: Princeton University Press, 1966.

Uitti, Karl D. *Story, Myth, and Celebration in Old French Narrative Poetry.* Princeton: Princeton University Press, 1973.

Vance, Eugene. *Reading the Song of Roland.* Englewood Cliffs, N.J.: Prentice-Hall, 1970.

———. "Spatial Structure in the *Chanson de Roland.*" *Modern Language Notes,* 82 (1967), 604–23.

Van Emden, Wolfgang C. "E cil de France le cleiment a guarant: Roland, Vivien, et le thème du *guarant.*" *Olifant,* 1 (1974), 21–47. Also in *Société Rencesvals, VIe Congrès International: Actes.* Aix-en-Provence: Université de Provence, 1974. Pp. 31–61.

———. "Pro Karolo Magno: In Response to William W. Kibler, 'Roland and Tierri.'" *Olifant,* 2 (1974–75), 175–82.

Verbruggen, J. F. *The Art of Warfare in Western Europe during the Middle Ages.* Amsterdam: North-Holland, 1977.

Vinaver, Eugène. *A la recherche d'une poétique médiévale.* Paris: Nizet, 1970.

———. *The Rise of Romance.* New York: Oxford University Press, 1971.

Vitz, Evelyn Birge. "Desire and Causality in Medieval Narrative." *Romanic Review,* 71 (1980), 213–43.

Vos, Marianne Cramer. "Ganelon's *mortel rage.*" *Olifant,* 2 (1974–75), 15–26.

Walpole, Ronald N. "Le Sens moral de la *Chanson de Roland.*" *Travaux de linguistique et de littérature* (Strasbourg), 4, no. 2 (1966), 7–21.

Waltz, Matthias. *Rolandslied, Wilhelmslied, Alexiuslied: Zur Struktur und geschichtlichen Bedeutung.* Heidelberg: Carl Winter, 1965.

Ward, Patricia. *The Medievalism of Victor Hugo.* University Park, Pa.: Pennsylvania State University Press, 1975.

Wendt, Michael. *Der Oxforder Roland: Heilsgeschehen und Teilidentität im 12. Jahrhundert.* Munich: Fink, 1970.

White, Julian Eugene. "*La Chanson de Roland:* Secular or Religious Inspiration?" *Romania,* 84 (1963), 398–408.

Whitehead, Frederick. "L'Ambiguïté de Roland." In *Studi in onore di Italo Siciliano.* Florence: Olschki, 1966. Pp. 1203–12.

———. "*La Chanson de Roland* et l'esprit héroïque." *Cahiers de civilisation médiévale,* 3 (1960), 115–17.

———. "Charlemagne's Second Dream." *Olifant,* 3 (1975–76), 189–95.

Williamson, Joan B. "Trust and Kinship in the *Chanson de Roland.*" In *VIII Congreso de la Société Rencesvals.* Pamplona: Institución Principe de Viana, 1981. Pp. 553–60.

Wilson, Guthrie. *Brave Company.* New York: Putnam's, 1950.

Wilson, W. Daniel. "Readers in Texts." *PMLA,* 96 (1981), 848–63.

Zaddy, Zara P. "The Problem of the Two Ganelons." In Peter Noble et al., eds., *The Medieval Alexander Legend and Romance Epic: Essays in Honour of David J. A. Ross.* Millwood, N.Y.: Kraus, 1982. Pp. 269–88.

Zumthor, Paul. *Essai de poétique médiévale.* Paris: Seuil, 1972.

———. "Etude typologique des *planctus* contenus dans la *Chanson de Roland.*" In *La Technique littéraire des chansons de geste.* Paris: Belles Lettres, 1959. Pp. 219–35.

———. *La Poésie et la voix dans la civilisation médiévale.* Paris: Presses Universitaires de France, 1984.

Index

Index

Library of Congress Cataloging-in-Publication Data

Cook, Robert Francis.
The sense of the Song of Roland.

Bibliography: p.
Includes index.
1. Chanson de Roland. 2. Roland (Legendary character) —Romances—History and criticism. 3. Roncesvalles, Battle of, 778, in literature. I. Title.
PQ1522.C66 1987 841'.1 87-5407
ISBN 0-8014-1930-1 (alk. paper)